Essentials of
Programming
Languages

second edition

Essentials of

Programming

Languages

second edition

Daniel P. Friedman

Mitchell Wand

Christopher T. Haynes

The MIT Press
Cambridge, Massachusetts
London, England

Typeset by the authors using LATEX 2_ε.
Printed and bound in the United States of America.

Library of Congress Cataloging-in-Publication Information Data

Friedman, Daniel P.
  Essentials of programming languages / Daniel P. Friedman, Mitchell Wand, Christopher T. Haynes—2nd ed.
    p.   cm.
  Includes bibliographical references and index.
  ISBN 0-262-06217-8 (hc. : alk. paper)
    1. Programming Languages (Elecronic computers). I. Wand, Mitchell.
  II. Haynes, Christopher Thomas. III. Title.

QA76.7.F73 2001
005.13—dc21   00-135246

Contents

Foreword

This book brings you face-to-face with the most fundamental idea in computer programming:

> *The interpreter for a computer language is just another program.*

It sounds obvious, doesn't it? But the implications are profound. If you are a computational theorist, the interpreter idea recalls Gödel's discovery of the limitations of formal logical systems, Turing's concept of a universal computer, and von Neumann's basic notion of the stored-program machine. If you are a programmer, mastering the idea of an interpreter is a source of great power. It provokes a real shift in mindset, a basic change in the way you think about programming.

I did a lot of programming before I learned about interpreters, and I produced some substantial programs. One of them, for example, was a large data-entry and information-retrieval system written in PL/I. When I implemented my system, I viewed PL/I as a fixed collection of rules established by some unapproachable group of language designers. I saw my job as not to modify these rules, or even to understand them deeply, but rather to pick through the (very) large manual, selecting this or that feature to use. The notion that there was some underlying structure to the way the language was organized, and that I might want to override some of the language designers' decisions, never occurred to me. I didn't know how to create embedded sublanguages to help organize my implementation, so the entire program seemed like a large, complex mosaic, where each piece had to be carefully shaped and fitted into place, rather than a cluster of languages, where the pieces could be flexibly combined. If you don't understand interpreters, you can still write programs; you can even be a competent programmer. But you can't be a master.

There are three reasons why as a programmer you should learn about interpreters.

First, you will need at some point to implement interpreters, perhaps not interpreters for full-blown general-purpose languages, but interpreters just the same. Almost every complex computer system with which people interact in flexible ways—a computer drawing tool or an information-retrieval system, for example—includes some sort of interpreter that structures the interaction. These programs may include complex individual operations—shading a region on the display screen, or performing a database search—but the interpreter is the glue that lets you combine individual operations into useful patterns. Can you use the result of one operation as the input to another operation? Can you name a sequence of operations? Is the name local or global? Can you parameterize a sequence of operations, and give names to its inputs? And so on. No matter how complex and polished the individual operations are, it is often the quality of the glue that most directly determines the power of the system. It's easy to find examples of programs with good individual operations, but lousy glue; looking back on it, I can see that my PL/I database program certainly had lousy glue.

Second, even programs that are not themselves interpreters have important interpreter-like pieces. Look inside a sophisticated computer-aided design system and you're likely to find a geometric recognition language, a graphics interpreter, a rule-based control interpreter, and an object-oriented language interpreter all working together. One of the most powerful ways to structure a complex program is as a collection of languages, each of which provides a different perspective, a different way of working with the program elements. Choosing the right kind of language for the right purpose, and understanding the implementation tradeoffs involved: that's what the study of interpreters is about.

The third reason for learning about interpreters is that programming techniques that explicitly involve the structure of language are becoming increasingly important. Today's concern with designing and manipulating class hierarchies in object-oriented systems is only one example of this trend. Perhaps this is an inevitable consequence of the fact that our programs are becoming increasingly complex—thinking more explicitly about languages may be our best tool for dealing with this complexity. Consider again the basic idea: the interpreter itself is just a program. But that program is written in some language, whose interpreter is itself just a program written in some language whose interpreter is itself .... Perhaps the whole distinction between program and programming language is a misleading idea, and future programmers will see themselves not as writing programs in particular, but as creating new languages for each new application.

Friedman, Wand, and Haynes have done a landmark job, and their book will change the landscape of programming-language courses. They don't just *tell* you about interpreters; they *show* them to you. The core of the book is a tour de force sequence of interpreters starting with an abstract high-level language and progressively making linguistic features explicit until we reach a state machine. You can actually run this code, study and modify it, and change the way these interpreters handle scoping, parameter-passing, control structure, etc.

Having used interpreters to study the execution of languages, the authors show how the same ideas can be used to analyze programs without running them. In two new chapters, they show how to implement type checkers and inferencers, and how these features interact in modern object-oriented languages.

Part of the reason for the appeal of this approach is that the authors have chosen a good tool—the Scheme language, which combines the uniform syntax and data-abstraction capabilities of Lisp with the lexical scoping and block structure of Algol. But a powerful tool becomes most powerful in the hands of masters. The sample interpreters in this book are outstanding models. Indeed, since they are *runnable* models, I'm sure that these interpreters and analyzers will find themselves at the cores of many programming systems over the coming years.

This is not an easy book. Mastery of interpreters does not come easily, and for good reason. The language designer is a further level removed from the end user than is the ordinary application programmer. In designing an application program, you think about the specific tasks to be performed, and consider what features to include. But in designing a language, you consider the various applications people might want to implement, and the ways in which they might implement them. Should your language have static or dynamic scope, or a mixture? Should it have inheritance? Should it pass parameters by reference or by value? Should continuations be explicit or implicit? It all depends on how you expect your language to be used, on which kinds of programs should be easy to write, and which you can afford to make more difficult.

Also, interpreters really *are* subtle programs. A simple change to a line of code in an interpreter can make an enormous difference in the behavior of the resulting language. Don't think that you can just skim these programs— very few people in the world can glance at a new interpreter and predict from that how it will behave even on relatively simple programs. So study these programs. Better yet, *run* them—this is working code. Try interpreting some simple expressions, then more complex ones. Add error messages. Modify the interpreters. Design your own variations. Try to really master these programs, not just get a vague feeling for how they work.

If you do this, you will change your view of your programming, and your view of yourself as a programmer. You'll come to see yourself as a designer of languages rather than only a user of languages, as a person who chooses the rules by which languages are put together, rather than only a follower of rules that other people have chosen.

Hal Abelson
Cambridge, MA
August, 2000

Preface

Goal

This book is an analytic study of programming languages. Our goal is to provide a deep, working understanding of the essential concepts of programming languages. These essentials have proved to be of enduring importance; they form a basis for understanding future developments in programming languages.

Most of these essentials relate to the semantics, or meaning, of program elements. Such meanings reflect how program elements are interpreted as the program executes. Programs called interpreters provide the most direct, executable expression of program semantics. They process a program by directly analyzing an abstract representation of the program text. We therefore choose interpreters as our primary vehicle for expressing the semantics of programming language elements.

The most interesting question about a program as object is, "What does it do?" The study of interpreters tells us this. Interpreters are critical because they reveal nuances of meaning, and are the direct path to more efficient compilation and to other kinds of program analyses.

Interpreters are also illustrative of a broad class of systems that transform information from one form to another based on syntax structure. Compilers, for example, transform programs into forms suitable for interpretation by hardware or virtual machines. Though general compilation techniques are beyond the scope of this book, we do develop several elementary program translation systems. These reflect forms of program analysis typical of compilation, such as control transformation, variable binding resolution, and type checking.

The following are some of the strategies that distinguish our approach.

1. Each new concept is explained through the use of a small language. These languages are often cumulative: later languages may rely on the features of earlier ones.

2. Language processors such as interpreters and type checkers are used to explain the behavior of programs in a given language. They express language design decisions in a manner that is both formal (unambiguous and complete) and executable.

3. When appropriate, we use interfaces and specifications to create data abstractions. In this way, we can change data representation without changing programs. We use this to investigate alternative implementation strategies.

4. Our language processors are written both at the very high level needed to produce a concise and comprehensible view of semantics and at the much lower level needed to understand implementation strategies.

5. We show how simple algebraic manipulation can be used to predict the behavior of programs and to derive their properties. In general, however, we make little use of mathematical notation, preferring instead to study the behavior of programs that constitute the implementations of our languages.

6. The text explains the key concepts, while the exercises explore alternative designs and other issues. For example, the text deals with static binding, but dynamic binding is discussed in the exercises. One thread of exercises applies the concept of lexical addressing to the various languages developed in the book.

We provide several views of programming languages using widely varying levels of abstraction. Frequently our interpreters provide a very high-level view that expresses language semantics in a very concise fashion, not far from that of formal mathematical semantics. At the other extreme, we demonstrate how programs may be transformed into a very low-level form characteristic of assembly language. By accomplishing this transformation in small stages, we maintain a clear connection between the high-level and low-level views.

Organization

The first two chapters provide the foundations for a careful study of programming languages. Chapter 1 emphasizes the connection between inductive data specification and recursive programming and introduces several notions related to the scope of variables. Chapter 2 introduces a data type facility. This leads to a discussion of data abstraction and examples of representational transformations of the sort used in subsequent chapters.

Chapter 3 uses these foundations to describe the behavior of programming languages. It introduces interpreters as mechanisms for explaining the run-time behavior of languages and develops an interpreter for a simple, lexically scoped language with first-class procedures, recursion, and assignment to variables. This interpreter is the basis for much of the material in the remainder of the book. The chapter then explores call-by-reference, call-by-need, and call-by-name parameter-passing mechanisms, and culminates with a sketch of an interpreter for an imperative language.

Chapter 4 extends the language of chapter 3 with type declarations. First we implement a type checker. Next we show how to use the types to enforce abstraction boundaries. Finally we show how the types in a program can be deduced by a unification-based type inference algorithm.

Chapter 5 presents the basic concepts of object-oriented languages, centered on classes (but ignoring types, which are deferred to chapter 6). We develop an efficient runtime architecture, which is used as the basis for the material in chapter 6.

Chapter 6 combines the ideas of the type checker of chapter 4 with those of the object-oriented language of chapter 5, leading to a conventional typed object-oriented language. This requires introducing new concepts including abstract classes, abstract methods, and casting.

Chapter 7 rewrites our basic interpreter in continuation-passing style. The control structure that is needed to run the interpreter thereby shifts from recursion to iteration. This exposes the control mechanisms of the interpreted language, and strengthens one's intuition for control issues in general. It also provides the means for extending the interpreter with exception-handling and multi-threading mechanisms. Finally, we use continuation-passing style to present logic programming.

Chapter 8 is the companion to the previous chapter. There we show how to transform our familiar interpreter into continuation-passing style; here we show how to accomplish this for a much larger class of programs. Continuation-passing style is a powerful programming tool, for it allows any sequential control mechanism to be implemented in almost any language. The algorithm is also a fine example of an abstractly specified source-to-source program transformation.

The dependencies of the various chapters are shown in the figure below.

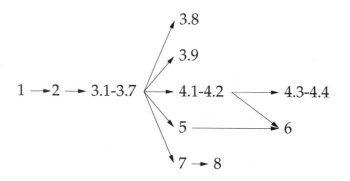

Finally, appendix A describes our SLLGEN parsing system.

Usage

This material has been used in both undergraduate and graduate courses. In addition, it has been used in continuing education courses for professional programmers. We assume background in data structures and experience both in a procedural language such as C, C++, or Java, and in Scheme.

Exercises are a vital part of the text and are scattered throughout. They range in difficulty from being trivial if related material is understood [⋆], to requiring many hours of thought and programming work [⋆⋆⋆]. A great deal of material of applied, historical, and theoretical interest resides within them. We recommend that each exercise be read and some thought be given as to how to solve it. Although we write our program interpretation and transformation systems in Scheme, any language that supports both first-class procedures and assignment (ML, Common Lisp, etc.) is adequate for working the exercises.

Exercise 0.1 [⋆] We often use phrases like "some languages have property *X*." For each such phrase, find one or more languages that have the property and one or more languages that do not have the property. Feel free to ferret out this information from any descriptive book on programming languages (say (Scott, 2000), (Sethi, 1996), or (Pratt & Zelkowitz, 1996)).

Exercise 0.2 [⋆] Determine the rationale for the existence of index items, such as `cons-prim`, that do not appear in the body of the book.

This is a hands-on book: everything discussed in the book may be implemented within the limits of a typical university course. Because the abstraction facilities of functional programming languages are especially suited to this sort of programming, we can write substantial language-processing systems that are nevertheless compact enough that one can understand and manipulate them with reasonable effort.

The web site, available through the publisher, includes complete Scheme code for all of the interpreters and analyzers in this book. The code is as compliant with R^{5}RS (Kelsey *et al.*, 1998) as we could make it. The site includes pointers to several Scheme implementations (some of which are freely available) and compatibility files that should allow our code to run without change on these implementations or any Scheme implementation that is R^{5}RS-compliant.

Acknowledgments

We are indebted to countless colleagues and students who used and critiqued the first edition of this book and provided invaluable assistance in the long gestation of this second edition. We are especially grateful for the contributions of the following individuals, to whom we offer a special word of thanks. Matthias Felleisen's keen analysis has improved the design of several chapters. Among these, his work with Amr Sabry on the CPS algorithm led to a far more elegant algorithm than we had in the earlier edition. Amr Sabry made many useful suggestions and found at least one extremely subtle bug in a draft of chapter 6. Benjamin Pierce offered a number of insightful observations after teaching from the first edition, almost all of which we have incorporated into the second edition. Gary Leavens provided exceptionally thorough and valuable comments on early drafts of this edition, including a large number of detailed suggestions for change. Jonathan Rossie suggested a subtle refinement of the CPS algorithm, which resulted in a simpler algorithmic structure and more compact output. Olivier Danvy helped in the development of a particularly interesting exercise in chapter 8. Anurag Mendhekar and Michael Levin contributed to the material on logic programming. Ryan Newton, in addition to reading a draft, assumed the onerous task of suggesting a difficulty level for each exercise. Kevin Millikin, Arthur Lee, Roger Kirchner, Max Hailperin, and Erik Hilsdale all used early drafts of this second edition. Their comments have been extremely valuable. Matthew Flatt, Shriram Krishnamurthi, Steve Ganz, Gregor Kiczales, Galen Williamson, Dipanwita Sarkar, Craig Citro, and Adam Foltzer also provided careful reading and useful comments.

Several people deserve special thanks for helping us with the various tools used in this book. Will Clinger urged us to write code to the Scheme standard. It was difficult, but thanks to his insistence we believe we have succeeded as far as possible and it has been well worth the effort. Jonathan Sobel and Erik Hilsdale built several prototype implementations and contributed many ideas as we experimented with the design of the `define-datatype` and `cases` syntactic extensions. The Rice Programming Language Team, especially Matthias Felleisen, Matthew Flatt, Robert Bruce Findler, and Shriram Krishnamurthi, were very helpful in providing compatibility with their DrScheme system. Kent Dybvig developed the exceptionally efficient and robust Chez Scheme implementation, which the authors have used for decades. Rob Henderson from the Indiana University Computer Science Department provided invaluable help in supporting Dan's computer systems.

Some have earned special mention for their thoughtfulness and concern for our well-being. George Springer, Larry Finkelstein, and Bob Filman have each supplied invaluable support. Robert Prior, our wonderful editor at MIT Press, deserves special thanks for his encouragement in getting us to attack the writing of this edition. Carrie Jadud's excellent copy-editing is much appreciated. Indiana University and Northeastern University created an environment that allowed us to undertake this project. Mary Friedman's gracious hosting of several week-long writing sessions did much to accelerate our progress. Finally, we are most grateful to our families for tolerating our passion for working on the book. Thank you Rob, Rachel, Sarah, and Mary; thank you Rebecca and Joshua Ben-Gideon, Jennifer, Joshua, and Barbara; and thank you Anne.

This edition has been in the works for a while and we have likely overlooked someone who has helped along the way. We regret any oversight. You see this written in books all the time and wonder why anyone would write it. Of course, you regret any oversight. But, when you have an army of helpers, you really feel a sense of obligation not to forget anyone. So, if you were overlooked, we are truly sorry.

— D.P.F., M.W., C.T.H.

1 *Inductive Sets of Data*

This chapter introduces recursive programming, along with its relation to mathematical induction. The notion of *scope*, which plays a primary role in programming languages, is also presented. Section 1.1 and section 1.2 introduce methods for inductively specifying data structures and show how such specifications may be used to guide the construction of recursive programs. Section 1.3 then introduces the notions of variable binding and scope.

The programming exercises are the heart of this chapter. They provide experience that is essential for mastering the technique of recursive programming upon which the rest of this book is based.

1.1 Recursively Specified Data

When writing code for a procedure, we must know precisely what kinds of values may occur as arguments to the procedure, and what kinds of values it is legal for the procedure to return. Often these sets of values are complex. In this section we introduce formal techniques for specifying sets of values.

1.1.1 Inductive Specification

Inductive specification is a powerful method of specifying a set of values. To illustrate this method, we use it to describe a certain subset of the natural numbers:

Definition 1.1.1 *Define the set S to be the smallest set of natural numbers satisfying the following two properties:*

1. $0 \in S$, and

2. Whenever $x \in S$, then $x + 3 \in S$.

A "smallest set" is the one that satisfies properties 1 and 2 and that is a subset of any other set satisfying properties 1 and 2. It is easy to see that there can be only one such set: if S_1 and S_2 both satisfy properties 1 and 2, and both are smallest, then $S_1 \subseteq S_2$ (since S_1 is smallest), and $S_2 \subseteq S_1$ (since S_2 is smallest), hence $S_1 = S_2$.

Let us see if we can describe some partial information about S to arrive at a non-inductive specification. We know that 0 is in S, by property 1. Since $0 \in S$, by property 2 we conclude that $3 \in S$. Then since $3 \in S$, by property 2 we conclude that $6 \in S$, and so on. So we see that all the multiples of 3 are in S. If we let M denote the set of all multiples of 3, we can restate this conclusion as $M \subseteq S$. But the set M itself satisfies properties 1 and 2. Since S is a subset of every set that satisfies properties 1 and 2, it must be that $S \subseteq M$. So we deduce that $S = M$, the set of multiples of 3. This is plausible: we know all the multiples of 3 must be in S, and anything else is extraneous.

This is a typical inductive definition. To specify a set S inductively, define it to be the smallest set satisfying two properties of the following form:

1. Some specific values must be in S.

2. If certain values are in S, then certain other values are also in S.

Sticking to this recipe guarantees that S consists precisely of those values inserted by property 1 and those values included by repeated application of property 2. As stated, this recipe is rather vague. It can be stated more precisely, but that would take us too far afield. Instead, let us see how this process works on some more examples.

Definition 1.1.2 *The set* list-of-numbers *is the smallest set of values satisfying the two properties:*

1. *The empty list is a list-of-numbers, and*

2. *If l is a list-of-numbers and n is a number, then the pair* (n . l) *is a list-of-numbers.*

From this definition we infer the following:

1. () is a list-of-numbers, because of property 1.

2. (14 . ()) is a list-of-numbers, because 14 is a number and () is a list-of-numbers.

3. `(3 . (14 . ()))` is a list-of-numbers, because 3 is a number and `(14 . ())` is a list-of-numbers.

4. `(-7 . (3 . (14 . ())))` is a list-of-numbers, because `-7` is a number and `(3 . (14 . ()))` is a list-of-numbers.

5. Nothing is a list-of-numbers unless it is built in this fashion.

Converting from dot notation to list notation, we see that `()`, `(14)`, `(3 14)`, and `(-7 3 14)` are all members of list-of-numbers.

1.1.2 Defining Sets of Values with Backus-Naur Form

The previous example is fairly straightforward, but it is easy to imagine how the process of describing more complex data types becomes quite cumbersome. To remedy this, we use a notation called *Backus-Naur Form*, or *BNF*. BNF was originally developed to specify the syntactic structure of programming languages, but we will use it to define sets of values as well by using the printed representation of those values.

For example, we can define the set list-of-numbers in BNF as follows:

$$\langle\text{list-of-numbers}\rangle ::= ()$$
$$\langle\text{list-of-numbers}\rangle ::= (\langle\text{number}\rangle \; . \; \langle\text{list-of-numbers}\rangle)$$

This set of rules is called a *grammar*.

Here we have two rules corresponding to the two properties in Definition 1.1.2 above. The first rule says that the empty list is in $\langle$list-of-numbers$\rangle$, and the second says that if n is in $\langle$number$\rangle$ and l is in $\langle$list-of-numbers$\rangle$, then $(n \; . \; l)$ is in $\langle$list-of-numbers$\rangle$.

Let us look at the pieces of this definition. In this definition we have:

- **Nonterminal Symbols.** These are the names of the sets being defined. These are customarily written with angle brackets around the name of the set, *e.g.* $\langle$list-of-numbers$\rangle$. In this case there is only one, but in general, there might be several sets being defined. These sets are sometimes called *syntactic categories*.

- **Terminal Symbols.** These are the characters in the external representation, in this case `.`, `(`, and `)`.

- **Productions.** The rules are often called *productions*. Each production has a left-hand side, which is a nonterminal symbol, and a right-hand side, which consists of terminal and nonterminal symbols. The left- and right-hand sides are usually separated by the symbol ::=, read *is* or *can be*. The right-hand side specifies a method for constructing members of the syntactic category in terms of other syntactic categories and *terminal symbols,* such as the left and right parentheses, and the period.

Often some syntactic categories mentioned in a BNF rule are left undefined when their meaning is sufficiently clear from context, such as ⟨number⟩.

BNF is often extended with a few notational shortcuts. One can write a set of rules for a single syntactic category by writing the left-hand side and ::= just once, followed by all the right-hand sides separated by the special symbol | (vertical bar, read *or*). A ⟨list-of-numbers⟩ can then be defined by

$$\langle\text{list-of-numbers}\rangle ::= \texttt{()} \mid \texttt{(}\langle\text{number}\rangle \texttt{ . } \langle\text{list-of-numbers}\rangle\texttt{)}$$

Another useful notation is to omit the left-hand side of a production when it is the same as the left-hand side of the preceding production. Using this convention our example would be written as:

$$\langle\text{list-of-numbers}\rangle ::= \texttt{()}$$
$$::= \texttt{(}\langle\text{number}\rangle \texttt{ . } \langle\text{list-of-numbers}\rangle\texttt{)}$$

Another shortcut is the *Kleene star,* expressed by the notation {...}*. When this appears in a right-hand side, it indicates a sequence of any number of instances of whatever appears between the braces. Using the Kleene star, the definition of ⟨list-of-numbers⟩ in list notation is simply

$$\langle\text{list-of-numbers}\rangle ::= \texttt{(}\{\langle\text{number}\rangle\}^*\texttt{)}$$

This includes the possibility of no instances at all. If there are zero instances, we get the empty list.

A variant of the star notation is *Kleene plus* {...}+, which indicates a sequence of *one* or more instances. Substituting + for * in the above example would define the syntactic category of non-empty lists of numbers. These notational shortcuts are just that—it is always possible to do without them by using additional BNF rules.

Yet another variant of the star notation is the *separated list* notation. If ⟨expression⟩ is a nonterminal, we write {⟨expression⟩}*(c) to denote a sequence of any number of instances of the nonterminal ⟨expression⟩, separated by the non-empty character sequence *c*. This includes the possibility of no instances at all. If there are zero instances, we get the empty string.

If a set is specified using BNF rules, a *syntactic derivation* may be used to prove that a given data value is a member of the set. Such a derivation starts with the nonterminal corresponding to the set. At each step, indicated by an arrow ⇒, a nonterminal is replaced by the right-hand side of a corresponding rule, or with a known member of its syntactic class if the class was left undefined. For example, the previous demonstration that (14 . ()) is a list of numbers may be formalized with the following syntactic derivation:

⟨list-of-numbers⟩
⇒ (⟨number⟩ . ⟨list-of-numbers⟩)
⇒ (14 . ⟨list-of-numbers⟩)
⇒ (14 . ())

The order in which nonterminals are replaced does not matter. Thus another possible derivation of (14 . ()) is

⟨list-of-numbers⟩
⇒ (⟨number⟩ . ⟨list-of-numbers⟩)
⇒ (⟨number⟩ . ())
⇒ (14 . ())

Exercise 1.1 [⋆]   Write a syntactic derivation that proves (-7 . (3 . (14 . ()))) is a list of numbers.

Let us consider the BNF definitions of some other useful sets. Many symbol manipulation procedures are designed to operate on lists that contain only symbols and other similarly restricted lists. We formalize this notion with these rules:

⟨s-list⟩   ::= ({⟨symbol-expression⟩}*)
⟨symbol-expression⟩ ::= ⟨symbol⟩ | ⟨s-list⟩

The literal representation of an s-list contains only parentheses and symbols. For example,

```
(a b c)
(an (((s-list)) (with () lots) ((of) nesting)))
```

A binary tree with numeric leaves and interior nodes labeled with symbols may be represented using three-element lists for the interior nodes as follows

⟨bintree⟩ ::= ⟨number⟩ | (⟨symbol⟩ ⟨bintree⟩ ⟨bintree⟩)

Examples of such trees follow:

```
1
2
(foo 1 2)
(bar 1 (foo 1 2))
(baz (bar 1 (foo 1 2)) (biz 4 5))
```

A simple mini-language that is often used to study the theory of programming languages is the *lambda calculus*. This language consists only of variable references, `lambda` expressions with a single formal parameter, and procedure calls. We can define it with the following grammar:

⟨expression⟩ ::= ⟨identifier⟩

::= (`lambda` (⟨identifier⟩) ⟨expression⟩)

::= (⟨expression⟩ ⟨expression⟩)

where ⟨identifier⟩ is any symbol other than `lambda`. This grammar defines the elements of ⟨expression⟩ as Scheme values, so it is convenient to write programs that manipulate them.

We can even use BNF to specify concisely the syntactic category of data in Scheme. In Scheme, numbers, symbols, booleans, and strings all have literal representations, which we associate with the syntactic categories ⟨number⟩, ⟨symbol⟩, ⟨boolean⟩, and ⟨string⟩, respectively. We can then use BNF to specify the representations for lists, improper lists (which end with dotted pairs), and vectors:

⟨list⟩	::=	({⟨datum⟩}*)
⟨dotted-datum⟩	::=	({⟨datum⟩}+ . ⟨datum⟩)
⟨vector⟩	::=	#({⟨datum⟩}*)
⟨datum⟩	::=	⟨number⟩ | ⟨symbol⟩ | ⟨boolean⟩ | ⟨string⟩
	::=	⟨list⟩ | ⟨dotted-datum⟩ | ⟨vector⟩

These four syntactic categories are all defined in terms of each other. This is legitimate because each of these compound data types contains components that may be numbers, symbols, booleans, strings, or other lists, improper lists or vectors.

To illustrate the use of this grammar, consider the following syntactic derivation that proves (#t (foo . ()) 3) is a list.

⟨list⟩
⇒ (⟨datum⟩ ⟨datum⟩ ⟨datum⟩)
⇒ (⟨boolean⟩ ⟨datum⟩ ⟨datum⟩)
⇒ (#t ⟨datum⟩ ⟨datum⟩)
⇒ (#t ⟨dotted-datum⟩ ⟨datum⟩)
⇒ (#t ({⟨datum⟩}⁺ . ⟨datum⟩) ⟨datum⟩)
⇒ (#t (⟨symbol⟩ . ⟨datum⟩) ⟨datum⟩)
⇒ (#t (foo . ⟨datum⟩) ⟨datum⟩)
⇒ (#t (foo . ⟨list⟩) ⟨datum⟩)
⇒ (#t (foo . ()) ⟨datum⟩)
⇒ (#t (foo . ()) ⟨number⟩)
⇒ (#t (foo . ()) 3)

All three elements of the outer list are introduced at once. This shortcut is possible because the grammar uses a Kleene star. Of course, the Kleene star and plus notation could be eliminated by introducing new nonterminals and productions, and the three list elements would then be introduced with three derivation steps instead of one.

Exercise 1.2 [⋆] Rewrite the ⟨datum⟩ grammar without using the Kleene star or plus. Then indicate the changes to the above derivation that are required by this revised grammar.

Exercise 1.3 [⋆] Write a syntactic derivation that proves (a "mixed" #(bag (of . data))) is a datum, using either the grammar in the book or the revised grammar from the preceding exercise. What is wrong with (a . b . c)?

BNF rules are said to be *context free* because a rule defining a given syntactic category may be applied in any context that makes reference to that syntactic category. Sometimes this is not restrictive enough: a node in a binary search tree is either empty or contains a key and two subtrees

⟨bin-search-tree⟩ ::= () | (⟨key⟩ ⟨bin-search-tree⟩ ⟨bin-search-tree⟩)

This correctly describes the structure of each node but fails to mention an important fact about binary search trees: all the keys in the left subtree are less than (or equal to) the key in the current node, and all the keys in the right subtree are greater than the key in the current node. Such constraints are said to be *context sensitive*, because they depend on the context in which they are used.

Context-sensitive constraints also arise when specifying the syntax of programming languages. For instance, in many languages every identifier must be declared before it is used. This constraint on the use of identifiers is sensitive to the context of their use. Formal methods can be used to specify context-sensitive constraints, but these methods are far more complicated than BNF. In practice, the usual approach is first to specify a context-free grammar using BNF. Context-sensitive constraints are then added using other methods, usually prose, to complete the specification of a context-sensitive syntax.

1.1.3 Induction

Having described sets inductively, we can use the inductive definitions in two ways: to prove theorems about members of the set and to write programs that manipulate them. Here we present an example of such a proof, using the example of binary trees from page 5; writing the programs is the subject of the next section.

Theorem 1.1.1 *Let $s \in \langle\text{bintree}\rangle$, where $\langle\text{bintree}\rangle$ is defined by*

$$\langle\text{bintree}\rangle ::= \langle\text{number}\rangle \mid (\langle\text{symbol}\rangle \ \langle\text{bintree}\rangle \ \langle\text{bintree}\rangle)$$

Then s contains an odd number of nodes.

Proof: The proof is by induction on the size of s, where we take the size of s to be the number of nodes in s. The induction hypothesis, $IH(k)$, is that any tree of size $\leq k$ has an odd number of nodes. We follow the usual prescription for an inductive proof: we first prove that $IH(0)$ is true, and we then prove that whenever k is a number such that IH is true for k, then IH is true for $k + 1$ also.

1. There are no trees with 0 nodes, so $IH(0)$ holds trivially.

2. Let k be a number such that $IH(k)$ holds, that is, any tree with $\leq k$ nodes actually has an odd number of nodes. We need to show that $IH(k + 1)$ holds as well: that any tree with $\leq k + 1$ nodes has an odd number of nodes. If s has $\leq k + 1$ nodes, there are exactly two possibilities according to the BNF definition of $\langle\text{bintree}\rangle$:

   (a) s could be of the form n, where n is a number. In this case, s has exactly one node, and one is odd.

(b) s could be of the form $(sym \; s_1 \; s_2)$, where sym is a symbol and s_1 and s_2 are trees. Now s_1 and s_2 must have fewer nodes than s. Since s has $\leq k+1$ nodes, s_1 and s_2 must have $\leq k$ nodes. Therefore they are covered by $IH(k)$, and they must each have an odd number of nodes, say $2n_1 + 1$ and $2n_2 + 1$ nodes, respectively. Hence the total number of nodes in the tree, counting the two subtrees and the root, is

$$(2n_1 + 1) + (2n_2 + 1) + 1 = 2(n_1 + n_2 + 1) + 1$$

which is once again odd.

This completes the proof of the claim that $IH(k+1)$ holds and therefore completes the induction. □

The key to the proof is that the substructures of a tree s are always smaller than s itself. Therefore the induction might be rephrased as follows:

1. IH is true on simple structures (those without substructures).

2. If IH is true on the substructures of s, then it is true on s itself.

This pattern of proof is called *structural induction*.

Exercise 1.4 [⋆⋆] Prove that if $e \in \langle \text{expression} \rangle$, then there are the same number of left and right parentheses in e (where $\langle \text{expression} \rangle$ is defined as in Section 1.1.2).

1.2   Recursively Specified Programs

In the previous section, we used the method of inductive definition to characterize complicated sets. Starting with simple members of the set, the BNF rules were used to build more and more complex members of the set. We now use the same idea to define procedures for manipulating those sets. First we define the procedure's behavior on simple inputs, and then we use this behavior to define its behavior on more complex arguments.

Imagine we want to define a procedure to find nonnegative powers of numbers, *e.g.* $e(n, x) = x^n$, where n is a nonnegative integer and $x \neq 0$. It is easy to define a sequence of procedures that compute particular powers: $e_0(x) = x^0$, $e_1(x) = x^1$, $e_2(x) = x^2$:

$$
\begin{aligned}
e_0(x) &= 1 \\
e_1(x) &= x \times e_0(x) \\
e_2(x) &= x \times e_1(x) \\
e_3(x) &= x \times e_2(x)
\end{aligned}
$$

In general, if n is a nonnegative integer,

$$e_n(x) = \begin{cases} 1 & n = 0 \\ x \times e_{n-1}(x) & n > 0. \end{cases}$$

At each stage, we use the fact that the problem has already been solved for smaller n. Next the subscript can be removed from e by making it a parameter:

1. If n is 0, $e(n, x) = 1$.

2. If n is greater than 0, we assume it is known how to solve the problem for $n - 1$. That is, we assume that $e(n - 1, x)$ is well defined. Therefore, $e(n, x) = x \times e(n - 1, x)$.

   This gives us the definition:

$$e(n, x) = \begin{cases} 1 & n = 0 \\ x \times e(n - 1, x) & n > 0. \end{cases}$$

To prove that $e(n, x) = x^n$ for any nonnegative integer n, we proceed by induction on n:

1. (Base Step) When $n = 0$, $e(0, x) = 1 = x^0$.

2. (Induction Step) Assume that the procedure works when its first argument is k, that is, $e(k, x) = x^k$ for some nonnegative integer k. Then we claim that $e(k + 1, x) = x^{k+1}$. We calculate as follows

$$\begin{aligned} e(k + 1, x) &= x \times e(k, x) & \text{(definition of } e) \\ &= x \times x^k & (\textit{IH} \text{ at } k) \\ &= x^{k+1} & \text{(fact about exponentiation)} \end{aligned}$$

This completes the induction.

We can write a program to compute e based upon the inductive definition

```
(define e
  (lambda (n x)
    (if (zero? n)
      1
      (* x
        (e (- n 1) x)))))
```

The two branches of the if expression correspond to the two cases detailed in the definition.

If we can reduce a problem to a smaller subproblem, we can call the procedure that solves the problem to solve the subproblem. The solution it returns for the subproblem may then be used to solve the original problem. This works because each time we call the procedure, it is called with a smaller problem, until eventually it is called with a problem that can be solved directly, without another call to itself.

When a procedure calls itself in this manner, it is said to be recursively defined. Such *recursive calls* are possible in Scheme and most other languages. The general phenomenon is known as *recursion,* and it occurs in contexts other than programming, such as inductive definitions. Later we shall study how recursion is implemented in programming languages.

Often an inductive proof can lead us to a recursive procedure. In Theorem 1.1.1, we showed that the number of nodes in a binary tree, defined by

$$\langle\text{bintree}\rangle ::= \langle\text{number}\rangle \mid (\langle\text{symbol}\rangle \langle\text{bintree}\rangle \langle\text{bintree}\rangle)$$

is always odd. Let us write a procedure count-nodes to count these nodes. If s is a number, then (count-nodes s) should be 1. If s is of the form (*sym s_1 s_2*), then (count-nodes s) should be (count-nodes s_1)+(count-nodes s_2)+1. This leads to the program

```
(define count-nodes
  (lambda (s)
    (if (number? s)
      1
      (+ (count-nodes (cadr s))
         (count-nodes (caddr s))
         1)))))
```

The procedure and the proof of the theorem have the same structure.

1.2.1 Deriving Programs from BNF Data Specifications

In the previous example, we used induction on integers, so the subproblem was solved by recursively calling the procedure with a smaller value of n. When manipulating inductively defined structures, subproblems are usually solved by calling the procedure recursively on a substructure of the original.

A BNF definition for the type of data being manipulated serves as a guide both to where recursive calls should be used and to which base cases need to be handled. This is a fundamental point:

Follow the Grammar!

When defining a program based on structural induction, the structure
of the program should be patterned after the structure of the data.

Typically this means that we will need one procedure for each syntactic
category in the grammar. Each procedure will examine the input to see which
production it corresponds to; for each nonterminal that appears in the right-
hand side, we will have a recursive call to the procedure for that nonterminal.

As an example, consider a procedure that determines whether a given list
is a member of ⟨list-of-numbers⟩.

A typical kind of program based on inductively defined structures is a
predicate that determines whether a given value is a member of a particular
set. Let us write a Scheme predicate `list-of-numbers?` that takes a list and
determines whether it belongs to the syntactic category ⟨list-of-numbers⟩.

```
> (list-of-numbers? '(1 2 3))
#t
> (list-of-numbers? '(1 two 3))
#f
> (list-of-numbers? '(1 (2) 3))
#f
```

We can define the set of lists as

$$\langle \text{list} \rangle ::= \text{()} \mid (\langle \text{datum} \rangle . \langle \text{list} \rangle)$$

and let us recall the definition of ⟨list-of-numbers⟩:

$$\langle \text{list-of-numbers} \rangle ::= \text{()} \mid (\langle \text{number} \rangle . \langle \text{list-of-numbers} \rangle)$$

We begin by writing down the simplest behavior of the procedure: what it
does when the input is the empty list.

```
(define list-of-numbers?
  (lambda (lst)
    (if (null? lst)
      ...
      ...)))
```

By the first production in the grammar for ⟨list-of-numbers⟩, the empty list
is a ⟨list-of-numbers⟩, so the answer should be `#t`.

```
(define list-of-numbers?
  (lambda (lst)
    (if (null? lst)
      #t
      ...)))
```

Throughout this book, bars in the left margin indicate lines that have changed since an earlier version of the same definition.

If the input is not empty, then by the grammar for ⟨list⟩, it must be of the form

$$(⟨\text{datum}⟩ . ⟨\text{list}⟩)$$

that is, a list whose car is a Scheme datum and whose cdr is a list. Comparing this to the grammar for ⟨list-of-numbers⟩, we see that such a datum can be an element of ⟨list-of-numbers⟩ if and only if its car is a number *and* its cdr is a list-of-numbers. To find out if the cdr is a list-of-numbers, we call `list-of-numbers?` recursively:

```
(define list-of-numbers?
  (lambda (lst)
    (if (null? lst)
      #t
      (and
        (number? (car lst))
        (list-of-numbers? (cdr lst))))))
```

To prove the correctness of `list-of-numbers?`, we would like to use induction on the length of `lst`.

1. The procedure `list-of-numbers?` works correctly on lists of length 0, since the only list of length 0 is the empty list, for which the correct answer, true, is returned.

2. Assuming `list-of-numbers?` works correctly on lists of length k, we show that it works on lists of length $k + 1$. Let `lst` be such a list. By the definition of ⟨list-of-numbers⟩, `lst` belongs to ⟨list-of-numbers⟩ if and only if its car is a number and its cdr belongs to ⟨list-of-numbers⟩. Since `lst` is of length $k + 1$, its cdr is of length k, so by the induction hypothesis we can determine the cdr's membership in ⟨list-of-numbers⟩ by passing it to `list-of-numbers?`. Hence `list-of-numbers?` correctly computes membership in ⟨list-of-numbers⟩ for lists of length $k + 1$, and the induction is complete.

The procedure terminates because every time `list-of-numbers?` is called, it is passed a shorter list. Every time the procedure recurs, it will be working on shorter and shorter lists, until it reaches the empty list.

Exercise 1.5 [⋆] This version of `list-of-numbers?` works properly only when its argument is a list. Extend the definition of `list-of-numbers?` so that it will work on an arbitrary Scheme ⟨datum⟩ and return #f on any argument that is not a list.

As a second example, we define a procedure `nth-elt` that takes a list `lst` and a zero-based index `n` and returns element number `n` of `lst`.

```
> (nth-elt '(a b c) 1)
b
```

The procedure `nth-elt` does for lists what `vector-ref` does for vectors.

Actually, Scheme provides the procedure `list-ref`, which is the same as `nth-elt` except for error reporting, but we choose another name because standard procedures should not be tampered with unnecessarily.

When `n` is 0, the answer is simply the car of `lst`. If `n` is greater than 0, then the answer is element $n - 1$ of `lst`'s cdr. Since neither the car nor cdr of `lst` exists if `lst` is the empty list, we must guard the `car` and `cdr` operations so that we do not take the car or cdr of an empty list.

```
(define nth-elt
  (lambda (lst n)
    (if (null? lst)
      (eopl:error 'nth-elt
        "List too short by ~s elements" (+ n 1))
      (if (zero? n)
        (car lst)
        (nth-elt (cdr lst) (- n 1))))))
```

The procedure `eopl:error` signals an error. Its first argument is a symbol that allows the error message to identify the procedure that called `eopl:error`. The second argument is a string that is then printed in the error message. There must then be an additional argument for each instance of the character sequence ~s in the string. The values of these arguments are printed in place of the corresponding ~s when the string is printed. After the error message is printed, the computation is aborted. `eopl:error` is not a standard Scheme procedure, but most implementations provide a similar facility.

Let us watch how `nth-elt` computes its answer:

```
  (nth-elt '(a b c d e) 3)
= (nth-elt   '(b c d e) 2)
= (nth-elt     '(c d e) 1)
= (nth-elt       '(d e) 0)
= d
```

Here `nth-elt` recurs on shorter and shorter lists, and on smaller and smaller numbers.

If error checking were omitted, we would have to rely on `car` and `cdr` to complain about being passed the empty list, but their error messages would be less helpful. For example, if we received an error message from `car`, we might have to look for uses of `car` throughout our program. Even this would not find the error if `nth-elt` were provided by someone else, so that its definition was not a part of our program.

Let us try one more example of this kind before moving on to harder examples. The standard procedure `length` determines the number of elements in a list.

```
> (length '(a b c))
3
> (length '((x) ()))
2
```

We write our own procedure, called `list-length`, to do the same thing. The length of the empty list is 0.

```
(define list-length
  (lambda (lst)
    (if (null? lst)
      0
      ...))))
```

The ellipsis is filled in by observing that the length of a non-empty list is one more than the length of its cdr.

```
(define list-length
  (lambda (lst)
    (if (null? lst)
      0
|     (+ 1 (list-length (cdr lst)))))))
```

The procedures `nth-elt` and `list-length` do not check whether their arguments are of the expected type. Programs such as this that fail to check that their input is properly formed are *fragile*. (Users think a program is broken if it behaves badly, even when it is being used improperly.) It is generally better to write *robust* programs that thoroughly check their arguments, but robust programs are often much more complicated.

The specification of a procedure should include the assumptions the procedure may make about its input, and what kinds of behavior are permitted if these assumptions fail. If a procedure is always called in a context that causes these assumptions to be satisfied, it is wasteful (and at worst impossible) for the procedure to check its input. If the context in which the procedure will be called is unknown, then a procedure that does not check its arguments may fail in unexpected and unwelcome ways.

As we are concerned in this book with concisely conveying ideas, rather than providing general purpose tools, many of our programs are fragile. Even when programs are written solely to test ideas, some error checking may be wise to facilitate debugging.

Exercise 1.6 [⋆] What happens if `nth-elt` and `list-length` are passed symbols when a list is expected? What is the behavior of `list-ref` and `length` in such cases? Write robust versions of `nth-elt` and `list-length`.

Exercise 1.7 [⋆⋆] The error message from `nth-elt` is uninformative. Rewrite `nth-elt` so that it produces a more informative error message, such as "(a b c) does not have an element 4." Hint: use `letrec` to create a local recursive procedure that does the real work.

1.2.2   Some Important Examples

In this section, we present some simple recursive procedures that will be used as examples later in this book. As in previous examples, they are defined so that (1) the structure of a program reflects the structure of its data and (2) recursive calls are employed at points where recursion is used in the set's inductive definition.

remove-first

The first procedure is `remove-first`, which takes two arguments: a symbol, `s`, and a list of symbols, `los`. It returns a list with the same elements arranged in the same order as `los`, except that the first occurrence of the symbol `s` is removed. If there is no occurrence of `s` in `los`, then `los` is returned.

```
> (remove-first 'a '(a b c))
(b c)
> (remove-first 'b '(e f g))
(e f g)
> (remove-first 'a4 '(c1 a4 c1 a4))
(c1 c1 a4)
> (remove-first 'x '())
()
```

Before we start on the program, we must complete the problem specification by defining the set ⟨list-of-symbols⟩. Unlike the s-lists introduced in the last section, these lists of symbols do not contain sublists.

$$\langle\text{list-of-symbols}\rangle ::= \text{()} \mid (\langle\text{symbol}\rangle \, . \, \langle\text{list-of-symbols}\rangle)$$

A list of symbols is either the empty list or a list whose car is a symbol and whose cdr is a list of symbols. If the list is empty, there are no occurrences of s to remove, so the answer is the empty list.

```
(define remove-first
  (lambda (s los)
    (if (null? los)
      '()
      ...))))
```

If los is non-empty, is there some case where we can determine the answer immediately? If $\text{los} = (s \, s_1 \, \ldots \, s_{n-1})$, the first occurrence of s is as the first element of los. So the result of removing it is just $(s_1 \, \ldots \, s_{n-1})$.

```
(define remove-first
  (lambda (s los)
    (if (null? los)
      '()
      (if (eqv? (car los) s)
        (cdr los)
        ...)))))
```

If the first element of los is not s, say $\text{los} = (s_0 \, s_1 \, \ldots \, s_{n-1})$, then we know that s_0 is not the first occurrence of s. Therefore the first element of the answer must be s_0. Furthermore, the first occurrence of s in los must be its first occurrence in $(s_1 \, \ldots \, s_{n-1})$. So the rest of the answer must be the result of removing the first occurrence of s from the cdr of los. Since the cdr of los is shorter than los, we may recursively call remove-first to remove s from the cdr of `los`. Thus the answer may be obtained by using `(cons (car los) (remove-first s (cdr los)))`. With this, the complete definition of `remove-first` follows.

```
(define remove-first
  (lambda (s los)
    (if (null? los)
      '()
      (if (eqv? (car los) s)
        (cdr los)
        (cons (car los) (remove-first s (cdr los)))))))
```

Exercise 1.8 [⋆] In the definition of `remove-first`, if the inner if's alternative (`cons ...`) were replaced by (`remove-first s (cdr los)`), what function would the resulting procedure compute?

remove

The second procedure is `remove`, defined over symbols and lists of symbols. It is similar to `remove-first`, but it removes *all* occurrences of a given symbol from a list of symbols, not just the first.

```
> (remove 'a4 '(c1 a4 d1 a4))
(c1 d1)
```

Since `remove-first` and `remove` work on the same input, their structure is similar. If the list `los` is empty, there are no occurrences to remove, so the answer is again the empty list. If `los` is non-empty, there are again two cases to consider. If the first element of `los` is not `s`, the answer is obtained as in `remove-first`.

```
(define remove
  (lambda (s los)
    (if (null? los)
      '()
      (if (eqv? (car los) s)
        ...
        (cons (car los) (remove s (cdr los)))))))
```

If the first element of `los` is the same as `s`, certainly the first element is not to be part of the result. But we are not quite done: all the occurrences of `s` must still be removed from the cdr of `los`. Once again this may be accomplished by invoking `remove` recursively on the cdr of `los`.

```
(define remove
  (lambda (s los)
    (if (null? los)
      '()
      (if (eqv? (car los) s)
        (remove s (cdr los))
        (cons (car los) (remove s (cdr los)))))))
```

Exercise 1.9 [⋆] In the definition of `remove`, if the inner `if`'s alternative `(cons ...)` were replaced by `(remove s (cdr los))`, what function would the resulting procedure compute?

`subst`

The third of our examples is `subst`. It takes three arguments: two symbols, `new` and `old`, and an s-list, `slist`. All elements of `slist` are examined, and a new list is returned that is similar to `slist` but with all occurrences of `old` replaced by instances of `new`.

```
> (subst 'a 'b '((b c) (b () d)))
((a c) (a () d))
```

Since `subst` is defined over s-lists, its organization reflects the definition of s-lists

$$\langle\text{s-list}\rangle \qquad ::= (\{\langle\text{symbol-expression}\rangle\}^*)$$
$$\langle\text{symbol-expression}\rangle ::= \langle\text{symbol}\rangle \mid \langle\text{s-list}\rangle$$

First we rewrite the grammar to eliminate the use of the Kleene star:

$$\langle\text{s-list}\rangle \qquad ::= ()$$
$$::= (\langle\text{symbol-expression}\rangle \ . \ \langle\text{s-list}\rangle)$$
$$\langle\text{symbol-expression}\rangle ::= \langle\text{symbol}\rangle \mid \langle\text{s-list}\rangle$$

This example is more complex than our previous ones because the grammar for its input contains two nonterminals, $\langle\text{s-list}\rangle$ and $\langle\text{symbol-expression}\rangle$. Our follow-the-grammar pattern says we should have two procedures, one for dealing with $\langle\text{s-list}\rangle$ and one for dealing with $\langle\text{symbol-expression}\rangle$:

```
(define subst
  (lambda (new old slist)
    ...))

(define subst-in-symbol-expression
  (lambda (new old se)
    ...))
```

Let us first work on subst. If the list is empty, there are no occurrences of
old to replace.

```
(define subst
  (lambda (new old slist)
    (if (null? slist)
      '()
      ...)))
```

If slist is non-empty, its car is a member of ⟨symbol-expression⟩ and its
cdr is another s-list. In this case, the answer should be a list whose car is
the result of changing old to new in the car of slist, and whose cdr is the
result of changing old to new in the cdr of slist. Since the car of slist
is an element of ⟨symbol-expression⟩, we solve the subproblem for the car
using subst-in-symbol-expression. Since the cdr of slist is an element
of ⟨s-list⟩, we recur on the cdr using subst:

```
(define subst
  (lambda (new old slist)
    (if (null? slist)
      '()
      (cons
        (subst-in-symbol-expression new old (car slist))
        (subst new old (cdr slist))))))
```

Now we can move on to subst-in-symbol-expression. From the grammar, we know that the symbol expression se is either a symbol or an s-list. If
it is a symbol, we need to ask whether it is the same as the symbol old. If it
is, the answer is new; if it is some other symbol, the answer is the same as se.
If se is an s-list, then we can recur using subst to find the answer.

```
(define subst-in-symbol-expression
  (lambda (new old se)
    (if (symbol? se)
      (if (eqv? se old) new se)
      (subst new old se))))
```

Since we have strictly followed the BNF definition of ⟨s-list⟩ and ⟨symbol-
expression⟩, this recursion is guaranteed to halt. Observe that subst and
subst-in-symbol-expression call each other recursively. Such procedures
are said to be *mutually recursive*.

The decomposition of subst into two procedures, one for each syntactic
category, is an important technique. It allows us to think about one syntactic
category at a time, which is important in more complicated situations.

Exercise 1.10 [⋆] In the last line of subst-in-symbol-expression, the recursion is on se and not a smaller substructure. Why is the recursion guaranteed to halt?

Exercise 1.11 [⋆] Eliminate the one call to subst-in-symbol-expression in subst by replacing it by its definition and simplifying the resulting procedure. The result will be a version of subst that does not need subst-in-symbol-expression. This technique is called *inlining*, and is used by optimizing compilers.

Exercise 1.12 [⋆⋆] In our example, we began by eliminating the Kleene star in the grammar for ⟨s-list⟩. When a production is expressed using Kleene star, often the recursion can be expressed using map. Write subst following the original grammar by using map.

notate-depth

Our next example is notate-depth. This procedure takes an s-list and produces a list similar to the original, except that each symbol is replaced by a list containing the symbol and a number equal to the depth at which the symbol appears in the original s-list. A symbol appearing at the top level of the s-list is at depth 0; a symbol appearing in an immediate sublist is at depth 1, etc. For example,

```
> (notate-depth '(a (b () c) ((d)) e))
((a 0) ((b 1) () (c 1)) (((d 2))) (e 0))
```

To solve this problem, we need to distinguish the s-list that is the input from an s-list that may appear as a sublist. Thus our grammar will be

$$
\begin{array}{lll}
\langle\text{top-level}\rangle & ::= & \langle\text{s-list}\rangle \\
\langle\text{s-list}\rangle & ::= & () \\
& ::= & (\langle\text{symbol-expression}\rangle \; . \; \langle\text{s-list}\rangle) \\
\langle\text{symbol-expression}\rangle & ::= & \langle\text{symbol}\rangle \mid \langle\text{s-list}\rangle
\end{array}
$$

We will have three procedures: notate-depth, notate-depth-in-s-list and notate-depth-in-symbol-expression, corresponding to the three nonterminals. The latter two procedures will take an additional parameter d that indicates what depth we are at. Initially, we are at depth 0.

```
(define notate-depth
  (lambda (slist)
    (notate-depth-in-s-list slist 0)))

(define notate-depth-in-s-list
  (lambda (slist d)
    ...))
```

```
(define notate-depth-in-symbol-expression
  (lambda (se d)
    ...))
```

To notate an s-list at depth d, we simply notate each of its elements:

```
(define notate-depth-in-s-list
  (lambda (slist d)
    (if (null? slist)
      '()
      (cons
        (notate-depth-in-symbol-expression (car slist) d)
        (notate-depth-in-s-list (cdr slist) d)))))
```

To notate a symbol-expression se at depth d, we first ask if se is a symbol. If so, we can return (list se d). If se is instead a list, then we need to notate its elements. But those elements are now at depth d+1 :

```
(define notate-depth-in-symbol-expression
  (lambda (se d)
    (if (symbol? se)
      (list se d)
      (notate-depth-in-s-list se (+ d 1)))))
```

This technique of passing additional arguments to keep track of the context in which a procedure is invoked is extremely useful. Such arguments are called *inherited attributes*. Our subst example uses a rudimentary form of this technique by passing the extra parameters old and new, but those parameters do not change as the procedure recurs.

Exercise 1.13 [★★] Rewrite the grammar for ⟨s-list⟩ to use Kleene star, and rewrite notate-depth-in-s-list using map.

1.2.3   Other Patterns of Recursion

Sometimes the grammar for the input may not provide sufficient structure for the program. As an example, we consider the problem of summing all the values in a vector.

If we were summing the values in a list, we could follow the grammar to recur on the cdr of the list to get a procedure like

```
(define list-sum
  (lambda (lon)
    (if (null? lon)
        0
        (+ (car lon)
           (list-sum (cdr lon))))))
```

But it is not possible to proceed in this way with vectors, because they do not decompose as readily.

Sometimes the best way to solve a problem is to solve a more general problem and use it to solve the original problem as a special case. For the vector sum problem, since we cannot decompose vectors, we generalize the problem to compute the sum of part of the vector. We define partial-vector-sum, which takes a vector of numbers, von, and a number, n, and returns the sum of the first n values in von.

```
(define partial-vector-sum
  (lambda (von n)
    (if (zero? n)
        0
        (+ (vector-ref von (- n 1))
           (partial-vector-sum von (- n 1))))))
```

Since n decreases steadily to zero, a proof of correctness for this program would proceed by induction on n. It is now a simple matter to solve our original problem

```
(define vector-sum
  (lambda (von)
    (partial-vector-sum von (vector-length von))))
```

Observe that von does not change. We can take advantage of this by rewriting the program using letrec:

```
(define vector-sum
  (lambda (von)
    (letrec
      ((partial-sum
         (lambda (n)
           (if (zero? n)
               0
               (+ (vector-ref von (- n 1))
                  (partial-sum (- n 1)))))))
      (partial-sum (vector-length von)))))
```

Exercise 1.14 [⋆⋆] Given the assumption $0 \leq n < length(\text{von})$, prove that `partial-vector-sum` is correct.

There are many other situations in which it may be helpful or necessary to introduce auxiliary variables or procedures to solve a problem. Always feel free to do so.

1.2.4   Exercises

Getting the knack of writing recursive programs involves practice. Thus we conclude this section with a number of exercises.

Exercise 1.15 [⋆] Define, test, and debug the following procedures. Assume that s is any symbol, n is a nonnegative integer, `lst` is a list, v is a vector, `los` is a list of symbols, `vos` is a vector of symbols, `slist` is an s-list, and x is any object; and similarly s1 is a symbol, `los2` is a list of symbols, x1 is an object, etc. Also assume that `pred` is a predicate, that is, a procedure that takes any Scheme object and returns either #t or #f. Make no other assumptions about the data unless further restrictions are given as part of a particular problem. For these exercises, there is no need to check that the input matches the description; for each procedure, assume that its input values are members of the specified sets.

To test these procedures, at the very minimum try all of the given examples. Also use other examples to test these procedures, since the given examples are not adequate to reveal all possible errors.

1. `(duple n x)` returns a list containing n copies of x.

   ```
   > (duple 2 3)
   (3 3)
   > (duple 4 '(ho ho))
   ((ho ho) (ho ho) (ho ho) (ho ho))
   > (duple 0 '(blah))
   ()
   ```

2. `(invert lst)`, where `lst` is a list of 2-lists (lists of length two), returns a list with each 2-list reversed.

   ```
   > (invert '((a 1) (a 2) (b 1) (b 2)))
   ((1 a) (2 a) (1 b) (2 b))
   ```

3. `(filter-in pred lst)` returns the list of those elements in `lst` that satisfy the predicate `pred`.

   ```
   > (filter-in number? '(a 2 (1 3) b 7))
   (2 7)
   > (filter-in symbol? '(a (b c) 17 foo))
   (a foo)
   ```

4. `(every? pred lst)` returns `#f` if any element of `lst` fails to satisfy `pred`, and returns `#t` otherwise.

```
> (every? number? '(a b c 3 e))
#f
> (every? number? '(1 2 3 5 4))
#t
```

5. `(exists? pred lst)` returns `#t` if any element of `lst` satisfies `pred`, and returns `#f` otherwise.

```
> (exists? number? '(a b c 3 e))
#t
> (exists? number? '(a b c d e))
#f
```

6. `(vector-index pred v)` returns the zero-based index of the first element of `v` that satisfies the predicate `pred`, or `#f` if no element of `v` satisfies `pred`.

```
> (vector-index (lambda (x) (eqv? x 'c)) '#(a b c d))
2
> (vector-ref '#(a b c)
    (vector-index (lambda (x) (eqv? x 'b)) '#(a b c)))
b
```

7. `(list-set lst n x)` returns a list like `lst`, except that the n-th element, using zero-based indexing, is x.

```
> (list-set '(a b c d) 2 '(1 2))
(a b (1 2) d)
> (list-ref (list-set '(a b c d) 3 '(1 5 10)) 3)
(1 5 10)
```

8. `(product los1 los2)` returns a list of 2-lists that represents the Cartesian product of `los1` and `los2`. The 2-lists may appear in any order.

```
> (product '(a b c) '(x y))
((a x) (a y) (b x) (b y) (c x) (c y))
```

9. `(down lst)` wraps parentheses around each top-level element of `lst`.

```
> (down '(1 2 3))
((1) (2) (3))
> (down '((a) (fine) (idea)))
(((a)) ((fine)) ((idea)))
> (down '(a (more (complicated)) object))
((a) ((more (complicated))) (object))
```

10. `(vector-append-list v lst)` returns a new vector with the elements of `lst` attached to the end of `v`. Do this without using `vector->list`, `list->vector`, and `append`.

```
> (vector-append-list '#(1 2 3) '(4 5))
#(1 2 3 4 5)
```

Exercise 1.16 [⋆⋆]

1. (up lst) removes a pair of parentheses from each top-level element of lst. If a top-level element is not a list, it is included in the result, as is. The value of (up (down lst)) is equivalent to lst, but (down (up lst)) is not necessarily lst.

```
> (up '((1 2) (3 4)))
(1 2 3 4)
> (up '((x (y)) z))
(x (y) z)
```

2. (swapper s1 s2 slist) returns a list the same as slist, but with all occurrences of s1 replaced by s2 and all occurrences of s2 replaced by s1.

```
> (swapper 'a 'd '(a b c d))
(d b c a)
> (swapper 'a 'd '(a d () c d))
(d a () c a)
> (swapper 'x 'y '((x) y (z (x))))
((y) x (z (y)))
```

3. (count-occurrences s slist) returns the number of occurrences of s in slist.

```
> (count-occurrences 'x '((f x) y (((x z) x))))
3
> (count-occurrences 'x '((f x) y (((x z) () x))))
3
> (count-occurrences 'w '((f x) y (((x z) x))))
0
```

4. (flatten slist) returns a list of the symbols contained in slist in the order in which they occur when slist is printed. Intuitively, flatten removes all the inner parentheses from its argument.

```
> (flatten '(a b c))
(a b c)
> (flatten '((a) () (b ()) () (c)))
(a b c)
> (flatten '((a b) c (((d)) e)))
(a b c d e)
> (flatten '(a b (() (c))))
(a b c)
```

5. (merge lon1 lon2), where lon1 and lon2 are lists of numbers that are sorted in ascending order, returns a sorted list of all the numbers in lon1 and lon2.

```
> (merge '(1 4) '(1 2 8))
(1 1 2 4 8)
> (merge '(35 62 81 90 91) '(3 83 85 90))
(3 35 62 81 83 85 90 90 91)
```

Exercise 1.17 [★★★]

1. (path n bst), where n is a number and bst is a binary search tree that contains
   the number n, returns a list of lefts and rights showing how to find the node
   containing n. If n is found at the root, it returns the empty list.

   ```
   > (path 17 '(14 (7 () (12 () ()))
                   (26 (20 (17 () ())
                           ())
                       (31 () ()))))
   (right left left)
   ```

2. (sort lon) returns a list of the elements of lon in increasing order.

   ```
   > (sort '(8 2 5 2 3))
   (2 2 3 5 8)
   ```

3. (sort predicate lon) returns a list of elements sorted by the predicate.

   ```
   > (sort < '(8 2 5 2 3))
   (2 2 3 5 8)
   > (sort > '(8 2 5 2 3))
   (8 5 3 2 2)
   ```

Exercise 1.18 [★★★] This exercise has three parts. Work them in order.

1. Define the procedure compose such that (compose p1 p2), where p1 and p2
   are procedures of one argument, returns the composition of these procedures,
   specified by this equation:

   ```
   ((compose p1 p2) x) = (p1 (p2 x))
   > ((compose car cdr) '(a b c d))
   b
   ```

2. (car&cdr s slist errvalue) returns an expression that, when evaluated,
   produces the code for a procedure that takes a list with the same structure as
   slist and returns the value in the same position as the leftmost occurrence of s
   in slist. If s does not occur in slist, then errvalue is returned. Do this so
   that it generates procedure compositions.

   ```
   > (car&cdr 'a '(a b c) 'fail)
   car
   > (car&cdr 'c '(a b c) 'fail)
   (compose car (compose cdr cdr))
   > (car&cdr 'dog '(cat lion (fish dog ()) pig) 'fail)
   (compose car (compose cdr (compose car (compose cdr cdr))))
   > (car&cdr 'a '(b c) 'fail)
   fail
   ```

3. Define car&cdr2, which behaves like car&cdr, but does not use compose in its
   output.

1.3   Scoping and Binding of Variables

We now apply these ideas to a group of important programming language concepts: the scoping and binding of variables.

In most programming languages, variables may appear in two different ways: as *references* or as *declarations*. A variable reference is a use of the variable. For example, in

```
(f x y)
```

all the variables, f, x, and y, appear as references. However, in

```
(lambda (x) ...)
```

or

```
(let ((x ...)) ...)
```

the occurrence of x is a declaration: it introduces the variable as a name for some value. In the `lambda` expression, the value of the variable will be supplied when the procedure is called; in the `let` expression the value of the variable is obtained from the value of the expression in the first "...".

We sometimes call the value named by a variable its *denotation*. The denotation must come from some declaration, and we say that the variable reference is *bound* by that declaration, or that it *refers* to that declaration.

Declarations in most programming languages have a limited scope, so that the same variable name may be used for different purposes in different parts of a program. For example, we have repeatedly used `lst` as a formal parameter, and in each case its scope was limited to the body of the corresponding lambda expression.

Every programming language must have some rules to determine the declaration to which each variable reference refers. These rules are typically called *binding* rules.

In Scheme, as in most other languages, the relation between a variable reference and the declaration to which it refers is a *static* property: it can be determined by analyzing the text of a program alone, without knowing the actual values to which the variable is bound. We say that such languages are *statically scoped*. By contrast, in some languages, the declaration to which a variable reference refers cannot be determined until the program is executed; such properties are called *dynamic*.

It is important to know whether a property is static, because static properties can be analyzed by a compiler to detect errors before run time and to improve the efficiency of object code. They are also usually easier for programmers to analyze, and this makes programs easier to understand.

In this section we study a number of static properties related to variable binding. We do this in the simplest possible context: the language of lambda calculus expressions, which we defined in section 1.1. Recall that this language consists only of variable references, `lambda` expressions with a single formal parameter, and procedure calls. It is defined by the grammar

$$\langle\text{expression}\rangle ::= \langle\text{identifier}\rangle$$
$$::= (\texttt{lambda}\ (\langle\text{identifier}\rangle)\ \langle\text{expression}\rangle)$$
$$::= (\langle\text{expression}\rangle\ \langle\text{expression}\rangle)$$

The binding rule for lambda calculus expressions is the following:

Definition 1.3.1 (Binding Rule for Lambda Calculus Expressions)
In `(lambda (`$\langle\text{identifier}\rangle$`))` $\langle\text{expression}\rangle$`)`, *the occurrence of* $\langle\text{identifier}\rangle$ *is a declaration that binds all occurrences of that variable in* $\langle\text{expression}\rangle$ *unless some intervening declaration of the same variable occurs.*

We spend the rest of this section exploring the consequences of this definition.

1.3.1 Free and Bound Variables

The first question one can ask about a variable and an expression is whether the variable occurs free or bound in that expression.

Definition 1.3.2 (Occurs Free, Occurs Bound)
A variable x occurs free in E if and only if there is some use of x in E that is not bound by any declaration of x in E.

A variable x occurs bound in an expression E if and only if there is some use of x in E that is bound by a declaration of x in E.

Thus in

```
((lambda (x) x) y)
```
(*)

x occurs bound, since the second occurrence of x is a reference bound by the first occurrence of x (a declaration). Similarly, y occurs free because its sole occurrence in this expression is not bound by any declaration of y.

A variable reference that is free in one context, such as (∗), may be bound in a larger surrounding context. For example, if (∗) were embedded in the body of a lambda calculus expression with formal parameter y, as in

```
(lambda (y)
  ((lambda (x) x) y))                                          (∗∗)
```

then the reference to y on the second line is bound by the declaration of the formal parameter y on the first line.

The value of an expression depends only on the values associated with the variables that occur free within the expression. The context that surrounds the expression must provide these values. For example, the value of the expression ((lambda (x) x) y) on the second line of (∗∗) depends only on the denotation of its single free variable y. The denotation of y comes from its associated declaration, the declaration of the formal parameter y on the first line. Hence the value of y will come from the argument to the procedure (∗∗).

Conversely, the value of an expression is independent of the bindings of variables that do not occur free in the expression. For example, the value of (∗) is independent of the denotation of x at the time that (∗) is evaluated. By the time the free occurrence of x in the body of (lambda (x) x) is evaluated, it will have a new binding (in (∗), the value associated with y).

Therefore, the meaning of an expression with no free variables is fixed. For instance, the meaning of (lambda (x) x) is always the same: it is the identity function that returns whatever value it is passed. Other lambda calculus expressions without free variables also have fixed meanings. For example, the value of

```
(lambda (f)
  (lambda (x)
    (f x)))
```

is a procedure that takes a procedure, f, and returns a procedure that takes a value x, applies f to it, and returns the result. *Lambda calculus* expressions without free variables are called *combinators.* Many combinators, such as the identity function and the application combinator above, are useful programming tools.

We formulated definition 1.3.2 for any programming language; for the language of lambda calculus expressions, we can make a much more specific definition.

Definition 1.3.3 (Occurs Free, Occurs Bound in Lambda Calculus Expressions)

A variable x occurs free *in a lambda calculus expression E if and only if*

1. *E is a variable reference and E is the same as x; or*

2. *E is of the form* (lambda (y) E'), *where y is different from x and x occurs free in E'; or*

3. *E is of the form* (E$_1$ E$_2$) *and x occurs free in E$_1$ or E$_2$.*

   A variable x occurs bound *in a lambda calculus expression E if and only if*

1. *E is of the form* (lambda (y) E'), *where x occurs bound in E' or x and y are the same variable and y occurs free in E'; or*

2. *E is of the form* (E$_1$ E$_2$) *and x occurs bound in E$_1$ or E$_2$.*

This definition says that *x* can occur bound in *E* only if *E* is a lambda-expression or an application; hence no variable occurs bound in an expression consisting of just a single variable.

From this definition, we can easily write procedures occurs-free? and occurs-bound? that take a variable and an expression and determine whether the variable occurs free or bound in the expression (figure 1.1). In each one we do a case analysis of the expression to determine which clause of the definition applies, and recur when the definition tells us to do so.

The procedures occurs-free? and occurs-bound? are not as readable as they might be. It is hard to tell, for example, that (caadr exp) refers to the declaration of a variable in a lambda expression, or that (caddr exp) refers to its body. We show how to improve this situation considerably in section 2.2.2.

Exercise 1.19 [★★] Write a procedure free-vars that takes a list structure representing an expression in the lambda calculus syntax given above and returns a set (a list without duplicates) of all the variables that occur free in the expression. Similarly, write a procedure bound-vars that returns a set of all the variables that occur bound in its argument.

Exercise 1.20 [★] Give an example of a lambda calculus expression in which a variable occurs free but which has a value that is independent of the value of the free variable.

Exercise 1.21 [★] Give an example of a lambda calculus expression in which the same variable occurs both bound and free.

```
(define occurs-free?
  (lambda (var exp)
    (cond
      ((symbol? exp) (eqv? exp var))
      ((eqv? (car exp) 'lambda)
       (and (not (eqv? (caadr exp) var))
            (occurs-free? var (caddr exp))))
      (else (or (occurs-free? var (car exp))
                (occurs-free? var (cadr exp)))))))

(define occurs-bound?
  (lambda (var exp)
    (cond
      ((symbol? exp) #f)
      ((eqv? (car exp) 'lambda)
       (or (occurs-bound? var (caddr exp))
           (and (eqv? (caadr exp) var)
                (occurs-free? var (caddr exp)))))
      (else (or (occurs-bound? var (car exp))
                (occurs-bound? var (cadr exp)))))))
```

Figure 1.1   occurs-free? and occurs-bound?

Exercise 1.22 [⋆] Scheme lambda expressions may have any number of formal parameters, and Scheme procedure calls may have any number of operands. Modify the formal definitions of occurs free and occurs bound to allow lambda expressions with any number of formal parameters and procedure calls with any number of operands. Then modify the procedures occurs-free? and occurs-bound? to follow these new definitions.

Exercise 1.23 [⋆] Extend the formal definitions of occurs free and occurs bound to include if expressions.

Exercise 1.24 [⋆⋆] Extend the formal definitions of occurs free and occurs bound to include Scheme let and let* expressions.

Exercise 1.25 [⋆] Extend the formal definitions of occurs free and occurs bound to include Scheme quotations (expressions of the form (quote ⟨datum⟩)).

Exercise 1.26 [⋆⋆] Extend the formal definitions of occurs free and occurs bound to include Scheme assignment (set!) expressions.

1.3.2   Scope and Lexical Address

The next problem is to associate with each variable reference the declaration to which it refers. It turns out to be easier to think about the reverse problem: given a declaration, which variable references refer to it?

Typically, the binding rules of a language associate with each declaration of a variable a region of the program within which the declaration is effective. For example, in the Scheme expression

```
(lambda (x) ...)
```

the region for x is the body of the lambda expression, and in a top-level definition

```
(define x ...)
```

the region is the whole program.

This is not the entire story, however, because many modern languages, including Scheme, allow regions to be *nested* within each other, as when one lambda expression appears in the body of another. Such languages are said to be *block-structured*, and the regions are sometimes called *blocks*.

For example, in Scheme the body of the lambda expression above might contain another declaration of x. In this case the inner declaration takes precedence over the outer one. Consider

```
> (define x                       ; call this x1
    (lambda (x)                   ; call this x2
      (map
        (lambda (x)               ; call this x3
          (+ x 1))                ; refers to x3
        x)))                      ; refers to x2
> (x '(1 2 3))                    ; refers to x1
(2 3 4)
```

Here the expression (+ x 1) is within the region of all three declarations of x. It therefore takes its binding from the innermost declaration of x, the one on the fourth line. Block-structured languages whose scope rules work in this way are said to use *lexical binding*.

We define the *scope* of a variable declaration to be the text within which references to the variable refer to the declaration. Thus the scope of a declaration is the region of text associated with the declaration, excluding any inner regions associated with declarations that use the same variable name. We say that the inner declaration of x *shadows* the outer declarations of x, or that the inner declaration creates a *hole* in the scope of the outer one. Alternatively, we may speak of the declarations that are *visible* at the point of a variable reference, meaning those that contain the variable reference within their scope.

The declaration of a variable *v* has a scope that includes all references to *v* that *occur free* in the region associated with the declaration. Those references to *v* that *occur bound* in the region associated with its declaration are shadowed by inner declarations.

Applying this to the preceding example, the region of the x declared on the first line is the read-eval-print loop's top level, which includes the body of the definition: however, its scope does not include the body of the defined procedure, since x does not occur free in the procedure (lambda (x) ...). The scope of the formal parameter x in the fourth line is the lambda expression's body, (+ x 1). This formal parameter creates a hole in the scope of the formal parameter x in the second line. The scope of the x in the second line includes the reference to x as the second argument to map, but not the reference to x as the first argument to +. The inner declarations of x shadow the outer declarations of x.

In a language with lexical binding, there is a simple algorithm for determining the declaration to which a variable reference refers. Search the regions enclosing the reference, starting with the innermost. As each successively larger region is encountered, check whether a declaration of the given variable is associated with the block. If one is found, it is the declaration of the variable. If not, proceed to the next enclosing region. If the outermost (top-level or global) region is reached and no declaration is found, the variable reference is free.

Exercise 1.27 [⋆] In the following expressions, draw an arrow from each variable reference to its associated formal parameter declaration.

```
(lambda (x)
  (lambda (y)
    ((lambda (x)
       (x y))
     x)))

(lambda (z)
  ((lambda (a b c)
     (a (lambda (a) (+ a c)) b))
   (lambda (f x)
     (f (z x)))))
```

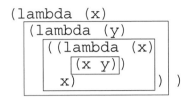

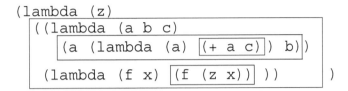

Figure 1.2 Contour diagrams

Exercise 1.28 [⋆] Repeat the above exercise with programs written in a block-structured language, other than Scheme.

It is sometimes more helpful to picture the borders of regions, rather than the interiors of regions. These borders are called *contours*. For example, the contours in the preceding exercise can be drawn as in figure 1.2.

Execution of the scoping algorithm may then be viewed as a journey outward from a variable reference. In this journey a number of contours may be crossed before arriving at the associated declaration. The number of contours crossed is called the *lexical* (or *static*) *depth* of the variable reference. It is customary to use "zero-based indexing," thereby not counting the last contour crossed. For example, in

```
(lambda (x y)
  ((lambda (a)
     (x (a y)))
   x))
```

the reference to x on the last line and the reference to a have lexical depth zero, while the references to x and y in the third line have lexical depth one.

The declarations associated with a region may be numbered in the order of their appearance in the text. Each variable reference may then be associated with two numbers: its lexical depth and its position, again using zero-based indexing, of its declaration in the declaring contour (its *declaration position*). Taken together, these two numbers are the variable reference's *lexical address*.

To illustrate lexical addresses, we may replace every variable reference v in an expression by

$$(v : d\ p)$$

where d is its lexical depth and p is its declaration position. The above example then becomes

```
(lambda (x y)
  ((lambda (a)
     ((x : 1 0) ((a : 0 0) (y : 1 1))))
   (x : 0 0)))
```

Since the lexical address completely specifies each variable reference, variable names are then superfluous! Thus variable references could be replaced by expressions of the form $(: d\ p)$, and formal parameter lists could be replaced by their length, as in

```
(lambda 2
  ((lambda 1
     ((: 1 0) ((: 0 0) (: 1 1))))
   (: 0 0)))
```

Names for lexically-bound variables are certainly a great help in writing and understanding programs, but they are not necessary in executing programs.

Exercise 1.29 [⋆] What is wrong with the following lexical-address expression?

```
(lambda (a)
  (lambda (a)
    (a : 1 0)))
```

Exercise 1.30 [⋆] Write a Scheme expression that is equivalent to the following lexical-address expression from which variable names have been removed.

```
(lambda 1
  (lambda 1
    (: 1 0)))
```

Compilers routinely calculate the lexical address of each variable reference. Once this has been done, the variable names may be discarded unless they are required to provide debugging information.

Exercise 1.31 [⋆⋆] Consider the subset of Scheme specified by the BNF rules

⟨expression⟩ ::= ⟨identifier⟩
               ::= (if ⟨expression⟩ ⟨expression⟩ ⟨expression⟩)
               ::= (lambda ({⟨identifier⟩}⋆) ⟨expression⟩)
               ::= ({⟨expression⟩}+)

Write a procedure `lexical-address` that takes any expression and returns the expression with every variable reference v replaced by a list $(v : d\ p)$, as above. If the variable reference v is free, produce the list $(v\ \texttt{free})$ instead.

```
> (lexical-address '(lambda (a b c)
                      (if (eqv? b c)
                        ((lambda (c)
                          (cons a c))
                         a)
                        b)))
(lambda (a b c)
  (if ((eqv? free) (b : 0 1) (c : 0 2))
    ((lambda (c)
       ((cons free) (a : 1 0) (c : 0 0)))
     (a : 0 0))
    (b : 0 1)))
```

Exercise 1.32 [⋆⋆] Write the procedure `un-lexical-address`, which takes lexical-address expressions with formal parameter lists and with variable references of the form `(: d p)`, or `(v free)` and returns an equivalent expression formed by substituting standard variable references for the lexical-address information, or `#f` if no such expression exists.

```
> (un-lexical-address '(lambda (a)
                         (lambda (b c)
                           ((: 1 0) (: 0 0) (: 0 1)))))
(lambda (a) (lambda (b c) (a b c)))
> (un-lexical-address '(lambda (a) (lambda (a) (: 1 0))))
#f
```

Exercise 1.33 [⋆⋆] Some languages do not allow an inner declaration to declare a variable already declared in an outer declaration. Write a procedure that takes a lambda calculus expression and checks to see if it contains such a redeclaration.

Further Reading

Scheme was introduced in (Sussman & Steele, 1975). Its development is recorded in (Steele & Sussman, 1978; Clinger *et al.*, 1985; Rees *et al.*, 1986; Clinger *et al.*, 1991; Kelsey *et al.*, 1998). The standard definitions of Scheme are provided by the IEEE standard (1991) and the *Revised[5] Report on the Algorithmic Language Scheme* (Kelsey *et al.*, 1998). (Dybvig, 1987; 1996) provides a short introduction to Scheme that includes a number of insightful examples.

Those new to recursive programming and symbolic computation might look at *The Little Schemer* (Friedman & Felleisen, 1996), or *The Little MLer* (Felleisen & Friedman, 1996), or for the more historically-minded, *The Little LISPer* (Friedman, 1974).

The lambda calculus was introduced in (Church, 1941) to study mathematical logic. Introductory treatments of the lambda calculus may be found in (Hankin, 1994), (Peyton Jones, 1987), or (Stoy, 1977). (Barendregt, 1981; 1991) provides an encyclopedic reference.

2 *Data Abstraction*

2.1 Specifying Data via Interfaces

Every time we decide to represent a certain set of quantities in a particular way, we are defining a new data type: the data type whose values are those representations and whose operations are the procedures that manipulate those entities.

The representation of these entities is often complex, so we do not want to be concerned with their details when we can avoid them. We may also decide to change the representation of the data. The most efficient representation is often a lot more difficult to implement, so we may wish to develop a simple implementation first and only change to a more efficient representation if it proves critical to the overall performance of a system. If we decide to change the representation of some data for any reason, we must be able to locate all parts of a program that are dependent on the representation. This is accomplished using the technique of *data abstraction*.

Data abstraction divides a data type into two pieces: an *interface* and an *implementation*. The interface tells us what the data of the type represents, what the operations on the data are, and what properties these operations may be relied on to have. The *implementation* provides a specific representation of the data and code for the operations that makes use of the specific data representation.

A data type that is abstract in this way is said to be an *abstract data type*. The rest of the program, the *client* of the data type, manipulates the new data only through the operations specified in the interface. Thus if we wish to change the representation of the data, all we must do is change the implementation of the operations in the interface.

This is a familiar idea: most of the time, we don't care how integers are actually represented inside the machine. Our only concern is that we can perform the arithmetic operations reliably. Similarly, a file descriptor in an operating system is a complex entity, but when we write programs we care only that we can invoke procedures that perform the open, close, read, and other typical operations on these files. The only time we need to worry about the representation of file descriptors is when we are modifying the implementation of a file system. When the client code does not rely on the representation of the values in the data type, manipulating them only through the procedures in the interface, we say that the code is *representation-independent*.

All the knowledge about how the data is represented must therefore reside in the code of the implementation. The most important part of an implementation is the specification of how the data is represented. We use the notation $\lceil v \rceil$ for "the representation of data v".

To make this clearer, let us consider a simple example: the data type of the nonnegative integers. The data to be represented are the nonnegative integers. The interface is to consist of four entities: a constant `zero` and three procedures, `iszero?`, `succ`, and `pred`. Of course, not just any value will be acceptable for `zero`, nor will any procedure be acceptable as an implementation of `iszero?`, `succ`, or `pred`. We can specify the intended behavior of these procedures as follows:

$$\texttt{zero} = \lceil 0 \rceil$$
$$(\texttt{iszero?}\ \lceil n \rceil) = \begin{cases} \texttt{\#t} & n = 0 \\ \texttt{\#f} & n \neq 0 \end{cases}$$
$$(\texttt{succ}\ \lceil n \rceil) = \lceil n + 1 \rceil \quad (n \geq 0)$$
$$(\texttt{pred}\ \lceil n + 1 \rceil) = \lceil n \rceil \quad (n \geq 0)$$

This specification does not dictate how these nonnegative integers are to be represented. It requires only that these procedures conspire to produce the specified behavior. Thus, `zero` must be bound to the representation of 0. The procedure `succ`, given the representation of the integer n, must return the representation of the integer $n + 1$, and so on. The specification says nothing about `(pred zero)`, so under this specification any behavior would be acceptable.

We can now write client programs that manipulate nonnegative integers, and we are guaranteed that they will get correct answers, no matter what representation is in use. For example,

```
(define plus
  (lambda (x y)
    (if (iszero? x)
      y
      (succ (plus (pred x) y)))))
```

will satisfy (plus $\lceil x \rceil$ $\lceil y \rceil$) = $\lceil x + y \rceil$, no matter what implementation of the nonnegative integers we use.

This would all be trivial if we did not have choices about the representation. Let us consider three possible representations:

1. *Unary representation:* In the unary representation, the nonnegative integer *n* is represented by a list of *n* #t's. Thus, 0 is represented by (), 1 is represented by (#t), 2 is represented by (#t #t), etc. We can define this representation inductively by:

   $$\lceil 0 \rceil = ()$$
   $$\lceil n+1 \rceil = (\text{cons \#t } \lceil n \rceil)$$

   In this representation, we can satisfy the specification by writing

   ```
   (define zero '())
   (define iszero? null?)
   (define succ (lambda (n) (cons #t n)))
   (define pred cdr)
   ```

2. *Scheme number representation:* In this representation, we simply use Scheme's internal representation of numbers (which might itself be quite complicated!). We let $\lceil n \rceil$ be the Scheme integer n, and define the four required entities by

   ```
   (define zero 0)
   (define iszero? zero?)
   (define succ (lambda (n) (+ n 1)))
   (define pred (lambda (n) (- n 1)))
   ```

3. *Bignum representation:* In the bignum representation, numbers are represented in base *N*, for some large integer *N*. The representation becomes a list consisting of numbers between 0 and *N* − 1 (sometimes called *bigits* rather than digits). This representation makes it easy to represent integers

much larger than can be represented in a machine word. For our purposes, it is convenient to keep the list with least-significant bigit first. We can define the representation inductively by

$$
\lceil n \rceil = \begin{cases} () & n = 0 \\ (\text{cons } r \lceil q \rceil) & n = qN + r,\ 0 \le r < N \end{cases}
$$

So if $N = 16$, then $\lceil 33 \rceil = (1\ 2)$ and $\lceil 258 \rceil = (2\ 0\ 1)$, since $258 = 1 \times 16^2 + 0 \times 16^1 + 2 \times 16^0$.

Exercise 2.1 [⋆] Implement the four required operations for bigits. Then use it to calculate the factorial of 10. How does the execution time vary as this argument changes? How does the execution time vary as the base changes? Explain why.

Exercise 2.2 [⋆⋆] Analyze each of these proposed representations critically. To what extent do they succeed or fail in satisfying the specification of the data type?

None of these implementations enforces data abstraction. There is nothing to prevent a client program from looking at the representation and determining whether it is a list or a Scheme integer. On the other hand, some languages provide direct support for data abstractions: they allow the programmer to create new interfaces and check that the new data is only manipulated through the procedures in the interface. If the representation of a type is hidden, so it cannot be exposed by any operation (including printing), the type is said to be *opaque*. Otherwise, it is said to be *transparent*.

Scheme does not provide a standard mechanism for creating new opaque types. Thus we settle for an intermediate level of abstraction: we will define interfaces and rely on the writer of the client program to be discreet and use only the procedures in the interfaces.

2.2   An Abstraction for Inductive Data Types

In chapter 1, we saw many examples of inductively defined sets of data. We will see many more such sets in the future, so it will be useful to have a standard interface for dealing with such data types. This interface is specified by the form `define-datatype`.

2.2.1   `define-datatype` and `cases`

Let us consider the definition of binary trees from section 1.1:

⟨bintree⟩ ::= ⟨number⟩ | (⟨symbol⟩ ⟨bintree⟩ ⟨bintree⟩)

This grammar defines the elements of ⟨bintree⟩ as Scheme values. But this is a particular representation choice. What should the interface for this data type look like? To manipulate values of this data type we will need the following:

- *constructors* that allow us to build each kind of binary tree,

- a predicate that tests to see if a value is a representation of a binary tree, and

- some way of determining, given a binary tree, whether it is a leaf or an interior node, and of extracting its components.

In this section we introduce a tool for specifying such inductive data types. This tool also provides a standard representation for these data types, including a standard method for discriminating between the alternatives and extracting the data in them.

This tool is called `define-datatype`. Before we consider the general properties of this tool, we demonstrate its use by specifying the data type of binary trees:

```
(define-datatype bintree bintree?
  (leaf-node
    (datum number?))
  (interior-node
    (key symbol?)
    (left bintree?)
    (right bintree?)))
```

This says that a `bintree` is either

- a `leaf-node` consisting of a number called the `datum` of the `bintree` or

- an `interior-node` consisting of a `key` that is a symbol, a `left` that is a `bintree`, and a `right` that is also a `bintree`.

It creates a data type with the following interface:

- a 1-argument procedure, `leaf-node`, for constructing a `leaf-node`. This procedure tests its argument with `number?`; if the argument does not pass this test, an error is reported.

- a 3-argument procedure, `interior-node`, for building an `interior-node`. This procedure tests its first argument with `symbol?` and its second and third arguments with `bintree?` to ensure that they are appropriate values.

- a 1-argument predicate `bintree?` that when passed a `leaf-node` or an `interior-node` returns true. For all other arguments, it returns false.

In addition, a new form of case construct (illustrated presently) makes it possible to conveniently distinguish between the two types of nodes and extract their contents.

We need some terminology before describing `define-datatype` in general. An *aggregate* data type is one that contains values of other types, such as an *array* or *record*. An array element is selected using a numerical index, while a record element, called a *field*, is selected via a *field name*.

A *union* type is one whose values are of one or the other of multiple given types. For example, the type of integers might be viewed as the union of the type of even integers and the type of odd integers. Values of a *discriminated union* type contain a value of one of the union's types and a tag indicating which type the value belongs to.

Scheme values belong to a discriminated union of all the primitive types provided by the Scheme implementation (such as integer, character, pair, empty list, vector, procedure, and so on). For the purpose of reasoning about Scheme programs, we may invent other abstract unions. For example, a list is a union of just the empty list and pair types.

Inductively defined data types are conveniently represented as a discriminated union of record types, sometimes called *variant records*. Each record type is called a *variant* of the type. The `define-datatype` facility is an extension of Scheme that makes it easy to define and use variant records.

A `define-datatype` declaration, which can only appear at the top-level of a program, has the general form

```
(define-datatype type-name type-predicate-name
  { (variant-name  { (field-name  predicate) }*) }*)
```

This creates a variant-record data type, named *type-name*. Each variant has a *variant-name* and zero or more fields, each with its own *field-name* and associated *predicate*. No two types may have the same name and no two variants, even those belonging to different types, may have the same name. Also, type names cannot be used as variant names. Each field predicate must be a Scheme predicate: a procedure of one argument that is used to assure that the field's values are valid.

For each variant a new procedure is created that is used to create data values belonging to that variant. These procedures are called *constructors* and are named after their variants. If there are *n* fields in a variant, its constructor takes *n* arguments, tests each of them with the associated predicate, and returns a new value of the given variant with the *i*-th field containing the *i*-th argument value.

The *type-predicate-name* is bound to a predicate. This predicate determines if its argument is a value belonging to the named type.

A record can be defined as a data type with a single variant. To distinguish data types with only one variant, we use a naming convention. When there is a single variant, the constructor is named a-*type-name* or an-*type-name*; otherwise, the constructors have names like *variant-description -type-name*.

Data types built by define-datatype may be mutually recursive. For example, consider the grammar for ⟨s-list⟩ from section 1.1:

$$\begin{aligned}
⟨\text{s-list}⟩ &::= (\{⟨\text{symbol-expression}⟩\}^*) \\
⟨\text{symbol-expression}⟩ &::= ⟨\text{symbol}⟩ \mid ⟨\text{s-list}⟩
\end{aligned}$$

The data in an s-list could be represented by the data type s-list defined by:

```
(define-datatype s-list s-list?
  (empty-s-list)
  (non-empty-s-list
    (first symbol-exp?)
    (rest s-list?)))

(define-datatype symbol-exp symbol-exp?
  (symbol-symbol-exp
    (data symbol?))
  (s-list-symbol-exp
    (data s-list?)))
```

The data type s-list gives its own representation of lists by using (empty-s-list) and non-empty-s-list in place of () and cons; if we wanted to specify that Scheme lists be used instead, we could have written

```
(define-datatype s-list s-list?
  (an-s-list
    (data (list-of symbol-exp?))))

(define list-of
  (lambda (pred)
    (lambda (val)
      (or (null? val)
          (and (pair? val)
               (pred (car val))
               ((list-of pred) (cdr val)))))))
```

Here (list-of *pred*) builds a predicate that tests to see if its argument is a list, and that each of its elements satisfies *pred*.

Exercise 2.3 [*] Implement vector-of, which is like list-of, but works for vectors instead of lists. Do this without using vector->list.

We use the form cases to determine the variant to which an object of a data type belongs, and to extract its components. To illustrate this form, consider again the set of binary trees, defined by

```
(define-datatype bintree bintree?
  (leaf-node
    (datum number?))
  (interior-node
    (key symbol?)
    (left bintree?)
    (right bintree?)))
```

We wish to find the sum of the integers in the leaves of such a tree. We can do this with cases by writing:

```
(define leaf-sum
  (lambda (tree)
    (cases bintree tree
      (leaf-node (datum) datum)
      (interior-node (key left right)
        (+ (leaf-sum left) (leaf-sum right))))))
```

The procedure leaf-sum takes a bintree that it refers to as tree. The (cases bintree ...) expression branches depending upon which variant of bintree the value tree belongs to. When a branch is taken, each of the variables in the branch is bound to the corresponding field of tree, and the expression in the branch is evaluated.

To see how this works, assume that tree is bound to a tree that was built by interior-node. For this binding of tree, the interior-node branch would be selected, left would be bound to the left subtree, right would be bound to the right subtree, and the expression (+ (leaf-sum left) (leaf-sum right)) would be evaluated. The recursive calls to leaf-sum would work similarly to finish the problem.

The form cases binds its variables *positionally*: the *i*-th variable is bound to the value in the *i*-th field. So we could just as well have written (leaf-node (n) n) instead of (leaf-node (datum) datum), etc.

Exercise 2.4 [⋆] Implement a `bintree-to-list` procedure for binary trees, so that `(bintree-to-list (interior-node 'a (leaf-node 3) (leaf-node 4)))` returns the list

```
(interior-node
  a
  (leaf-node 3)
  (leaf-node 4))
```

Exercise 2.5 [⋆⋆] Use `cases` to write `max-interior`, which takes a binary tree of numbers with at least one interior node and returns the symbol associated with an interior node with a maximal leaf sum.

```
> (define tree-a
    (interior-node 'a (leaf-node 2) (leaf-node 3)))
> (define tree-b
    (interior-node 'b (leaf-node -1) tree-a))
> (define tree-c
    (interior-node 'c tree-b (leaf-node 1)))
> (max-interior tree-b)
a
> (max-interior tree-c)
c
```

The last invocation of `max-interior` might also have returned a, since both the a and c nodes have a leaf sum of 5.

The general syntax of `cases` is

```
(cases type-name expression
  {(variant-name ({field-name}*) consequent)}*
  (else default))
```

The form specifies the type, the expression yielding the value to be examined, and a sequence of clauses. Each clause is labeled with the name of a variant of the given type and the names of its fields. The `else` clause is optional. First, *expression* is evaluated, resulting in some value v of *type-name*. If v is a variant of *variant-name*, then the corresponding clause is selected. Each of the *field-names* is bound to the value of the corresponding field of v. Then the *consequent* is evaluated within the scope of these bindings and its value returned. If v is not one of the variants, and an `else` clause has been specified, *default* is evaluated and its value returned. If there is no `else` clause, then there *must* be a clause for every variant of that data type.

The form `define-datatype` provides a convenient way of defining an inductive data type, but it is not the only way. Depending on the application, it may be valuable to use a special purpose representation that is more compact or efficient, taking advantage of special properties of the data. These advantages are gained at the expense of having to write the procedures in the interface by hand. We shall see some examples of this in section 2.3.

2.2.2   Abstract Syntax and its Representation

In section 1.1 we introduced the language of lambda calculus expressions, defined by the grammar

$$\langle expression \rangle ::= \langle identifier \rangle$$
$$::= (\texttt{lambda} \ (\langle identifier \rangle) \ \langle expression \rangle)$$
$$::= (\langle expression \rangle \ \langle expression \rangle)$$

Following the pattern we used for ⟨bintree⟩, we can represent every lambda calculus expression using the data type defined by

```
(define-datatype expression expression?
  (var-exp
    (id symbol?))
  (lambda-exp
    (id symbol?)
    (body expression?))
  (app-exp
    (rator expression?)
    (rand expression?)))
```

Here the names var-exp, id, app-exp, rator, and rand abbreviate *variable expression, identifier, application expression, operator,* and *operand,* respectively.

A BNF definition specifies a particular representation of an inductive data type: one that uses the particular strings or values generated by the grammar. Such a representation is called *concrete syntax,* or *external* representation.

In order to process such data, we need to convert it to an *internal* representation. In abstract syntax, terminals such as parentheses need not be stored, because they convey no information. On the other hand, we want to make sure that the data structure allows us to determine easily what kind of lambda calculus expression it represents, and to extract its components easily. The data type expression provides exactly this.

To create an abstract syntax for a given concrete syntax, we must name each production of the concrete syntax and each occurrence of a nonterminal in each production. For the grammar of lambda calculus expressions, we can

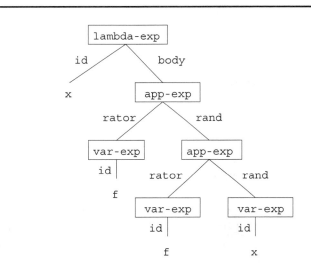

Figure 2.1   Abstract syntax tree for (lambda (x) (f (f x)))

summarize the choices we have made using the following concise notation:

⟨expression⟩ ::= ⟨identifier⟩
    var-exp (id)

::= (lambda (⟨identifier⟩) ⟨expression⟩)
    lambda-exp (id body)

::= (⟨expression⟩ ⟨expression⟩)
    app-exp (rator rand)

Such notation, which specifies both concrete and abstract syntax, is used throughout this book.

Given the abstract syntax name choices reflected in this notation, it is straightforward to generate define-datatype declarations for the abstract syntax. One declaration is used for each nonterminal, using the nonterminal name as the data type name.

The abstract syntax representation of an expression is most readily viewed as an *abstract syntax tree*. For example, see figure 2.1 for the abstract syntax tree of the lambda calculus expression (lambda (x) (f (f x))). Each node of the tree corresponds to a step in a syntactic derivation of the expression, with internal nodes labeled with their associated production name. Edges are labeled with the name of the corresponding nonterminal occurrence. Leaves correspond to terminal strings.

Exercise 2.6 [⋆] Draw the abstract syntax tree for the lambda calculus expression

```
((lambda (a) (a b)) c)
```

Abstract syntax trees are useful in programming-language processing systems because programs that process other programs, such as interpreters or compilers, are almost always *syntax directed*. What is done with each part of a program is guided by knowledge of the grammar rule associated with that part, and any subparts corresponding to nonterminals in the grammar rules should be readily accessible. For example, when processing the lambda calculus expression `(lambda (x) (f (f x)))`, we must first recognize it as a lambda calculus expression, corresponding to the BNF rule

$$\langle \text{expression} \rangle ::= \texttt{(lambda (} \langle \text{identifier} \rangle \texttt{)} \langle \text{expression} \rangle \texttt{)}$$

Then the formal parameter is x and the body is `(f (f x))`. The body must in turn be recognized as an application, and so on. Converting the program to an abstract syntax tree enables the processing system to make such decisions easily.

For example, the procedure `occurs-free?` in section 1.3 can be:

```
(define occurs-free?
  (lambda (var exp)
    (cases expression exp
      (var-exp (id) (eqv? id var))
      (lambda-exp (id body)
        (and (not (eqv? id var))
             (occurs-free? var body)))
      (app-exp (rator rand)
        (or (occurs-free? var rator)
            (occurs-free? var rand)))))))
```

The use of the abstract syntax avoids the use of obscure car-cdr chains to extract the components of the expression.

As another example, we may consider the problem of converting an abstract syntax tree back to a list-and-symbol representation. If we do this, the Scheme print routines will then display it in its concrete syntax. This is performed by `unparse-expression`:

```
(define unparse-expression
  (lambda (exp)
    (cases expression exp
      (var-exp (id) id)
      (lambda-exp (id body)
        (list 'lambda (list id)
          (unparse-expression body)))
      (app-exp (rator rand)
        (list (unparse-expression rator)
              (unparse-expression rand)))))))
```

If a program is represented as a string of characters, it may be a complex undertaking to derive the corresponding abstract syntax tree. This task, which is called *parsing*, is unrelated to whatever we may wish to do with the abstract syntax tree. Thus the job of parsing is best performed by a separate program, called a *parser*. Since abstract syntax trees are produced by parsers, they are also known as *parse trees*.

If the concrete syntax of a language happens also to be list structures (including symbols and numbers), the parsing process is greatly simplified. For example, every expression specified by our lambda calculus grammar is both a string and a list structure. The Scheme `read` routine automatically parses strings into lists and symbols. It is then easier to parse these list structures into abstract syntax trees as in `parse-expression`.

```
(define parse-expression
  (lambda (datum)
    (cond
      ((symbol? datum) (var-exp datum))
      ((pair? datum)
       (if (eqv? (car datum) 'lambda)
         (lambda-exp (caadr datum)
           (parse-expression (caddr datum)))
         (app-exp
           (parse-expression (car datum))
           (parse-expression (cadr datum)))))
      (else (eopl:error 'parse-expression
              "Invalid concrete syntax ~s" datum)))))
```

Where a Kleene star or plus is used in concrete syntax, it is most convenient to use a *list* of associated subtrees when constructing an abstract syntax tree. For example, consider a variant of the exercise 1.31 syntax in figure 2.2. Here `ids` and `rands` are associated with lists of formal parameters and operand expressions, respectively. The predicate for the `rands` field can be `(list-of expression?)`.

⟨expression⟩ ::= ⟨number⟩

> `lit-exp (datum)`

::= ⟨var-exp⟩

> `var-exp (id)`

::= (if ⟨expression⟩ ⟨expression⟩ ⟨expression⟩)

> `if-exp (test-exp true-exp false-exp)`

::= (lambda ({⟨identifier⟩}*) ⟨expression⟩)

> `lambda-exp (ids body)`

::= (⟨expression⟩ {⟨expression⟩}*)

> `app-exp (rator rands)`

Figure 2.2   Lists of formal parameters and operand expressions

Exercise 2.7 [★★] Define the data type and parse and unparse procedures for the above grammar. Then implement `lexical-address` of exercise 1.31 using abstract syntax. It will be helpful to add two new variants

```
(lex-info
  (id symbol?)
  (depth number?)
  (position number?))

(free-info
  (id symbol?))
```

representing the translation of a given bound or free variable reference. The value returned by `lexical-address` may then be generated using an unparse procedure that takes an abstract syntax tree of the form indicated by the above grammar, but with `lex-info` and `free-info` variants in place of `var-exp` variants.

Exercise 2.8 [★] Rewrite the solution to exercise 1.19 using abstract syntax. Then compare this version to the original solution.

Exercise 2.9 [★] The procedure `parse-expression` is fragile: it does not detect several possible syntactic errors, such as (a b c), and aborts with inappropriate error messages for other expressions, such as (lambda). Modify it so that it is robust, accepting any datum and issuing an appropriate error message if the datum does not represent a lambda calculus expression.

Exercise 2.10 [⋆] Consider the definition of `fresh-id`:

```
(define fresh-id
  (lambda (exp s)
    (let ((syms (all-ids exp)))
      (letrec
        ((loop (lambda (n)
                 (let ((sym (string->symbol
                              (string-append s
                                (number->string n)))))
                   (if (memv sym syms) (loop (+ n 1)) sym)))))
        (loop 0)))))
```

Implement `fresh-id` by defining `all-ids`, which finds all the symbols in an expression. This includes the free occurrences, the bound occurrences, and the lambda identifiers for which there are no bound occurrences.

```
> (fresh-id
    (app-exp
      (lambda-exp 'w2
        (app-exp (var-exp 'w1) (var-exp 'w0)))
      (var-exp 'w3))
    "w")
w4
```

Exercise 2.11 [⋆⋆] Let us assume that our lambda calculus expression has been enhanced with the constants 3, *, and +. Extend `parse-expression` and `unparse-expression` to support this enhancement.

Next, consider substituting `(* p 3)` for x in `(lambda (p) (+ p x))` and `(lambda (q) (+ q x))`. The resulting expressions are `(lambda (p) (+ p (* p 3)))` and `(lambda (q) (+ q (* p 3)))`.

This is wrong, because we know that changing the name of a bound variable shouldn't make a difference: `(lambda (p) (+ p x))` and `(lambda (q) (+ q x))` should behave the same way, and the terms after substitution will definitely behave differently. In the first example, we say that the p in `(* p 3)` has been *captured* by the binding occurrence.

We can fix this problem by renaming the bound variable to some fresh name, say p0, so the result of the substitution becomes `(lambda (p0) (+ p0 (* p 3)))`. Capture is thereby avoided; it no longer matters whether the original bound variable was p or q. Here is the notation we use for this thoughout: $E_1[E_2/x]$. The resultant expression is the same as E_1 with free occurrences of the identifer x replaced by the expression E_2.

Below is the definition of a procedure that substitutes `subst-exp` for all occurrences of `subst-id` in exp, but without renaming.

```
(define lambda-calculus-subst
  (lambda (exp subst-exp subst-id)
    (letrec
      ((subst
        (lambda (exp)
          (cases expression exp
            (var-exp (id)
              (if (eqv? id subst-id) subst-exp exp))
            (lambda-exp (id body)
              (lambda-exp id (subst body)))
            (app-exp (rator rand)
              (app-exp (subst rator) (subst rand)))
            (lit-exp (datum)
              (lit-exp datum))
            (primapp-exp (prim rand1 rand2)
              (primapp-exp prim (subst rand1) (subst rand2)))
            ))))
      (subst exp)))))
```

Fix lambda-calculus-subst so that it performs renaming when necessary. Hint: use fresh-id from the previous exercise.

Exercise 2.12 [⋆] In the previous exercise, we presented the lambda calculus substitution operator, $E_1[E_2/x]$. Here, we define three new operators that rely on it: α, β, and η.

- (lambda (y) E) α-converts to (lambda (x) E[x/y]), if x is not free in E
- ((lambda (x) E_1) E_2) β-converts to $E_1[E_2/x]$
- (lambda (x) (E x)) η-converts to E, if x is not free in E.

Implement these operators. Do they use recursion explicitly?

Exercise 2.13 [⋆] Define a *term* to be either a variable, a constant (either a string, a number, a boolean, or the empty list), or a list of terms. We can use the following data type to define the abstract syntax of terms.

```
(define-datatype term term?
  (var-term
    (id symbol?))
  (constant-term
    (datum constant?))
  (app-term
    (terms (list-of term?))))
```

We represent a term using symbols for variables and lists for app terms, while treating everything else as a constant. Thus the term

```
("append" ("cons" w x) y ("cons" w z))
```

represents an abstract syntax tree that can be built by

```
(app-term
  (list
    (constant-term "append")
    (app-term
      (list
        (constant-term "cons") (var-term 'w) (var-term 'x)))
    (var-term 'y)
    (app-term
      (list
        (constant-term "cons") (var-term 'w) (var-term 'z)))))
```

Implement parse-term, unparse-term, and all-ids (exercise 2.10) for this term language.

2.3   Representation Strategies for Data Types

We have seen that when data abstraction is used, programs have the property of representation independence: programs are independent of the particular representation used to implement an abstract data type. It is then possible to change the representation by redefining the small number of procedures belonging to the interface. We frequently use this property in later chapters.

In this section we introduce some strategies for representing data types. We illustrate these choices using a data type of *environments*. An environment associates a value with each element of a finite set of symbols. An environment may be used to associate variables with their values in a programming language implementation. A *symbol table*, which among other things may associate variable names with lexical address information at compile time, is another use of an environment.

2.3.1   The Environment Interface

An environment is a function whose domain is a finite set of Scheme symbols, and whose range is the set of all Scheme values. If we adopt the usual mathematical convention that a function is a set of ordered pairs, then we need to represent all sets of the form $\{(s_1, v_1), \ldots, (s_n, v_n)\}$ where the s_i are distinct symbols and the v_i are any Scheme values.

The interface to this data type has three procedures, specified as follows:

```
(empty-env)         = ⌈∅⌉
(apply-env ⌈f⌉ s)   = f(s)
(extend-env
   '(s₁ ... sₖ)
   '(v₁ ... vₖ)
   ⌈f⌉)             = ⌈g⌉,
```

$$\text{where } g(s') = \begin{cases} v_i & \text{if } s' = s_i \text{ for some } i, 1 \leq i \leq k \\ f(s') & \text{otherwise} \end{cases}$$

The procedure `empty-env`, applied to no arguments, must produce a representation of the empty environment; `apply-env` applies a representation of an environment to an argument; and (`extend-env` '(s_1 ...s_n) '(v_1 ...v_n) *env*) produces a new environment that behaves like *env*, except that its value at symbol s_i is v_i. For example, the environment $\{(d, 6), (x, 7), (y, 8)\}$ may be constructed and accessed as follows:

```
> (define dxy-env
    (extend-env '(d x) '(6 7)
      (extend-env '(y) '(8)
        (empty-env)))))
> (apply-env dxy-env 'x)
7
```

Most interfaces will contain some *constructors* that build elements of the data type, and some *observers* that extract information from values of the data type. In this example, `empty-env` and `extend-env` are the constructors, and `apply-env` is the only observer.

Exercise 2.14 [⋆⋆] Consider the data type of *stacks* of values, with an interface consisting of the procedures `empty-stack`, `push`, `pop`, `top`, and `empty-stack?`. Write a specification for these operations in the style of the example above. Which operations are constructors and which are observers?

2.3.2   Procedural Representation

A *first-class* object is one that can be passed as an argument, returned as a value, and stored in a data structure. In languages such as Scheme in which procedures are first-class, it is often advantageous to represent data as procedures, particularly when the data type has multiple constructors, but only a single observer.

```
(define empty-env
  (lambda ()
    (lambda (sym)
      (eopl:error 'apply-env "No binding for ~s" sym))))

(define extend-env
  (lambda (syms vals env)
    (lambda (sym)
      (let ((pos (list-find-position sym syms)))
        (if (number? pos)
          (list-ref vals pos)
          (apply-env env sym))))))

(define apply-env
  (lambda (env sym)
    (env sym)))

(define list-find-position
  (lambda (sym los)
    (list-index (lambda (sym1) (eqv? sym1 sym)) los)))

(define list-index
  (lambda (pred ls)
    (cond
      ((null? ls) #f)
      ((pred (car ls)) 0)
      (else (let ((list-index-r (list-index pred (cdr ls))))
              (if (number? list-index-r)
                (+ list-index-r 1)
                #f))))))
```

Figure 2.3   Procedural representation of environments

An environment may be represented as a Scheme procedure that takes a symbol and returns its associated value. With this representation, the environment interface may be defined as in figure 2.3.

If the empty environment, created by invoking `empty-env`, is passed any symbol whatsoever, it indicates with an error message that the given symbol is not in its domain. The procedure `extend-env` returns a new procedure that represents the extended environment. This procedure, when passed a symbol sym, first uses the auxiliary procedure list-find-position to determine the position of sym in syms. The procedure list-find-position, in turn, uses list-index to accomplish this. If sym is in syms, then list-index returns an integer representing its position, and the corresponding element of vals is returned using the procedure list-ref. If sym is not in syms, then list-index returns #f, and sym is looked up in the old environment env, in accordance with the specification.

Very often the set of values in the data type can be represented as a set of procedures. In this case, we can extract the interface and the procedural representation by the following steps:

1. Identify the lambda expressions in the client code whose evaluation yields values of the type. Create a constructor procedure for each such lambda expression. The parameters of the constructor procedure will be the free variables of the lambda expression. Replace each such lambda expression in the client code by an invocation of the corresponding constructor.

2. Define an apply- procedure like apply-env above. Identify all the places in the client code, including the bodies of the constructor procedures, where a value of the type is applied. Replace each such application by an invocation of the apply- procedure.

If these steps are carried out, the interface will consist of all the constructor procedures and the apply- procedure, and the client code will be representation-independent: it will not rely on the representation, and we will be free to substitute another implementation of the interface, such as those we are about to describe.

Exercise 2.15 [⋆] Implement the stack data type of exercise 2.14 using a procedural representation.

Exercise 2.16 [⋆] Implement the procedure list-find-last-position, which is like list-find-position except that it returns the position of the rightmost matching symbol. For example, in the list (c a b a c a d e), the list-find-position of a is 1, whereas list-find-last-position of a is 5. Do this without using reverse or list->vector. When can list-find-position be used in place of list-find-last-position?

Interfaces created in this way will have only one observer. If more than one observer is needed, a single procedure as described here may not be enough to represent all the data. In general, if there are *n* observers in the interface the procedural representation will require a record of *n* procedures, one for each observer.

Exercise 2.17 [⋆⋆] Add to the environment interface a predicate called has-association? that takes an environment *env* and a symbol *s* and tests to see if *s* has an associated value in *env*. Extend the procedural representation to implement this by representing the environment by two procedures: one that returns the value associated with a symbol and one that returns whether or not the symbol has an association.

2.3.3 Abstract Syntax Tree Representation

This procedural representation is easy to understand, but it requires that procedures be first-class objects. Another representation can be obtained by observing that every environment is built by starting with the empty environment and applying extend-env *n* times, for some $n \geq 0$. Thus every environment can be built by an expression like

```
(extend-env symsn valsn
  ...
    (extend-env syms1 vals1
      (empty-env))...)
```

These expressions can be described by the grammar

⟨env-rep⟩ ::= (empty-env)
            empty-env-record

      ::= (extend-env ({⟨symbol⟩}*) ({⟨value⟩}*) ⟨env-rep⟩)
             extended-env-record (syms vals env)

The abstract syntax trees for this grammar can be defined by

```
(define-datatype environment environment?
  (empty-env-record)
  (extended-env-record
    (syms (list-of symbol?))
    (vals (list-of scheme-value?))
    (env environment?)))

(define scheme-value? (lambda (v) #t))
```

We can implement the environment abstraction by redefining the procedures empty-env and extend-env to build the appropriate variants and by redefining apply-env to interpret the information in these records and perform the actions specified by the body of the appropriate (lambda (sym) ...) expression. The implementation of the environment data type using this new representation is:

```
(define empty-env
  (lambda ()
    (empty-env-record)))

(define extend-env
  (lambda (syms vals env)
    (extended-env-record syms vals env)))

(define apply-env
  (lambda (env sym)
    (cases environment env
      (empty-env-record ()
        (eopl:error 'apply-env "No binding for ~s" sym))
      (extended-env-record (syms vals env)
        (let ((pos (list-find-position sym syms)))
          (if (number? pos)
            (list-ref vals pos)
            (apply-env env sym)))))))
```

The consequent expressions of the cases expression are *exactly* the same as the bodies of the respective (lambda (sym) ...) expressions in the procedural representation, and the variant fields correspond *exactly* to the lexically-bound free variables in these lambda expressions.

With this representation, the last transcript might continue as follows.

```
> (environment-to-list dxy-env)
(extended-env-record (d x) (6 7)
  (extended-env-record (y) (8)
    (empty-env-record)))
```

The result is a list representation of an abstract syntax tree that shows how the tree was constructed using empty-env and extend-env.

Exercise 2.18 [⋆] Implement environment-to-list.

This example illustrates a general technique for transforming a procedural representation into an abstract syntax tree representation. The key steps in the transformation are:

1. Identify the constructors for new values of the type, and create a data type with one variant for each constructor. Each variant should have one field for each parameter of the constructor. If the type has been derived from a set of procedures, as described at the end of section 2.3.2, then the fields will be the same as the free variables of the original lambda expression.

2. Define the constructors to build the appropriate variant of the data type.

3. Define the `apply-` procedure for the type using (cases *type-name* ...) with one clause per variant, where the variable list of each clause lists the parameters of the constructor and the consequent expression of each clause is the body of the corresponding lambda expression.

Exercise 2.19 [⋆] Implement the stack data type of exercise 2.14 using an abstract syntax tree representation.

Exercise 2.20 [⋆] Add `has-association?` of exercise 2.17 to the abstract syntax tree representation.

2.3.4 Alternative Data Structure Representations

As we mentioned above, `define-datatype` provides a convenient general implementation of trees. In many cases, however, we can exploit patterns in the data to obtain additional simplifications.

For example, as we noted above, every environment is built by starting with the empty environment and applying `extend-env` some number of times: that is, by an expression in the grammar

⟨env-exp⟩ ::= (empty-env)
       ::= (extend-env ({⟨symbol⟩}*) ({⟨value⟩}*) ⟨env-exp⟩)

We need to represent the abstract syntax trees of this grammar. We could represent them by a data type, but we can use any representation in which we can always tell what kind of tree we have and from which we can extract the pieces.

Here, we have a single constant constructor and a single non-trivial constructor. So the tag information in the abstract syntax trees is redundant. We could simply represent these trees by list structures given by the grammar

⟨env-rep⟩ ::= ()
       ::= ((({⟨symbol⟩}*) ({⟨value⟩}*)) . ⟨env-rep⟩)

We can always tell which kind of environment we have: an empty list represents the empty environment, and a non-empty list represents an environment built by `extend-env`.

For a data structure representation, the constructors simply build the appropriate list structure. An observer examines the data structure it is given, determines which kind of structure it is, extracts the components, and performs the same operations on the components that it did in the abstract syntax tree representation. Thus our running example becomes:

```
> (define dxy-env
    (extend-env '(d x) '(6 7)
      (extend-env '(y) '(8)
        (empty-env))))
> dxy-env
(((d x) (6 7)) ((y) (8)))
```

Exercise 2.21 [⋆] What list structure does (extend-env '() '() (empty-env)) produce?

We use these definitions to implement our environment interface:

```
(define empty-env
  (lambda ()
    '()))

(define extend-env
  (lambda (syms vals env)
    (cons (list syms vals) env)))

(define apply-env
  (lambda (env sym)
    (if (null? env)
        (eopl:error 'apply-env "No binding for ~s" sym)
        (let ((syms (car (car env)))
              (vals (cadr (car env)))
              (env (cdr env)))
          (let ((pos (list-find-position sym syms)))
            (if (number? pos)
                (list-ref vals pos)
                (apply-env env sym)))))))
```

This representation is called the *ribcage* representation. The environment is represented as a list of lists called *ribs*; the car of each rib is a list of symbols and the cadr of each rib is the corresponding list of values.

Some efficiency may be gained by observing that we are always using an index to retrieve values from the values list. If the values were stored in a vector instead of a list, this lookup would be constant (using vector-ref) rather than linear time (using list-ref). We also take this opportunity to change the representation of a rib from a list of two elements to a single pair. For this new representation, we modify our previous code to become

```
(define extend-env
  (lambda (syms vals env)
|   (cons (cons syms (list->vector vals)) env)))

(define apply-env
  (lambda (env sym)
    (if (null? env)
      (eopl:error 'apply-env "No binding for ~s" sym)
      (let ((syms (car (car env)))
|           (vals (cdr (car env)))
            (env (cdr env)))
        (let ((pos (list-find-position sym syms)))
          (if (number? pos)
|             (vector-ref vals pos)
              (apply-env env sym)))))))
```

Figure 2.4 shows an environment represented in this way. This figure also illustrates why this is called a ribcage representation. (See exercise 2.22.)

If environment lookup is based on lexical distance information, we can eliminate the symbol lists, representing environments simply as a list of vectors as in `apply-env-lexical` below.

```
(define extend-env
  (lambda (syms vals env)
|   (cons (list->vector vals) env)))

(define apply-env-lexical
  (lambda (env depth position)
    (if (null? env)
      (eopl:error 'apply-env-lexical
        "No binding for depth = ~s position = ~s"
        depth position)
      (if (zero? depth)
        (vector-ref (car env) position)
        (apply-env-lexical (cdr env) (- depth 1) position)))))
```

Exercise 2.22 [⋆] Design a 2-element rib data type and use it to implement the environment interface.

Exercise 2.23 [⋆ ⋆] A simpler representation of environments would consist of a single pair of ribs: a list of symbols and a list of values. Implement the environment interface for this representation.

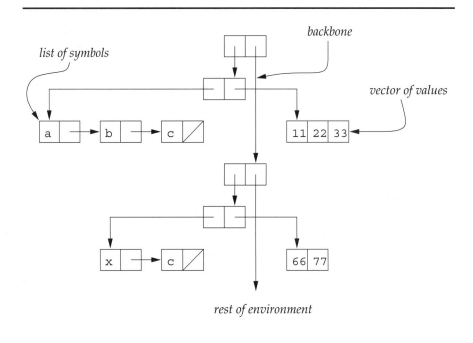

Figure 2.4   Ribcage environment structure with vectors

Exercise 2.24 [⋆⋆] Define a *substitution* to be a function whose domain is the set of Scheme symbols and whose range is the set of all terms (exercise 2.13). The interface for substitutions consists of (empty-subst), which binds its argument to a variable term of its argument, referred to as a *trivial association*; (apply-subst s i), which returns the value of symbol *i* in substitution *s*; and (extend-subst i t s), which returns a new substitution like *s*, except that symbol *i* is associated with term *t*.

Implement the data type of substitutions with both a procedural representation and an abstract syntax tree representation.

Then implement a procedure subst-in-term that takes a term and a substitution and walks through the term replacing each variable with its association in the substitution, much like the procedure subst of section 1.2.2. Finally, implement subst-in-terms that takes a list of terms.

Exercise 2.25 [⋆⋆] An important use of substitutions is in the *unification problem*. The unification problem is: given two terms *t* and *u*, can they be made equal? More precisely, is there a substitution *s* such that (subst-in-term t s) and (subst-in-term u s) are equal? We say that such an *s unifies t* and *u*. There may be many such unifiers, but there will always be one that is the most general.

The code below shows part of an algorithm to find the most general unifying substitution. If no such unifier exists, it returns #f.

```
(define unify-term
  (lambda (t u)
    (cases term t
      (var-term (tid)
        (if (or (var-term? u) (not (memv tid (all-ids u)))))
          (unit-subst tid u)
          #f))
      (else
        (cases term u
          (var-term (uid) (unify-term u t))
          (constant-term (udatum)
            (cases term t
              (constant-term (tdatum)
                (if (equal? tdatum udatum) (empty-subst) #f))
              (else #f)))
          (app-term (us)
            (cases term t
              (app-term (ts) (unify-terms ts us))
              (else #f)))))))))

(define unify-terms
  (lambda (ts us)
    (cond
      ((and (null? ts) (null? us)) (empty-subst))
      ((or (null? ts) (null? us)) #f)
      (else
        (let ((subst-car (unify-term (car ts) (car us))))
          (if (not subst-car)
            #f
            (let ((new-ts (subst-in-terms (cdr ts) subst-car))
                  (new-us (subst-in-terms (cdr us) subst-car)))
              (let ((subst-cdr (unify-terms new-ts new-us)))
                (if (not subst-cdr)
                  #f
                  (compose-substs subst-car subst-cdr)))))))))))
```

Complete the algorithm by extending the substitution interface with the two procedures unit-subst and compose-substs. The application (unit-subst i t) returns a substitution that replaces symbol i with term t and replaces any other symbol by its trivial association. The application (compose-substs s_1 s_2) returns a substitution s' such that for any term t, (subst-in-term t s') returns the same term as (subst-in-term (subst-in-term t s_1) s_2).

The memv test in unify-term is called the *occurs check*. Create an example to illustrate that this test is necessary.

2.4   A Queue Abstraction

As a final example of the use of data abstraction, consider queues. An interface for queues might include operations for setting the queue to empty, testing it for empty, placing a value on the queue, and removing an object from the queue.

In a functional setting, these operations might take queues as arguments and return queues as results. However, we often want queues to be shared from widely separate procedures, so it would be difficult to pass the queues as arguments from one procedure to another. In this situation it is more convenient for the procedures to refer to a shared queue with state.

The representation of the queue is hidden, so the interface consists of a procedure for creating a queue and procedures that will return each of the operations that will act on the shared hidden state of the queue.

This interface consists of the following procedures:

- `(create-queue)` creates a queue object.

- `(queue-get-reset-operation q)` returns a procedure that sets the queue to empty.

- `(queue-get-empty?-operation q)` returns a procedure that determines whether the queue is empty.

- `(queue-get-enqueue-operation q)` returns the enqueue operation on the queue.

- `(queue-get-dequeue-operation q)` returns the dequeue operation on the queue.

The code in figure 2.5 creates such a queue. It creates four procedures with access to a shared hidden state consisting of the variables `q-in` and `q-out`. Instead of assigning these procedures to global variables, we return a vector containing these four procedures. Then client code can use this vector like this:

```
(let ((q1 (create-queue)) (q2 (create-queue)))
  (let ((enq1 (queue-get-enqueue-operation q1))
        (enq2 (queue-get-enqueue-operation q2))
        (deq1 (queue-get-dequeue-operation q1))
        (deq2 (queue-get-dequeue-operation q2)))
    (begin
      (enq1 33) (enq2 (+ 1 (deq1))) (deq2))))
```

```
(define create-queue
  (lambda ()
    (let ((q-in '())
          (q-out '()))
      (letrec
        ((reset-queue
           (lambda ()
             (set! q-in '())
             (set! q-out '())))
         (empty-queue?
           (lambda ()
             (and (null? q-in)
                  (null? q-out))))
         (enqueue
           (lambda (x)
             (set! q-in (cons x q-in))))
         (dequeue
           (lambda ()
             (if (empty-queue?)
                 (eopl:error 'dequeue
                   "Not on an empty queue")
                 (begin
                   (if (null? q-out)
                       (begin
                         (set! q-out (reverse q-in))
                         (set! q-in '())))
                   (let ((ans (car q-out)))
                     (set! q-out (cdr q-out))
                     ans))))))
        (vector reset-queue empty-queue? enqueue dequeue)))))

(define queue-get-reset-operation
  (lambda (q) (vector-ref q 0)))
(define queue-get-empty?-operation
  (lambda (q) (vector-ref q 1)))
(define queue-get-enqueue-operation
  (lambda (q) (vector-ref q 2)))
(define queue-get-dequeue-operation
  (lambda (q) (vector-ref q 3)))
```

Figure 2.5   A data type of queues

This creates two queues, initially empty. It binds the enqueue and dequeue operations on these queues to convenient names. Then it places the number 33 on the first queue, removes it, adds one to it, places it on the second queue, and then removes it, producing the answer 34.

The code in figure 2.5 has a useful but non-obvious property: it uses *amortized linear time*. The dequeue operation may take longer than constant time, because it may need to reverse q-in, but it can be shown that this occurs so rarely that the queue takes only $O(n)$ steps to execute n requests. The proof of this property is beyond the scope of this book.

The idea of sharing a small hidden state among a bundle of procedures is important. Such a package is often called an *object*, and the procedures that act on the state are called *methods*. This is the main idea of object-oriented programming, which we study in chapters 5 and 6. In the context of operating systems, methods are sometimes called *capabilities*.

Exercise 2.26 [⋆⋆] A cell interface consists of these four operations: cell, cell?, contents, and setcell. The procedure cell stores its argument in a memory location; cell? determines if its argument is a cell; contents retrieves the value of the cell; and setcell stores its second argument in the first argument, which must be a cell. Use the data type reference with a one-element vector to implement the cell interface. Then use the queue interface style to encapsulate these definitions.

```
(define-datatype reference reference?
  (a-ref
    (position integer?)
    (vec vector?)))
```

Further Reading

The idea of data abstraction was a prime innovation of the 1970s and has a large literature, from which we mention only (Parnas, 1972) on the importance of interfaces as boundaries for information-hiding.

Our define-datatype and cases "consconstructs were inspired by ML's datatype and pattern-matching facilities described in (Milner, Tofte, & Harper, 1989) and (Milner, Tofte, Harper, & MacQueen, 1997).

We learned about the representation of sets of procedures as data structures from (Reynolds, 1972). This idea is formalized under the name of *super-combinators* in (Hughes, 1982). For more detail, see (Peyton Jones, 1987).

The concept of unification was brought into computer science in (Robinson, 1965) for use in automatic theorem proving. The implementation of queues in section 2.4 is presented in (Okasaki, 1998).

3 *Environment-Passing Interpreters*

In this chapter we study the *semantics*, or meaning, of some of the most common and fundamental programming languages features. Our primary tool for this study is *interpreters*. Figure 3.1(a) shows the setup for using an interpreter. Program text (a program in the source language) is passed through a front end that converts it to a syntax tree. The syntax tree is then passed to the interpreter, which is a program that looks at a data structure and performs some actions that depend on its structure. In the case of a language-processing system, the interpreter takes the abstract syntax tree and converts it, possibly using external inputs, to an answer.

An alternative organization is shown in Figure 3.1(b). There the interpreter is replaced by a compiler, which translates the abstract syntax tree into some other language (the target language), which in turn is executed by an interpreter. Most often, this other language is a machine language, which is interpreted by a hardware machine, but some language implementations use a special-purpose target language that is simpler than the original and for which it is relatively simple to write an interpreter. This allows the program to be compiled once and then executed on many different hardware platforms.

A compiler is typically divided into two parts: an analyzer that attempts to deduce useful information about the program, and a translator that does the translation, possibly using information from the analyzer. We study some simple analyzers and translators in chapters 4, 6, and 8.

Other than those chapters, our language processors will be interpreters. They allow us to specify the behavior of language features in a high-level fashion without also having to deal with the peculiarities of a target language.

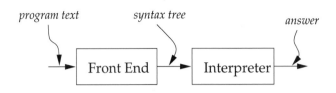

(a) Execution via interpreter

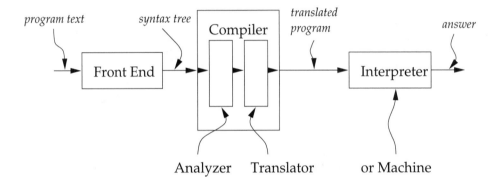

(b) Execution via Compiler

Figure 3.1   Block diagrams for a language-processing system

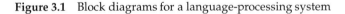

We develop interpreters for a series of simple languages. Each interpreter is a data-driven procedure. We have already developed several such procedures. These include `occurs-free?`, `lambda-calculus-subst`, `parse-expression`, and `unparse-expression` of section 2.2.2, and the `apply-` procedures of section 2.3. Each of these procedures takes data and performs some action determined by the form of the data.

The semantics of variable binding mechanisms is of primary importance in these langauges. We are also interested in seeing how these bindings are made concrete using environments.

3.1   A Simple Interpreter

In this section we develop a simple interpreter that reflects the fundamental semantics of many modern programming languages and is the basis for most of the material in the rest of this book. We build this interpreter in stages, starting with the simplest forms: literals, variables, and primitive applications. Then we add other forms one at a time.

An important part of the specification of any programming language is the set of values that the language manipulates. Each language has at least two such sets: the *expressed values* and the *denoted values*. The expressed values are the possible values of expressions, and the denoted values are the values bound to variables. In Scheme, for example, there are many kinds of expressed values, such as numbers, pairs, characters, and strings, but there is only one kind of denoted value: locations containing expressed values.

In our first language the expressed values are the integers, and the denoted values are the same as the expressed values. We write this as follows:

$$\text{Expressed Value} = \text{Number}$$
$$\text{Denoted Value} = \text{Number}$$

We use equations like this as informal reminders of the expressed and denoted values for each of our interpreters.

We also need to distinguish two languages: the *defined language* (or *source language*), which is the language we are specifying with our interpreter, and the *defining language* (or *host language*), which is the language in which we write the interpreter. In our case the defining language is Scheme with `define-datatype` and `cases`. The equations above describe the expressed and denoted values of the defined language.

We start with the following syntax:

⟨program⟩   ::= ⟨expression⟩
```
a-program (exp)
```

⟨expression⟩ ::= ⟨number⟩
```
lit-exp (datum)
```

::= ⟨identifier⟩
```
var-exp (id)
```

::= ⟨primitive⟩ ({⟨expression⟩}*⁽ʼ⁾)
```
primapp-exp (prim rands)
```

⟨primitive⟩ ::= + | - | * | add1 | sub1

A program is just an expression. An expression is either a number, an identifier, or a *primitive application* consisting of a primitive operator, a left parenthesis, a list of expressions separated by commas, and a right parenthesis. Typical expressions in our language are

```
3
x
+(3,x)
add1(+(3,x))
```

The abstract syntax trees are built, as before, of records with type definitions based on the abstract syntax names given with the grammar.

```
(define-datatype program program?
  (a-program
    (exp expression?)))

(define-datatype expression expression?
  (lit-exp
    (datum number?))
  (var-exp
    (id symbol?))
  (primapp-exp
    (prim primitive?)
    (rands (list-of expression?)))
  )

(define-datatype primitive primitive?
  (add-prim)
  (subtract-prim)
  (mult-prim)
  (incr-prim)
  (decr-prim))
```

The second field of a `primapp-exp` record contains a list of abstract syntax trees for the application's operands. For the primitive operations, we have one variant for each primitive.

Exercise 3.1 [*] Cosider the fourth example above. Then implement the procedure `program-to-list` so that it returns the list

```
(a-program
  (primapp-exp
    (incr-prim)
    ((primapp-exp
      (add-prim)
      ((lit-exp 3)
       (var-exp x))))))
```

Our first interpreter is shown in figure 3.2. It follows the grammar, so it has three procedures, `eval-program`, `eval-expression`, and `apply-primitive`, which correspond to the three nonterminals, ⟨program⟩, ⟨expression⟩, and ⟨primitive⟩. In addition it has two auxiliary procedures, `eval-rands` and `init-env`, which simplify the presentation.

The main procedure, `eval-program`, is passed the abstract syntax tree of a program and returns its value. It follows a familiar pattern, branching on the type of record at the root of the tree. Since a program always consists of an expression, there is only one possibility, but we still need to use `cases` to extract this expression from the abstract syntax tree. The procedure `eval-program` passes this expression to `eval-expression`, along with a suitable environment in which to find the values of any identifiers that appear in the expression. The auxiliary procedure `init-env` is called to build this environment; we have chosen to put a few arbitrary bindings in the initial environment.

The most interesting procedure is `eval-expression`. It takes an expression and an environment, and returns the value of the expression using that environment to find the values of any variables. Like `eval-program`, it branches on the type of the root of the tree:

- The first case is easy: If `exp` is a literal, the datum is returned.

- If `exp` is a node that represents a variable, we look up the identifier in the environment to find its value.

- The last possibility is that `exp` is a node that represents an application of a primitive operation to some operands. We first evaluate the operands, using the auxiliary procedure `eval-rands`, and then pass them and the primitive operation to `apply-primitive` to determine the actual value.

The procedure `eval-rands` takes a list of operands and an environment. It evaluates each operand using `eval-rand`, which in turn calls `eval-expression`. We need to pass the environment to both `eval-rands` and `eval-rand` so that they will have the information they need to evaluate any variables that appear in the subexpressions. We need not pass the environment to `apply-primitive`, however, because that procedure deals only with values, not with expressions that might contain variables.

The procedure `apply-primitive` takes a primitive operation and a list of values and produces the value that should be obtained by applying the primitive operation to the list of values. Like `eval-program` and

```
(define eval-program
  (lambda (pgm)
    (cases program pgm
      (a-program (body)
        (eval-expression body (init-env))))))

(define eval-expression
  (lambda (exp env)
    (cases expression exp
      (lit-exp (datum) datum)
      (var-exp (id) (apply-env env id))
      (primapp-exp (prim rands)
        (let ((args (eval-rands rands env)))
          (apply-primitive prim args)))
      )))

(define eval-rands
  (lambda (rands env)
    (map (lambda (x) (eval-rand x env)) rands)))

(define eval-rand
  (lambda (rand env)
    (eval-expression rand env)))

(define apply-primitive
  (lambda (prim args)
    (cases primitive prim
      (add-prim () (+ (car args) (cadr args)))
      (subtract-prim () (- (car args) (cadr args)))
      (mult-prim () (* (car args) (cadr args)))
      (incr-prim () (+ (car args) 1))
      (decr-prim () (- (car args) 1))
      )))

(define init-env
  (lambda ()
    (extend-env
      '(i v x)
      '(1 5 10)
      (empty-env))))
```

Figure 3.2   A simple interpreter

`eval-expression`, it branches on the form of the primitive operation to decide what actual operation to perform on these values.

This completes the discussion of our first interpreter.

Exercise 3.2 [⋆⋆] In what order are the subexpressions in a primitive application evaluated? Is there a way to determine this empirically? Can the order affect the result?

3.2   The Front End

Before we can conveniently test our interpreter, however, we need a *front end* that converts programs into abstract syntax trees. Because programs are just strings of characters, our front end needs to group these characters into meaningful units. This grouping is usually divided into two stages: *scanning* and *parsing*.

Scanning is the process of dividing the sequence of characters into words, numbers, punctuation, comments, and the like. These units are called *lexical items*, *lexemes*, or most often *tokens*. We refer to the way in which a program should be divided up into tokens as the *lexical specification* of the language. The scanner takes a sequence of characters and produces a sequence of tokens.

Parsing is the process of organizing the sequence of tokens into hierarchical syntactic structures such as expressions, statements, and blocks. This is like organizing (diagramming) a sentence into clauses. We refer to this as the *syntactic* or *grammatical* structure of the language. The parser takes a sequence of tokens from the scanner and produces an abstract syntax tree.

The standard approach to building a front end is to use a *parser generator*. A parser generator is a program that takes as input a lexical specification and a grammar, and produces as output a scanner and parser for them. Appendix A describes SLLGEN, a parser-generator system for Scheme that we use in this book. In SLLGEN, the scanner and grammar for our example language are specified in figure 3.3.

The first definition is the lexical specification. It says that white space in the defined language (here called `white-sp`) is defined to be the same as any Scheme whitespace character and should be skipped; that a comment begins with a % character and consists of an arbitrary number of characters until the end of the line is reached; that an identifier consists of a letter followed by an arbitrary number of letters, digits, or question marks; and that a number consists of a digit followed by an arbitrary number of digits. The second

```
(define scanner-spec-3-1
  '((white-sp
     (whitespace)                        skip)
    (comment
     ("%" (arbno (not #\newline)))       skip)
    (identifier
     (letter (arbno (or letter digit "?"))) symbol)
    (number
     (digit (arbno digit))               number)))

(define grammar-3-1
  '((program
     (expression)
     a-program)
    (expression
     (number)
     lit-exp)
    (expression
     (id)
     var-exp)
    (expression
     (primitive "(" (separated-list expression ",") ")" )
     primapp-exp)
    (primitive ("+")
     add-prim)
    (primitive ("-")
     subtract-prim)
    (primitive ("*")
     mult-prim)
    (primitive ("add1")
     incr-prim)
    (primitive ("sub1")
     decr-prim)))
```

Figure 3.3   scanner-spec-3-1 and grammar-3-1

```
> (define scan&parse
    (sllgen:make-string-parser
      scanner-spec-3-1
      grammar-3-1))
> (sllgen:make-define-datatypes scanner-spec-3-1 grammar-3-1)
> (define run
    (lambda (string)
      (eval-program
        (scan&parse string))))
> (scan&parse "add1(2)")
(a-program (primapp-exp (incr-prim) ((lit-exp 2))))
> (run "add1(2)")
3
> (define read-eval-print
    (sllgen:make-rep-loop   "--> " eval-program
      (sllgen:make-stream-parser
        scanner-spec-3-1
        grammar-3-1)))
> (read-eval-print)
--> 5
5
--> add1(2)
3
--> +(add1(2),-(6,4))
5
```

Figure 3.4   Read-eval-print loop for string syntax

definition corresponds to the productions of the grammar in the preceding
section. Each production is given a name, which becomes the name of the
corresponding node type in the abstract syntax tree.

The procedure sllgen:make-define-datatypes can be used to automatically generate the define-datatype declarations from the grammar, or
else these declarations can be generated by hand. The SLLGEN procedure sllgen:make-string-parser is used to construct a scanner and parser
based on the lexical and grammatical specifications. It returns a procedure
that takes a string and produces an abstract syntax tree (figure 3.4.)

Parser generator systems are available for most major languages. If no
parser generator is available, or none is suitable for the application, one can

```
> (define run
    (lambda (x)
      (eval-program (parse-program x))))
> (run '5)
5
> (run '(add1 2))
3
> (define read-eval-print
    (lambda ()
      (begin
        (display "--> ")
        (write (eval-program (parse-program (read))))
        (newline)
        (read-eval-print)))))
> (read-eval-print)
--> 5
5
--> (add1 2)
3
--> (+ (add1 2) (- 6 4))
5
```

Figure 3.5   Read-eval-print loop for Scheme-like syntax

choose to build a scanner and parser by hand. This process is described in most compiler textbooks. The parsing technology and associated grammars used in this book are designed for simplicity in the context of our very specialized needs.

Another approach is to ignore the details of the concrete syntax and to write our expressions as list structures, as we did in section 1.3. Thus, instead of writing add1(+(3,n)), we might write (add1 (+ 3 n)). For this approach, we need a procedure parse-program, which takes a Scheme list, symbol, or number and returns the corresponding abstract syntax tree. A test of this front end, using run, appears in figure 3.5.

While this approach is simple, it may lead to confusion between the defined language and the defining language. It may also require more cumbersome syntax than the original string-oriented syntax. When using this approach in doing exercises expressed in terms of string-grammar syntax, feel free to invent appropriate list-structure syntax for use instead.

The interactive user interface provided by most implementations of Scheme (and other languages suitable for interactive use) is a *read-eval-print loop*. The system reads an expression or definition, evaluates it, prints the result, and then loops to repeat these actions. (See the second definition in figure 3.5.) A read-eval-print loop for our interpreters makes it easier to run a number of tests.

By utilizing the SLLGEN procedures `sllgen:make-stream-parser` and `sllgen:make-rep-loop` to connect the parser to the stream of characters coming from the standard input, we can define a read-eval-print loop using the string-syntax front end, as in figure 3.4. Since we will be using SLLGEN, henceforth, if the prompt `-->` appears in a transcript, it indicates that the current version of `eval-program` is performing the evaluation.

Exercise 3.3 [⋆] Write `parse-program`. See section 2.2.2.

Exercise 3.4 [⋆] Test `eval-program` using both `run` and a read-eval-print loop.

Exercise 3.5 [⋆] Extend the language by adding a new primitive operator `print` that takes one argument, prints it, and returns the integer 1.

Exercise 3.6 [⋆] Extend the language by adding a new primitive operator `minus` that takes one argument, n, and returns $-n$.

```
--> minus(+(minus(5),9))
-4
```

Exercise 3.7 [⋆] Add list processing primitives to the language, including `cons`, `car`, `cdr`, `list`, and a new variable, `emptylist`, which is bound to the empty list. Since there is no support for symbols, lists can contain only numbers and other lists. How does this change the expressed and denoted values of the language?

```
--> list(1,2,3)
(1 2 3)
--> car(cons(4,emptylist))
4
```

Exercise 3.8 [⋆] Add a new primitive `setcar`, which side-effects the car field of a cons pair. How does this change the expressed and denoted values of the language?

Exercise 3.9 [⋆] Modify the interpreter so that invoking a primitive operation on the wrong number of arguments causes an error to be reported. (Since this check involves only static information, it could be done prior to run-time, which is preferable for many reasons. We encourage the use of such an approach.)

3.3   Conditional Evaluation

To study the semantics and implementation of a wide range of programming language features, we now begin adding these features to our defined language. For each feature, we add a production to the grammar for ⟨expression⟩, specify an abstract syntax for that production, and then add an appropriate `cases` clause to `eval-expression` to handle the new type of abstract syntax tree node. First we add a conditional expression syntax:

⟨expression⟩ ::= `if` ⟨expression⟩ `then` ⟨expression⟩ `else` ⟨expression⟩
            `if-exp (test-exp true-exp false-exp)`

To avoid adding booleans as a new type of expressed value, we let zero represent false and any other value represent true and use the procedure `true-value?`, which abstracts this decision:

```
(define true-value?
  (lambda (x)
    (not (zero? x))))
```

If the value of the `test-exp` subexpression is a true value, the value of the entire `if-exp` should be the value of the `true-exp` subexpression; otherwise it should be the value of the `false-exp` subexpression. For example,

```
--> if 1 then 2 else 3
2
--> if -(3,+(1,2)) then 2 else 3
3
```

This behavior is obtained by adding the following clause in `eval-expression`:

```
          (if-exp (test-exp true-exp false-exp)
            (if (true-value? (eval-expression test-exp env))
              (eval-expression true-exp env)
              (eval-expression false-exp env)))
```

This code uses the `if` form of the defining language to define the `if` form of the defined language. This illustrates how we are dependent on our understanding of the defining language: if we do not know what Scheme's `if` does, this code would not help us understand the new language. In this case, of course, we do understand Scheme's `if`, and our code provides some additional information on the defined language's conditional expression as it considers any nonzero value to be true.

Exercise 3.10 [⋆] Test `if` forms by extending the interpreter of figure 3.2.

Exercise 3.11 [⋆] Add to the defined language numeric equality, zero-testing, and order predicates `equal?`, `zero?`, `greater?` and `less?` to the set of primitive operations. These predicates should use 1 to represent true.

```
--> equal?(3,3)
1
--> zero?(sub1(5))
0
--> if greater?(2,3) then 5 else 6
6
```

Exercise 3.12 [⋆] Add to the defined language the facilities of exercise 3.7, along with the predicate `null?`.

Exercise 3.13 [⋆] Add to the defined language a facility that extends `if` as `cond` does in Scheme. Use the grammar

⟨expression⟩ ::= cond {⟨expression⟩ ==> ⟨expression⟩}* end
> cond-exp (test-exps conseq-exps)

If none of the tests succeeds, the expression should return 0.

Exercise 3.14 [⋆] Add boolean values to the expressed and denoted values of the language, so we have

$$\begin{aligned} \text{Expressed Value} &= \text{Number} + \text{Bool} \\ \text{Denoted Value} &= \text{Number} + \text{Bool} \end{aligned}$$

Modify the predicates of exercise 3.11 to use these new booleans. Then modify `eval-expression` to produce an error if the test produces a non-boolean.

Exercise 3.15 [⋆⋆] As an alternative to the preceding exercise, add a new nonterminal ⟨bool-exp⟩ of boolean expressions to the language. Change the production for conditional expressions to say

⟨expression⟩ ::= if ⟨bool-exp⟩ then ⟨expression⟩ else ⟨expression⟩

Write suitable productions for ⟨bool-exp⟩ and implement `eval-bool-exp`. Where do the predicates of exercise 3.11 wind up in this organization?

3.4 Local Binding

Next we address the problem of creating new variable bindings with a `let` form. We add to the interpreted language a syntax in which the keyword `let` is followed by a series of declarations, the keyword `in`, and the body. For example,

```
let x = 5
    y = 6
in +(x,y)
```

The entire `let` form is an expression, as is its body, so `let` expressions may
be nested. The usual lexical binding rules for block structure apply: the binding region of a `let` declaration is the body of the `let` expression, and inner
bindings create holes in the scope of outer bindings. Thus in

```
let x = 1
in let x = +(x,2)
   in add1(x)
```

the reference to x in the first application refers to the outer declaration,
whereas the reference to x in the second application refers to the inner declaration, and hence the value of the entire expression is 4.

The concrete syntax of the `let` form is

⟨expression⟩ ::= let {⟨identifier⟩ = ⟨expression⟩}* in ⟨expression⟩

$\boxed{\text{let-exp (ids rands body)}}$

The abstract syntax now looks like

```
(define-datatype expression expression?
  (lit-exp
    (datum number?))
  (var-exp
    (id symbol?))
  (primapp-exp
    (rator primitive?)
    (rands (list-of expression?)))
  (if-exp
    (test-exp expresson?)
    (true-exp expression?)
    (false-exp expression?))
  (let-exp
    (ids (list-of symbol?))
    (rands (list-of expression?))
    (body expression?)))
```

When a `let` expression is evaluated, the subexpressions on the right-hand
side of its declarations are evaluated first. Since the scope of these declarations is restricted to the `let` expression's body, the right-hand side subexpressions are evaluated in `env`, the environment of the entire `let` expression.

```
(define eval-expression
  (lambda (exp env)
    (cases expression exp
      (lit-exp (datum) datum)
      (var-exp (id) (apply-env env id))
      (primapp-exp (prim rands)
        (let ((args (eval-rands rands env)))
          (apply-primitive prim args)))
      (if-exp (test-exp true-exp false-exp)
        (if (true-value? (eval-expression test-exp env))
            (eval-expression true-exp env)
            (eval-expression false-exp env)))
      (let-exp (ids rands body)
        (let ((args (eval-rands rands env)))
          (eval-expression body (extend-env ids args env)))))
      )))
```

Figure 3.6   Interpreter with `if` and `let`

Then the body of the `let` expression is evaluated in an environment in which the declared variables are bound to the values of the expressions on the right-hand sides of the declarations, whereas other bindings should be obtained from the environment in which the entire `let` expression is evaluated.

We obtain this behavior by adding the `let-exp` clause in figure 3.6. First, `eval-rands` is used to evaluate the right-hand side expressions in the environment `env`. Then, the body is evaluated in a new environment obtained by extending the current environment with bindings that associate the declared variables with the values of their right-hand-side expressions.

As expected for a lexical-binding language, a fixed region of text, `body`, is associated with the new environment bindings. Also, if `extend-env` creates a binding for an already bound variable, the new binding takes precedence over the old. Inner declarations thus shadow, or create holes in the scope of, outer declarations. For example, the subexpression `add1(x)` is evaluated in a new environment obtained by extending an environment binding x to 1 with a binding of x to 3. Since the binding of x to 3 takes precedence, the reference to x in `add1(x)` yields 3 and the final value is 4. This satisfies the lexical binding rule associated with block-structured languages: a variable reference is associated with the nearest lexically enclosing binding of the variable.

Exercise 3.16 [⋆] Test the `let` form of the interpreter of figure 3.6.

Exercise 3.17 [⋆] Add to the defined language the facilities of exercise 3.7 and the primitive procedure `eq?`, which should correspond to the Scheme procedure `eq?`. Why could this predicate not be adequately tested until now?

Exercise 3.18 [⋆] Add an expression to the defined language:

⟨expression⟩ ::= unpack {⟨identifier⟩}* = ⟨expression⟩ in ⟨expression⟩
    unpack-exp (ids exp body)

so that `unpack x y z = lst in ...` binds `x`, `y`, and `z` to the elements of `lst` if `lst` is a list of exactly three elements, and reports an error otherwise.

3.5 Procedures

So far our language has only the primitive operations that were included in the original language. For our interpreted language to be at all useful, we must allow new procedures to be created. We use the following syntax for procedure creation and application:

⟨expression⟩ ::= proc ({⟨identifier⟩}*⁽ʼ⁾) ⟨expression⟩
    proc-exp (ids body)

        ::= (⟨expression⟩ {⟨expression⟩}*)
    app-exp (rator rands)

Thus we can write programs like

```
let f = proc (y, z) +(y,-(z,5))
in (f 2 28)
```

Since the `proc` form may be used anywhere an expression is allowed, we can also write `(proc(y, z)+(y,-(z,5)) 2 28)`. This is the application of the procedure `proc(y, z)+(y,-(z,5))` to the literals 2 and 28.

We wish procedures to be first-class values in our language. Thus we want

Expressed Value = Denoted Value = Number + ProcVal

where ProcVal is the set of values representing procedures. Our next task is to determine what information must be included in a value representing a procedure. To do this, we consider what happens at procedure-application time.

When a procedure is applied, its body is evaluated in an environment that binds the formal parameters of the procedure to the arguments of the application. Variables occurring free in the procedure should also obey the lexical binding rule. This requires that they retain the bindings that were in force *at the time the procedure was created*. Consider the following example:

```
let x = 5
in let f = proc (y, z) +(y,-(z,x))
       x = 28
   in (f 2 x)
```

When f is called, its body should be evaluated in an environment that binds y to 2, z to 28, and x to 5. Recall that the scope of the inner declaration of x does not include the procedure declaration. Thus from the position of the reference to x in the procedure's body, the nearest lexically enclosing declaration of x is the outer declaration, which associates x with 5.

In order for a procedure to retain the bindings that its free variables had at the time it was created, it must be a *closed* package, independent of the environment in which it is used. Such a package is called a *closure*. In order to be self-contained, a closure must contain the procedure body, the list of formal parameters, and the bindings of its free variables. It is convenient to store the entire creation environment, rather than just the bindings of the free variables, but see exercise 3.27 for an alternative. We sometimes say the procedure is *closed over* or *closed in* its creation environment.

We can think of ProcVal as a data type; the interface consists of closure, which tells how to build a procedure value, and apply-procval, which tells how to apply a procedure value. When a procedure is applied, its body is evaluated in an environment that binds the formal parameters of the procedure to the arguments of the application. Therefore these procedures should satisfy the condition

```
(apply-procval (closure ids body env) args)
= (eval-expression body (extend-env ids args env))
```

According to the methodology described in section 2.3.2, we can employ a procedural representation for procedures by defining closure to have a value that is a procedure that expects an argument list.

```
(define closure
  (lambda (ids body env)
    (lambda (args)
      (eval-expression body (extend-env ids args env)))))
```

```
(define apply-procval
  (lambda (proc args)
    (proc args)))
```

Alternatively, since closures are the only kind of procedure values in our language, we can define ProcVal as an abstract syntax tree representation by writing

```
(define-datatype procval procval?
  (closure
    (ids (list-of symbol?))
    (body expression?)
    (env environment?)))
```

In the abstract syntax tree representation for procedures, `apply-procval` uses `cases` to take the closure apart and then invokes the body of the closure in the appropriately extended environment:

```
(define apply-procval
  (lambda (proc args)
    (cases procval proc
      (closure (ids body env)
        (eval-expression body (extend-env ids args env))))))
```

Now we can see how to modify `eval-expression` to handle programmer-defined procedures. This client code manipulates procedures only through the ProcVal interface, so it is independent of the representation of procedures.

When a `proc` expression is evaluated, all that is done is to build a closure and return it immediately.

```
(define eval-expression
  (lambda (exp env)
    (cases expression exp
      (proc-exp (ids body) (closure ids body env))
      ...)))
```

The body of the procedure is not evaluated here: it cannot be evaluated until the values of the formal parameters are known, when the closure is applied to some arguments.

When an application is evaluated, the operator and the operands are evaluated, and the results are sent to `apply-procval`, which knows about the representation of procedures:

```
(define eval-expression
  (lambda (exp env)
    (cases expression exp
      (app-exp (rator rands)
        (let ((proc (eval-expression rator env))
              (args (eval-rands rands env)))
          (if (procval? proc)
            (apply-procval proc args)
            (eopl:error 'eval-expression
              "Attempt to apply non-procedure ~s" proc))))
      ...)))
```

The operands are also called the *actual parameters*. These are expressions, and should not be confused with their values, which we consistently call the *arguments* to the procedure, nor should they be confused with the *bound variables* or *formal parameters* of the procedure that will be bound to them.

The interpreter is shown in figure 3.7. To see how all this fits together, let us consider a simple calculation. In this calculation, we write *«exp»* to denote the abstract syntax tree associated with the expression *exp*, and we write [x=*a*,y=*b*] *env* in place of (extend-env '(x y) '(*a b*) *env*).

```
(eval-expression <<let x = 5
                   in let x = 38
                          f = proc (y, z) *(y,+(x,z))
                          g = proc (u) +(u,x)
                      in (f (g 3) 17)>>
                 env0)
= bind x and evaluate the body of the let
(eval-expression <<let x = 38
                       f = proc (y, z) *(y,+(x,z))
                       g = proc (u) +(u,x)
                   in (f (g 3) 17)>>
                 env1)
   where env1 = [x = 5]env0
= bind x, f, and g and evaluate the body of the let
(eval-expression <<(f (g 3) 17)>> env2)
   where env2 =
           [x = 38,
            f = (closure (y z) <<*(y,+(x,z))>> env1),
            g = (closure (u) <<+(u,x)>> env1)
           ]env1
= rule for app-exp in eval-expression
(let ((proc (eval-expression <<f>> env2))
      (args (eval-rands '(<<(g 3)>> <<17>>) env2)))
  (apply-procval proc args))
```

```
(define eval-expression
  (lambda (exp env)
    (cases expression exp
      (lit-exp (datum) datum)
      (var-exp (id) (apply-env env id))
      (primapp-exp (prim rands)
        (let ((args (eval-rands rands env)))
          (apply-primitive prim args)))
      (if-exp (test-exp true-exp false-exp)
        (if (true-value? (eval-expression test-exp env))
          (eval-expression true-exp env)
          (eval-expression false-exp env)))
      (let-exp (ids rands body)
        (let ((args (eval-rands rands env)))
          (eval-expression body (extend-env ids args env))))
      (proc-exp (ids body) (closure ids body env))
      (app-exp (rator rands)
        (let ((proc (eval-expression rator env))
              (args (eval-rands rands env)))
          (if (procval? proc)
            (apply-procval proc args)
            (eopl:error 'eval-expression
              "Attempt to apply non-procedure ~s" proc)))))
    )))
```

Figure 3.7   Interpreter with user-defined procedures

Before finishing this calculation, let us work on (g 3) in env2:

```
(eval-expression <<(g 3)>> env2)
= rule for app-exp in eval-expression
(let ((proc (eval-expression <<g>> env2))
      (args (eval-rands '(<<3>>) env2)))
  (apply-procval proc args))
= evaluate the rator and the rands
(let ((proc '(closure (u) <<+(u,x)>> env1))
      (args '(3)))
  (apply-procval proc args))
= substitute the values of proc and args
(apply-procval
  '(closure (u) <<+(u,x)>> env1)
  '(3))
```

```
=  definition of apply-procval
(eval-expression <<+(u,x)>> [u = 3]env1)
= 3 + 5 = 8
```

Now we can finish the main calculation:

```
(let ((proc '(closure (y z) <<*(y,+(x,z))>> env1))
      (args '(8 17)))
  (apply-procval proc args))
=  substitute the values of proc and args
(apply-procval
  '(closure (y z) <<*(y,+(x,z))>> env1)
  '(8 17))
=  definition of apply-procval
(eval-expression <<*(y,+(x,z))>> [y = 8, z = 17]env1)
= 8 * (5 + 17) = 8 * 22 = 176
```

Exercise 3.19 [⋆] Test user-defined procedures with the interpreter of figure 3.7.

Exercise 3.20 [⋆⋆] Modify the interpreter to signal an error if a closure is called with the wrong number of arguments.

First-class procedures are extremely powerful. Consider the following program:

```
let makemult = proc (maker, x)
                 if x
                 then +(4,(maker maker -(x,1)))
                 else 0
in let times4 = proc (x) (makemult makemult x)
   in (times4 3)
```

This program calculates a multiple of 4 by repeated additions, essentially simulating a recursive program.

Exercise 3.21 [⋆] Use the tricks of the program above to write a procedure for factorial in the defined language of this section.

Exercise 3.22 [⋆⋆] Use the tricks of the program above to write the pair of mutually-recursive procedures, odd and even as in section 3.6, in the defined language of *this* section.

In an implementation that uses a ribcage implementation for environments, the lexical address of a variable reference, as calculated in section 1.3.2, tells us exactly where in the environment the variable reference will appear: if the variable reference v gets lexical address $(d\ p)$, then the variable will appear in the d-th rib at position p.

Exercise 3.23 [⋆⋆] Write a lexical-address calculator, like that of exercise 1.31, for the language of this section. The calculator should take an abstract syntax tree and produce a similar abstract syntax tree, except that every occurrence of (var-exp *v*) should be replaced by (lexvar-exp *v* *d* *p*), where (*d p*) is the lexical address for this occurrence of the variable *v*. Add lexvar-exp as a new variant of the data type expression. With SLLGEN, an easy way to do this is to add a new production to the grammar. Alternatively, write out the define-datatype by hand instead of using sllgen:make-define-datatypes. (Hint: edit the list produced by sllgen:list-define-datatypes).

Exercise 3.24 [⋆] Instrument the interpreter to illustrate the fact that each variable is found at the position predicted by its lexical address. To do this, modify the interpreter to take the output of the lexical-address calculator from the preceding exercise. Then modify eval-expression so that it sends to apply-env both the identifier and the lexical address for each variable reference. The procedure apply-env should look up the variable using the identifier in the usual way. It should then compare the lexical address to the actual rib and position in which the variable is found, and print an informative message.

A consequence of this observation is that lexically-bound variables need not appear at all in the syntax trees processed by the interpreter. One can simply replace each lexically-bound variable with its lexical address.

Exercise 3.25 [⋆⋆] Implement the language of this section using this idea. Modify the lexical-address analyzer of exercise 3.23 so that its output for a variable reference includes the lexical address but not the variable name. Then create a nameless-environment abstraction with interface

```
(empty-nameless-env)
(extend-nameless-env vals env)
(apply-nameless-env env depth position)
```

Applying the procedure apply-nameless-env to env, depth, and position looks up the position-th variable in the depth-th rib of env, in the fashion of the procedure apply-env-lexical of section 2.3.4. Last, modify eval-expression, closure, and apply-procval to use nameless environments.

Exercise 3.26 [⋆⋆] Repeat the preceding exercises for an implementation using flat environments (exercise 2.23). Modify the lexical-address analyzer to predict where in a flat environment the variable reference will be found. The resulting lexical address will be an integer. Modify the interpreter to use these integers as lexical addresses, as in the preceding exercise.

Exercise 3.27 [⋆] When we build a closure, we have kept the entire environment in the closure. But of course all we need are the bindings for the free variables. Modify the interpreter to use the following definition of closure:

```
(define closure
  (lambda (ids body env)
    (let ((freevars (set-diff (free-vars body) ids)))
      (let ((saved-env
              (extend-env
                freevars
                (map
                  (lambda (v)
                    (apply-env env v))
                  freevars)
                (empty-env))))
        (lambda (args)
          (eval-expression body
            (extend-env ids args saved-env)))))))
```

where set-diff takes the difference of two sets. This is called the *flat closure* representation. The environment of such a closure consists of exactly one rib comprising its free variables and their values. What would the analogous representation look like if we used an abstract syntax tree representation?

Exercise 3.28 [★★★] Modify the lexical-address analyzer to predict where in the environment of each flat closure each free variable reference will be located. The lexical-address analyzer and closure will have to agree on the order in which the free variables appear in the rib. Then modify the interpreter to use these lexical addresses instead of variable names.

Exercise 3.29 [★] Add a new kind of procedure called a traceproc to the language. A traceproc works exactly like a proc, except that it prints a trace message on entry and on exit. Use this facility to trace the behavior of the times4 program above.

Exercise 3.30 [★★] *Dynamic binding* (or *dynamic scoping*) is an alternative design for procedures, in which the procedure body is evaluated in an environment obtained by extending the environment at the point of call. For example in

```
let a = 3
in let p = proc (x) +(x,a)
       a = 5
   in *(a,(p 2))
```

the a in the procedure body would be bound to 5, not 3. Modify the interpreter of figure 3.7 to use dynamic binding. Represent defined-language procedures with Scheme procedures of the form (lambda (args env) ...). Do these procedures have any free lexical variables?

Exercise 3.31 [★★] Another approach to implementing dynamic binding is to store all environment bindings on a global stack, which pairs variable names with their values. Bindings are pushed onto this stack when a procedure is called and popped from the stack when the procedure returns. Modify the interpreter of figure 3.7 to implement dynamic binding in this way. How does the efficiency of this binding method compare with lexical binding, both when lexical distance analysis is used with lexical binding and when it is not?

Exercise 3.32 [⋆] With dynamic binding, recursive procedures may be bound by `let`; no special mechanism is necessary for recursion. This is of historical interest, because in the early years of programming language design other approaches to recursion, such as those discussed in section 3.6, were not widely understood. To demonstrate recursion via dynamic binding, test the program

```
let fact = proc (n) add1(n)
in let fact = proc (n)
                 if zero?(n)
                 then 1
                 else *(n,(fact sub1(n)))
   in (fact 5)
```

using both lexical and dynamic binding.   Write the mutually-recursive procedures `even` and `odd` as in section 3.6 in the defined language with dynamic binding.

Exercise 3.33 [⋆ ⋆] Unfortunately, programs that use dynamic binding may be exceptionally difficult to understand. For example, under lexical binding, consistently renaming the bound variables of a procedure can never change the behavior of a program: we can even remove all identifiers and replace them by their lexical addresses, as in exercise 3.25.

For example, under dynamic binding, the procedure `proc  ()  a` returns the value of the variable a in its caller's environment. Thus, the program

```
let a = 3
    p = proc () a
in let f = proc (x) (p)
       a = 5
   in (f 2)
```

returns 5, since a's value at the call site is 5. What if f's formal parameter were a?

3.6   Recursion

We look now at how recursion may be added to our interpreter. In most languages only procedures may be defined recursively. Allowing other possibilities, as in Scheme, is sometimes useful but presents additional complications. Therefore we use a variation on Scheme's syntax that restricts the right-hand side to `proc`-like expressions as presented in the grammar:

⟨expression⟩ ::= `letrec`
          `{`⟨identifier⟩ `(`{⟨identifier⟩}*⁽ʼ⁾`)` `=` ⟨expression⟩`}`*
          `in` ⟨expression⟩

```
letrec-exp
 (proc-names idss bodies
  letrec-body)
```

The left-hand side of a recursive declaration is the name of the recursive procedure and a list of formal parameters. To the right of the = is the procedure body. Here are a couple of familiar examples.

```
letrec
  fact(x) = if zero?(x) then 1 else *(x,(fact sub1(x)))
in (fact 6)

letrec
  even(x) = if zero?(x) then 1 else (odd sub1(x))
  odd(x)  = if zero?(x) then 0 else (even sub1(x))
in (odd 13)
```

To evaluate a `letrec` expression, we evaluate the body of the expression in an environment that has the desired behavior:

```
(define eval-expression
  (lambda (exp env)
    (cases expression exp
      (letrec-exp (proc-names idss bodies letrec-body)
        (eval-expression letrec-body
          (extend-env-recursively
            proc-names idss bodies env)))
      ...)))
```

The complete definition of `eval-expression` is shown in figure 3.8.

The new procedure `extend-env-recursively` is added to the environment interface. We specify the behavior of `(extend-env-recursively proc-names idss bodies env)` as follows:

Let e' be `(extend-env-recursively proc-names idss bodies` e`)`. Then

1. If `name` is one of the names in `proc-names`, and `ids` and `body` are the corresponding formal parameter list and procedure body, then `(apply-env` e' `name)` = `(closure ids body` e'`)`.

2. If not, then `(apply-env` e' `name)` = `(apply-env` e `name)`.

```
(define eval-expression
  (lambda (exp env)
    (cases expression exp
      (lit-exp (datum) datum)
      (var-exp (id) (apply-env env id))
      (primapp-exp (prim rands)
        (let ((args (eval-rands rands env)))
          (apply-primitive prim args)))
      (if-exp (test-exp true-exp false-exp)
        (if (true-value? (eval-expression test-exp env))
          (eval-expression true-exp env)
          (eval-expression false-exp env)))
      (let-exp (ids rands body)
        (let ((args (eval-rands rands env)))
          (eval-expression body (extend-env ids args env))))
      (proc-exp (ids body) (closure ids body env))
      (app-exp (rator rands)
        (let ((proc (eval-expression rator env))
              (args (eval-rands rands env)))
          (if (procval? proc)
            (apply-procval proc args)
            (eopl:error 'eval-expression
              "Attempt to apply non-procedure ~s" proc))))
      (letrec-exp (proc-names idss bodies letrec-body)
        (eval-expression letrec-body
          (extend-env-recursively
            proc-names idss bodies env)))
      )))
```

Figure 3.8   Interpreter with `letrec`

We can implement `extend-env-recursively` in any way that satisfies
these requirements, including those of section 2.3. Representing environments with the procedural representation of section 2.3.2, using `letrec` itself,
we can write `extend-env-recursively` (figure 3.9).

Given a symbol `sym`, we first determine if it is among the names used
in `proc-names`. If it is present, we return a closure consisting of the corresponding formal-parameter list, the corresponding body, and the recursive
environment. Otherwise, we look up the symbol in the old environment
`old-env`. This implements the behavior specified above.

```
(define extend-env-recursively
  (lambda (proc-names idss bodies old-env)
    (letrec
      ((rec-env
         (lambda (sym)
           (let ((pos (rib-find-position sym proc-names)))
             (if (number? pos)
               (closure
                 (list-ref idss pos)
                 (list-ref bodies pos)
                 rec-env)
               (apply-env old-env sym)))))))
      rec-env)))
```

Figure 3.9 Recursive environments

If we represent environments using the abstract syntax representation of section 2.3.3, then we add a new variant for this new environment constructor, and move the code above into `apply-env`. See figure 3.10.

In each of these implementations, we build a new closure each time a procedure is retrieved from the environment. This is unnecessary since the environment for the closure is always the same. If we use a ribcage representation like that of figure 2.4, we can build the closures only once, by building an environment with a circular structure like that of figure 3.11.

Figure 3.12 shows the code that builds the run-time structure of figure 3.11. This takes us back to the original two-variant environment data type. To create a recursive environment, we first build a vector to hold the values, and then an environment `env` with a new `extended-env-record` that contains the list of procedure names and the new vector. Then, for each procedure declaration, we create a closure containing the procedure's formal parameters, its body, and `env`, and we insert this closure into the corresponding position in the vector. This creates a structure like that shown in figure 3.11. Last, we return this new environment. The procedure `iota` takes a positive integer n and builds a list of integers from 0 to $n - 1$.

Exercise 3.34 [★★] Extend exercise 3.25 to handle `letrec`.

Exercise 3.35 [★★] Implement a version of `letrec` that builds each closure at most once. If the closure is never retrieved, it should never be built.

```
(define-datatype environment environment?
  (empty-env-record)
  (extended-env-record
    (syms (list-of symbol?))
    (vals vector?)
    (env environment?))
  (recursively-extended-env-record
    (proc-names (list-of symbol?))
    (idss (list-of (list-of symbol?)))
    (bodies (list-of expression?))
    (env environment?)))

(define extend-env-recursively
  (lambda (proc-names idss bodies old-env)
    (recursively-extended-env-record
      proc-names idss bodies old-env)))

(define apply-env
  (lambda (env sym)
    (cases environment env
      (empty-env-record ()
        (eopl:error 'empty-env "No binding for ~s" sym))
      (extended-env-record (syms vals old-env)
        (let ((pos (rib-find-position sym syms)))
          (if (number? pos)
            (vector-ref vals pos)
            (apply-env old-env sym))))
      (recursively-extended-env-record (proc-names idss
                                        bodies old-env)
        (let ((pos (rib-find-position sym proc-names)))
          (if (number? pos)
            (closure
              (list-ref idss pos)
              (list-ref bodies pos)
              env)
            (apply-env old-env sym)))))))
```

Figure 3.10   Abstract syntax tree representation of recursive environments

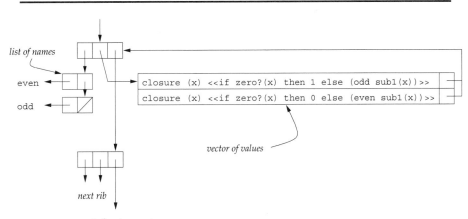

list of names

even

odd

closure (x) <<if zero?(x) then 1 else (odd sub1(x))>>

closure (x) <<if zero?(x) then 0 else (even sub1(x))>>

vector of values

next rib

rest of environment

The boxes with two fields represent `cons` cells; the ones with three fields represent `extended-env-record` nodes.

Figure 3.11   Circular environment structure for even and odd

```
(define extend-env-recursively
  (lambda (proc-names idss bodies old-env)
    (let ((len (length proc-names)))
      (let ((vec (make-vector len)))
        (let ((env (extended-env-record
                      proc-names vec old-env)))
          (for-each
            (lambda (pos ids body)
              (vector-set! vec pos (closure ids body env)))
            (iota len) idss bodies)
          env)))))) 
```

Figure 3.12   Circular data structure representation of recursive environments

Exercise 3.36 [⋆ ⋆] Write a program that behaves differently under the implementation of figure 3.12 than it does under the other two implementations shown in this section. (Hint: retrieve a recursive procedure from an environment twice, and use eq? (exercise 3.17) to see if the same closure is returned.) How can this difference be reconciled with the contention that all three implementations satisfy the specification of `extend-env-recursively`?

3.7   Variable Assignment

We next extend our language to allow assignments to variables. This means that each identifier must denote the address of a mutable location in memory. We call such an address a reference, and it is the contents of these references that are modified by variable assignment. Thus denoted values are references whose contents are expressed values:

$$
\begin{array}{rcl}
\text{Denoted Value} & = & \text{Ref(Expressed Value)} \\
\text{Expressed Value} & = & \text{Number} + \text{ProcVal}
\end{array}
$$

References or locations are sometimes called *L-values*. This reflects their association with variables appearing on the left-hand side of assignment statements. Analogously, expressed values, such as the values of the right-hand side expressions of assignment statements, are known as *R-values*.

We choose the concrete syntax

$$\langle expression \rangle ::= \texttt{set}\ \langle identifier \rangle\ \texttt{=}\ \langle expression \rangle$$
$$\boxed{\texttt{varassign-exp (id rhs-exp)}}$$

This adds a new variant to our data type for expressions. The new variant can be written as

```
(varassign-exp
  (id symbol?)
  (rhs-exp expression?))
```

What is the difference between assignment and binding? A binding creates a new association of a name with a value, while an assignment changes the value of an existing binding. Binding is about the association of names with values; assignment is about the *sharing* of values between different procedures. When a binding is shared by multiple procedures, a change by one is seen by all. Consider the following program in the defined language:

```
let x = 0
in letrec
     even() = if zero?(x)
               then 1
               else let d = set x = sub1(x)
                    in (odd)
     odd()  = if zero?(x)
               then 0
               else let d = set x = sub1(x)
                    in (even)
   in let d = set x = 13 in (odd)
```

Here the idiom let d = *exp* in *exp* where d is a dummy variable, is used to accomplish sequencing (exercise 3.39).

The two procedures even and odd share the variable x. They communicate not by passing data explicitly, as the similar program of section 3.6 does, but by changing the state of the variable they share. This is convenient when two procedures might share many quantities; one needs to assign only to the few quantities that change from one call to the next. Similarly, one procedure might call another procedure not directly but through a long chain of procedure calls. They could communicate data directly through a shared variable, without the intermediate procedures needing to know about it. Thus communication through a shared variable can be a kind of information hiding.

For example, consider the redirection of input and output. I/O operations usually use "standard" input and output ports (connected, say, to a keyboard and the display), unless a specific port is indicated. But we may want all the output generated as a result of invoking a particular procedure call, such as (p 1 2), to be directed to a port associated with a new file, say port, instead of the standard output port. How could the output procedure know what port to use? It would be necessary to pass the port as an argument to p. The procedure p would then have to pass the port to any procedures it calls that might do output, and these procedures would have to do the same. Some of these procedures may not do any output directly, but they must still receive and pass on the output port if any procedure they call does output, either directly or by calling other procedures. This seems to violate modularity, especially since there may be other parameters to pass, such as line lengths, fonts, etc. If the output procedure were constructed to obtain its port and other parameters from non-local variables, then the procedure p could communicate this information directly by assigning to these variables, and the intermediate procedures need not be concerned.

Another use of assignment is to create hidden state directly through the use of private variables. Consider the following program:

```
let g = let count = 0
        in proc ()
              let d = set count = add1(count)
              in count
in +((g),(g))
```

Here the procedure g keeps a private variable that stores the number of times g has been called, so this program evaluates to 3. We use a similar technique to generate symbols in section 8.4.

For our example language, we choose to create a new reference for each formal parameter at every procedure call. This policy is known as *call-by-value*. Under call-by-value, when we assign to a formal parameter, the assignment is local to the procedure. For example,

```
let x = 100
in let p = proc (x) let d = set x = add1(x)
                    in x
   in +((p x),(p x))
```

returns 202, because a new reference is created for x at each of the procedure calls. Thus, at each procedure call, the assignment affects only the inner binding. This is in contrast to the preceding example, in which all the calls to the procedure g shared the same variable count.

In order to implement variable assignment, we introduce the reference data type. The operations on this data type are deref and setref!, which access or store the value in the mutable location.

We begin with a simple implementation of references. We assume the familiar environment representation with a value vector in each rib. References are then elements of rib vectors, which are assignable using vector-set!. Since a vector element is not a Scheme object, we represent a reference as a data type containing the vector and the position of the desired L-value within this vector.

```
(define-datatype reference reference?
  (a-ref
    (position integer?)
    (vec vector?)))
```

A picture of a reference is shown in figure 3.13. The operations for this implementation are deref and setref!. We define these in terms of

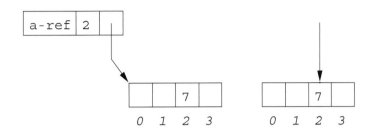

A primitive reference to a location in a Scheme vector, containing 7. We depict such a reference graphically by drawing a pointer to the middle of the structure, as shown on the right-hand side of the diagram.

Figure 3.13 Representation of references

primitive-deref and primitive-setref! because we reuse the latter two procedures in our later implementations of references.

```
(define primitive-deref
  (lambda (ref)
    (cases reference ref
      (a-ref (pos vec) (vector-ref vec pos)))))

(define primitive-setref!
  (lambda (ref val)
    (cases reference ref
      (a-ref (pos vec) (vector-set! vec pos val)))))

(define deref
  (lambda (ref)
    (primitive-deref ref)))

(define setref!
  (lambda (ref val)
    (primitive-setref! ref val)))
```

Exercise 3.37 [*] Add to the interface for references a constructor newrefs, which takes a list of values and returns a list of references; each reference initially contains the corresponding value as its contents. Why would an interface containing newrefs as a constructor be better than one containing a-ref?

```
(define apply-env
  (lambda (env sym)
    (deref (apply-env-ref env sym)))))

(define apply-env-ref
  (lambda (env sym)
    (cases environment env
      (empty-env-record ()
        (eopl:error 'apply-env-ref "No binding for ~s" sym))
      (extended-env-record (syms vals env)
        (let ((pos (rib-find-position sym syms)))
          (if (number? pos)
            (a-ref pos vals)
            (apply-env-ref env sym)))))))))
```

Figure 3.14 `apply-env` and `apply-env-ref`

Exercise 3.38 [⋆] Why is it that we do not need to include a constructor in the interface for references?

We revisit our environment abstraction so we can make use of references. We assume that the denoted values in an environment are of the form Ref(X) for some set X. We reveal this structure by introducing the operation `apply-env-ref` into the interface. The procedure `apply-env-ref` is very similar to the previous definition of `apply-env`, but when it finds the matching identifier, it returns the reference instead of its value. The procedure `apply-env` can then be defined in terms of `apply-env-ref` and `deref`. See figure 3.14.

To implement variable assignment, we now simply add the following clause to `eval-expression`:

```
(varassign-exp (id rhs-exp)
  (begin
    (setref!
      (apply-env-ref env id)
      (eval-expression rhs-exp env))
    1))
```

We explicitly return 1 because the return value of `setref!` is unspecified, and we must always return an expressed value.

```
(define eval-expression
  (lambda (exp env)
    (cases expression exp
      (lit-exp (datum) datum)
      (var-exp (id) (apply-env env id))
      (primapp-exp (prim rands)
        (let ((args (eval-rands rands env)))
          (apply-primitive prim args)))
      (if-exp (test-exp true-exp false-exp)
        (if (true-value? (eval-expression test-exp env))
            (eval-expression true-exp env)
            (eval-expression false-exp env)))
      (let-exp (ids rands body)
        (let ((args (eval-rands rands env)))
          (eval-expression body (extend-env ids args env))))
      (proc-exp (ids body) (closure ids body env))
      (app-exp (rator rands)
        (let ((proc (eval-expression rator env))
              (args (eval-rands rands env)))
          (if (procval? proc)
              (apply-procval proc args)
              (eopl:error 'eval-expression
                "Attempt to apply non-procedure ~s" proc))))
      (letrec-exp (proc-names idss bodies letrec-body)
        (eval-expression letrec-body
          (extend-env-recursively
            proc-names idss bodies env)))
      (varassign-exp (id rhs-exp)
        (begin
          (setref!
            (apply-env-ref env id)
            (eval-expression rhs-exp env))
          1))
      )))
```

Figure 3.15 Interpreter with variable assignment using call-by-value

Exercise 3.39 [⋆] Add the expression `begin` to the language.

⟨expression⟩ ::= `begin` ⟨expression⟩ {`;` ⟨expression⟩}* `end`
> `begin-exp (exp exps)`

A `begin` expression may contain one or more subexpressions separated by semi-colons. These are evaluated in order and the value of the last is returned. Implement this by modifying `eval-expression`.

Exercise 3.40 [⋆⋆] Define a *form* to be a *definition* or expression using the following concrete syntax

⟨form⟩ ::= `define` ⟨identifier⟩ = ⟨expression⟩
      ::= ⟨expression⟩

This syntax intentionally prevents definitions (as opposed to local declarations) from appearing inside expressions.

Modify the read-eval-print loop so that it reads a sequence of forms, with definitions performed and expressions evaluated as they are encountered. A definition is performed by first evaluating the given expression in the initial environment. If the initial environment already contains a binding for the given variable, the expression's value is assigned to this binding as if by a top-level assignment. If the given variable is not bound in the initial environment, the initial environment should be extended to bind the variable to a location containing the expression's value; this will require some changes in the environment abstraction. After performing a definition, the next prompt is printed without printing any value. After evaluation of an expression, the value of the expression should be printed, as usual, before prompting for the next definition or expression. Implement and test `even` and `odd` (from section 3.6) as definitions.

Exercise 3.41 [⋆⋆] Another design for assignment is to have locations become expressed values, and have allocation, dereferencing, and assignment be explicit in the program. Then we would have

Expressed Value = Number + ProcVal + Ref(Expressed Value)
Denoted Value = Expressed Value

Modify the interpreter of figure 3.15 to use this set of expressed values, with new primitives `cell`, `contents`, and `setcell` for creating, dereferencing, and mutating cells as in exercise 2.26. In this language, our procedure with a private counter (page 100) would look something like

```
let g = let count = cell(0)
        in proc ()
             begin
               setcell(count,add1(contents(count)));
               contents(count)
             end
in +((g),(g))
```

Exercise 3.42 [★★]   Add arrays to this language. Introduce new primitives `array`, `arrayref`, and `arrayset` that create, dereference, and update arrays. This leads to

$$\text{Arr} = (\text{Ref(Expressed Value)})^*$$
$$\text{Expressed Value} = \text{Number} + \text{ProcVal} + \text{Arr}$$
$$\text{Denoted Value} = \text{Ref(Expressed Value)}$$

where the first occurrence of Ref can be a different implementation of references (perhaps using the fact that a Scheme array is already a sequence of references) than the one described in this section. What should be the result of the following program?

```
let a = array(2)
    p = proc (x)
            let v = arrayref(x,1)
            in arrayset(x,1,add1(v))
in begin
    arrayset(a,1,0);
    p(a);
    p(a);
    arrayref(a,1)
  end
```

Here `array(2)` is intended to build an array of size 2.

Exercise 3.43 [★★] Modify the interpreter of figure 3.15 by defining primitives `deref` and `setref` using deref and setref!, respectively. Then add a new production

$$\langle\text{expression}\rangle ::= \texttt{ref}\ \langle\text{identifier}\rangle$$
$$\boxed{\texttt{ref-exp (id)}}$$

This differs from the language of exercise 3.41, since references are only of variables. This allows us to write familiar programs such as `swap` within our call-by-value language. What should be the value of this expression?

```
let a = 3
    b = 4
    swap = proc (x,y)
            let temp = deref(x)
            in begin
                    setref(x,deref(y));
                    setref(y,temp)
                end
in begin
    (swap ref a ref b);
    -(a,b)
  end
```

What are the expressed and denoted values of this language?

Exercise 3.44 [⋆] Now that variables are mutable, we can build recursive procedures by assignment. For example

```
letrec times4(x) = if x
                      then +(4,(times4 sub1(x)))
                      else 0
in (times4 3)
```

can be replaced by

```
let times4 = 0
in begin
     set times4 = proc (x)
                     if x
                     then +(4,(times4 sub1(x)))
                     else 0;
     (times4 3)
   end
```

Trace this by hand and verify that this translation works.

Exercise 3.45 [⋆⋆] In the interpreter of figure 3.15, all variable bindings are mutable (as in Scheme). Another alternative is to allow both mutable and immutable variable bindings:

$$\begin{array}{rcl}
\text{Expressed Value} & = & \text{Number} + \text{ProcVal} \\
\text{Denoted Value} & = & \text{Ref(Expressed Value)} + \text{Expressed Value}
\end{array}$$

Variable assignment should work only when the variable to be assigned to has a mutable binding. Dereferencing occurs implicitly when the denoted value is a reference.

Modify this interpreter and its accompanying environment abstraction so that `let` introduces immutable bindings, but `letmutable` introduces mutable bindings. The `letmutable` expression is a new special form, with a syntax similar to the `let` form.

⟨expression⟩ ::= letmutable {⟨identifier⟩ = ⟨expression⟩}* in ⟨expression⟩
                  ⎢letmutable-exp (ids rands body)⎥

Exercise 3.46 [⋆⋆] Adapt the interpreter of figure 3.15 to use the representation of closures from exercise 3.27, in which only the bindings of free variables are kept in the closure.

Exercise 3.47 [⋆⋆] We suggested earlier the use of assignment to make a program more modular by allowing one procedure to communicate information to a distant procedure without requiring intermediate procedures to be aware of it. Very often

such an assignment should only be temporary, lasting for the execution of a procedure call. Add to the language a facility for *dynamic assignment* (also called *fluid
binding*) to accomplish this. Use the production

⟨expression⟩ ::= setdynamic ⟨identifier⟩ = ⟨expression⟩ during ⟨expression⟩

                 `setdynamic-exp (id rhs-exp body)`

The effect of the `setdynamic` expression is to assign temporarily the value of
`rhs-exp` to `id`, evaluate `body`, re-assign `id` to its original value, and return the value
of `body`. The identifier `id` must already be bound. For example, in

```
let x = 4
in let p = proc (y) +(x,y)
   in +(setdynamic x = 7 during (p 1),
        (p 2))
```

the value of x, which is free in procedure p, is 7 in the call `(p 1)`, but is reset to 4 in
the call `(p 2)`, so the value of the expression is $8 + 6 = 14$.

Exercise 3.48 [⋆⋆⋆] Our understanding of assignment, as expressed in the interpreter of figure 3.15, depends on the semantics of side effects in Scheme. In particular,
it depends on *when* these effects take place. If we could model assignment without
using Scheme's side-effecting operations, our understanding would not be dependent on Scheme in this way. We can do this by modeling the state of a program not
as a collection of mutable locations but as a function, called the *store*. The domain
of the store function is some arbitrary set of addresses (say the nonnegative integers)
that represents locations, and its range is the set of expressed values. Mutation of a
location in the store is then modeled by extending this function to associate the location with the new value. This new association supersedes any earlier associations
for the same location. Assume that each invocation of (location) produces an
unused integer. Alternatively, model the store as an abstract syntax tree and use the
"length" of the store to retrieve the next unused location.

In order for the new store to be used in subsequent evaluation, it must be returned by
`eval-expression` and then passed as an additional argument to interpreter procedures (`eval-expression`, `eval-rands`, `apply-procval`, etc.) that might need it.
Consider figure 3.16. Every procedure that might modify the store returns not just its
usual value but an `answer` consisting of the value and a new store. The trickiest procedure to modify is `eval-rands`. It can no longer just use `map`. Instead, it must evaluate the operands in some specific order, with the store resulting from each evaluation
being used in the next evaluation. Complete this definition of `eval-expression`.

3.8 Parameter-Passing Variations

The language design of section 3.7, in which formal parameters are bound
to locations of operand values, has used call-by-value. This is the most commonly used form of parameter passing, and is the standard against which

```
(define-datatype answer answer?
  (an-answer
    (val expval?)
    (store store?)))

(define eval-expression
  (lambda (exp env store)
    (cases expression exp
      (var-exp (id)
        (an-answer (apply-store store (apply-env env id))
          store))
      (varassign-exp (id rhs-exp)
        (cases answer (eval-expression rhs-exp env store)
          (an-answer (val new-store)
            (an-answer 1
              (extend-store (apply-env env id) val store)))))
      (if-exp (test-exp true-exp false-exp)
        (cases answer (eval-expression test-exp env store)
          (an-answer (val new-store)
            (if (true-value? val)
              (eval-expression true-exp env new-store)
              (eval-expression false-exp env new-store)))))
      ...)))
```

Figure 3.16   Store-passing interpreter for exercise 3.48

other parameter-passing mechanisms are usually compared. In this section
we explore alternative parameter-passing mechanisms.

Consider the following expression:

```
let a = 3
    p = proc (x) set x = 4
in begin (p a); a end
```

Under call-by-value semantics, the denoted value associated with x is a reference that initially contains the same value as the reference associated with
a, but these references are distinct. Thus the assignment to x has no effect on
the contents of a's reference, so the value of the entire expression is 3.

With call-by-value semantics it is a big help to know that when a procedure assigns a new value to one of its parameters, this cannot possibly be
seen by its caller. Of course, if the parameter passed to the caller contains a

reference to a mutable location, as in exercise 3.42, and the procedure modifies this location, the resulting modification will still be seen by the caller in subsequent uses of the reference.

Though this isolation between the caller and callee is generally desirable, there are times when it is valuable to allow a procedure to be passed variables with the expectation that they will be assigned by the procedure. This may be accomplished by passing the procedure a reference to the location of the caller's variable, rather than the contents of the variable. This parameter-passing mechanism is called *call-by-reference*. If an operand is simply a variable reference, a reference to the variable's location is passed. The formal parameter of the procedure is then bound to this location. If the operand is some other kind of expression, then the formal parameter is bound to a new location containing the value of the operand, just as in call-by-value. Using call-by-reference in the above example, the assignment of 4 to x has the effect of assigning 4 to a, so the entire expression would return 4, not 3.

One common use of call-by-reference is to return multiple values. A procedure can return one value in the normal way and assign others to parameters that are passed by reference. For another sort of example, consider the common programming need for swapping the values in two variables:

```
let a = 3
    b = 4
    swap = proc (x, y)
               let temp = x
               in begin
                      set x = y;
                      set y = temp
                  end
in begin
    (swap a b);
    -(a,b)
   end
```

Under call-by-reference, this swaps the values of a and b, so it returns 1. If this program were run with our existing call-by-value interpreter, however, it would return -1, because the assignments inside the swap procedure then have no effect on variables a and b.

Under call-by-reference, identifiers still denote references to expressed values, just as they did under call-by-value:

$$\begin{aligned} \text{Denoted Value} &= \text{Ref(Expressed Value)} \\ \text{Expressed Value} &= \text{Number} + \text{ProcVal} \end{aligned}$$

The only change occurs when new references are created. Under call-by-value, a new reference is created for every evaluation of an operand; under call-by-reference, a new reference is created for every evaluation of an operand *other than a variable*.

Because call-by-value creates a new location for every operand in a procedure application, we could put the values of all the operands in a vector, and have `apply-env-ref` create a reference to the location at variable-lookup time. Under call-by-reference, however, we will need a new location for some operands and not for others, so we need a different representation for references.

For our implementation of call-by-reference, we will use the implementation of references shown in figure 3.17. A reference will be, as before, a reference to a location within a vector. But the vector, instead of containing expressed values, will contain either expressed values or references to expressed values. We call these two kinds of targets *direct targets* and *indirect targets*, respectively. A direct target corresponds to the behavior of call-by-value, in which a new location is created; an indirect target corresponds to the new behavior of call-by-reference, in which no new location is created. The new definitions of `deref` and `setref!` look at the kind of target to determine the expressed value to return or the location to mutate.

The procedures `extend-env` and `apply-env-ref` are unchanged: `extend-env` will take a list of targets and return a vector containing those targets, and `apply-env-ref` looks up an identifier and creates a reference to the location containing the appropriate target.

Now we can implement call-by-reference. We consider each place where subexpressions are evaluated. For primitive applications, we simply need to evaluate the subexpressions and pass the values to `apply-primitive`, so in `eval-expression` we write

```
(primapp-exp (prim rands)
  (let ((args (eval-primapp-exp-rands rands env)))
    (apply-primitive prim args)))
```

where `eval-primapp-exp-rands` is defined by

```
(define eval-primapp-exp-rands
  (lambda (rands env)
    (map (lambda (x) (eval-expression x env)) rands)))
```

For `let`-bound variables, we choose to retain the call-by-value behavior, so in `eval-expression` we write

```
(define-datatype target target?
  (direct-target
    (expval expval?))
  (indirect-target
    (ref ref-to-direct-target?)))

(define expval?
  (lambda (x)
    (or (number? x) (procval? x))))

(define ref-to-direct-target?
  (lambda (x)
    (and
      (reference? x)
      (cases reference x
        (a-ref (pos vec)
          (cases target (vector-ref vec pos)
            (direct-target (v) #t)
            (indirect-target (v) #f)))))))

(define deref
  (lambda (ref)
    (cases target (primitive-deref ref)
      (direct-target (expval) expval)
      (indirect-target (ref1)
        (cases target (primitive-deref ref1)
          (direct-target (expval) expval)
          (indirect-target (p)
            (eopl:error 'deref
              "Illegal reference: ~s" ref1)))))))

(define setref!
  (lambda (ref expval)
    (let ((ref (cases target (primitive-deref ref)
                 (direct-target (expval1) ref)
                 (indirect-target (ref1) ref1))))
      (primitive-setref! ref (direct-target expval)))))
```

Figure 3.17 Implementation of references for call-by-reference

```
(let-exp (ids rands body)
  (let ((args (eval-let-exp-rands rands env)))
    (eval-expression body (extend-env ids args env)))))
```

where `eval-let-exp-rands` and `eval-let-exp-rand` are defined by

```
(define eval-let-exp-rands
  (lambda (rands env)
    (map (lambda (x) (eval-let-exp-rand x env)) rands)))

(define eval-let-exp-rand
  (lambda (rand env)
    (direct-target (eval-expression rand env))))
```

For procedure applications, we continue to evaluate each operand using `eval-rand`.

```
(define eval-rand
  (lambda (rand env)
    (cases expression rand
      (var-exp (id)
        (indirect-target
          (let ((ref (apply-env-ref env id)))
            (cases target (primitive-deref ref)
              (direct-target (expval) ref)
              (indirect-target (ref1) ref1)))))
      (else
        (direct-target (eval-expression rand env))))))
```

Here we must be a bit more careful. If the operand is a non-variable, then we create a new location, as before, by returning a direct target. If the operand is a variable, it denotes a location containing an expressed value, so we want to return an indirect target pointing to that location. This is a bit trickier than it first appears. If a variable is bound to a location containing a direct target (which must contain an expressed value, like 5), then a reference to the location is returned as an indirect target. But, if the variable is bound to another reference, then that reference is returned. This maintains the invariant that a reference contains either an expressed value or a reference to an expressed value.

We show the operation of `eval-rand` in figure 3.18 where we depict the value ribs in the environment of the innermost procedure body in the program

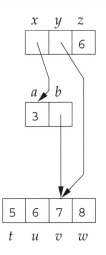

Figure 3.18 Environments built by call-by-reference

```
(proc (t, u, v, w)                    % call this p1
   (proc (a, b)                       % call this p2
      (proc (x, y, z)                 % call this p3
         set y = 13
         a b 6)
      3 v)
   5 6 7 8)
```

First the procedure p1 is applied to 5, 6, 7, and 8, yielding the value vector at
the bottom of the figure. Next p2 is applied to the operands 3 and v, yielding the value vector in the middle. This vector contains 3 and a reference to
the location containing 7. In each vector element, there is a direct-target
wrapped around each expressed value and an indirect-target wrapped
around each reference; these are not depicted to preserve the clarity of the
picture. Finally, p3 is invoked on a, b, and 6. The variable a contains a
direct target, so x is bound to an indirect target containing a pointer to a.
The variable b contains an indirect target, so y is bound to an indirect target
containing a pointer to the target of b. Last, 6 is an expressed value, so z is
bound to a direct target containing 6.

Exercise 3.49 [⋆] Redraw figure 3.18 using the format of the left-hand side of figure 3.13. Include the direct-target and indirect-target data structures.

Exercise 3.50 [★★] Implement the call-by-reference interpreter and test it with examples including primitive application and `letrec`.

Exercise 3.51 [★★] Rewrite the preceding definition of `eval-rand` so that targets are reused rather than reconstructed whenever possible.

Exercise 3.52 [★] More than one call-by-reference parameter may refer to the same location, as in the following program.

```
let b = 3
    p = proc (x, y)
          begin
            set x = 4;
            y
          end
in (p b b)
```

This yields 4 since both x and y refer to the same location, which is the binding of b. This phenomenon is known as *variable aliasing*. Here x and y are aliases (names) for the same location. Aliasing makes it very difficult to understand programs. Generally, we do not expect an assignment to one variable to change the value of another. Virtually all rules for reasoning formally about programs are invalid in the presence of aliasing.

Test the call-by-reference interpreter with programs that demonstrate aliasing.

Exercise 3.53 [★★] In languages supporting call-by-reference it is usual for call-by-value to be supported also, with a method for specifying which is to be used for each formal parameter. Extend the implementation of this section in this way.

Exercise 3.54 [★★★] Most languages support arrays, in which case array references are generally treated like variable references under call-by-reference. That is, if an operand is an array reference, the location referred to, rather than its contents, is passed to the called procedure. This allows, for example, a swap procedure to be used in commonly occurring situations in which the values in two array elements are to be exchanged. Add array primitives like those of exercise 3.42 to the call-by-reference language of this section, and extend `eval-rand` to handle this case, so that, for example, a procedure application like (swap (arrayref a i) (arrayref a j)) will work as expected.

Exercise 3.55 [★] *Call-by-value-result* is a variation on call-by-reference. In call-by-value-result, the actual parameter must be a variable. When a parameter is passed, the formal parameter is bound to a new reference initialized to the value of the actual parameter, just as in call-by-value. The procedure body is then executed normally. When the procedure body returns, however, the value in the new reference is copied back into the reference denoted by the actual parameter. This may be more efficient than call-by-reference because it can improve memory locality. Implement call-by-value-result and test it with a program that produces different answers using call-by-value-result and call-by-reference.

We now turn to a very different form of parameter passing, called *lazy evaluation*. Sometimes in a given call a procedure never refers to one or more of its formal parameters. In this case time devoted to evaluating the corresponding operands is wasted. It may even be that evaluation of such an operand would result in an error or never terminate. For example, were it not for such problems, `if` could be a procedure, instead of having to be a syntactic form.

In a language such as Scheme that supports first-class procedures, one can delay (perhaps indefinitely) the evaluation of an operand by encapsulating it as the body of a *thunk*, a procedure of no arguments. Whenever a variable is referenced, the corresponding procedure must be invoked. The actions of forming thunks and evaluating them are called *freezing* and *thawing*, respectively.

A few languages support a parameter-passing mechanism called *lazy evaluation* that automates this technique. Lazy evaluation mechanisms may differ in how they handle multiple references to the same parameter. A naive approach would invoke the thunk every time the parameter is referred to. This policy is called, for historical reasons, *call-by-name*. In the absence of side effects this is a waste of time, since the same value is returned each time. A more sophisticated approach, called *call-by-need*, records the value of each thunk the first time it is invoked, and thereafter refers to the saved value instead of re-invoking the thunk. This is an example of a more general technique known as *memoization*.

In the absence of side-effects, call-by-name and call-by-need always give the same answer. In the presence of side-effects, however, it is easy to distinguish these two mechanisms. Consider, for example, the expression

```
let g = let count = 0
        in proc ()
             begin
               set count = add1(count);
               count
             end
in (proc (x) +(x,x)
    (g))
```

The procedure g returns the number of times it is called. Under call-by-name each reference to the variable x invokes g, so the first x evaluates to 1, the second x evaluates to 2, and the result is 3. Under call-by-need, g is invoked only once, for the first reference to x, so both occurrences of x evaluate to 1, and the result is 2.

An attraction of lazy evaluation in all its forms is that in the absence of side-effects it supports reasoning about programs in a particularly simple way. The effect of a procedure call can be modeled by replacing the call with the body of the procedure, with every reference to a formal parameter in the body replaced by the corresponding operand. This evaluation strategy is the basis for the lambda calculus, in which it is referred to as *β-reduction*. (See exercise 2.12.) In other languages it is sometimes called the *copy rule*.

Even with call-by-need there can be considerable overhead associated with so much freezing and thawing activity. It is, however, possible to reduce this overhead to often-acceptable levels, primarily by not making thunks when it can be proved that the result will not be changed.

A more important reason why call-by-name is not popular is that it generally makes it difficult to determine the flow of control (order of evaluation), which in turn is essential to understanding a program with side effects. On the other hand, if there are no side effects, the flow of control does not affect the result of a program, so this is not a problem. Thus lazy evaluation is popular in purely-functional programming languages (those with no side-effects), and rarely found elsewhere.

We now add lazy evaluation to our language. As before, variables denote references to expressed values:

$$\begin{aligned} \text{Denoted Value} \quad &= \quad \text{Ref(Expressed Value)} \\ \text{Expressed Value} \quad &= \quad \text{Number} + \text{ProcVal} \end{aligned}$$

We implement lazy evaluation by extending our data type of references to add a third kind of target, called a *thunk target*. A thunk target is like a direct target, except that instead of containing an expressed value it contains a thunk that evaluates to an expressed value. If deref is given a reference containing a thunk (either as a direct or indirect target), it evaluates the thunk using eval-thunk, which evaluates the expression contained in the thunk and returns the corresponding expressed value; further, if the system is using call-by-need, eval-thunk updates the location containing the thunk to contain instead a direct target with the expressed value. See figures 3.19 and 3.20.

In eval-rand we recognize literals and procedures and do not bother to freeze them, since they evaluate quickly. We also give special treatment to operands that are variables, as in call-by-reference and we treat thunk targets in the same way that we treat direct targets. Last and most important, all other operands are frozen by creating a thunk that delays their evaluation until needed (figure 3.21). Thus, under call-by-need, in the expression

```
(define-datatype target target?
  (direct-target
    (expval expval?))
  (indirect-target
    (ref ref-to-direct-target?))
  (thunk-target
    (exp expression?)
    (env environment?)))

(define ref-to-direct-target?
  (lambda (x)
    (and
      (reference? x)
      (cases reference x
        (a-ref (pos vec)
          (cases target (vector-ref vec pos)
            (direct-target (v) #t)
            (indirect-target (p) #f)
            (thunk-target (exp env) #t)))))))))
```

Figure 3.19   Implementation of references for call-by-name and call-by-need (part 1)

```
(proc (a, b)
  (proc (x)
    (proc (y)
      (proc (z) +(+(x,y),z) y)
    x)
  +(a,b))
 15 20)
```

the operand +(a,b) gets evaluated only when the first variable is referenced in +(+(x,y),z), regardless of which variable is evaluated first, and it is evaluated only once. Each of the other two variables refers to the same already-evaluated thunk.

Exercise 3.56 [⋆⋆] Implement the call-by-need interpreter, but leave if out of the language syntax and implement it as a primitive procedure.

Exercise 3.57 [⋆⋆] Revise the call-by-need interpreter of the previous exercise so that it becomes a call-by-name interpreter. Then include variable asignment. Test it with a program that uses assignment in such a way that two references to the same parameter return different values.

```
(define deref
  (lambda (ref)
    (cases target (primitive-deref ref)
      (direct-target (expval) expval)
      (indirect-target (ref1)
        (cases target (primitive-deref ref1)
          (direct-target (expval) expval)
          (indirect-target (p)
            (eopl:error 'deref
              "Illegal reference: ~s" ref1))
          (thunk-target (exp env) (eval-thunk ref1))))
      (thunk-target (exp env) (eval-thunk ref)))))

(define eval-thunk
  (lambda (ref)
    (cases target (primitive-deref ref)
      (thunk-target (exp env)
        (let ((val (eval-expression exp env)))
          (primitive-setref! ref (direct-target val))
          val))
      (else
        (eopl:error 'eval-thunk "Impossible!")))))

(define setref!
  (lambda (ref expval)
    (let ((ref (cases target (primitive-deref ref)
                 (direct-target (expval1) ref)
                 (indirect-target (ref1) ref1)
                 (thunk-target (exp env) ref))))
      (primitive-setref! ref (direct-target expval)))))
```

Figure 3.20   Implementation of references for call-by-name and call-by-need (part 2)

Exercise 3.58 [★★] Add let to the call-by-need interpreter. Use a test program that demonstrates that this let is lazy.

Exercise 3.59 [★★] Add strictlet to the call-by-need interpreter. This is similar to the lazy let of exercise 3.58, but forces the evaluation of each of its bindings.

Exercise 3.60 [★★] When is it possible to avoid invoking indirect-target from within eval-rand?

```
(define eval-rand
  (lambda (rand env)
    (cases expression rand
      (var-exp (id)
        (let ((ref (apply-env-ref env id)))
          (indirect-target
            (cases target (primitive-deref ref)
              (direct-target (expval) ref)
              (indirect-target (ref1) ref1)
              (thunk-target (exp env) ref)))))
      (lit-exp (datum) (direct-target datum))
      (proc-exp (ids body)
        (direct-target (closure ids body env)))
      (else (thunk-target rand env)))))
```

Figure 3.21 eval-rand for call-by-need

```
let conz = proc (x, y) proc (m) if m then x else y
    caz = proc (b) (b 1)
    cdz = proc (b) (b 0))
in let lz = (conz random(10) 0)
  in let u = (caz lz)
    in zero?(-((caz lz),u))
```

Figure 3.22 Example for exercise 3.61

Exercise 3.61 [★★★] The power of lazy evaluation is greatly enhanced in the presence of primitive data constructors that do not thaw one or more of their arguments until their value is extracted from the structure. One way to accomplish this is to represent the data constructors as procedures. The program in figure 3.22 illustrates this approach by defining a lazy version of cons, with corresponding car and cdr operations. With call-by-need semantics, the answer is always true, because u and (caz lz) will always be bound to the first answer returned by random(10). With call-by-name semantics, there is a good chance that the result will be false, since the calls to u and (caz lz) in zero?(-((caz lz),u)) will each invoke random(10), and there is a reasonably good chance that they will not yield the same random value.

Add conz, caz, cdz and random as primitives.

3.9   Statements

So far our languages have been expression-oriented: the primary syntactic category of interest has been expressions, and we have primarily been interested in their values. In this section we extend our interpreter to model a simple statement-oriented language.

In our statement language, the expressed values are integers and ProcVals; the denoted values are locations containing expressed values. The syntax of the language is given in figure 3.23. Here ⟨expression⟩ refers to the language of expressions of section 3.7. The informal semantics is straightforward. A program is a statement. A program does not return a value, but works by printing. Assignment statements work in the usual way. A print statement evaluates its actual parameter and prints the result. The compound, if, and while statements work in the usual way. Tests use the same convention about truth as does the language of section 3.3: 0 counts as false and all other values count as true. A block statement binds each of the declared identifiers to an uninitialized location and then executes the body of the block. The scope of these bindings is the body. Here are some examples.

```
var x,y; {x = 3; y = 4; print(+(x,y))}

var x,y,z; {x = 3; y = 4; z = 0;
            while x do {z = +(z,y); x = sub1(x)};
            print(z)}

var x; {x = 3; print(x);
        var x; {x = 4; print(x)};
        print(x)}

var f,x; {f = proc (x, y) *(x,y);
          x = 3;
          print((f 4 x))}
```

The first example prints 7. The second example prints 12 and illustrates a while loop, where its statement is executed so long as its expression is true. The third example prints 3, then 4, and then 3 again and shows the scoping of the block statement. The fourth example prints 12 and demonstrates the interaction between statements and expressions. A procedure value is created and stored in the variable f. In the last line, this procedure is applied to the actual parameters 4 and x; since x is bound to a location, it is dereferenced to obtain 3. Our syntax requires the two sets of parentheses here: the outer set are from the print-statement production and the inner ones are from the app production for expressions.

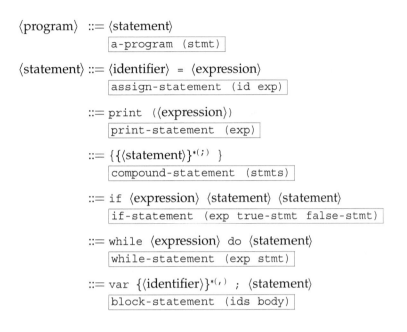

Figure 3.23   Grammar for language of statements

It is straightforward to implement an interpreter for this language. See figure 3.24. As usual, we follow the grammar, writing one procedure for each nonterminal. Since programs and statements are executed for their effect rather than evaluated for their value, we call these procedures `execute-program` and `execute-statement`. In the code for compound statements, we rely on the fact that the Scheme procedure `for-each` is guaranteed to process its second argument from left to right. In the while statement, we use a one-armed `if` to avoid having to return an arbitrary value.

Exercise 3.62 [⋆] Add `read` statements of the form `read` (⟨identifier⟩) to this language. This statement reads a nonnegative integer from the input and stores it in the given variable.

Exercise 3.63 [⋆] A do-while statement is like a `while` statement, except that the test is performed *after* the execution of the body. Add do-while statements to the interpreter of figure 3.24.

Exercise 3.64 [⋆] Extend the block statement to allow variables to be initialized. In the solution, does the scope of a variable include the initializer for variables declared later in the same block statement?

Exercise 3.65 [⋆⋆] Extend the block statement to allow a procedure to be declared in a block, and add a statement that calls a procedure with actual parameters. A procedure body should be within the scope of any variables declared earlier in the same block statement.

Exercise 3.66 [⋆⋆⋆] Extend the solution to the previous exercise so that procedures declared in a single block are mutually recursive. Feel free to restrict the language so that all the variable declarations in a block are followed by all the procedure declarations.

Exercise 3.67 [⋆⋆] Extend the language of the last exercise to include *subroutines*. In our usage a subroutine is like a procedure, except that it does not return a value and its body is a statement, rather than expression. Also, add subroutine calls as a new kind of statement and extend the syntax of blocks so that they may be used to declare both procedures and subroutines. How does this affect the denoted and expressed values? What happens if a procedure is referenced in a subroutine call, or vice versa?

Further Reading

The wide use of interpreters as a vehicle for explaining the behavior of programming languages dates back to (McCarthy, 1960; 1965), which uses a metacircular interpreter (an interpreter written in the defined language itself) as an illustration of the power of Lisp. Our interpreters are not metacircular, but the concept of metacircularity has been thoroughly explored in (Smith, 1982; 1984), which characterizes metacircular interpreters as an infinite tower of interpreters.

Fortran (Backus *et al.*, 1957) was the first language to use call-by-reference, Algol 60 (Naur *et al.*, 1963) was the first language to use call-by-name, and Haskell (Hudak *et al.*, 1990) was the first practical language to use call-by-need. (Plotkin, 1975) shows how to model call-by-value and call-by-name in the lambda calculus.

```
(define execute-program
  (lambda (pgm)
    (cases program pgm
      (a-program (statement)
        (execute-statement statement (init-env))))))

(define execute-statement
  (lambda (stmt env)
    (cases statement stmt
      (assign-statement (id exp)
        (setref!
          (apply-env-ref env id)
          (eval-expression exp env)))
      (print-statement (exp)
        (write (eval-expression exp env))
        (newline))
      (compound-statement (statements)
        (for-each
          (lambda (statement)
            (execute-statement statement env))
          statements))
      (if-statement (exp true-statement false-statement)
        (if (true-value? (eval-expression exp env))
          (execute-statement true-statement env)
          (execute-statement false-statement env)))
      (while-statement (exp statement)
        (let loop ()
          (if (true-value? (eval-expression exp env))
            (begin
              (execute-statement statement env)
              (loop)))))
      (block-statement (ids statement)
        (execute-statement statement
          (extend-env ids ids env)))
      )))
```

Figure 3.24   Interpreter for the language of statements

4 *Types*

The data that programs manipulate come in many types: integers, characters, procedures, lists, *etc.* Some operations are appropriate on some types of values, and others are not. An attempt to apply an operation to inappropriate data is called a *type error*. In this chapter we show the same ideas we use to interpret programs can be used to analyze our programs to ensure that no type error can occur during execution.

In section 4.1 we explore some of the subtleties in determining whether or not an operation is appropriate, and outline the major approaches for dealing with inappropriate operations. The remainder of this chapter deals with the most important of those approaches, *static typing*. In section 4.2 we consider *type checking*, a simple design for static typing in which the programmer must supply key type information for the type analyzer. In section 4.3 we show how type analysis can be used to enforce abstraction boundaries of the sort considered in section 2.1. Last, in section 4.4 we explore *type inference*, a strategy in which the analyzer deduces the type of each variable on the basis of its use in the program.

4.1 Typed Languages

Typed languages typically approach the problem of type analysis as follows:

1. They define a set of types for the language, and we define what it means for an expressed value v to be of type t.

2. An analysis step is introduced into the language-processing model (figure 3.1). The analyzer assigns a type to each expression in the program. Usually, the goal is to do this in such a way that if expression e is assigned

type *t*, then whenever *e* is executed, its value will be of type *t*. If the type system has this property, we say that it is *sound*.

3. As it works, the analyzer inspects each invocation of an operation in the program. Each operand of the operation is an expression of some type, and therefore we know that the value of that operand will be of that type. If the arguments are not known to be of the appropriate types, we say that this invocation of an operation is a potential *type error*. The specification of the kinds of errors which are to be detected in this way is part of the design of the language.

4. If type errors are detected, the analyzer can take some action, which is typically also part of the language design. It can refuse to execute the program, or it can apply some corrective measures.

Each of these steps allows a variety of design choices. The first issue is what the types are, whether a value can have more than one type, and if so whether that type can be determined readily at run time. In some languages, every run-time value includes a tag (or some other run-time information) to indicate its type. This is called *latent* or *dynamic* typing. Scheme is a latently-typed language: every value in Scheme has a tag to indicate its type. These tags are checked by `number?`, `string?`, etc. Similarly, in our earlier languages we arranged our data representations to distinguish procedures from other values, and we had a run-time check to prevent `apply-procval` from trying to apply a value that was not a procedure.

In a language with dynamic typing, one can tell at run time when an operation is appropriate or inappropriate: simply check the tags. One shortcoming of dynamic typing is that inserting and checking the tags can add run-time overhead. Clever design of data structures can minimize this overhead.

A more serious limitation of dynamic typing is that it does not support data abstraction. For example, it might seem appropriate to take the cdr of a list, but it would be inappropriate to do so if that list happened to be a bignum representation of a number (section 2.1), and we were not inside the implementation of the number data type. We study this issue in section 4.3.

In other languages, a run-time value might represent (say) both an integer and character. Such languages are said to have an *untyped* execution model. Data abstraction, as exemplified by an example of a list that is also a bignum, is one way in which such overlaps might arise.

We could have implemented the language of section 3.5 in an untyped execution model. We could have represented procedures by integers that point-

```
(define-datatype closure-record closure-record?
  (a-closure-record
    (ids (list-of symbol?))
    (body expression?)
    (env environment?)))

(define procval? integer?)

(define all-closures (make-vector 1000))
(vector-set! all-closures 0 1)

(define closure
  (lambda (ids body env)
    (let ((free-ptr (vector-ref all-closures 0)))
      (vector-set! all-closures free-ptr
        (a-closure-record ids body env))
      (vector-set! all-closures  0 (+ 1 free-ptr))
      free-ptr)))

(define apply-procval
  (lambda (proc args)
    (cases closure-record (vector-ref all-closures proc)
      (a-closure-record (ids body env)
        ...))))
```

Figure 4.1   Implementing procedures in an untyped execution model

ed into an array of closures. See figure 4.1. Here `all-closures` is a vector of closure records, with its first element acting as a free-cell counter. In this representation, given a piece of data, there is no reliable way of determining whether it was intended to represent an integer or a procedure.

Languages with untyped execution models typically make no attempt to detect inappropriate operations at run time. If operations are applied to inappropriate data, the results are unspecified. In such a language one might be able to multiply 2 characters; the result is whatever the hardware happens to do with the representation of characters. We call this a *laissez-faire* design.

Typed languages avoid these difficulties by analyzing the program before execution, to determine whether any particular call site in the program might result in an inappropriate operation at run time. This is called *static type checking.* If a potential type error is detected, the analyzer may produce a warning, insert run-time checking code (if the run-time model permits it), or reject the program. Static type checking may be used either with or without latent typing, but it is critical for languages with an untyped execution model, since run-time type checking is infeasible for such languages.

In this chapter we study static type checking. We present several algorithms for assigning types to expressions and checking that no expression can possibly cause an operation to be performed on inappropriate arguments. Our checkers either produce a type for the program or reject it and raise an error.

The types of our first language have a very simple structure:

$\langle$type-exp$\rangle$ ::= `int`
    | `int-type-exp  ()` |

$\langle$type-exp$\rangle$ ::= `bool`
    | `bool-type-exp  ()` |

$\langle$type-exp$\rangle$ ::= `({`$\langle$type-exp$\rangle$`}`$^{*(*)}$ `->` $\langle$type-exp$\rangle$`)`
    | `proc-type-exp  (arg-texps  result-texp)` |

When types appear in programs, they are called *type expressions*. For the remainder of this section, we ignore the difference between type expressions and types; we consider the distinction in more detail in section 4.2.

Our types include base types for integers and booleans and types for procedures. The type of a procedure consists of the types of its arguments (separated by *'s) and the type of its result. The property of an expressed value v being of type t is defined by induction on t:

Definition 4.1.1 *An expressed value is of type* `int` *iff it is an integer; it is of type* `bool` *iff it is a boolean; and it is of type* $(t_1 * \ldots * t_n \text{ -> } t)$ *iff it is a ProcVal that expects exactly n arguments, and when given n arguments of types* $t_1, \ldots, t_n$, *it returns a value of type t.*

Thus, in our language, each expressed value has at most one type, but it is not always possible to determine the type of a value at run time, because one may not be able to determine the type of the value returned by a procedure.

We could use these types to describe Scheme values. For example:

```
(int -> bool)                          type of even?
(int * int -> int)                     type of +
(int -> (int -> int))                  type of (lambda (x)
                                                 (lambda (y) (+ x y)))
((int -> int) * int -> bool)           type of (lambda (f x)
                                                 (even? (f (+ x 1)))))
```

where we mean these to be the types of the *values* of these expressions, not of the expressions themselves; we haven't said what it means for an expression to have a type.

Our languages will be *strongly statically typed*, meaning that no program that passes the checker will ever make a type error. For our languages, a type error is defined as one of the following:

1. an attempt to apply an integer or a boolean to an argument,

2. an attempt to apply a procedure or primitive to the wrong number of arguments,

3. an attempt to apply a primitive expecting an integer to a non-integer, or

4. an attempt to use a non-boolean as the test in a conditional expression.

We do not include other kinds of errors, such as division by zero, as type errors because our techniques do not allow us to ensure the absence of such errors prior to run time.

Our goal is to write a procedure `type-of-expression` which, given an expression *exp* and a *type environment* (call it *tenv*) mapping each variable to a type, assigns to *exp* a type *t* with the property that:

> Whenever *exp* is executed in an environment in which each variable has the type specified for it by *tenv*, the resulting value has type *t*.

We will write several versions of `type-of-expression`. Our analyses will be based on the principle that if we know the types of the value of each of the variables in an expression, we can deduce the type of the value of the expression. We will then assign that type as the type of the expression.

It is easy to write down how `type-of-expression` should behave for the most common expressions. If the expression is a number, then the result is always an integer, and if the expression is a variable, then the result is of the type specified by *tenv*:

```
(type-of-expression «n» tenv) = int
(type-of-expression «id» tenv) = (apply-env tenv id)
```

When the expression is an application we can predict the type of the result by looking at the type of the operator and types of the operands. For the application to succeed, the type of the operator must be a procedure type. If the type of the operator is $(t_1 * t_2 * \ldots * t_n \rightarrow t)$, then there must be exactly n operands, and the type of the i-th operand must be t_i for each i, so that the procedure is given arguments of the right type. If these conditions hold, then the result of the application will be the result type of the procedure, namely t. We can summarize this by writing

$$
\begin{array}{l}
\text{if } (\texttt{type-of-expression } «\textit{rator}» \; \textit{tenv}) = (t_1 * t_2 * \ldots * t_n \rightarrow t) \\
\text{and } (\texttt{type-of-expression } «\textit{rand}_1» \; \textit{tenv}) = t_1 \\
\text{and } (\texttt{type-of-expression } «\textit{rand}_2» \; \textit{tenv}) = t_2 \\
\ldots \\
\underline{\text{and } (\texttt{type-of-expression } «\textit{rand}_n» \; \textit{tenv}) = t_n} \\
\text{then } (\texttt{type-of-expression } « (\textit{rator } \textit{rand}_1 \; \textit{rand}_2 \ldots \textit{rand}_n)» \; \textit{tenv}) = t
\end{array}
$$

This is an example of a *conditional specification*. It says that if all the hypotheses (listed above the line) are true, then the conclusion (shown below the line) must also be true. We often omit the "if," "and"s and "then," since they are implicit in the format of the rule. We call this the *typing rule* for application. Such rules are a standard way of specifying the typing behavior of a language.

As another example of this kind of reasoning, let us consider the typing rule for conditional expressions. In the languages of chapter 3, the test expression of a conditional expression can return any value. Here, since we have a type of booleans available, we restrict conditional expressions so that the test expression must return a boolean. This leads us to the following rule:

$$
\begin{array}{l}
(\texttt{type-of-expression } «\textit{test-exp}» \; \textit{tenv}) = \texttt{bool} \\
(\texttt{type-of-expression } «\textit{true-exp}» \; \textit{tenv}) = t \\
\underline{(\texttt{type-of-expression } «\textit{false-exp}» \; \textit{tenv}) = t} \\
(\texttt{type-of-expression} \\
\quad «\texttt{if } \textit{test-exp } \texttt{then } \textit{true-exp } \texttt{else } \textit{false-exp}» \\
\quad \textit{tenv}) = t
\end{array}
$$

For a conditional expression to be well-typed, the test must have type `bool`, and the two branches must have the same type t. The value of the conditional expression will be the value of one of its branches, so no matter what the value of the test, the value of the entire expression will have type t.

We next turn to finding the type of a procedure expression. Consider the procedure expression `proc` $(x_1, \ldots, x_n)$ *exp*. To say that this procedure expression has type $(t_1 * t_2 * \ldots * t_n \rightarrow t)$ is to say that it expects n arguments, of types $t_1, \ldots, t_n$, and given such arguments it will return a value of type t.

To check that this procedure actually has this behavior, we must show that if the body is executed with the variables $x_1, \ldots, x_n$ having values of types $t_1, \ldots, t_n$, then it will produce a value of type t. Of course, the body *exp* may have other variables, but those will have the values (and hence the types) that they had at closure-construction time.

This suggests the following rule, where we use the same notation about environment extension that we used in section 3.5; we write $[x = t_1, y = t_2]$*tenv* in place of `(extend-tenv '(x y) '(`t_1 t_2`)` *tenv*`)`.

$$\frac{\text{(type-of-expression «}exp\text{» } [x_1 = t_1, \ldots, x_n = t_n]tenv) = t}{\begin{array}{l} \text{(type-of-expression «proc } (x_1, \ldots, x_n) \ exp\text{» } tenv) \\ \quad = (t_1 * t_2 * \ldots * t_n \rightarrow t) \end{array}}$$

This example reveals a fundamental problem with this approach: if we are trying to compute the type of a `proc` expression, how are we going to find the types $t_1, \ldots, t_n$ of the bound variables? They are nowhere to be found.

There are two basic strategies for rectifying this situation.

- *type checking*: In this approach the programmer is required to supply the missing information about the types of bound variables, and the type checker deduces the types of the other expressions and checks them for consistency.

- *type inference*: In this approach the type checker attempts to *infer* the types for the bound variables based on how the variables are used in the program. If the language is carefully designed, the type checker can infer all or most of the types of the bound variables.

We study type checking in sections 4.2 and 4.3, and type inference in section 4.4. Type checking is the approach taken in most commonly used programming languages, but type inference illustrates some important ideas.

⟨expression⟩ ::= proc ({⟨type-exp⟩ ⟨identifier⟩}*⁽ʼ⁾) ⟨expression⟩
> proc-exp (arg-texps ids body)

⟨expression⟩ ::= letrec
>   {⟨type-exp⟩ ⟨identifier⟩
>   ({⟨type-exp⟩ ⟨identifier⟩}*⁽ʼ⁾) = ⟨expression⟩}*
>   in ⟨expression⟩
> letrec-exp
>   (result-texps proc-names
>   arg-texpss idss bodies
>   letrec-body)

⟨expression⟩ ::= true
> true-exp ()

⟨expression⟩ ::= false
> false-exp ()

Figure 4.2   Grammar for expressions with types

Exercise 4.1 [⋆] Find at least two languages in which it is possible to multiply two characters. What, if anything, can be deduced about representation of characters by analyzing the output?

4.2   Type Checking

In a type-checked language, we require the programmer to include the types of all bound variables. For letrec-bound variables, we require the programmer to specify the result type of the procedure as well; we see later why this is needed. We modify our grammar to embody these requirements in figure 4.2.

Here we have changed the productions for proc-exp and letrec-exp. We have also added productions for true-exp and false-exp, which are of boolean type. With this syntax, typical programs look like

```
proc (int x) add1(x)
```

and

```
letrec
  int fact (int x) =
        if zero?(x) then 1 else *(x,(fact sub1(x)))
in fact
```

A procedure expression looks like

$$\text{proc } (t_1\ x_1, t_2\ x_2, \ldots, t_n\ x_n)\ exp$$

where t_1, ..., t_n are type expressions. The result type of `fact` is `int`, but the type of `fact` itself is (`int -> int`).

Type expressions are syntactic in nature; we introduce *types* as the corresponding analysis-time semantic notion, as we use closures as the run-time semantic notion corresponding to procedure expressions. For the language of this section, we take types to be the same as type expressions; types are given more structure in sections 4.3 and 4.4.

A type is either an atomic type with a name or a procedure type with a list of argument types and a result type. Using named atomic types enables us to add new atomic types later. The procedure `expand-type-expression` converts type expressions to types in the obvious way. Our checker calls `expand-type-expression` whenever we convert from something syntactic (that is, something from the abstract syntax tree) to something we want to analyze. The constants `int-type` and `bool-type` are convenient abbreviations. See figure 4.3.

We have enough tools to write `type-of-expression`. See figure 4.5. The first few clauses implement the rules for literals and variables. We use a procedure `apply-tenv` similar to `apply-env` but with a distinctive error message. The clause for `if-exp` implements the rule for conditional expressions. It calls the procedure `check-equal-type!`, which succeeds if its first two arguments are equal types and otherwise raises an error. The third argument to `check-equal-type!` is used for error reporting. We use the procedure `type-to-external-form` to convert a type back into a list structure like

```
(int * (int -> bool) -> int)
```

for better readability (figure 4.4).

Exercise 4.2 [*] The Scheme procedure `equal?` is more powerful than needed here. Rewrite `check-equal-type!` to do an explicit recursive traversal of the types.

```
(define-datatype type type?
  (atomic-type
    (name symbol?))
  (proc-type
    (arg-types (list-of type?))
    (result-type type?)))

(define int-type (atomic-type 'int))
(define bool-type (atomic-type 'bool))

(define expand-type-expression
  (lambda (texp)
    (cases type-exp texp
      (int-type-exp () int-type)
      (bool-type-exp () bool-type)
      (proc-type-exp (arg-texps result-texp)
        (proc-type
          (expand-type-expressions arg-texps)
          (expand-type-expression result-texp))))))

(define expand-type-expressions
  (lambda (texps)
    (map expand-type-expression texps)))
```

Figure 4.3   Representation of types

We can now write auxiliary procedures to implement each of the other rules. The rule for procedure expressions in our language is given by

$$\frac{(\text{type-of-expression } «exp» \; [x_1 = t_1, \ldots, x_n = t_n]tenv) = t}{(\text{type-of-expression } «\text{proc } (t_1 \; x_1, \ldots, t_n \; x_n) \; exp » \; tenv)} \\ = (t_1 * t_2 * \ldots * t_n \text{ -> } t)$$

This differs from our previous attempt at a rule for procedures only by the specification of the types of the formal parameters in the conclusion.

This rule is implemented by `type-of-proc-exp`. Given a `proc` expression `proc` $(t_1 \; x_1, t_2 \; x_2, \ldots, t_n \; x_n) \; exp$, `type-of-proc-exp` first converts the type expressions $t_1, \ldots t_n$ into the list of types `arg-types`. It then checks the body in the specified type environment and binds the resulting type to `result-type`. Last, it constructs a procedure type out of the appropriate parts (figure 4.6), following the specification of the typing rule.

```
(define check-equal-type!
  (lambda (t1 t2 exp)
    (or (equal? t1 t2)
        (eopl:error 'check-equal-type!
          "Types didn't match: ~s != ~s in~%~s"
          (type-to-external-form t1)
          (type-to-external-form t2)
          exp))))

(define type-to-external-form
  (lambda (ty)
    (cases type ty
      (atomic-type (name) name)
      (proc-type (arg-types result-type)
        (append
          (arg-types-to-external-form arg-types)
          '(->)
          (list (type-to-external-form result-type)))))))
```

Figure 4.4   Checking for equal types

We next turn to application. Given either a primitive application or a procedure application, `type-of-expression` finds the types of the operator and the operands and then calls `type-of-application` to apply the rule

$$
\begin{array}{l}
(\texttt{type-of-expression} \text{ «}rator\text{» } tenv) = (t_1 * t_2 * \ldots * t_n \to t) \\
(\texttt{type-of-expression} \text{ «}rand_1\text{» } tenv) = t_1 \\
(\texttt{type-of-expression} \text{ «}rand_2\text{» } tenv) = t_2 \\
\qquad \ldots \\
\underline{(\texttt{type-of-expression} \text{ «}rand_n\text{» } tenv) = t_n} \\
(\texttt{type-of-expression} \text{ « } (rator\ rand_1\ rand_2 \ldots\ rand_n)\text{» } tenv) = t
\end{array}
$$

The definition of `type-of-application` is shown in figure 4.6. This procedure first checks to see that the type of the operator is a procedure type. Then it checks to see that the number of arguments expected by the procedure matches the number of arguments supplied. Then, in the `for-each` loop, it checks to see that the type of each expected argument is equal to the type of the corresponding operand. It does this by passing each triple of (rand-type, argument-type, rand) to `check-equal-type!`. If these checks succeed, then the type of the application is the result type of the procedure.

```
(define type-of-expression
  (lambda (exp tenv)
    (cases expression exp
      (lit-exp (number) int-type)
      (true-exp () bool-type)
      (false-exp () bool-type)
      (var-exp (id) (apply-tenv tenv id))
      (if-exp (test-exp true-exp false-exp)
        (let ((test-type (type-of-expression test-exp tenv))
              (false-type (type-of-expression false-exp tenv))
              (true-type (type-of-expression true-exp tenv)))
          (check-equal-type! test-type bool-type test-exp)
          (check-equal-type! true-type false-type exp)
          true-type))
      (proc-exp (texps ids body)
        (type-of-proc-exp texps ids body tenv))
      (primapp-exp (prim rands)
        (type-of-application
          (type-of-primitive prim)
          (types-of-expressions rands tenv)
          prim rands exp))
      (app-exp (rator rands)
        (type-of-application
          (type-of-expression rator tenv)
          (types-of-expressions rands tenv)
          rator rands exp))
      (let-exp (ids rands body)
        (type-of-let-exp ids rands body tenv))
      (letrec-exp (result-texps proc-names texpss idss bodies
                   letrec-body)
        (type-of-letrec-exp
          result-texps proc-names texpss idss bodies
          letrec-body tenv))
      )))

(define types-of-expressions
  (lambda (rands tenv)
    (map (lambda (exp) (type-of-expression exp tenv)) rands)))
```

Figure 4.5 type-of-expression for a type checker

```
(define type-of-proc-exp
  (lambda (texps ids body tenv)
    (let ((arg-types (expand-type-expressions texps)))
      (let ((result-type
              (type-of-expression body
                (extend-tenv ids arg-types tenv))))
        (proc-type arg-types result-type)))))

(define type-of-application
  (lambda (rator-type rand-types rator rands exp)
    (cases type rator-type
      (proc-type (arg-types result-type)
        (if (= (length arg-types) (length rand-types))
          (begin
            (for-each
              check-equal-type!
              rand-types arg-types rands)
            result-type)
          (eopl:error 'type-of-expression
            (string-append
              "Wrong number of arguments in expression ~s:"
              "~%expected ~s~%got ~s")
            exp
            (map type-to-external-form arg-types)
            (map type-to-external-form rand-types))))
      (else
        (eopl:error 'type-of-expression
          "Rator not a proc type:~%~s~%had rator type ~s"
          rator (type-to-external-form rator-type))))))

(define type-of-primitive
  (lambda (prim)
    (cases primitive prim
      (add-prim ()
        (proc-type (list int-type int-type) int-type))
      (incr-prim ()
        (proc-type (list int-type) int-type))
      (zero-test-prim ()
        (proc-type (list int-type) bool-type))
      ...)))
```

Figure 4.6   Checking procedures, application, and primitives

```
(define type-of-let-exp
  (lambda (ids rands body tenv)
    (let ((tenv-for-rands
            (extend-tenv
              ids
              (types-of-expressions rands tenv)
              tenv)))
      (type-of-expression body tenv-for-rands)))))
```

Figure 4.7   Checking `let`

To deal with primitive applications, we need `type-of-primitive`, which takes a primitive and returns its type (figure 4.6).

Exercise 4.3 [⋆] The specification of the types in `type-of-primitive` is less readable than one might like. Modify `type-of-primitive` so that the types of primitives are specified using list structures like `(int * (int -> bool) -> int)`. Include a list-structure parser to convert a list structure like the one above.

What about `let` and `letrec`? Typing `let` is easy. We can compute the types of each of the right-hand sides, and use those types in the type environment for the body. The typing rule is:

$$
\begin{array}{l}
\text{(type-of-expression «}e_1\text{» } tenv) = t_1 \\
\text{(type-of-expression «}e_2\text{» } tenv) = t_2 \\
\quad\cdots \\
\text{(type-of-expression «}e_n\text{» } tenv) = t_n \\
\underline{\text{(type-of-expression «}body\text{» } [x_1 = t_1, \ldots, x_n = t_n]tenv) = t} \\
\text{(type-of-expression «let } x_1 = e_1 \ldots x_n = e_n \text{ in } body\text{» } tenv) = t
\end{array}
$$

The code for this is in figure 4.7. The `letrec` expression is a little more challenging. A typical `letrec` expression looks like

$$
\begin{array}{l}
\text{letrec} \\
\quad t_1 \ p_1 \ (t_{11} \ x_{11}, \ldots, t_{1,n_1} \ x_{1,n_1}) = e_1 \\
\quad t_2 \ p_2 \ (t_{21} \ x_{21}, \ldots, t_{2,n_2} \ x_{2,n_2}) = e_2 \\
\quad\quad \cdots \\
\text{in } body
\end{array}
$$

This expression declares a set of procedures named $p_1, p_2, \ldots$, with bodies $e_1, e_2, \ldots$. The procedure p_i has n_i parameters; its j-th formal parameter is named x_{ij} and has type t_{ij}; and its result type is t_i. Hence the type of p_i should be $(t_{i1} * t_{i2} * \ldots * t_{i,n_i} \rightarrow t_i)$.

The body of the letrec and each of the procedure bodies $e_1, e_2, \ldots$ must be checked in a type environment where each variable is given its correct type. We can use our scoping rules to determine what variables are in scope, and hence what types should be associated with them.

In the body of the letrec, the procedure names $p_1, p_2, \ldots$ are in scope. As suggested above, the procedure p_i is declared to have type $(t_{i1} * t_{i2} \ldots \rightarrow t_i)$. Hence the body should be checked in the type environment

$$tenv_{body} = [p_1 = (t_{11} * t_{12} \ldots \rightarrow t_1),$$
$$p_2 = (t_{21} * t_{22} \ldots \rightarrow t_2),$$
$$\ldots$$
$$]tenv$$

We have to check each of the right-hand sides. But in what type environment? In the i-th procedure body e_i, the variables $p_1, p_2, \ldots$ are in scope, and they should have the same types they have in $tenv_{body}$. In addition, the formal parameters $x_{i1}, x_{i2}, \ldots$ are in scope, and they should have types $t_{i1}, t_{i2}, \ldots$. Hence the type environment for e_i should be

$$tenv_i = [x_{i1} = t_{i1}, x_{i2} = t_{i2}, \ldots]tenv_{body}$$

Furthermore, in this type environment, e_i should have result type t_i. This leads us to the following rule for letrec:

$$\text{(type-of-expression «}e_1\text{» } tenv_1) = t_1$$
$$\text{(type-of-expression «}e_2\text{» } tenv_2) = t_2$$
$$\ldots$$
$$\underline{\text{(type-of-expression «}body\text{» } tenv_{body}) = t}$$
$$\text{(type-of-expression}$$
$$\text{« letrec}$$
$$t_1\ p_1\ (t_{11}\ x_{11}, \ldots, t_{1,n_1}\ x_{1,n_1}) = e_1$$
$$t_2\ p_2\ (t_{21}\ x_{21}, \ldots, t_{2,n_2}\ x_{2,n_2}) = e_2$$
$$\ldots$$
$$\text{in } body \text{ »}$$
$$tenv) = t$$

We must include the result types t_i in the program. We cannot just compute the type of each e_i, as we did for let, because we need *all* of the t_j's to compute the type of each e_i.

```
(define type-of-letrec-exp
  (lambda (result-texps proc-names texpss idss bodies
            letrec-body tenv)
    (let ((arg-typess
            (map
              (lambda (texps)
                (expand-type-expressions texps))
              texpss))
          (result-types
            (expand-type-expressions result-texps)))
      (let ((the-proc-types
              (map proc-type arg-typess result-types)))
        (let ((tenv-for-body
                (extend-tenv proc-names the-proc-types tenv)))
          (for-each
            (lambda (ids arg-types body result-type)
              (check-equal-type!
                (type-of-expression
                  body
                  (extend-tenv ids arg-types tenv-for-body))
                result-type
                body))
            idss arg-typess bodies result-types)
          (type-of-expression letrec-body tenv-for-body)))))))
```

Figure 4.8 Checking `letrec`

The code for `type-of-letrec-exp` is shown in figure 4.8. The type expressions for the arguments and for the result are first converted to types. The variable `the-proc-types` is then bound to the list of types of the procedures, and $tenv_{body}$ is computed and is bound to `tenv-for-body`. Then the type of each procedure body is computed and is compared to the specified result type. If all of these tests are passed, then the type of the `letrec` body is computed and is returned as the type of the entire expression.

The top level of the checker is `type-check`, which is defined as

```
(define type-check
  (lambda (string)
    (type-to-external-form
      (type-of-program
        (scan&parse string)))))
```

Exercise 4.4 [★★] Complete the implementation of the checker, and test it on expressions that exercise all aspects of the checker. These tests should, of course, include programs that are rejected by the checker.

Exercise 4.5 [★★★] Construct a test harness that takes a set of expressions, along with their correct types (or #f for expressions that should report a type error), runs the checker on each, and verifies that the checker returns the correct type for each expression that should be typed and that it reports an error for each expression that should be rejected. Hint: this will require using more of the Scheme language than we have used for our interpreters.

Exercise 4.6 [★] Extend the checker to handle `varassign-exp` from section 3.7.

Exercise 4.7 [★★] Add `pair` types to the language. Say that a value is of type (pair t_1 t_2) if it is a pair consisting of a value of type t_1 and a value of type t_2. Add to the language the following productions:

⟨type-exp⟩   ::= `pair` ⟨type-exp⟩ ⟨type-exp⟩
              ┌─────────────────────────┐
              │ `pair-type (texp1 texp2)` │
              └─────────────────────────┘

⟨expression⟩ ::= `pair` (⟨expression⟩ , ⟨expression⟩)
              ┌─────────────────────────┐
              │ `pair-exp (exp1 exp2)` │
              └─────────────────────────┘

⟨expression⟩ ::= `unpack` ⟨identifier⟩ ⟨identifier⟩ = ⟨expression⟩
              `in` ⟨expression⟩
              ┌─────────────────────────────┐
              │ `unpack-exp (id1 id2 exp body)` │
              └─────────────────────────────┘

A `pair` expression creates a pair; an `unpack` expression (like exercise 3.18) binds its two identifiers to the two parts of the expression; the scope of these identifiers is the body. The typing rules for `pair` and `unpack` are:

$$\frac{\begin{array}{l}(\texttt{type-of-expression } «e_1» \; tenv) = t_1 \\ (\texttt{type-of-expression } «e_2» \; tenv) = t_2\end{array}}{(\texttt{type-of-expression } «\texttt{pair}(e_1,e_2)» \; tenv) = (\texttt{pair } t_1 \; t_2)}$$

$$\frac{\begin{array}{l}(\texttt{type-of-expression } «exp» \; tenv) = (\texttt{pair } t_1 \; t_2) \\ (\texttt{type-of-expression } body\,[x_1 = t_1, x_2 = t_2]tenv) = t\end{array}}{(\texttt{type-of-expression } «\texttt{unpack } x_1 \; x_2 = exp \texttt{ in } body» \; tenv) = t}$$

Extend `type-of-expression` to implement these rules.

Exercise 4.8 [★★] Add `list` types to the language, with operations like those of exercise 3.7. A value is of type `(list t)` if and only if it is a list and all of its elements are of type *t*. Extend the language with the following productions:

$$\langle\text{type-exp}\rangle \quad ::= \text{list} \ \langle\text{type-exp}\rangle$$
$$\boxed{\texttt{list-type-exp (texp)}}$$

$$\langle\text{expression}\rangle ::= \text{list} \ (\{\langle\text{expression}\rangle\}^{*(\prime)})$$
$$\boxed{\texttt{list-exp (exps)}}$$

$$\langle\text{expression}\rangle ::= \text{cons} \ (\langle\text{expression}\rangle \ , \ \langle\text{expression}\rangle)$$
$$\boxed{\texttt{cons-exp (exp1 exp2)}}$$

$$\langle\text{expression}\rangle ::= \text{null?} \ (\langle\text{expression}\rangle)$$
$$\boxed{\texttt{null-exp (exp)}}$$

$$\langle\text{expression}\rangle ::= \text{emptylist} \ [\ \langle\text{type-exp}\rangle \ ]$$
$$\boxed{\texttt{emptylist-exp (texp)}}$$

with types given by the following four rules:

$$\frac{\begin{array}{l}(\texttt{type-of-expression} \ «e_1» \ tenv) = t \\ \ldots \\ (\texttt{type-of-expression} \ «e_n» \ tenv) = t, \quad n > 0\end{array}}{(\texttt{type-of-expression} \ «\texttt{list} \ (e_1,\ldots,e_n)» \ tenv) = (\texttt{list} \ t)}$$

$$\frac{\begin{array}{l}(\texttt{type-of-expression} \ «e_1» \ tenv) = t \\ (\texttt{type-of-expression} \ «e_2» \ tenv) = (\texttt{list} \ t)\end{array}}{(\texttt{type-of-expression} \ «\texttt{cons} \ (e_1,e_2)» \ tenv) = (\texttt{list} \ t)}$$

$$\frac{(\texttt{type-of-expression} \ «e» \ tenv) = (\texttt{list} \ t)}{(\texttt{type-of-expression} \ «\texttt{null?} \ (e)» \ tenv) = \texttt{bool}}$$

$$(\texttt{type-of-expression} \ «\texttt{emptylist}[t]» \ tenv) = (\texttt{list} \ t)$$

Write similar rules for `car` and `cdr`, and extend the checker to handle these as well as the other expressions. These rules should guarantee that `car` and `cdr` are applied to lists, but they should not guarantee that the lists be non-empty. Why would it be unreasonable for the rules to guarantee that the lists be non-empty? Why is the type parameter in `emptylist` necessary?

4.3 Enforcing Abstraction Boundaries

The presence of data abstraction in a language makes the definition of "inappropriate" more difficult. We can probably agree that in Scheme `(3 x)` and `(car 3)` are inappropriate, but what about `(- #\a #\b)` or `(- #\a 1)`? If a particular implementation of the character interface used integers as a representation, then these might be appropriate inside the implementation of the data type of characters, but they would likely be inappropriate outside the implementation, since the client code is not supposed to know, or be able to take advantage of, the representation of the data. And even `(car 3)` might be appropriate inside the implementation of numbers, if the implementation used a unary or a bignum representation.

We'd like to add to our language a facility for building and enforcing abstraction boundaries. Our language will use types to ensure that client code does not manipulate the values of the data type except through the procedures in the interface of the type.

We establish an abstraction boundary with a `lettype` expression, which looks like

$$\texttt{lettype } tid = t$$
$$t_1 \; p_1 \; (t_{11} \; x_{11}, \ldots, t_{1,n_1} \; x_{1,n_1}) = e_1$$
$$t_2 \; p_2 \; (t_{21} \; x_{21}, \ldots, t_{2,n_2} \; x_{2,n_2}) = e_2$$
$$\cdots$$
$$\texttt{in } body$$

This defines a new type named *tid*, represented by the type *t*. The names $p_1, p_2, \ldots$ make up the interface. The bodies $e_1, e_2, \ldots$ of these procedures constitute the implementation, and *body* is the client or user of the type. The idea is that the definitions of $p_1, p_2, \ldots$ know that a value of type *tid* is really implemented as a value of type *t*, but *body* will see *tid* as a new atomic type, manipulable only by the procedures named $p_1, p_2, \ldots$.

For example, figure 4.9 (top) is a definition of a type `myint` that implements the interface like that of the nonnegative integers from section 2.1. It uses the built-in integers of our language, except that zero is represented by 1. In the implementations of the procedures, `myint` is the same as `int`, so we can invoke `add1` or `sub1` on a value of type `myint`. In *body*, however, `myint` is a new data type, on which we can use only the operations `zero` (a 0-ary procedure that returns a representation of 0), `succ`, `pred`, and `iszero?`. So in the body `(succ (zero))` is legal, but `add1((zero))` is not, nor is `zero?((zero))`.

For another example, consider a data type like the type of environments. Since we do not have symbols in our language, we consider instead the data type of finite functions from integers to integers in figure 4.9 (middle). The interface consists of the names `zero-ff`, `extend-ff`, and `apply-ff`. The procedure `zero-ff` takes no arguments and returns the function that always returns 0. The procedure `extend-ff` changes the value of the function for a single integer. The functions built by `zero-ff` and `extend-ff` are finite in that they return non-zero answers for only finitely many arguments. The procedure `apply-ff` applies a finite function to an argument.

We cannot write the code in figure 4.9 (bottom), however. The procedure application (`f k`) in `apply-ff` is acceptable, since inside the implementation we know that finite functions are represented as procedures. Indeed, inside `extend-ff` we could have written (`old-ff k1`) in place of (`apply-ff old-ff k1`). But such an application is not acceptable in the body, since that would mean that the body relies on this representation.

Our idea for implementing this is to use *type identifiers* in our type expressions, and to put bindings for the type identifiers in our type environments. In the preceding examples, `myint` (or `ff`) is a type identifier. We check the implementation in a type environment where `myint` (or `ff`) is bound to its representation type, but we check the client code in a type environment in which `myint` (or `ff`) is bound to a new atomic type.

To implement this idea, we add to the grammar two new productions:

⟨expression⟩ ::= `lettype` ⟨identifier⟩ = ⟨type-exp⟩
                       {⟨type-exp⟩ ⟨identifier⟩
                       ({⟨type-exp⟩ ⟨identifier⟩}*$^{(,)}$) = ⟨expression⟩}*
                       `in` ⟨expression⟩

```
lettype-exp
 (type-name texp result-texps proc-names
  arg-texpss idss bodies
  lettype-body)
```

⟨type-exp⟩ ::= ⟨identifier⟩

```
tid-type-exp (id)
```

The first of these is the production for `lettype`. The second production introduces type identifiers into the language of type expressions.

At run time, a `lettype` expression will act like a `letrec` expression. The scope of the declared procedures consists of the procedure bodies and the body of the `lettype`.

```
lettype myint = int
  myint zero  () = 1
  myint succ  (myint x) = add1(x)
  myint pred  (myint x) = sub1(x)
  bool  iszero? (myint x) = zero?(sub1(x))
in body

lettype ff = (int -> int)
  ff zero-ff () = proc (int k) 0
  ff extend-ff (int k, int val, ff old-ff) =
      proc (int k1)
        if zero?(-(k1,k))
        then val
        else (apply-ff old-ff k1)
  int apply-ff (ff f, int k) = (f k)
in let ff1 = (extend-ff 1 11
                (extend-ff 2 22
                  (zero-ff)))
   in (apply-ff ff1 2)

lettype ff = (int -> int)
  ff zero-ff () = proc (int k) 0
  ff extend-ff (int k, int val, ff old-ff) =
      proc (int k1)
        if zero?(-(k1,k))
        then val
        else (apply-ff old-ff k1)
  int apply-ff (ff f, int k) = (f k)
in let ff1 = (extend-ff 1 11
                (extend-ff 2 22
                  (zero-ff)))
|  in (ff1 2)
```

Figure 4.9 lettype expressions

We add to our type environments a new kind of binding, so that the type environment binds ordinary identifiers to types and type identifiers to types. The latter get added one at a time, so we create a new kind of rib:

```
(define apply-tenv
  (lambda (tenv sym)
    (cases type-environment tenv
      (empty-tenv-record ()
        (eopl:error 'apply-tenv
          "Variable ~s unbound in type environment" sym))
      (extended-tenv-record (syms vals tenv)
        (let ((pos (list-find-position sym syms)))
          (if (number? pos)
              (list-ref vals pos)
              (apply-tenv tenv sym))))
      (typedef-record (name type tenv)
        (apply-tenv tenv sym)))))
```

Figure 4.10   Adding a new kind of rib to type environment

```
(define-datatype type-environment type-environment?
  (empty-tenv-record)
  (extended-tenv-record
    (syms (list-of symbol?))
    (vals (list-of type?))
    (tenv type-environment?))
  (typedef-record
    (name symbol?)
    (definition type?)
    (tenv type-environment?)))

(define empty-tenv empty-tenv-record)
(define extend-tenv extended-tenv-record)
(define extend-tenv-with-typedef typedef-record)
```

Having a new kind of rib means that we can use the same name both for a type identifier and an ordinary identifier (figure 4.10).

Exercise 4.9 [⋆] The error behavior of `apply-tenv` can be improved by including the original type environment in the error message. Rewrite `apply-tenv` to do this.

The definition of types is unchanged from section 4.2, but we modify `expand-type-expression` to take a type environment and expand the bindings of any type identifiers it sees (hence the name *expand*). See figure 4.11.

```
(define expand-type-expression
  (lambda (texp tenv)
    (cases type-exp texp
      (tid-type-exp (id) (find-typedef tenv id))
      (int-type-exp () (atomic-type 'int))
      (bool-type-exp () (atomic-type 'bool))
      (proc-type-exp (arg-texps result-texp)
        (proc-type
          (expand-type-expressions arg-texps tenv)
          (expand-type-expression result-texp tenv))))))

(define expand-type-expressions
  (lambda (texps tenv)
    (map
      (lambda (texp)
        (expand-type-expression texp tenv))
      texps)))
```

Figure 4.11   Expanding type expressions

Every use of `expand-type-expression` is now modified to take the type environment as a parameter. For example, we write:

```
(define type-of-proc-exp
  (lambda (texps ids body tenv)
    (let ((arg-types (expand-type-expressions texps tenv)))
      (let ((result-type
              (type-of-expression body
                (extend-tenv ids arg-types tenv))))
        (proc-type arg-types result-type)))))
```

The procedure `type-of-lettype-exp` works like `type-of-letrec-exp`, except that when it checks the procedure declarations, it does so in an environment where the type identifier is bound to its representation, and when it checks the body, it does so in an environment where the type identifier is bound to a new atomic type.

Recall that a typical `lettype` expression looks like

$$
\begin{aligned}
&\texttt{lettype } tid = t \\
&\quad t_1 \; p_1 \; (t_{11} \; x_{11}, \ldots, t_{1,n_1} \; x_{1,n_1}) = e_1 \\
&\quad t_2 \; p_2 \; (t_{21} \; x_{21}, \ldots, t_{2,n_2} \; x_{2,n_2}) = e_2 \\
&\qquad \cdots \\
&\texttt{in } body
\end{aligned}
$$

To check this expression, we build two type environments. The type environment $tenv_{implementation}$ is used as a basis for checking the procedure bodies e_i that form the implementation of the data type. The type environment $tenv_{client}$ is used for checking *body*, which forms the client or user of the data type.

$$
\begin{aligned}
tenv_{implementation} &= [tid = t]tenv \\
tenv_{client} &= [tid = \langle \text{fresh atomic type} \rangle]tenv
\end{aligned}
$$

We must also bind each ordinary identifier to its type according to the usual scoping rules. To do this, we proceed by analogy with `letrec`. As with `letrec`, the procedure body is checked in an environment in which the procedure's formal parameters and all the `letrec`-bound procedure names are bound to their declared types. Furthermore, the type expressions should be expanded using $tenv_{implementation}$, because the procedure body e_i is inside the abstraction boundary, and so the representation of the type tid as t should be visible. Hence the type environment for e_i should be

$$
\begin{aligned}
tenv_i = \\
[x_{i1} = t_{i1}^*, \; x_{i2} = t_{i2}^*, \ldots] \\
[p_1 = (t_{11} * t_{12} \ldots * \text{ -> } t_1)^*, \\
p_2 = (t_{21} * t_{22} \ldots * \text{ -> } t_2)^*, \\
\cdots \\
]tenv_{implementation}
\end{aligned}
$$

where t^* means the expansion of the type expression t in $tenv_{implementation}$.

Similarly, the type environment for the body of the `lettype` should be

$$
\begin{aligned}
tenv_{body} = \\
[p_1 = (t_{11} * t_{12} \ldots \text{ -> } t_1)^{\dagger}, \\
p_2 = (t_{21} * t_{22} \ldots \text{ -> } t_2)^{\dagger}, \\
\cdots \\
]tenv_{client}
\end{aligned}
$$

where $t^{\dagger}$ denotes the expansion of the type expression t in $tenv_{client}$. This is the correct expansion, because the body is outside the abstraction boundary, and therefore should see *tid* as an atomic type, on which the only available operations are the p_i.

Every time we extend a type environment, we do so with a type expression that is expanded in the same type environment. Therefore we define the auxiliary procedures

```
(define extend-tenv-with-typedef-exp
  (lambda (typename texp tenv)
    (extend-tenv-with-typedef typename
      (expand-type-expression texp tenv)
      tenv)))

(define extend-tenv-with-type-exps
  (lambda (ids texps tenv)
    (extend-tenv ids
      (expand-type-expressions texps tenv)
      tenv)))
```

The code is shown in figure 4.12. We proceed much as we did for `type-of-letrec-exp`. The procedure first extracts the various portions of the `lettype`. The variable `rhs-texps` is bound to the list of type expressions associated with the procedures. We must use type expressions here, rather than types, because these type expressions will be expanded differently in the procedure bodies than in the body of the `lettype`.

The type environments `tenv-for-implementation`, `tenv-for-client`, `tenv-for-proc`, and `tenv-for-body` are then built. In `tenv-for-client`, the type name is bound to a fresh atomic type. This code uses `fresh-type`, which creates a new type with a name similar to its argument:

```
(define fresh-type
  (let ((counter 0))
    (lambda (s)
      (set! counter (+ counter 1))
      (atomic-type
        (string->symbol
          (string-append
            (symbol->string s)
            (number->string counter)))))))
```

Successive evaluations of `(fresh-type 'xx)` will return `(atomic-type xx1)`, `(atomic-type xx2)`, etc.

Once the various type environments are constructed, the type of each of the procedure bodies is computed and compared to the specified result type,

```
(define type-of-lettype-exp
  (lambda (type-name texp
            result-texps proc-names arg-texpss idss bodies
            lettype-body tenv)
    (let ((the-new-type (fresh-type type-name))
          (rhs-texps
            (map proc-type-exp arg-texpss result-texps)))
      (let ((tenv-for-implementation
              (extend-tenv-with-typedef-exp
                type-name texp tenv))
            (tenv-for-client
              (extend-tenv-with-typedef
                type-name the-new-type tenv)))
        (let ((tenv-for-proc
                (extend-tenv-with-type-exps
                  proc-names rhs-texps
                  tenv-for-implementation))
              (tenv-for-body
                (extend-tenv-with-type-exps
                  proc-names rhs-texps tenv-for-client)))
          (for-each
            (lambda (ids arg-texps body result-texp)
              (check-equal-type!
                (type-of-expression
                  body
                  (extend-tenv-with-type-exps
                    ids arg-texps tenv-for-proc))
                (expand-type-expression
                  result-texp tenv-for-proc)
                body))
            idss arg-texpss
            bodies result-texps)
          (type-of-expression lettype-body tenv-for-body)))))))
```

Figure 4.12 `type-of-lettype-exp`

```
lettype myint = int
  myint zero () = 1
  myint succ (myint x) = add1(x)
  myint pred (myint x) = sub1(x)
  bool  iszero? (myint x) =  zero?(-(x,1))
in (succ (zero))
type: myint8

lettype myint = int
  myint zero () = 1
  myint succ (myint x) = add1(x)
  myint pred (myint x) = sub1(x)
  bool  iszero? (myint x) =  zero?(-(x,1))
in add1((zero))
types didn't match: int != myint9 in
(app-exp (var-exp zero) ())

lettype ff = (int -> int)
  ff zero-ff () = proc (int k) 0
  ff extend-ff (int k, int val, ff old-ff) =
      proc (int k1) if zero?(-(k1,k))
                    then val
                    else (apply-ff old-ff k1)
  int apply-ff (ff f, int k) = (f k)
in let ff1 = (extend-ff 1 11 (extend-ff 2 22 (zero-ff)))
   in (apply-ff ff1 2)
type: int

lettype ff = (int -> int)
  ff zero-ff () = proc (int k) 0
  ff extend-ff (int k, int val, ff old-ff) =
      proc (int k1) if zero?(-(k1,k))
                    then val
                    else (apply-ff old-ff k1)
  int apply-ff (ff f, int k) = (f k)
in let ff1 = (extend-ff 1 11 (extend-ff 2 22 (zero-ff)))
   in (ff1 2)
rator not a proc type:
(var-exp ff1)
had rator type ff117
```

Figure 4.13   Examples of type checking using `lettype`

using `tenv-for-proc`, which extends `tenv-for-implementation`. If all of these tests are passed, then the type of the `lettype` body is computed in `tenv-for-body`, which extends `tenv-for-client`, and is returned as the type of the entire expression.

The results of this system on the examples from the beginning of the section are shown in figure 4.13. Each attempt to break the abstraction boundary by performing an illegal operation is detected as a type error.

Exercise 4.10 [⋆] Complete the implementation of the checker of this section.

Exercise 4.11 [⋆ ⋆] How many of the other calls to `expand-tenv` can be replaced with `extend-tenv-with-type-exps`?

Exercise 4.12 [⋆] Extend the test harness from exercise 4.5 for this checker. Be careful to handle fresh types correctly; for instance, the first example in figure 4.13 might return `myint1` or `myint2` or `myint3`, etc.

Exercise 4.13 [⋆ ⋆ ⋆] In our examples, the client program (the body of the `lettype`) appears together with the code that implements the abstract data type. It is more typical for the client code to be separate from the implementation. Thus a program unit might look like

```
importtype ff
  ff zero-ff ()
  ff extend-ff (int k, int val, ff old-ff)
  int apply-ff (ff f, int k)
in body
```

Modify this checker to check such program units. Devise a complementary syntax for `exporttype` to export a type, and a syntax for combining such program units.

4.4   Type Inference

Writing down the types in the program may be helpful for design and documentation, but it can be time-consuming. Another approach is to have the compiler figure out the types of all the variables, based on observing how they are used, and utilizing any hints the programmer might give. Surprisingly, for our simple languages, the compiler can *always* infer the types of the variables. This strategy is called *type inference*.

To do this, we change the language so that all the type expressions are optional. In place of a missing type expression, we use the marker `?`. Hence a typical program looks like

```
letrec
  ? even(? odd, ? x) =
      if zero?(x) then 1 else (odd sub1(x))
in letrec
    ? odd(? x) =
        if zero?(x) then 0 else (even odd sub1(x))
  in (odd 13)
```

Each of the five question marks indicates a place where a type must be inferred.

Since the type expressions are optional, we may fill in some of the ?'s with types, as in

```
letrec
  ? even(? odd, int x) =
      if zero?(x) then 1 else (odd sub1(x))
in letrec
    bool odd(? x) =
            if zero?(x) then 0 else (even odd sub1(x))
  in (odd 13)
```

Exercise 4.14 [⋆] What is wrong with this expression?

```
letrec
  ? even(? odd, ? x) =
      if zero?(x) then 1 else (odd sub1(x))
in letrec
    ? odd(bool x) =
        if zero?(x) then 0 else (even odd sub1(x))
  in (odd 13)
```

We add the following productions to our grammar:

$$\langle\text{optional-type-exp}\rangle ::= \langle\text{type-exp}\rangle$$

$$\boxed{\texttt{a-type-exp (texp)}}$$

$$\langle\text{optional-type-exp}\rangle ::= \text{?}$$

$$\boxed{\texttt{no-type-exp ()}}$$

An ⟨optional-type-exp⟩ is either a type expression or a ?. To use optional type expressions in ordinary expressions, we change the productions for proc-exp and letrec-exp to use ⟨optional-type-exp⟩:

⟨expression⟩ ::= proc ({⟨optional-type-exp⟩ ⟨identifier⟩}*⁽ʼ⁾) ⟨expression⟩

```
proc-exp (optional-arg-texps ids body)
```

⟨expression⟩ ::= letrec
         {⟨optional-type-exp⟩ ⟨identifier⟩
          ({⟨optional-type-exp⟩ ⟨identifier⟩}*⁽ʼ⁾) = ⟨expression⟩}*
         in ⟨expression⟩

```
letrec-exp
  (optional-result-texps proc-names
   optional-arg-texpss idss bodies
   letrec-body)
```

To deal with the ?'s, we add a new kind of type, called a *type variable*. A type variable stands for a type that is not yet known. Each type variable contains a serial number that identifies it uniquely, and a container, which is a vector of length 1. The vector's single element can be either (), meaning that nothing is known about this type: *empty*, or else a type: *full*. The checker will fill the type variable when it deduces something about the type. Once a type variable is full, its contents will never be changed. Such a variable is sometimes called *single-assignment* or *write-once*. The procedures that deal with types treat a type variable as a placeholder for the type it contains (if any).

The procedures for manipulating type variables are shown in figure 4.14. The procedure fresh-tvar creates a fresh type variable, with a globally unique value for its counter, and with its vector initialized to (), meaning that nothing is known yet about this type.

Type variables should not be confused with the type identifiers of section 4.3. Type identifiers have lexical scope and are kept in type environments, but type variables are global and are kept in Scheme's heap.

We change all calls to the procedure expand-type-expression so that they instead call expand-optional-type-expression. This change is necessary to match the grammar. When the procedure expand-optional-type-expression encounters a type expression, it calls expand-type-expression; when it encounters a ?, it emits a type variable.

We next modify check-equal-type! to handle type variables. The new version of check-equal-type! will perform a task that may be described as "check to see if the two types *can be made* equal, and if so, adjust the contents of the type variables to make them equal."

```
(define-datatype type type?
  (atomic-type (name symbol?))
  (proc-type
    (arg-types (list-of type?))
    (result-type   type?))
  (tvar-type
    (serial-number integer?)
    (container vector?)))

(define expand-optional-type-expression
  (lambda (otexp tenv)
    (cases optional-type-exp otexp
      (no-type-exp () (fresh-tvar))
      (a-type-exp (texp) (expand-type-expression texp tenv)))))

(define fresh-tvar
  (let ((serial-number 0))
    (lambda ()
      (set! serial-number (+ 1 serial-number))
      (tvar-type serial-number (vector '())))))

(define tvar->contents
  (lambda (ty)
    (vector-ref (tvar-type->container ty) 0)))

(define tvar-set-contents!
  (lambda (ty val)
    (vector-set! (tvar-type->container ty) 0 val)))

(define tvar-non-empty?
  (lambda (ty)
    (not (null? (vector-ref (tvar-type->container ty) 0)))))

(define tvar-type->container
  (lambda (ty)
    (cases type ty
      (tvar-type (sn vec) vec)
      (else (eopl:error 'tvar-type->container
             "Not a tvar-type: ~s" ty)))))
```

Figure 4.14   Definition of types and type variables

With the new behavior for `check-equal-type!`, `type-of-expression` recursively walks through the program. As it walks through the program, it calls `check-equal-type!` to take careful note of how each symbol is used and to make whatever deductions are possible about the types.

This equality-centered approach can be used to simplify the code for `type-of-application`:

```
(define type-of-application
  (lambda (rator-type actual-types rator rands exp)
    (let ((result-type (fresh-tvar)))
      (check-equal-type!
        rator-type
        (proc-type actual-types result-type)
        exp)
      result-type)))
```

This version makes a type variable `result-type` for the as-yet-unknown type of the entire application. It then checks to see that the operator is a procedure that accepts arguments of the same types as the operands and that produces a result that is the same as the type of the application. As a result of this matching, some deductions will be made about `result-type`, and those deductions will be stored in `result-type` where they will be visible to everyone. The remainder of the code for `type-of-expression` and its auxiliary procedures can be used unchanged, since each subexpression is considered exactly once.

Before considering the details of `check-equal-type!`, let's see how we might do this process by hand.

As `type-of-expression` walks through the code, it introduces one type variable for each formal parameter whose type is not declared, and one additional type variable for each application. For each node in the abstract syntax tree of the expression we get some equations between types and type variables.

For example, when typing a conditional expression if e_0 then e_1 else e_2 in *tenv*, we must have

$$(\texttt{type-of-expression } «e_0» \ tenv) = \texttt{bool}$$
$$(\texttt{type-of-expression } «e_1» \ tenv)$$
$$= (\texttt{type-of-expression } «e_2» \ tenv)$$
$$= (\texttt{type-of-expression } «\texttt{if } e_0 \text{ then } e_1 \text{ else } e_2» \ tenv)$$

and when typing an application $(\textit{rator rand}_1 \ldots \textit{rand}_n)$ in *tenv*, it must be that

    (type-of-expression «*rator*» *tenv*) =
    ((type-of-expression «*rand*$_1$» *tenv*)
    * ... *
    (type-of-expression «*rand*$_n$» *tenv*)
    ->
    (type-of-expression «$(\textit{rator rand}_1 \ldots \textit{rand}_n)$» *tenv*))

This says that at each application, the operator must be a procedure that maps the types of the operands to the type of the entire application.

Finally, when typing proc expression proc $(x_1 \ldots x_n)$ *exp* in *tenv*, we must have

    (type-of-expression «proc $(x_1 \ldots x_n)$ *exp*» *tenv*) =
    ((type-of-expression x_1 *tenv*$_{body}$)
    * ... *
    (type-of-expression x_n *tenv*$_{body}$)
    ->
    (type-of-expression «*exp*» *tenv*$_{body}$))

where *tenv*$_{body}$ is the type environment in which the body *exp* is to be typed.

So to deduce the type of an expression, we'll introduce a type variable for each bound variable and each application, and write out an equation for each compound expression using the rules above. Since we type each subexpression in exactly one type environment, we don't need to worry about the different values of *tenv*.

Then all we have to do is solve the resulting equations. The code solves these equations by calling check-equal-type!, but we first consider how to solve these equations by hand.

As an example, consider proc(f,x) (f +(1,x) zero?(x)). Let's start by making a table of all the bound variables and applications in this expression, and assigning a type variable to each one:

Expression	Type Variable
f	tf
x	tx
(f +(1,x) zero?(x))	t1
+(1,x)	t2
zero?(x)	t3

We know, by the procedure rule, that the type of the entire expression is (tf * tx -> t1). We must find the types tf, tx, and t1.

Now, for each compound expression (either an application or a conditional; in this example we have only applications), we can deduce a type equation:

```
Expression                   Type Equation
(f +(1,x) zero?(x))          tf = (t2 * t3 -> t1)
+(1,x)                       (int * int -> int) = (int * tx -> t2)
zero?(x)                     (int -> bool) = (tx -> t3)
```

The first equation says that the procedure f must be prepared to take a first argument of the same type as +(1,x) and a second argument of the same type as zero?(x), and its result must be of the same type as the application. The other equations follow similarly: in each case the left-hand side is the type of the operator, and the right-hand side is a type constructed from the types of the operands and the type of the application. The right-hand side is the type of those procedures that "fit" in this application.

We can fill in tf, tx, t1, t2, and t3 in any way we like, so long as they satisfy the three type equations:

```
tf = (t2 * t3 -> t1)
(int * int -> int) = (int * tx -> t2)
(int -> bool) = (tx -> t3)
```

We can solve such equations by systematic inspection. From the second equation, we conclude

```
tx = int
t2 = int
```

Substituting these values into the remaining equations, we get

```
tf = (int * t3 -> t1)
(int -> bool) = (int -> t3)
```

From the last equation, we deduce

```
t3 = bool
```

and substituting this into the first equation yields

```
tf = (int * bool -> t1)
```

We have now solved for all the type variables, except t1:

```
tf = (int * bool -> t1)
tx = int
t2 = int
t3 = bool
```

This process of repeated inspection and substitution is called *unification*.

We conclude from this calculation that we could assign our original term `proc(f,x)(f +(1,x) zero?(x))` the type `(tf * tx -> t1)` or the type `((int * bool -> t1) * int -> t1)` for any choice of t1. This code will work for any type t1; we say it is *polymorphic* in t1.

This is reasonable, since the first argument f must be a procedure of two arguments. Its first argument must be an int (because + always produces an int, and its second argument must be a bool, but its output could be anything. The second argument x must be an int because it is used both as an argument to + and as an argument to zero?. The output from the entire procedure will be the same as the output from f.

Let us consider the same example, but with the + changed to a cons, with type `(int * (list int) -> (list int))`. Then the equations would be

```
Expression                 Type Equation
(f cons(1,x) zero?(x))     tf = (t2 * t3 -> t1)
cons(1,x)                  (int * (list int) -> (list int))
                             = (int * tx -> t2)
zero?(x)                   (int -> bool) = (tx -> t3)
```

From the second equation, we deduce

```
tx = (list int)
t2 = (list int)
```

Substituting these values into the third equation, we get

```
(int -> bool) = ((list int) -> t3)
```

But there is no value for t3 that will make these types the same: for them to be equal, we must have `int = (list int)`, which is false.

So this is an example where `check-equal-type!` reports an error. This is the correct behavior, since the expression is inconsistent in its use of x: the first occurrence of x requires it to be a list of ints, and the second occurrence requires it to be an int. So the expression should be rejected.

Exercise 4.15 [★★] How can this approach be extended to do type inference by hand for a `let` expression? For a `letrec` expression?

Exercise 4.16 [★] Write down and solve the type equations for the following examples.

1. `proc (f,g,p,x) if (p (f x)) then (g 1 x) else add1((f x))`
2. `proc (x,p,f) if (p x) then add1(x) else (f p x)`
3. `proc (x,p,f,g) if (p add1(x)) then add1((f x)) else (g f x)`
4. `let x = 3 f = proc (x) add1(x) in (f x)`

Treat `add1` as if it were a procedure of type `(int -> int)`, and + as if it were a procedure of type `(int * int -> int)`.

How does `check-equal-type!` solve equations like the ones in the preceding examples? Instead of simply calling `equal?`, `check-equal-type!` will recursively traverse the type structures it is asked to equate. If it encounters a type variable that contains a type, it recurs on that type. If it encounters a type variable that is empty, then it fills the type variable with the other type.

Figure 4.15 shows this algorithm at work on the example of page 157. In the initial equation, the left-hand side is the type variable tf, so `check-equal-type!` fills it by inserting a reference to the right-hand side (shown in the figure as a dashed line). The resulting data structure is shown in figure 4.15(a).

Figure 4.15(b) shows the data structure after processing the second equation. The equation is set up as shown. The type variable t2 is shared by the first and second equations. The procedure `check-equal-type!` does a recursive traversal of the two trees. It observes that both sides are 2-argument procedure types, and both have first argument int. For the second argument, one side is int and the other is tx, so it fills tx with int. It then observes that the result type on one side is int and on the other is t2, so it fills t2 with int, yielding the structure shown in the figure.

After processing the third equation, the data structure looks like figure 4.15(c). Again, `check-equal-type!` observes that both sides are 1-argument procedure types. The argument on the left side is int. The argument on the right side is also int, because the right-side argument is tx, which has already been filled with int. Thus the step in the manual algorithm of substituting the new values into the remaining equations is unnecessary here because the substitution is done automatically in the data structure. Last, `check-equal-type!` observes that the result type is bool on the

left and t3 on the right, so it fills t3 with bool. Thus, check-equal-type!
simulates the hand solution shown earlier and gets the same information.

Figure 4.15(d) shows the data structures built by check-equal-type! for
the example on page 159. Here the first two equations have been processed,
and check-equal-type! has begun to process the third equation. Comparing the types of the first argument, it discovers int on the left, but tx
which is (list int) on the right. Since there are no type variables in int
or (list int), there is no way to make these two types equal. Therefore
check-equal-type! reports that the equations cannot be solved.

Though both the checker of section 4.2 and the inferencer of this section
use a recursive traversal of the program to be checked, they work very differently. The checker always computes the type of an expression from the
type of its subexpressions. The type inferencer recursively walks through
the program, taking careful note of how each symbol is used and making
deductions about the types whenever possible. In the manual system we
have used above, the notes take the form of equations. In the implemented system, the note-taking is automated, and takes the form of new equations, introduced with check-equal-type!. Solving the equations consists
of recursively walking through the equations and making substitutions as
necessary. Setting the contents of a type variable effectively substitutes the
new value for the type variable everywhere it appears.

The code for check-equal-type! is shown in figure 4.16. The procedure
checks each way in which t1 and t2 can be equal:

1. It first determines whether t1 and t2 are the same Scheme value. If so,
   it succeeds and returns an unspecified value.

2. If t1 is a type variable, it calls the procedure check-tvar-equal-type!
   on t1 and t2, passing exp for error-reporting purposes.

3. Symmetrically, if t2 is a type variable, it calls check-tvar-equal-type!
   on t2 and t1.

4. If t1 and t2 are atomic types, it determines whether they have the same
   name; if not, they cannot be equal, and an error is reported.

5. If t1 and t2 are both procedure types, it determines whether they have
   the same number of arguments. If so, it recurs on each of the argument
   types and on the result type.

6. Otherwise, t1 and t2 cannot be equal, so an error is reported.

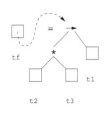

(a) after processing first equation

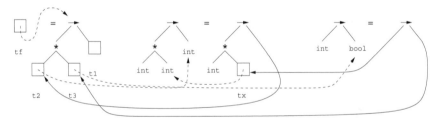

(b) after processing second equation

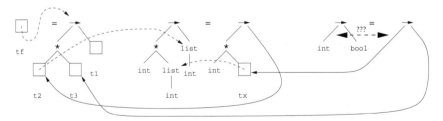

(c) after processing third equation

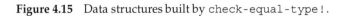

(d) about to discover an unsatisfiable equation

Figure 4.15   Data structures built by check-equal-type!.

```
(define check-equal-type!
  (lambda (t1 t2 exp)
    (cond
      ((eqv? t1 t2))
      ((tvar-type? t1) (check-tvar-equal-type! t1 t2 exp))
      ((tvar-type? t2) (check-tvar-equal-type! t2 t1 exp))
      ((and (atomic-type? t1) (atomic-type? t2))
       (if (not
             (eqv?
               (atomic-type->name t1)
               (atomic-type->name t2)))
         (raise-type-error t1 t2 exp)))
      ((and (proc-type? t1) (proc-type? t2))
       (let ((arg-types1 (proc-type->arg-types t1))
             (arg-types2 (proc-type->arg-types t2))
             (result-type1 (proc-type->result-type t1))
             (result-type2 (proc-type->result-type t2)))
         (if (not
               (= (length arg-types1) (length arg-types2)))
           (raise-wrong-number-of-arguments t1 t2 exp)
           (begin
             (for-each
               (lambda (t1 t2)
                 (check-equal-type! t1 t2 exp))
               arg-types1 arg-types2)
             (check-equal-type!
               result-type1 result-type2 exp)))))
      (else (raise-type-error t1 t2 exp)))))

(define check-tvar-equal-type!
  (lambda (tvar ty exp)
    (if (tvar-non-empty? tvar)
      (check-equal-type! (tvar->contents tvar) ty exp)
      (begin
        (check-no-occurrence! tvar ty exp)
        (tvar-set-contents! tvar ty)))))
```

Figure 4.16 The unifier `check-equal-type!`

Figure 4.17   Creating a circular type

The procedure `check-tvar-equal-type!` deals with the case of equating a type variable `tvar` and a type `ty`. If `tvar` contains a type, then we recur on its contents, calling `check-equal-type!` to equate that type to `ty`.

If `tvar` is empty, we would like to set the contents of `tvar` to `ty`, thus making them equal. However, we have one more important detail to address: `check-equal-type!` recurs on the structure of its arguments. So if the contents of the type variables create a cyclic structure, `check-equal-type!` might fail to terminate. So we first call `check-no-occurrence!` to make sure that the type variable `tvar` does not occur within the type `ty`.

For example, consider the equation

```
t1 = (int -> t1)
```

If we filled in `t1`, as shown in figure 4.17, we would get a cycle, which would cause `check-equal-type!` to loop the next time it encountered `t1`.

After first saving `ty` for error-reporting purposes, `check-no-occurrence!` recurs on the structure of `ty`. If `ty` is an atomic type, then `tvar` cannot occur in it. If `ty` is itself a type variable, then the code checks to see if it is the same variable as `tvar`; if it is, an error is reported. Last, if `ty` is a procedure type, then we recur on the argument types and the result type. (See figure 4.18.)

There is only one more place in the inferencer where we need to be concerned about type variables. That is in `type-to-external-form` (figure 4.19). If `type-to-external-form` is given a type variable, then if the variable is empty, it should produce a suitable symbol; if the variable contains a type, the result should be obtained by recurring on that type.

Exercise 4.17 [⋆⋆] Complete the implementation of the type inferencer.

Exercise 4.18 [⋆] Why won't the previous version of `type-of-application` work here? Why is this the only `type-of-` procedure that needs to be modified?

```
(define check-no-occurrence!
  (lambda (tvar ty exp)
    (letrec
      ((loop
         (lambda (ty1)
           (cases type ty1
             (atomic-type (name) #t)
             (proc-type (arg-types result-type)
               (begin
                 (for-each loop arg-types)
                 (loop result-type)))
             (tvar-type (num vec)
               (if (eqv? tvar ty1)
                 (raise-occurrence-check tvar ty exp)))))))
      (loop ty)))))
```

Figure 4.18   check-no-occurrence!

```
(define type-to-external-form
  (lambda (ty)
    (cases type ty
      (atomic-type (name) name)
      (proc-type (arg-types result-type)
        (append
          (arg-types-to-external-form arg-types)
          '(->)
          (list (type-to-external-form result-type))))
      (tvar-type (serial-number container)
        (if (tvar-non-empty? ty)
          (type-to-external-form (tvar->contents ty))
          (string->symbol
            (string-append
              "tvar"
              (number->string serial-number))))))))
```

Figure 4.19   type-to-external-form

Exercise 4.19 [⋆⋆] Extend the inferencer to handle pair types, as in exercise 4.7.

Exercise 4.20 [⋆⋆] Extend the inferencer to handle list types, as in exercise 4.8. Modify the language so that `emptylist` no longer needs a type. (Hint: create a type variable in place of t).

Exercise 4.21 [⋆] Write a translator that erases all the types from a program, so that it can be interpreted by one of the interpreters from chapter 3.

Exercise 4.22 [⋆⋆⋆] If the procedure `check-equal-type!` processes a series of equations between type variables, such as $t_1 = t_2, t_2 = t_3, t_3 = t_4$, etc., it will generate a chain where t_1 contains a reference to t_2, t_2 contains a reference to t_3, etc. The procedure `check-equal-type!` will then have to traverse these links before finding out any useful information about t_1. Write an expression that causes this situation to arise. Then modify `check-equal-type!` so that whenever t_1 points to some type (other than a type variable) via some chain of references, all the type variables on the path are modified to point directly to the end point of the chain; this will save later pointer traversals. This technique is called *path compression* and is known to improve the asymptotic complexity of the unification algorithm.

Exercise 4.23 [⋆⋆⋆] Our inferencer is very useful, but it is not powerful enough to allow the programmer to define procedures that are polymorphic, like the polymorphic primitives `pair` or `cons`, which can be used at many types. For example, one would like to write programs like

```
letrec
  ? map (? f, ? x) =
     if null?(x)
     then emptylist
     else cons((f car(x)), (map f cdr(x)))
  ? even (? y) =
     if zero?(y) then true else (odd sub1(y))
  ? odd (? y) =
     if zero?(y) then false else (even sub1(y))
in pair((map add1 cons(3,cons(5,emptylist))),
        (map even cons(3,cons(5,emptylist))))
```

This expression uses map twice, once producing a list of `int`s and once producing a list of `bool`s. Therefore it needs two different types for the two uses. Since the inferencer of this section will find at most one type for map, it will detect the clash between `int` and `bool` and reject the program. (See exercises 4.7 and 4.8.)

Invent or discover through reading a technique for declaring procedures that are polymorphic.

Further Reading

Most current work in typed programming languages can be traced back to (Milner, 1978), which introduces types in ML as a way of guaranteeing the reliability of computer-generated proofs. (Ullman, 1997) gives a good short introduction; a complementary treatment is (Felleisen & Friedman, 1996). The use of types to enforce data abstractions appears in (Reynolds, 1975) and is used in CLU (Liskov, Snyder, Atkinson, & Schaffert, 1977). ML has a module system that enforces similar boundaries; see (Paulson, 1996) for a good discussion with some interesting applications.

Type inference has been discovered several times. The standard reference is (Hindley, 1969), though Hindley remarks that the results were known to Curry in the 1950s. (Morris, 1968) also presents type inference, but the widespread use of type inference did not happen until Milner's 1978 paper.

5 *Objects and Classes*

Many programming tasks require the program to manage some piece of state through an interface. For example, a file system has internal state, but we access and modify that state only through the file system interface. Our queue abstraction in section 2.4 is an additional example of this paradigm. In each case, the piece of state spans several variables, and changes to those variables must be coordinated in order to maintain the consistency of the state. One therefore needs some technology to ensure that the various variables that constitute the state are updated in a coordinated manner. *Object-oriented programming* is a useful technology for accomplishing this task.

In object-oriented programming, each managed piece of state is called an *object*. An object consists of several stored quantities, called its *fields*, with associated *methods* (functions) that have access to the fields. The operation of calling a method is often viewed as sending the method name and arguments as a message to the object; this is sometimes called the *message-passing* view of object-oriented programming.

Most often, one needs to manage several pieces of state with similar methods. For example, one might have several file systems or several queues in a program. To facilitate the sharing of methods, object-oriented programming systems typically provide *classes*, which are structures that specify the fields and methods of each such object. Each object is created as an *instance* of some class.

Often, one wishes to define a new class as a small modification of an existing class by adding or changing the behavior of some methods, or by adding fields. In this case, we say the new class *inherits from* or *extends* the old class, since the rest of the class's behavior is inherited from the original class.

This program organization is useful because it permits a straightforward translation from the objects of the physical world or other application domain to the objects of the program. Real-world objects typically have some *state* and some *behavior* that either controls or is controlled by that state. For example, cats can eat, purr, jump, and lie down, and these activities are controlled by their current state, including how hungry and tired they are. Real-world objects are conveniently grouped into classes containing objects that behave similarly except for differences that can be explained by their state. A particular cat shares general behavioral characteristics with all cats, and also has state that changes with time. Classes may be arranged hierarchically, reflecting for example that cats belonging to the same breed share certain characteristics of the breed, as well as more general characteristics of all cats. Similarly, cats all have characteristics common to mammals. This is easily modeled by inheritance.

Whether program elements are modeling real-world objects or artificial aspects of a system's state, a program's structure is often clarified if it can be composed of objects that combine both behavior and state. It is also natural to associate behaviorally-similar objects with the same class.

Closures give one example of the power of programming with objects. A closure is an object whose state is contained in its free variables. A closure has a single behavior: it may be invoked on some arguments. More often, however, one wants an object to have several behaviors. Object-oriented programming languages provide support for this ability.

Another important feature of object-oriented languages is *polymorphism*, which means the ability of an entity to have more than one form. In programming languages it often means the ability of a value to have more than one type. In the context of object-oriented languages, the most common kind of polymorphism is the ability of an instance of a subclass to play the role of an object of its superclass, so that it may be used anywhere an instance of the superclass may be used. Another form of polymorphism is introduced in exercise 5.13. We study polymorphism in more detail in chapter 6.

There is much debate over which attributes a language must have to be considered object-oriented, but there is general agreement that the four elements just discussed are central:

- *objects* encapsulate behavior (methods) and state (stored in fields),

- *classes* group objects that differ only in their state,

- *inheritance* allows new classes to be derived from existing ones, and

- *polymorphism* allows messages to be sent to objects of different classes.

```
class c1 extends object
  field i
  field j
  method initialize (x)
    begin
      set i = x;
      set j = -(0,x)
    end
  method countup (d)
    begin
      set i = +(i,d);
      set j = -(j,d)
    end
  method getstate () list(i,j)
let t1 = 0
    t2 = 0
    o1 = new c1(3)
in begin
      set t1 = send o1 getstate();
      send o1 countup(2);
      set t2 = send o1 getstate();
      list(t1,t2)
    end
```

Figure 5.1   A simple object-oriented program

Though languages may support any combination of these features, there is great synergy in combining all four.

In this chapter we study the primary run-time structures of object-oriented programming. We present four implementations of the same language, ranging from a very simple implementation to one that incorporates most features of a realistic implementation.

5.1   Object-Oriented Programming

Object-oriented languages use a variety of different words to describe similar concepts. We begin with an example to establish our terminology and to illustrate alternatives. Figure 5.1 shows a simple program in our object-oriented language. It declares `c1` to be a class that inherits from `object`. We study inheritance in section 5.2. Each object of class c1 contains two fields named i and j. The fields are sometimes called *members* or *instance variables*. The class c1 supports three *methods*, sometimes called *member functions*, named initialize, countup, and getstate. Each method consists of its *method name*, its *method ids* (also called *method parameters*), and its *method body*. The method names correspond to the kinds of *messages* to which instances of c1 can respond. We sometimes refer to "c1's countup method."

In this example, each of the methods of the class maintains the integrity constraint or *invariant* that $i = -j$. A real programming example would, of course, likely have far more complex integrity constraints.

We next turn to execution of the program in figure 5.1. The expression first creates two variables, t1 and t2, and an object o1 of the class. When an object is created, its initialize method is invoked, in this case setting i to 3 and j to -3. The getstate method of o1 is then invoked, returning the list (3 -3). Next, o1's countup method is invoked, changing the value of the two fields to 5 and -5. Then the getstate method is invoked, returning the list (5 -5). Last, the value of list(t1,t2), which is ((3 -3) (5 -5)), is returned as the value of the entire program.

In the program in figure 5.2 we have a tree with two kinds of nodes, interior_node and leaf_node. To find the sum of the leaves of a node, we send it the sum message. Generally, we do not know what kind of node we are sending the message to. Instead, each node accepts the sum message and uses its sum method to do the right thing. This is called *dynamic dispatch*, and is used to implement subclass polymorphism. Here the expression builds a tree with two interior nodes and three leaf nodes. It sends a sum message to the node o1; o1 sends sum messages to its subtrees, and so on, returning 12 at the end.

A method body can invoke other methods by using the identifier self, which is bound to the object on which the method has been invoked. In some languages this is called this instead of self. Thus use of self allows methods to be mutually recursive. For example, in

```
class oddeven extends object
  method initialize () 1
  method even (n)
    if zero?(n) then 1 else send self odd(sub1(n))
  method odd (n)
    if zero?(n) then 0 else send self even(sub1(n))
let o1 = new oddeven()
in send o1 odd(13)
```

```
class interior_node extends object
  field left
  field right
  method initialize (l, r)
    begin
      set left = l;
      set right = r
    end
  method sum () +(send left sum(),send right sum())
class leaf_node extends object
  field value
  method initialize (v) set value = v
  method sum () value
let o1 = new interior_node(
          new interior_node(
            new leaf_node(3),
            new leaf_node(4)),
          new leaf_node(5))
in send o1 sum()
```

Figure 5.2 Object-oriented program for summing the leaves of a tree

the methods even and odd invoke each other recursively, because when they are executed, self is bound to an object that contains them both. This is much like the dynamic-binding implementation of recursion in exercise 3.32.

5.2 Inheritance

Inheritance allows the programmer to define new classes by incremental modification of old ones. This is extremely useful in practice. Inheritance supports hierarchical classifications of objects; for example, every colorpoint is a point, but not vice versa. This can be modeled using inheritance, as in the classic example in figure 5.3.

If class c2 extends class c1, we say that c1 is the *parent* of c2 or that c2 is a *child* of c1. Since inheritance defines c2 as an extension of c1, c1 must be defined before c2. To get things started, we introduce a class object with no methods or fields. Since object has no initialize method, it is impossible to create an object of class object. Each class (other than object) has a single

```
class point extends object
  field x
  field y
  method initialize (initx, inity)
    begin
      set x = initx;
      set y = inity
    end
  method move (dx, dy)
    begin
      set x = +(x,dx);
      set y = +(y,dy)
    end
  method get_location () list(x,y)
class colorpoint extends point
  field color
  method set_color (c) set color = c
  method get_color () color
let p = new point(3, 4)
    cp = new colorpoint(10, 20)
in begin
    send p move(3, 4);
    send cp set_color(87);
    send cp move(10, 20);
    list(send p get_location(),    % returns (6 8)
         send cp get_location(),    % returns (20 40)
         send cp get_color())       % returns 87
  end
```

Figure 5.3   Classic example of inheritance: colorpoint

parent, but it may have many children. Thus the relation extends imposes a tree structure on the set of classes, with object at the root.

The genealogical analogy is the source of the term *inheritance*. The analogy is often pursued so that we speak of the *ancestors* of a class (the chain from a class's parent to the root class object) or its *descendants*.

If class *c*2 inherits from class *c*1, all the fields and methods of *c*1 will be visible from the methods of *c*2, unless they are redeclared in *c*2.

Since a class inherits all the methods and fields of its parent, an instance of a child class can be used anywhere an instance of its parent can be used.

Similarly, any instance of any descendant of a class can be used anywhere an instance of the class can be used. This is sometimes called *subclass polymorphism*. If $c2$ is a descendant of $c1$, we sometimes say that $c2$ is a *subclass* of $c1$, and write $c2 < c1$, because the objects that can be used in place of an object of class $c2$ are a subset of the objects that can be used in place of an object of class $c1$. Conversely, we sometimes say that $c1$ is a *superclass* of $c2$.

Since each class has at most one immediate superclass, this is a *single-inheritance* language. Some languages allow classes to inherit from multiple superclasses. Such *multiple inheritance* is powerful, but it is also problematic; we consider some of the difficulties in the exercises.

If a field of $c1$ is redeclared in one of its subclasses $c2$, the new declaration *shadows* the old one, just as in lexical binding. For example, consider

```
class c1 extends object
  field x
  field y
  method initialize () 1
  method setx1 (v) set x = v
  method sety1 (v) set y = v
  method getx1 () x
  method gety1 () y
class c2 extends c1
  field y
  method sety2 (v) set y = v
  method getx2 () x
  method gety2 () y
let o2 = new c2()
in begin
     send o2 setx1(101);
     send o2 sety1(102);
     send o2 sety2(999);
     list(send o2 getx1(),      % returns 101
          send o2 gety1(),      % returns 102
          send o2 getx2(),      % returns 101
          send o2 gety2())      % returns 999
   end
```

Here an object of class c2 has two fields named x: the one declared in c1 and the one declared in c2. The methods declared in c1 see c1's fields x and y. In c2, the x in getx2 refers to c1's field x, but the y in gety2 refers to c2's field y.

If a method *m* of a class $c1$ is redeclared in one of its subclasses $c2$, we say that the new method *overrides* the old one. If an object of class $c2$ is sent an *m* message, then the new method should be used. This rule is simple, but it has subtle consequences. Consider the following example:

```
class c1 extends object
  method initialize () 1
  method m1 () 1
  method m2 () send self m1()
class c2 extends c1
  method m1 () 2
let o1 = new c1()
    o2 = new c2()
in list(send o1 m1(),
        send o2 m1(),
        send o2 m2())
```

We expect `send o1 m1()` to return 1, since `o1` is an instance of `c1`. Similarly, we expect `send o2 m1()` to return 2, since `o2` is an instance of `c2` and its method should clearly have priority in this case.

Now what about `send o2 m2()`? Method `m2` immediately calls method `m1`, but which one? The call happens in class `c1`, so it is possible that the programmer intended `send self m1()` as a call to `c1`'s `m1`, as in the `oddeven` example on page 172. This interpretation is called *static method dispatch*, because the method to be executed can be determined from the text of the declaration of class `c1`, which is static information.

The alternate interpretation is that the programmer intended that any invocation of method `m1` on an object of class `c2` should get `c2`'s method for `m1`, returning 2. Since `self` is `o2`, which is of class `c2`, the call `send self m1()` should return 2. This interpretation is called *dynamic method dispatch*, because the actual method to be executed for any given method call cannot be determined without knowing the actual class of the object on which the method is invoked, and this will only be known at run time.

To further illustrate the interaction of `self` and inheritance, consider the example in figure 5.4.

When `o2` is sent the message `m3`, the method body in `c1` is evaluated, with `self` bound to `o2`. But `o2`'s method for `m2` is the one in `c2`, since `o2` is an instance of class `c2`. This is an important consequence of the use of dynamic dispatch, which is a vital part of the object-oriented programming paradigm.

In general, static method dispatch is meaningful only in a language with static types. In a language without types, static method dispatch is meaningful only when the object of the call is `self` (or in a super call, discussed

```
class c1 extends object
  method initialize () 1
  method m1 () 1
  method m2 () 100
  method m3 () send self m2()
class c2 extends c1
  method initialize () 1
  method m2 () 2
let o1 = new c1()
    o2 = new c2()
in list(send o1 m1(),    % returns 1
        send o1 m2(),    % returns 100
        send o1 m3(),    % returns 100
        send o2 m1(),    % returns 1 (from c1)
        send o2 m2(),    % returns 2 (from c2)
        send o2 m3())    % returns 2 (c1's m3 calls c2's m2)
```

Figure 5.4   Example illustrating interaction of `self` and inheritance

presently). We therefore use dynamic method dispatch for the language of this section.

There is one occasion in which a form of static method dispatch is required, as the program in figure 5.5 illustrates.

We have supplied the class `colorpoint` with an overly specialized `initialize` method that sets the field `color` as well as the fields `x` and `y`. However, the body of the new method duplicates the code of the overridden one. This might be acceptable in our small example, but in a large example this would clearly be bad practice. (Why?) Furthermore, if `colorpoint` declared a field `x`, there would be no way to initialize the field `x` of `point`, just as there is no way to initialize the first `y` in the example on page 175.

The solution is to replace the duplicated code in the body of `colorpoint`'s `initialize` method with a *super call* of the form `super initialize()`. Then the `initialize` method in `colorpoint` would read

```
method initialize (initx, inity, initcolor)
  begin
    super initialize(initx, inity);
    set color = initcolor
  end
```

```
class point extends object
  field x
  field y
  method initialize (initx, inity)
    begin
      set x = initx;
      set y = inity
    end
  method move (dx, dy)
    begin
      set x = +(x,dx);
      set y = +(y,dy)
    end
  method get_location () list(x,y)
class colorpoint extends point
  field color
  method initialize (initx, inity, initcolor)
    begin
      set x = initx;
      set y = inity;
      set color = initcolor
    end
  method set_color (c) set color = c
  method get_color () color
let o1 = new colorpoint(3, 4, 172)
in send o1 get_color()
```

Figure 5.5   Example demonstrating a need for static method dispatch

To explain the operation of a super call, we introduce the notion of a host class. We call the class in which a method is declared that method's *host class*. Similarly, define the host class of an expression to be the host class of the method (if any) in which the expression occurs.

A super call, super $s(\ldots)$, in the body of a method m invokes a method s of the parent of m's host class. This is not necessarily the parent of the class of self. To illustrate this distinction, consider figure 5.6. Sending an m3 message to an object o3 of class c3 finds c2's method for m3, which executes super m1(). If super m1() were dynamically dispatched, it would execute the m1 method of the parent of the class of o3. The class of o3 is c3, whose parent is c2. So the super call would invoke c2's method for m1, returning

```
class c1 extends object
  method initialize () 1
  method m1 () send self m2()
  method m2 () 13
class c2 extends c1
  method m1 () 22
  method m2 () 23
  method m3 () super m1()
class c3 extends c2
  method m1 () 32
  method m2 () 33
let o3 = new c3()
in send o3 m3()
```

Figure 5.6   Example illustrating interaction of `super` call with `self`

22. But that is not what happens. The correct interpretation of the super call uses static method dispatch. Since this call occurs in class c2, it executes the m1 method of c2's parent c1, which invokes o3's m2 method. But o3 is an object of class c3, so it is c3's m2 method that is found, returning 33.

Though the object of a super method call is `self`, method dispatch is static, because the specific method to be invoked can be determined from the text, independent of the class of `self`.

5.3   The Language

We have so far presented object-oriented programming in terms of a set of examples. In order to proceed with an implementation, we need to be more precise.

For our language, we extend the language of section 3.7 with the additional productions shown in figure 5.7. A program is a sequence of class declarations followed by an expression to be executed. A class declaration has a name, an immediate superclass name, zero or more field declarations, and zero or more method declarations. A method declaration, like a procedure declaration in a `letrec`, has a name, a list of formal parameters, and a body.

$\langle\text{program}\rangle \quad ::= \{\langle\text{class-decl}\rangle\}^* \ \langle\text{expression}\rangle$

```
a-program (class-decls body)
```

$\langle\text{class-decl}\rangle \quad ::= \text{class} \ \langle\text{identifier}\rangle \ \text{extends} \ \langle\text{identifier}\rangle$
$\qquad\qquad\qquad \{\text{field} \ \langle\text{identifier}\rangle\}^* \ \{\langle\text{method-decl}\rangle\}^*$

```
a-class-decl
 (class-name super-name
   field-ids method-decls)
```

$\langle\text{method-decl}\rangle ::= \text{method} \ \langle\text{identifier}\rangle \ (\{\langle\text{identifier}\rangle\}^{*(,)}) \ \langle\text{expression}\rangle$

```
a-method-decl (method-name ids body)
```

$\langle\text{expression}\rangle \quad ::= \text{new} \ \langle\text{identifier}\rangle \ (\{\langle\text{expression}\rangle\}^{*(,)})$

```
new-object-exp (class-name rands)
```

$\langle\text{expression}\rangle \quad ::= \text{send} \ \langle\text{expression}\rangle \ \langle\text{identifier}\rangle \ (\{\langle\text{expression}\rangle\}^{*(,)})$

```
method-app-exp (obj-exp method-name rands)
```

$\langle\text{expression}\rangle \quad ::= \text{super} \ \langle\text{identifier}\rangle \ (\{\langle\text{expression}\rangle\}^{*(,)})$

```
super-call-exp (method-name rands)
```

Figure 5.7   New productions for a simple object-oriented programming language

We add objects and lists as expressed values, so we have

Expressed Value $\quad=\quad$ Number + ProcVal + Obj + List(Expressed Value)
Denoted Value $\quad\ \ =\quad$ Ref(Expressed Value)

We write List(Expressed Value) to indicate that the lists may contain any expressed value. The operations on lists are as in exercise 3.7. Last, we assume that we have a begin expression, as in exercise 3.39, that evaluates its subexpressions from left to right and returns the value of the last one.

The definition of Obj depends on our choice of implementation. Classes are neither denotable nor expressible in our language: they may appear as part of objects but never as the binding of a variable or the value of an expression. (But, see exercise 5.22.)

We have added three expressions. The new expression creates an object of the named class. The initialize method is then invoked to initialize the fields of the object. The `rands` are evaluated and passed as parameters to the `initialize` method. The value returned by this method call is thrown away and the new object is returned as the value of the `new` expression.

A `send` expression consists of an expression that should evaluate to an object, a method name, and zero or more operands. The object's class should include the named method, which is passed the arguments obtained by evaluating the operands. As with procedure calls, the method body is then evaluated within the scope of lexical bindings associating the method's parameters with the corresponding arguments. Though not enforced, we refrain from sending an `initialize` method.

A super call expression invokes a method found by looking at the super-class of the expression's host class. A super call consists of a method name and zero or more arguments. The object of the `send` expression that caused the host method's body to be evaluated continues as the object as if it were a `send` expression. In all other respects, the `super` expression is treated the same as a `send` expression.

In the next section, we present four implementations of this language. They share a basis that implements all of the non-object-oriented features of the language, including `eval-program` and `eval-expression`.

When a program is evaluated, the class declarations are processed by `elaborate-class-decls!`, and then the expression is evaluated.

```
(define eval-program
  (lambda (pgm)
    (cases program pgm
      (a-program (c-decls exp)
        (elaborate-class-decls! c-decls)
        (eval-expression exp (init-env))))))
```

Each implementation must supply a value for `elaborate-class-decls!`. The job of this procedure is to store the class declarations in some form that makes them accessible when needed later in the computation.

The procedure `eval-expression` contains, as usual, a clause for each kind of expression in the language, including a clause for each of the three new productions. We consider each new kind of expression in turn.

When a `send` expression is evaluated, the operands and the object expression are evaluated. Then the method associated with the method name is found in the method declaration of the object and then that method is applied to its arguments. This is the work of `find-method-and-apply`, whose second argument is the name of the class where the method is to be looked up. The corresponding clause in `eval-expression` is

```
(method-app-exp (obj-exp method-name rands)
  (let ((args (eval-rands rands env))
        (obj (eval-expression obj-exp env)))
    (find-method-and-apply
      method-name (object->class-name obj) obj args)))
```

The procedure `find-method-and-apply` takes four arguments: a method name, the name of the class in which to begin searching for the method, the value for `self`, and the list of arguments. Here the search begins in the class of the object. Each implementation must supply its own definition for this procedure. Similarly, each implementation must supply a definition for `object->class-name`.

Super method invocation is similar to ordinary method invocation except that the method is looked up in the superclass of the host class of the expression. In our implementations, we make sure that the name of this class is bound to a special variable named `%super`. This is not a legal variable name in our language, so there is no possibility of confusion, nor need we expand denoted values to include class names. The `self` will be the current self, which will likewise be bound in the environment. It is the job of `find-method-and-apply` to establish these bindings correctly. The clause in `eval-expression` is

```
(super-call-exp (method-name rands)
  (let ((args (eval-rands rands env))
        (obj (apply-env env 'self)))
    (find-method-and-apply
      method-name (apply-env env '%super) obj args)))
```

Our last task is to create objects. When a `new` expression is evaluated, the operands are evaluated and a new object is created from the class name. Then its initialize method is called, but its value is ignored. Finally, the object is returned.

```
(new-object-exp (class-name rands)
  (let ((args (eval-rands rands env))
        (obj (new-object class-name)))
    (find-method-and-apply
      'initialize class-name obj args)
    obj))
```

So each implementation must supply its own `elaborate-class-decls!`, `find-method-and-apply`, `object->class-name`, and `new-object`, and, of course, any data structures and other procedures that these four procedures require.

5.4   Four implementations

We present four implementations. The first is a naive implementation. The
second chooses a more realistic representation for objects. The third recog-
nizes that most of the work that happens at either object-construction time
or method-application time can be done at class-construction time, so that
this work is accomplished once per program execution rather than once per
object-creation or method application. The last compresses a hierarchy of
methods into a single structure for more convenient searching.

5.4.1   A Simple Implementation

We begin with a very simple implementation.

In this implementation, we observe that a class declaration already contains the information that we need, including the class's name, its immediate
superclass's name, its field identifiers, and its method declarations. Hence
we represent classes and methods by their declarations. We build a reposito-
ry of class declarations by using a Scheme global variable, `the-class-env`:

```
(define the-class-env '())

(define elaborate-class-decls!
  (lambda (c-decls)
    (set! the-class-env c-decls)))
```

The procedure `lookup-class` looks up a class name in `the-class-env`
and returns the corresponding declaration.

We represent an object as a list of *parts*, with one part corresponding to each
class in the inheritance chain. Each part consists of class name and a vector
to hold the state of the part. The class declaration of the first `part` of the list
represents the lowest point on the class chain, and the further down the list
we move, the closer we get to the top of the hierarchy. For example, in the
program of figure 5.8, `o3` will be represented by three parts, each representing
the contributions of one of `c1`, `c2`, and `c3`. The representation of `o3` is shown
in figure 5.9. Each part is defined by the data type

```
(define-datatype part part?
  (a-part
    (class-name symbol?)
    (fields vector?)))
```

To build an object, we construct a list of parts, given a class name. If the
class name is `object`, then we know that we have reached the top of the

```
class c1 extends object
  field x
  field y
  method initialize ()
    begin
      set x = 11;
      set y = 12
    end
  method m1 () ... x ... y ...
  method m2 () ... send self m3() ...
class c2 extends c1
  field y
  method initialize ()
    begin
      super initialize();
      set y = 22
    end
  method m1 (u,v) ... x ... y ...
  method m3 () ...
class c3 extends c2
  field x
  field z
  method initialize ()
    begin
      super initialize();
      set x = 31;
      set z = 32
    end
  method m3 () ... x ... y ... z ...
let o3 = new c3()
in send o3 m1(7,8)
```

Figure 5.8   Sample program for OOP implementations

inheritance chain and there are no parts to construct. Otherwise, we find the class declaration corresponding to the given class name, and we return a list whose car is the first part and whose cdr is obtained by recurring on the superclass. The first part is constructed from the name of the current class and a vector containing as many elements as there are fields declared in the current class. When we are done, we have a list of uninitialized parts.

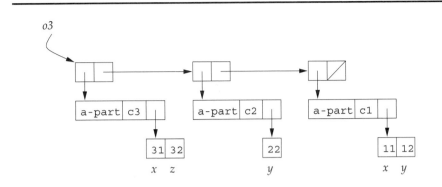

Figure 5.9   An object in the simple implementation

```
(define new-object
  (lambda (class-name)
    (if (eqv? class-name 'object)
        '()
        (let ((c-decl (lookup-class class-name)))
          (cons
            (make-first-part c-decl)
            (new-object (class-decl->super-name c-decl)))))))

(define make-first-part
  (lambda (c-decl)
    (a-part
      (class-decl->class-name c-decl)
      (make-vector (length (class-decl->field-ids c-decl))))))
```

In this code, we use simple procedures to access individual fields of a node
in the syntax tree. We give these procedures names that include "->" to
suggest their behavior. For example,

```
(define class-decl->super-name
  (lambda (c-decl)
    (cases class-decl c-decl
      (a-class-decl (class-name super-name field-ids m-decls)
        super-name))))
```

We often generalize these "->" accessors to allow for compositions of accessors, and to use lookup-class when necessary. For example, we write

```
(define class-name->method-decls
  (lambda (class-name)
    (class-decl->method-decls (lookup-class class-name))))
```

Exercise 5.1 [⋆] Use these techniques to define the procedures part->fields and part->field-ids.

Our next challenge is to implement find-method-and-apply. We search the classes along the inheritance chain until we find a class that declares a method matching the method name. When we do, we call apply-method with the found method declaration, the name of the host class, self, and the arguments.

```
(define find-method-and-apply
  (lambda (m-name host-name self args)
    (if (eqv? host-name 'object)
      (eopl:error 'find-method-and-apply
        "No method for name ~s" m-name)
      (let ((m-decl (lookup-method-decl m-name
                      (class-name->method-decls host-name))))
        (if (method-decl? m-decl)
          (apply-method m-decl host-name self args)
          (find-method-and-apply m-name
            (class-name->super-name host-name)
            self args))))))
```

The procedure lookup-method-decl takes a method name and a list of method declarations and returns the matching method declaration or false if no matching method declaration is found.

Applying a method is much like applying a closure. We must execute the body of the method in an environment in which each variable is bound to the proper value. To do this, we build an environment in which the first rib contains the bindings for %super, for self, and for the formal parameters of the method. The rest of the environment provides a binding for each field variable that is visible from the method. The field variables visible from the method are those of the parts of the object starting with the host class. Consider the example in figure 5.8. If we execute send o3 m1(7,8), then the fields visible from method m1 are those starting at the part of o3 that corresponds to m1's host class c2. In this way, a class name gives a *view* of the object; we can find the view with the procedure view-object-as:

```
(define view-object-as
  (lambda (parts class-name)
    (if (eqv? (part->class-name (car parts)) class-name)
      parts
      (view-object-as (cdr parts) class-name))))
```

From this view of the object, we can generate an environment consisting of one rib for each part. Each rib binds the field variables of one part to the fields of that part, using the already-constructed vector:

```
(define build-field-env
  (lambda (parts)
    (if (null? parts)
      (empty-env)
      (extend-env-refs
        (part->field-ids (car parts))
        (part->fields    (car parts))
        (build-field-env (cdr parts))))))

(define extend-env-refs
  (lambda (syms vec env)
    (extended-env-record syms vec env)))
```

Now we can write `apply-method`:

```
(define apply-method
  (lambda (m-decl host-name self args)
    (let ((ids (method-decl->ids m-decl))
          (body (method-decl->body m-decl))
          (super-name (class-name->super-name host-name)))
      (eval-expression body
        (extend-env
          (cons '%super (cons 'self ids))
          (cons super-name (cons self args))
          (build-field-env
            (view-object-as self host-name)))))))
```

Figure 5.10 contains the environment built for the evaluation of the method body in `send o3 m1(7,8)`. We have now written the four required procedures, so our implementation is complete.

5.4.2 Flat Objects

We don't want to have to build all these ribs at every method call. It would be better to represent all the storage managed by an object as a single vector, instead of spreading it over a list of parts. This leads to the definition

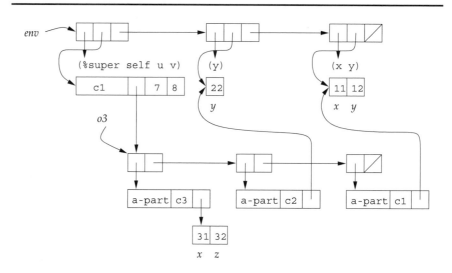

Figure 5.10   Environment for method application in simple implementation

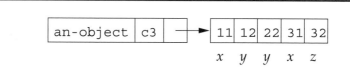

Figure 5.11   An object in the flat representation

```
(define-datatype object object?
  (an-object
    (class-name symbol?)
    (fields vector?)))
```

We choose to lay out the storage with the fields from the "oldest" class first. Thus in figure 5.8, an object of class c1 would have its fields laid out as (x y); an object of class c2 would lay out its fields as (x y y), with the second y being the one belonging to c2, and an object of class c3 would be laid out as (x y y x z). The representation of object o3 from figure 5.8 is shown in figure 5.11.

This strategy has the useful property that any subclass of c3 will have these
fields in the same positions in the vector, because any fields added later will
appear to the right of these fields. What is the position of x in a method that
is defined in any subclass of c3? Assuming that x is not redefined, we know
that the position of x must be 3 throughout all such methods. Thus, when a
field identifier is declared, the position of the corresponding value remains
unchanged unless the field identifier is redeclared.

Of course, we want the methods in class c3 to refer to the field x declared
in c3, not the one declared in c1. To do this, we change the implementation of
environments. In each rib, we use the position corresponding to the *rightmost*
occurrence of the variable name. So if the rib is (x y y x z), x will refer to
the rightmost x, which is the one in c3.

To support this, we redefine rib-find-position.

```
(define rib-find-position
  (lambda (name symbols)
    (list-find-last-position name symbols)))
```

Exercise 5.2 [⋆] Why do the lexical environments of chapter 3 still work with the
above definition of rib-find-position? See exercise 2.16 for a hint.

Since we have changed neither the representation of classes nor the representation of methods, we need consider only the two procedures new-object
and find-method-and-apply. We start with new-object.

```
(define new-object
  (lambda (class-name)
    (an-object
      class-name
      (make-vector (roll-up-field-length class-name)))))

(define roll-up-field-length
  (lambda (class-name)
    (if (eqv? class-name 'object)
      0
      (+
        (roll-up-field-length
          (class-name->super-name class-name))
        (length (class-name->field-ids class-name))))))
```

The procedure roll-up-field-length is a recursive procedure that starts
with a class name and finds the total number of fields that must be allocated
for an object of that class: if the class name is object, there are no fields;

otherwise the number of fields is the sum of the number of fields needed for the class's parent and the number of fields declared in the class itself.

The procedure `find-method-and-apply` is unchanged, since it does not deal with the representation of objects, but we must redefine `apply-method`. Since there is only one vector of field values, we modify `apply-method` to build only a single rib for the fields.

```
(define apply-method
  (lambda (m-decl host-name self args)
    (let ((ids (method-decl->ids m-decl))
          (body (method-decl->body m-decl))
          (super-name (class-name->super-name host-name))
          (field-ids (roll-up-field-ids host-name))
          (fields (object->fields self)))
      (eval-expression body
        (extend-env
          (cons '%super (cons 'self ids))
          (cons super-name (cons self args))
          (extend-env-refs field-ids fields (empty-env)))))))
```

The procedure `apply-method` calls `roll-up-field-ids` to build a matching list of field identifiers. Like `roll-up-field-length`, it recurs up the inheritance chain, building up the list of field identifiers using `append`. The order of the arguments to `append` guarantees that the old field names precede the new ones, so for c2 in figure 5.8 we get `(x y y)`, as desired.

```
(define roll-up-field-ids
  (lambda (class-name)
    (if (eqv? class-name 'object)
      '()
      (append
        (roll-up-field-ids
          (class-name->super-name class-name))
        (class-name->field-ids class-name)))))
```

Figure 5.12 shows the environment built for the evaluation of the method body in `send o3 m1(7,8)` in figure 5.8. This figure shows that the vector may be longer than the list of identifiers: the list of identifiers is just `(x y y)`, since those are the only field variables visible from method `m1` in c2, but the vector in the environment is the vector of the entire object. However, since the values of these three field variables are in the first three elements of the vector, this still works, and since `apply-env` uses `list-find-last-position`, the method `m1` will associate the variable `y` with the `y` declared in c2, as desired.

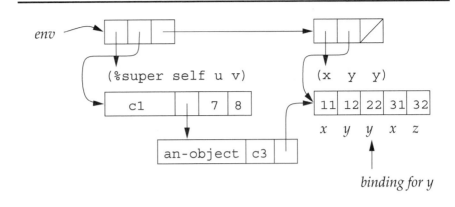

Figure 5.12   Environment for method application in the flat object representation

The list of identifiers is generally of the same length as the vector of field variables when the host class and the class of self are the same. If the host class is higher up the class chain, then there may be more vector elements than field identifiers, but the values corresponding to the field identifiers will be at the beginning of the vector. The position of the identifier in the list, as reported by `list-find-last-position`, will always give the correct position for the field variable.

This implementation is quite inefficent, however, since we search the class chain whenever we build an object (`roll-up-field-length`) or invoke a method (`roll-up-field-ids`). We address this in our next implementation.

5.4.3   Moving the Work to Class-Declaration Time

To avoid calling `roll-up-field-ids` at every method call, we need to compute this information and store it with the method. While we're at it, we also store the name of the method's superclass, for use in super calls. We create a new data type in which to keep this information:

```
(define-datatype method method?
  (a-method
    (method-decl method-decl?)
    (super-name symbol?)
    (field-ids (list-of symbol?))))
```

This information is *static*: it does not depend on any expressed or denoted values that might show up when the program is executed. So it would be much better to compute it exactly once per class. To do this, we need a data type in which to keep the information:

```
(define-datatype class class?
  (a-class
    (class-name symbol?)
    (super-name symbol?)
    (field-length integer?)
    (field-ids (list-of symbol?))
    (methods method-environment?)))
```

We use an easy representation for method environments:

```
(define method-environment? (list-of method?))
```

In this representation the `methods` slot contains only the methods declared in this class.

We build these classes at class-construction time by redefining the procedure `elaborate-class-decls!`:

```
(define elaborate-class-decls!
  (lambda (c-decls)
    (for-each elaborate-class-decl! c-decls)))

(define elaborate-class-decl!
  (lambda (c-decl)
    (let ((super-name (class-decl->super-name c-decl)))
      (let ((field-ids (append
                          (class-name->field-ids super-name)
                          (class-decl->field-ids c-decl))))
        (add-to-class-env!
          (a-class
            (class-decl->class-name c-decl)
            super-name
            (length field-ids)
            field-ids
            (roll-up-method-decls
              c-decl super-name field-ids)))))))
```

Here the roll-up operations are so simple that they are not worth making into separate procedures. The field identifiers are obtained by appending the fields of the current class declaration to those of the superclass, which have already been computed and stored in the superclass's class structure. The number of fields is calculated by taking the length of `field-ids`.

The procedure `initialize-class-env!` initializes the class environment to be empty by setting `the-class-env` to the empty list, and the procedure `add-to-class-env!` adds the newly-constructed class to the list of classes `the-class-env`. The procedure `roll-up-method-decls` turns each method declaration into a `method`, and returns the list of methods:

```
(define roll-up-method-decls
  (lambda (c-decl super-name field-ids)
    (map
      (lambda (m-decl)
        (a-method m-decl super-name field-ids))
      (class-decl->method-decls c-decl))))
```

Figure 5.13 shows the class and method structures built for the evaluation of the class declarations in figure 5.8. For simplicity, the figure does not include the `initialize` methods; neither does it show the tags on the structures nor the details of the method declarations.

We must adjust `find-method-and-apply` and `apply-method` to use this new representation. The procedure `find-method-and-apply` is unchanged, except that every reference to a method declaration is changed to a method. The procedure `apply-method` now takes a method instead of a method declaration as its first argument, and it gets the list of field identifiers from the method instead of calling `roll-up-field-ids`. Similarly, we extract the binding for `%super` directly from the method, so the `host-name` argument is not used.

```
(define apply-method
  (lambda (method host-name self args)
    (let ((ids (method->ids method))
          (body (method->body method))
          (super-name (method->super-name method))
          (field-ids (method->field-ids method))
          (fields (object->fields self)))
      (eval-expression body
        (extend-env
          (cons '%super (cons 'self ids))
          (cons super-name (cons self args))
          (extend-env-refs field-ids fields (empty-env)))))))
```

Exercise 5.3 [⋆] Rewrite `find-method-and-apply` and `apply-method` so that the host name is not passed as an argument to `apply-method`.

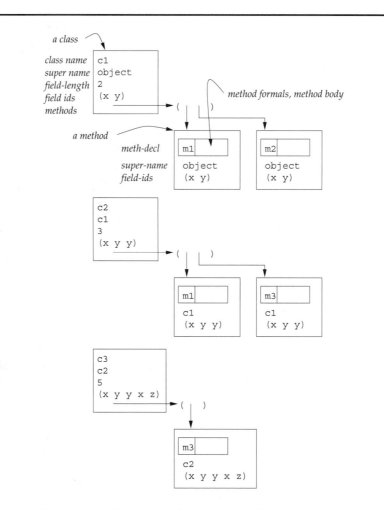

Figure 5.13   Class and method structures for sample program

Last, we change `new-object` to get the required information from the class, rather than calling `roll-up-field-length`:

```
(define new-object
  (lambda (class-name)
    (an-object
      class-name
      (make-vector (class-name->field-length class-name)))))
```

5.4.4 Flat Method Environments

In this section we modify the representation of classes so that each class contains not just the methods declared in the class, but also those methods of its ancestors that may be invoked on objects of the class. Thus, in the definition of a class

```
(define-datatype class class?
  (a-class
    (class-name symbol?)
    (super-name symbol?)
    (field-length integer?)
    (field-ids (list-of symbol?))
    (methods method-environment?)))
```

the method environment will include *all* the methods that are reachable for objects of this class, not merely the ones that are declared in this class. This is analogous to the transformation in section 5.4.2 that replaced a list of field vectors by a single vector. This representation makes method searching faster, and is used in chapter 6.

If the class structures contain information about all the reachable methods, then we no longer need a loop in `find-method-and-apply`:

```
(define find-method-and-apply
  (lambda (m-name host-name self args)
    (let ((method (lookup-method m-name
                    (class-name->methods host-name))))
      (if (method? method)
        (apply-method method host-name self args)
        (eopl:error 'find-method-and-apply
          "No method for name ~s" m-name)))))
```

To accomplish this, we must alter `roll-up-method-decls`, which is responsible for filling the method-environment slot in each class structure:

```
(define roll-up-method-decls
  (lambda (c-decl super-name field-ids)
    (merge-methods
      (class-name->methods super-name)
      (map
        (lambda (m-decl)
          (a-method m-decl super-name field-ids))
        (class-decl->method-decls c-decl)))))
```

The procedure `roll-up-method-decls` combines the methods of the superclass with those declared in the current class, using the auxiliary procedure `merge-methods`.

```
(define merge-methods
  (lambda (super-methods methods)
    (cond
      ((null? super-methods) methods)
      (else
        (let ((overriding-method
                (lookup-method
                  (method->method-name (car super-methods))
                  methods)))
          (if overriding-method
            (cons overriding-method
              (merge-methods (cdr super-methods)
                (remove-method overriding-method methods)))
            (cons (car super-methods)
              (merge-methods (cdr super-methods)
                methods)))))))))
```

It is the job of `merge-methods` to determine the order in which the methods are listed in the class. We adopt a strategy similar to that used in section 5.4.2: methods are placed in their order of declaration, from oldest to youngest. If a method of a superclass class is overridden, however, the newer method is installed in place of the superclass's method. Hence in each class there is at most one method for each method name. This strategy yields the representation shown in figure 5.14. Here the representation for class `c1` is as before. For class `c2`, method `m3` is added at the end, but the new version of `m1` appears in the first position. For `c3`, the methods `m1` and `m2` are as they were in `c2`, but `m3` is replaced by the new definition. Of course, the methods are shared, not copied, but the diagram shows them as if they were copied for readability.

Exercise 5.4 [★★] Redraw figure 5.14 to show the sharing of methods. Which of the `field-ids` lists are shared?

As with the field layouts of section 5.4.2, this strategy has the property that in any subclass of `c3`, the methods `m1`, `m2`, and `m3` will always appear in the first three positions of the method environment. This property will be crucial for the optimizations to be considered in chapter 6.

The arguments to `merge-methods` are the methods of the superclass and the current methods. There are three cases to consider. The first case is the

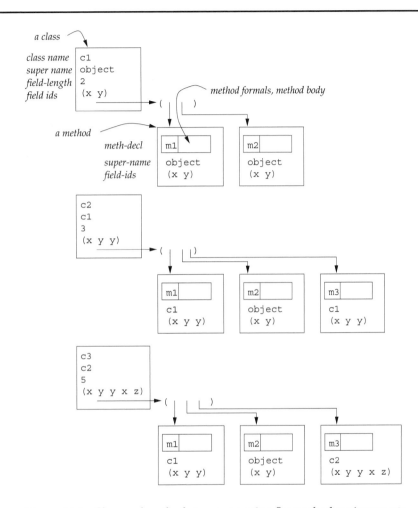

Figure 5.14   Class and method structures using flat method environments

simplest. If there are no super methods, then we simply return the remaining current methods. Next we determine if a super method is being overridden. In that case, we replace the overridden method by the overriding one. As part of the recursion, we remove the overriding one from the current list of methods to be merged in. As a result of this organization, we know that the super method of a particular method is guaranteed to be in the same position thoughout the inheritance chain. If it is not being overridden, we simply add it to the list. So, these methods are in the same position as the ones in the super methods. The effect is to append the non-overriding methods to the tail end of the super methods, and to replace those super methods that are being overridden.

We have revised `elaborate-class-decls!` and `find-method-and-apply`; `new-object` and `object->class` are unchanged, so this completes our fourth and final implementation.

5.4.5   Exercises

This section contains a variety of exercises based on the language and interpreters of this chapter. Most can be done with any of the interpreters.

Exercise 5.5 [⋆⋆] Complete each of these implementations of the language.

Exercise 5.6 [⋆] Test the implementation from the previous exercise by running the test program in figure 5.15. It should result in a list with the following attributes: 15 appears twice, 35 appears 5 times, 50 appears once, 100 appears twice, 200 appears twice, 300 appears once, and there are 6 sets of parentheses.

Exercise 5.7 [⋆] The interpreter of section 5.4.1 stores the superclass name of a method's host class in the lexical environment. It could instead store the host class name. Then it could retrieve the superclass name from the host class name. Make this change to each of the four implementations.

Exercise 5.8 [⋆] Implement the following using the language of this section:

1. The queue abstraction of figure 2.5.
2. Extend the queue class with a counter that counts the number of operations that have been performed on the current queue.
3. Extend the queue class with a counter that counts the total number of operations that have been performed on all the queues in the class. (Hint: pass a shared counter object at initialization time.)

Exercise 5.9 [⋆⋆⋆] Implement lexical addressing for this language. First, write a lexical-address calculator like that of exercise 1.31 for the language of this section. It should produce abstract syntax trees. Then modify the implementation of environments so that the field identifiers are not kept in the ribs, and modify `eval-expression` so that `apply-env` takes a lexical address instead of a symbol, as in exercise 3.25. Of course, the lexical addresses calculated for the layered representation of objects (section 5.4.1) will be different from those generated for the flat object representation used in the other implementations.

Exercise 5.10 [⋆⋆⋆] Can anything equivalent to the optimizations of the preceding exercise be done for method invocations? Discuss why or why not.

```
class a extends object
  field i
  field j
  method initialize () 1
  method setup ()
    begin
      set i = 15;
      set j = 20;
      50
    end
  method f () send self g()
  method g () +(i,j)
class b extends a
  field j
  field k
  method setup ()
    begin
      set j = 100;
      set k = 200;
      super setup();
      send self h()
    end
  method g () list(i,j,k)
  method h () super g()
class c extends b
  method g () super h()
  method h () +(k,j)
let p = proc (o)
          let u = send o setup()
          in list(u,send o g(), send o f())
in list((p new a()),(p new b()),(p new c()))
```

Figure 5.15   Test program for exercise 5.6

Exercise 5.11 [⋆] Add to our language the expression instanceof (*exp*, *class-name*).
It is true if and only if the object obtained by evaluating *exp* is an instance of *class-name*
or of one of its subclasses. In our framework, why must this be an expression rather
than a primitive?

Exercise 5.12 [⋆] In our language, the environment for a method includes bindings
for the field variables declared in the host class *and* its superclasses. Limit them to
just the host class.

Exercise 5.13 [★★] Object-oriented languages frequently allow *overloading* of methods. This feature allows a class to have multiple methods of the same name, provided they have distinct *signatures*. A method's signature is typically the method name plus the types of its parameters. Since we do not have types in our current language, we might overload based simply on the method name and number of parameters. For example, a class might have two `initialize` methods, one with no parameters for use when initialization with a default field value is desired, and another with one parameter for use when a particular field value is desired. Extend our interpreter to allow overloading based on the number of method parameters.

Exercise 5.14 [★★] Add to our language a new expression,

$$\texttt{fieldref}\ \ obj\ \ field\text{-}id$$

that retrieves the contents of the given field of the object. Add also

$$\texttt{fieldset}\ \ obj\ \ field\text{-}id\ \ exp$$

which sets the given field to the value of *exp*.

Exercise 5.15 [★★] Many object-oriented languages divide an object's fields into private fields, which are only accessible lexically from within the class declaration, and public fields, which are accessible from anywhere. Add this language feature to the language of the previous exercise. Hint: use the ideas in exercise 5.7.

Exercise 5.16 [★] Extend the results of exercise 5.14 to include super field references and super field assignments.

Exercise 5.17 [★★] Extend the syntax of our language so that each method declaration requires one of the modifiers `public`, `protected`, or `private`. A public method may be called from anywhere. A protected method may be called only from the class in which it is declared or one of its subclasses. A private method may be called only from its host class.

Exercise 5.18 [★] In sections 5.4.3 and 5.4.4, redefine `method-environment?` to be `(vector-of method?)`. What other procedures must be altered to accomodate this change?

Exercise 5.19 [★★] In section 5.4.4, could we have defined `merge-methods` to be something very simple, like `append`? What would be lost in doing so?

Exercise 5.20 [★] In our interpreters, the class `object` is a special case because it is not explicitly represented in the class environment. What procedures must be aware of this special case? Eliminate these special cases by placing a class whose name is `object` into the initial class environment. Give the class `object` an `initialize` method, so that it is possible to create an object of class `object`, and so that there is a default `initialize` method.

Exercise 5.21 [★★] In the languages of chapter 3, the process of creating procedures was separate from the process of binding a procedure to a name, so a closure did not contain its name, even in a `letrec`. Modify the representations used in this section so that the representation of a class or method no longer contains its name, and modify class and method environments to resemble more closely the environments that were used in chapter 3. Then modify the representation of objects so that they contain a class rather than a class name.

Exercise 5.22 [★★★] Design and implement an object-oriented language without explicit classes, using the observation that in the representation of the preceding exercise, each object contains its own methods and fields. Therefore we can replace each class by an object with the correct set of methods and fields. Such an object is called a *prototype*. Replace the class object by a prototype object with no methods or fields. Extend a class by adding methods and fields to its prototype, yielding a new prototype. Thus we might write let c2 = extend c1 ... instead of class c2 extends c1 .... Replace the new operation with an operation clone that takes an object and simply copies its methods and fields. Methods in this language occur inside a lexical scope, so they should have access to lexically visible variables, as usual, as well as field variables. What shadowing relation should hold when a field variable of a superprototype has the same name as a variable in a containing lexical scope?

Exercise 5.23 [★★] Many object-oriented languages include a provision for *static* or *class* variables. Static variables associate some state with a class; all the instances of the class share this state. For example, one might write:

```
class c1
  static next_serial_number = 1
  field my_serial_number
  method get_serial_number () my_serial_number
  method initialize ()
    begin
      set my_serial_number = next_serial_number;
      set next_serial_number = add1(next_serial_number)
    end
let o1 = new c1()
    o2 = new c1()
in list(send o1 get_serial_number(),
        send o2 get_serial_number())
```

Each new object of class c1 receives a new consecutive serial number.

Add static variables to our language. Since static variables can appear in a method body, apply-method must add an additional rib in the environment it constructs. What environment should be used for the evaluation of the initializing expression for a static variable (1 in the example above)?

Exercise 5.24 [★★★] Modify the representation of environments so that self is always easily accessible, even from an interior scope of the method body. (One way of doing this is to make self an additional argument to the interpreter.) Then extend the lexical-address translator of exercise 5.9 so that variables that are bound to fields are accessed as vector references from self, rather than being handled as a separate rib. The result should be an interpreter in which any field variable is accessible in constant time.

Exercise 5.25 [★★] In exercise 5.13, we added overloading to the language by extending the interpreter. Another way to support overloading is not to modify the interpreter, but to use a syntactic preprocessor. Write a preprocessor that changes the name of every method *m* to one of the form *m*:@*n*, where *n* is the number of parameters in the method declaration. It must similarly change the name in every method call, based on the number of operands. We assume that :@ is not used by programmers in method names, but is accepted by the interpreter in method names. Compilers frequently use such a technique to implement method overloading. This is an instance of a general trick called *name mangling*.

Exercise 5.26 [★★★] Using the first example of inheritance from figure 5.5, we include a method in the class point that determines if two points have the same x and y coordinates. We add the method similarpoints to the point class as follows:

```
method similarpoints (pt)
  if equal?(send pt getx(),x)
  then equal?(send pt gety(),y)
  else 0
```

This works for both kinds of points. Since getx, gety, and similarpoints are defined in class point, by inheritance, they are defined in colorpoint. Test similarpoints to compare points with points, points with color points, color points with points, and color points with color points.

Next consider a small extension. We add a new similarpoints method to the colorpoint class. We expect it to return true if both points are collocated, and further, in case both are color points, they have the same color. Otherwise it returns false. Here is an incorrect solution.

```
method similarpoints (pt)
  if super similarpoints(pt)
  then equal?(send pt getcolor(),color)
  else 0
```

Test this extension. Determine why it does not work on all the cases. Fix it so that all the tests return the correct values.

The difficulty of writing a procedure that relies on more than one object is known as the *binary method problem*. It demonstrates that the class-centric model of object-oriented programming, which this chapter explores, leaves something to be desired when there are multiple objects. It is called the *binary* method problem because the problem shows up with just two objects, but it gets progressively worse as the number of objects increases.

Exercise 5.27 [★★★] We have treated super calls as if they were lexically bound. But we can do better: we can determine super calls *statically*. Since a super call refers to a method in a class's parent, and the parent, along with its methods, is known prior to the start of execution, we can determine the exact method to which any super call refers at the same time we do lexical-addressing and other analyses. Write a translator that takes each super call and replaces it with an abstract syntax tree node containing the actual method to be invoked.

Exercise 5.28 [★ ★ ★] Dynamic method dispatch implies that at any method application site, the class of the object to which the message is sent may vary from one call to the next. Though this flexibility is vital, in practice for many call sites the class of the target object does not change, or changes only occasionally. We may take advantage of this behavior by caching at the call site the class of the last object of that call and the position at which the method was found for that call. With each new call the class of the call's object is compared with the class of the last call. If they are the same (a *cache hit*) the method position is known without doing a new method table lookup. This technique is called *method caching*. Implement caching in our interpreter.

Exercise 5.29 [★ ★] Some object-oriented languages include facilities for named-class method invocation and field references. In a named-class method invocation, one might write named-send c1 o m1(). This would invoke c1's m1 method on o, so long as o was an instance of c1 or of one of its subclasses, even if m1 were overridden in o's actual class. Thus this is a form of static method dispatch. Named-class field reference provides a similar facility for field reference. Add named-class method invocation, field reference, and field setting to the language of this section. How do these facilities fit in with the idea of classes as abstractions?

Exercise 5.30 [★ ★ ★] Write a translator that replaces method names in named method calls as in exercise 5.29 with numbers indicating the offset of the named method in the run-time method vector of the named class. Implement an interpreter for the translated code in which named method access is constant time.

Exercise 5.31 [★ ★ ★] Multiple inheritance, in which a class can have more than one parent, can be useful, but may introduce serious complications. What if two inherited classes both have methods of the same name? This can be disallowed, or resolved by enumerating the methods in the class by some arbitrary rule, such as depth-first left-to-right, or by requiring that the ambiguity be resolved at the point such a method is called. The situation for fields is even worse. Consider the following situation, in which class c4 is to inherit from c2 and c3, both of which inherit from c1:

```
class c1 extends object
   field x
class c2 extends c1
class c3 extends c1
class c4 extends c2, c3
```

Does an instance of c4 have one instance of field x shared by c2 and c3, or does c4 have two x fields: one inherited from c2 and one inherited from c3? Some languages opt for sharing, some not, and some provide a choice, at least in some cases. The complexity of this problem has led to a design trend favoring single inheritance of classes, but multiple inheritance only for interfaces, which avoids most of these difficulties.

Add multiple inheritance to the language. Extend the syntax as necessary. Indicate clearly what issues arise when resolving method and field name conflicts. Characterize the sharing issue and its resolution.

Exercise 5.32 [★ ★ ★] Invent, or discover through reading, a technique for simulating multiple inheritance given single inheritance. Demonstrate the technique by writing and testing a sample program that uses this simulation technique.

Further Reading

Simula 67 (Birtwistle, Dahl, Myhrhaug, & Nygaard, 1979) is generally regarded as the first object-oriented language. The object-oriented metaphor was extended by Smalltalk in (Goldberg & Robson, 1983) and by Actors in (Hewitt, 1977). Both use human interaction and sending and receiving messages as the metaphor for explaining their ideas. Scheme grew out of Sussman and Steele's attempts to understand Hewitt's work. (Springer & Friedman, 1989) and (Abelson, Sussman, & Sussman, 1985; 1996) both provide further examples of object-oriented programming in Scheme and discuss when functional and imperative programming styles are most appropriate. (Steele, 1990) and (Kiczales, des Rivières, & Bobrow, 1991) describe CLOS, the powerful object-oriented programming facility of Common Lisp. The derivation at the end of the chapter is based on the implementation of C++ method tables in (Ellis & Stroustrup, 1992).

6 *Objects and Types*

In chapter 4, we showed how a type system could inspect a program to guarantee that it would never execute an inappropriate operation. No program that passes the checker will ever attempt to apply a non-procedure to an argument, or to apply a procedure or primitive to the wrong number of arguments or to an argument of the wrong type.

In this chapter, we apply this technology to an object-oriented language. In addition to the safety properties listed above, no program that passes our checker will ever send a message to an object for which there is no corresponding concrete method, or send a message to an object with the wrong number of arguments or with arguments of the wrong type.

In addition to guaranteeing these safety properties, our type analyzer produces information that can be used to optimize programs in our language.

In section 6.1 we present this language and discuss its syntax and semantics. In section 6.2 we present a checker that guarantees these safety properties. Last, in section 6.3, we show how the type information can be used to produce significant optimizations in the execution of our programs.

6.1   A Simple Typed Object-Oriented Language

A sample program in our typed object-oriented language is shown in figure 6.1. This program defines a class `tree`, which has a `sum` method that finds the sum of the values in the leaves, as in figure 5.2, and an `equal` method, which takes another tree and recursively descends through the trees to determine if they are equal. We consider the latter method in more detail below.

The major new features of the language are:

- Fields and methods are specified with their types, using a syntax similar to that used in chapter 4.

- The concept of *abstract* classes and methods is introduced.

- The concept of *casting* is introduced, and the `instanceof` test from exercise 5.11 is incorporated into the language.

- The concept of *subtype polymorphism* is added to the language.

We consider each of these items in turn.

The new productions for the language are shown in figure 6.2. We add a `void` type as the type of a `set` operation, and list types as in exercise 4.8. As in section 4.3, we add identifiers to the set of type expressions, but for this chapter, an identifier used as a type is associated with the class of the same name. We consider this correspondence in more detail below. Classes take an optional abstraction specifier. Methods require their result type to be specified, along with the types of their arguments, using a syntax similar to that used in chapter 4. A new kind of method, called an *abstract* method, is added. An abstract method does not have a body. Last, two new expressions are added, `cast` and `instanceof`.

An abstract class is one which is not intended to be instantiated. For example, in figure 6.1, the intention is that every tree is either an interior node or a leaf node; there are never any objects of class `tree`. This restriction can be enforced by a run-time check whenever a new object is created. A class that is not abstract is said to be *concrete* (or *instantiable*).

An abstract method is a placeholder for methods to be supplied by each subclass of a class. For example, in figure 6.1, we need to be sure that every object of class `tree` has a `sum` method. Therefore we include an abstract `sum` method in class `tree`. In our interpreter, an abstract method is just another kind of method, and `apply-method` will signal an error if an abstract method is applied. The checker, however, will verify that every concrete subclass of `tree` supplies a concrete `sum` method, so that no well-typed program will ever attempt to apply an abstract method.

The next feature we add to the language is `instanceof`. The expression `instanceof` *exp name* returns a true value whenever the object obtained by evaluating *exp* is an instance of *name* or of one of its descendants. Casting complements `instanceof`. For example, our sample program includes the method

```
abstract class tree extends object
  method int initialize () 1
  abstractmethod int sum ()
  abstractmethod bool equal (tree t)

class interior_node extends tree
  field tree left
  field tree right
  method void initialize (tree l, tree r)
    begin
      set left = l;
      set right = r
    end
  method tree getleft () left
  method tree getright () right
  method int sum () +(send left sum(),send right sum())
  method bool equal (tree t)
    if instanceof t interior_node
    then if send left
            equal(send cast t interior_node getleft())
         then send right
              equal(send cast t interior_node getright())
         else false
    else false

class leaf_node extends tree
  field int value
  method void initialize (int v) set value = v
  method int sum () value
  method int getvalue () value
  method bool equal (tree t)
    if instanceof t leaf_node
    then zero?(-(value,send cast t leaf_node getvalue()))
    else false

let o1 = new interior_node(
           new interior_node(
             new leaf_node(3),
             new leaf_node(4)),
           new leaf_node(5))
in list(send o1 sum(),
        if send o1 equal(o1) then 100 else 200)
```

Figure 6.1   A sample program in the typed object-oriented language

⟨type-exp⟩   ::= void
```
void-type-exp ()
```

⟨type-exp⟩   ::= list ⟨type-exp⟩
```
list-type-exp (texp)
```

⟨type-exp⟩   ::= ⟨identifier⟩
```
class-type-exp (class-name)
```

⟨class-decl⟩   ::= ⟨abstraction-specifier⟩ class ⟨identifier⟩
                          extends ⟨identifier⟩
                          {field ⟨type-exp⟩ ⟨identifier⟩}*
                          {⟨method-decl⟩}*
```
a-class-decl
  (specifier class-name super-name
   local-field-texps local-field-ids
   method-decls)
```

⟨abstraction-specifier⟩ ::=
```
concrete-specifier ()
```

⟨abstraction-specifier⟩ ::= abstract
```
abstract-specifier ()
```

⟨method-decl⟩   ::= method ⟨type-exp⟩ ⟨identifier⟩
                          ({⟨type-exp⟩ ⟨identifier⟩}*⁽ʼ⁾) ⟨expression⟩
```
a-method-decl
  (type-exp name
   id-texps ids body)
```

⟨method-decl⟩   ::= abstractmethod ⟨type-exp⟩ ⟨identifier⟩
                          ({⟨type-exp⟩ ⟨identifier⟩}*⁽ʼ⁾)
```
an-abstract-method-decl
  (type-exp name
   id-texps ids)
```

⟨expression⟩   ::= cast ⟨expression⟩ ⟨identifier⟩
```
cast-exp (obj-exp name)
```

⟨expression⟩   ::= instanceof ⟨expression⟩ ⟨identifier⟩
```
instanceof-exp (obj-exp name)
```

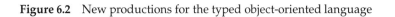

Figure 6.2   New productions for the typed object-oriented language

```
method bool equal(tree t)
  if instanceof t interior_node
  then if send left
          equal(send cast t interior_node getleft())
        then send right
            equal(send cast t interior_node getright())
        else false
    else false
```

The expression `cast t interior_node` checks to see if the value of `t` is in
fact an instance of `interior_node`. If it is, the value of `t` is returned; if not,
an error is signalled. An `instanceof` expression returns a true value if and
only if the corresponding `cast` would succeed. Hence in this example the
cast is guaranteed to succeed, since it is guarded by the `instanceof`. The
cast, in turn, guards the use of `send ... getleft()`. The cast expression is
guaranteed to return a value of class `interior_node`, and therefore it will be
safe to send this value a `getleft` message.

Exercise 6.1 [⋆⋆] Write an equality predicate for the class `tree` that does not use
`instanceof` or `cast`. Hint: what is needed here is a *double dispatch*, in place of the
single dispatch provided by the usual methods. This can be simulated as follows:
Instead of asking the class of the argument `t`, the current tree should send back to `t`
a message that encodes its own class, along with parameters containing the values of
the appropriate fields.

The last new concept in the language is *subtype polymorphism*. This refers to
the idea that an object of a certain class can also be regarded as a value of any
of its ancestor classes. This idea is used, for example, in `instanceof`. We see
it in our example: `interior_node` requires two arguments of type `tree`, but
there are no objects of class `tree`. There are only objects of subclasses of `tree`.
Subtype polymorphism means that a procedure or method that expects an
argument of a certain class can also take an argument of any subclass of that
class. This comes for free in the interpreter, but it requires some modifications
to the checker, which we discuss in section 6.2.

For our implementation, we begin with the interpreter of section 5.4.4.
Since most of the interpreter's activity is independent of types, we modify it
as little as possible, and adopt a laissez-faire strategy whenever we can. Since
it is impossible to apply an abstract method, we modify `method-decl->body`
to raise an error when the program attempts to do so. See figure 6.3.

Finally, we add two new clauses to `eval-expression` to evaluate
`instanceof` and `cast` expressions:

```
(define apply-method
  (lambda (method host-name self args)
    (let ((ids (method->ids method))
          (body (method->body method))
          (super-name (method->super-name method))
          (field-ids (method->field-ids method))
          (fields (object->fields self)))
      (eval-expression body
        (extend-env
          (cons '%super (cons 'self ids))
          (cons super-name (cons self args))
          (extend-env-refs field-ids fields (empty-env)))))))))

(define method->body
  (lambda (method)
    (method-decl->body (method->method-decl method))))

(define method-decl->body
  (lambda (md)
    (cases method-decl md
      (a-method-decl (result-texp name arg-type-exps ids
                       method-body)
        method-body)
      (an-abstract-method-decl (result-texp name
                                  arg-type-exps ids)
        (eopl:error 'method-decl->body
          "Can't take body of abstract method")))))
```

Figure 6.3   apply-method in the presence of abstract methods

```
(cast-exp (exp name)
  (let ((obj (eval-expression exp env)))
    (if (is-subclass? (object->class-name obj) name)
      obj
      (eopl:error 'eval-expression
        "Can't cast object to type ~s:~%~s"))))

(instanceof-exp (exp name)
  (let ((obj (eval-expression exp env)))
    (if (is-subclass? (object->class-name obj) name)
      the-true-value
      the-false-value)))
```

The procedure `is-subclass?` traces the parent link of the first class structure until it either finds the second one or stops at `object`:

```
(define is-subclass?
  (lambda (name1 name2)
    (if (eqv? name1 name2)
        #t
        (let ((class (lookup-class name1)))
          (let ((super-name (class->super-name class)))
            (if (eqv? super-name 'object)
                #f
                (is-subclass? super-name name2)))))))
```

This completes the modification of the interpreter for the language of this section.

Exercise 6.2 [⋆ ⋆] Complete the implementation of this interpreter, and test it on a substantial body of programs.

Exercise 6.3 [⋆] Devise a test plan for this interpreter so that every clause is exercised.

Exercise 6.4 [⋆] Augment the interpreter so that it detects any attempt to create an object of an abstract class.

6.2   The Type Checker

We now turn to the checker for this language. The goal of the checker is to guarantee a set of safety properties. For our language, these properties are those of the underlying procedural language, plus the following properties of the object-oriented portion of the language: no program that passes our type checker will ever

- send a message to an object for which there is no corresponding method,

- send a message to an object with the wrong number of arguments or with arguments of the wrong type, or

- attempt to create an object of an abstract class, or an object of a concrete class in which one of the required abstract methods of a superclass has not been supplied.

Since the fields of an object are created uninitialized, and we make no attempt to verify that the `initialize` methods actually initialize all the fields, it will still be possible for a program to reference an uninitialized field.

Hence our safety properties do not preclude attempting to operate on an uninitialized value. Similarly, because it is in general impossible to predict the type of an `initialize` method, our checker will not prevent the explicit invocation of an `initialize` method with the wrong number of arguments or arguments of the wrong type, but the implicit invocation of `initialize` by `new` will always be correct. We discuss these issues in more detail below.

In chapter 4, we emphasized a rule-based derivation of types: for each kind of expression, we wrote down a rule that showed how to derive the type of the entire expression from the types of its subexpressions. In more complex situations, however, it may not be entirely clear what the rule should be for a given expression. In that case, we need some principles to help us decide on the rule the checker should use.

The goal of the checker is to predict successfully the type of each expression, given the types of its free variables. As a result, the procedure `type-of-expression` bore a considerable resemblance to `eval-expression`: instead of evaluating each expression in an environment containing the values of the variables, `type-of-expression` processed each expression in a type environment containing the types of the variables. The analogy between ordinary computation and such a partial computation, getting partial information about the answers from partial information about the inputs, is called the principle of *abstract interpretation*.

We develop our checker using the principle of abstract interpretation. At every stage we proceed as if we were writing an interpreter, except that we have only the types of the variables available to us. We reuse as much as possible of the code and data structures of the original interpreter, except that we have only the type information available.

We begin with the types. In chapter 4, it was a fairly simple matter to determine when a value was of the right type: an integer value was of type `int`, a boolean value was of type `bool`, and a procedure value was of type `(t1 * ... * tn -> t)` if and only if whenever it was given arguments of types `t1, ..., tn` it would produce a value of type `t`.

In the object-oriented paradigm, the situation is more complicated because we have two competing notions: type and class. Every object has a class. At first glance, the class of an object appears to be like a type in a dynamic type system: it is a tag that identifies the set to which the object belongs. This notion, however, is not enough. In an object-oriented system, if class $c2$ extends $c1$, then an object of class $c2$ can be used in any context in which an object of class $c1$ can appear: the $c2$ object has all the methods of the $c1$ object, so it can accept any message that the $c1$ object could accept. For example, in the program of figure 6.1, the `equal` method must accept both interior nodes and leaves, that is, it must accept any object whose class is a subclass of `tree`. This is *subclass polymorphism*.

Hence we adopt the following policy: we introduce a type *c* for each class *c*, and we say that an object is a value of *type c* whenever its class is either *c* or a class that is a subclass of *c*. Using this terminology, we can say that `instanceof` *x c* tests whether the value of *x* has type *c*, not whether it has class *c*.

To implement this policy, we add to the types of section 4.2 a new type for each class. For convenience in testing, we also include list types, as in exercise 4.8.

```
(define-datatype type type?
  (atomic-type
    (name symbol?))
  (list-type
    (value-type type?))
  (class-type
    (name symbol?))
  (proc-type
    (arg-types (list-of type?))
    (result-type type?)))
```

We interpret an identifier in a type position as describing a class; this is done by adding the production

$$\langle \text{type-exp} \rangle ::= \langle \text{identifier} \rangle$$

```
class-type-exp (class-name)
```

in figure 6.2, and modifying `expand-type-exp` to map a `class-type-exp` to a `class-type` (figure 6.4).

The checker begins with the implementation of `type-of-program`. By the principle of abstract interpretation, `type-of-program` should be as similar as possible to `eval-program`. Where the interpreter has an environment `env` mapping identifiers to values, the checker will have a type environment `tenv` mapping identifiers to types. Where the interpreter has a class environment mapping class names to class structures, the checker will have a static class environment mapping class names to static classes, which will contain the static information about each class. Compare `type-of-program` to `eval-program`:

```
(define expand-type-expression
  (lambda (texp)
    (cases type-exp texp
      (int-type-exp () int-type)
      (bool-type-exp () bool-type)
      (void-type-exp () void-type)
      (list-type-exp (texp)
        (list-type (expand-type-expression texp)))
      (class-type-exp (name) (class-type name))
      (proc-type-exp (arg-texps result-texp)
        (proc-type
          (expand-type-expressions arg-texps)
          (expand-type-expression  result-texp)))))))
```

Figure 6.4   `expand-type-expression`

```
(define eval-program
  (lambda (pgm)
    (cases program pgm
      (a-program (c-decls exp)
        (elaborate-class-decls! c-decls)
        (eval-expression exp (init-env))))))

(define type-of-program
  (lambda (pgm)
    (cases program pgm
      (a-program (c-decls exp)
        (statically-elaborate-class-decls! c-decls)
        (type-of-expression exp (empty-tenv))))))
```

The procedure `statically-elaborate-class-decls!`, which checks all of the class declarations and sets up the static class environment that will be used by the rest of the checker, is invoked by `type-of-program`. Then `type-of-expression` finds the type of the program body.

Next we consider what will be in the static class environment. The ordinary class environment maps each class name to a class containing its fields, methods, and the name of its parent. Hence the static class environment should map each class name to a static class containing the types of its fields, the types of its methods, and its parent. As before, each class contains all of the fields and methods accessible from that class, not just the ones declared in the class. We also keep track of whether the class is concrete or abstract.

For each method, we construct a static method, consisting of its static information, including its name, whether or not it is abstract, its type (as a `proc-type`), and the name of its superclass.

```
(define-datatype static-class static-class?
  (a-static-class
    (class-name symbol?)
    (super-name symbol?)
    (specifier abstraction-specifier?)
    (field-ids (list-of symbol?))
    (field-types (list-of type?))
    (methods static-method-environment?)))

(define-datatype static-method-struct static-method-struct?
  (a-static-method-struct
    (method-name symbol?)
    (specifier abstraction-specifier?)
    (type type?)
    (super-name symbol?)))

(define static-method-environment?
  (list-of static-method-struct?))
```

We build the static class environment by initializing it to an empty environment, and then processing each class and adding it in turn.

```
(define statically-elaborate-class-decls!
  (lambda (c-decls)
    (initialize-static-class-env!)
    (for-each statically-elaborate-class-decl! c-decls)))
```

The procedure `statically-elaborate-class-decl!` processes a class declaration. First it finds the names and types of all the fields of this class, consulting the superclass if needed. It uses `statically-lookup-class` to look up the superclass in the static class environment, since the ordinary class environment does not exist. It then collects all the method declarations, using the procedure `statically-roll-up-method-decls` to model the overriding of methods, and adds the static class information to the static class environment. Then it verifies, using `check-for-abstract-methods!`, that if the current class is concrete, then all its methods are concrete. Finally, it checks each of the methods. See figure 6.5.

Exercise 6.5 [★★] Why must the class information be added to the static class environment before the methods are checked? (Hint: what happens if a method body invokes a method on `self`?)

```
(define statically-elaborate-class-decl!
  (lambda (c-decl)
    (cases class-decl c-decl
      (a-class-decl (specifier class-name super-name
                    field-texps field-ids m-decls)
        (let ((field-ids
                (append
                  (if (eqv? super-name 'object)
                    '()
                    (static-class->field-ids
                      (statically-lookup-class super-name)))
                  field-ids))
              (field-types
                (append
                  (if (eqv? super-name 'object)
                    '()
                    (static-class->field-types
                      (statically-lookup-class super-name)))
                  (expand-type-expressions field-texps)))
              (methods
                (statically-roll-up-method-decls
                  m-decls
                  specifier
                  class-name
                  super-name)))
          (add-to-static-class-env!
            (a-static-class
              class-name
              super-name
              specifier
              field-ids
              field-types
              methods))
          (check-for-abstract-methods!
            specifier methods class-name)
          (for-each
            (lambda (m-decl)
              (typecheck-method-decl! m-decl
                class-name super-name field-ids field-types))
            m-decls))))))
```

Figure 6.5 `statically-elaborate-class-decl!`

```
(define statically-roll-up-method-decls
  (lambda (m-decls specifier self-name super-name)
    (statically-merge-methods self-name
      (if (eqv? super-name 'object)
        '()
        (static-class->methods
          (statically-lookup-class super-name)))
      (map
        (lambda (m-decl)
          (method-decl-to-static-method-struct
            m-decl specifier self-name super-name))
        m-decls)))))
```

Figure 6.6 `statically-roll-up-method-decls`

Exercise 6.6 [⋆] Write `check-for-abstract-methods!`.

We next consider `statically-roll-up-method-decls`, shown in figure 6.6. It is the static version of `roll-up-method-decls` (section 5.4.4). It produces a list of static methods by calling `statically-merge-methods` on the class name, the list of static methods from the superclass, and a static method for each method declared in the current class. The procedure `method-decl-to-static-method-struct` expands the type expressions and rearranges the data to produce a static method from a method declaration. See figure 6.7.

The procedure `statically-merge-methods` (figure 6.8) produces a list of static methods, taking inheritance into account, in the same order in which `merge-methods` creates the list of methods at run time. Methods are placed in their order of declaration, from oldest to youngest. However, if a method of an ancestor class is overridden, the newer method is installed in place of the ancestor method. Hence in each class there is at most one method for each method name, as shown in figure 5.14.

The arguments to `statically-merge-methods` are the static structures for the methods of the superclass and the static structures for the methods of the host class. There are three cases to consider. The first case is the simplest. If there are no super methods, then we simply return the remaining current methods.

```
(define method-decl-to-static-method-struct
  (lambda (m-decl specifier self-name super-name)
    (cases method-decl m-decl
      (a-method-decl (result-texp name id-texps ids body)
        (a-static-method-struct
          name
          (concrete-specifier)
          (proc-type
            (expand-type-expressions id-texps)
            (expand-type-expression result-texp))
          super-name))
      (an-abstract-method-decl (result-texp name id-texps ids)
        (a-static-method-struct
          name
          (abstract-specifier)
          (proc-type
            (expand-type-expressions id-texps)
            (expand-type-expression result-texp))
          super-name)))))
```

Figure 6.7   `method-decl-to-static-method-struct`

Next we consider whether the first super method is being overridden. In
that case, we must check to see whether the type of the overriding method is
the same as that of the method being overridden. We must check this because
when we invoke a method of some object, say of type c, we know only that
the object will be either of c or of one of its subclasses. If the type of the
method were different in the subclass, we would have no way of guaranteeing that it was being called with correct arguments.

The one exception to this rule is the method `initialize`. The type of
`initialize` will generally change as we go from class to subclass, as in figure 6.1. Hence it is impossible to predict the type of an object's `initialize`
method given only the type of the object. So, our checker cannot prevent
an explicit invocation of an `initialize` method with incorrect arguments.
Since `initialize` is typically called only at object creation time, this is not a
serious flaw. If the overriding method has the same type as the overridden
one, or if we are dealing with `initialize` method, we replace the overridden method by the overriding one. As part of the recursion, we remove the
overriding one from the current list of methods to be merged in.

```
(define statically-merge-methods
  (lambda (class-name super-methods methods)
    (cond
      ((null? super-methods) methods)
      (else
        (let ((overriding-method
                (statically-lookup-method
                  (static-method->method-name
                    (car super-methods))
                  methods)))
          (if overriding-method
            (if (or
                  (eqv?
                    'initialize
                    (static-method->method-name
                      (car super-methods)))
                  (equal?
                    (static-method->type overriding-method)
                    (static-method->type
                      (car super-methods))))
              (cons overriding-method
                (statically-merge-methods
                  class-name
                  (cdr super-methods)
                  (remove-method overriding-method methods)))
              (eopl:error 'statically-merge-methods
                (string-append
                  "~%Overriding method ~s in class ~s of"
                  "wrong type~% original: ~s~%new:       ~s")
                (static-method->method-name overriding-method)
                class-name
                (static-method->type (car super-methods))
                (static-method->type overriding-method)))
            (cons (car super-methods)
              (statically-merge-methods
                class-name
                (cdr super-methods)
                methods)))))))))
```

Figure 6.8 `statically-merge-methods`

```
(define typecheck-method-decl!
  (lambda (m-decl specifier self-name super-name field-ids
              field-types)
    (cases method-decl m-decl
      (a-method-decl (result-texp name id-texps ids body)
        (let ((id-types (expand-type-expressions id-texps)))
          (let ((tenv
                  (extend-tenv
                    (cons '%super (cons 'self ids))
                    (cons (class-type super-name)
                      (cons (class-type self-name)
                        id-types))
                    (extend-tenv
                      field-ids field-types (empty-tenv)))))
            (let ((body-type (type-of-expression body tenv)))
              (check-is-subtype!
                body-type
                (expand-type-expression result-texp)
                m-decl)))))
      (an-abstract-method-decl (result-texp name id-texps ids)
        #t)))))
```

Figure 6.9 `typecheck-method-decl!`

Last, if the super method is not being overridden, we place it in the output and remove it from the list of super methods.

A consequence of this organization is that the super method of a particular method is guaranteed to be in the same position throughout the inheritance chain. The effect is to append the non-overriding methods to the end of the super methods, and replace those super methods that are being overridden.

Once all the static method information is collected, the static class information is added to the static class environment. Then each of the method declarations is checked, using `typecheck-method-decl!`. We build a type environment that matches the run-time environment built by `apply-method`, and then verify that the type of the body matches its declared type. For an abstract method, there is nothing to check. See figure 6.9.

By the principle of subtype polymorphism, the result of the body can be of any subtype of the specified result type. Hence in place of `check-equal-type!`, we call `check-is-subtype!`, which in turn calls `is-subtype?`, to compare the calculated and specified types of the body.

```
(define check-is-subtype!
  (lambda (t1 t2 exp)
    (if (is-subtype? t1 t2)
      #t
      (eopl:error 'check-is-subtype!
        "~%~s is not a subtype of ~s in ~%~s"
        (type-to-external-form t1)
        (type-to-external-form t2)
        exp))))
```

```
(define is-subtype?
  (lambda (t1 t2)
    (cases type t1
      (class-type (name1)
        (cases type t2
          (class-type (name2)
            (statically-is-subclass? name1 name2))
          (else #f)))
      (else (equal? t1 t2)))))
```

The static class environment built for the sample program of figure 6.1 is shown in figure 6.10. The static classes are in reverse order, reflecting the order in which the class environment is built. Each of the three classes has its methods in the same order, with the same type, as desired.

Once all the method declarations are checked, we check the body of the program, using `type-of-expression`.

Before adding any clauses to `type-of-expression`, we must modify this procedure to deal with subtype polymorphism. If class `c2` extends `c1`, then an object of class `c2` can be used in any context in which an object of class `c1` can appear. For example, in the program of figure 6.1, the `initialize` method of `interior_node` must accept as arguments both interior nodes and leaves. The same considerations apply to any procedure. If we wrote a procedure `proc (tree t) 1`, that procedure should be able to take as an actual parameter `new leaf(3)`, despite the fact that the procedure was of type `(tree -> int)` and the argument was of type `leaf`. The application should be legal whenever the type of each actual is a subtype of the corresponding formal parameter.

So we must modify `type-of-application` to allow this. Luckily, only one line need be changed:

```
((a-static-class leaf_node tree (concrete-specifier)
   (value) ((atomic-type int))
   ((a-static-method-struct
      initialize
      (concrete-specifier)
      (proc-type ((atomic-type int)) (atomic-type void))
      tree)
    (a-static-method-struct
      sum
      (concrete-specifier)
      (proc-type () (atomic-type int))
      tree)))
 (a-static-class interior_node tree (concrete-specifier)
   (left right) ((class-type tree) (class-type tree))
   ((a-static-method-struct
      initialize
      (concrete-specifier)
      (proc-type
        ((class-type tree) (class-type tree))
        (atomic-type void))
      tree)
    (a-static-method-struct
      sum
      (concrete-specifier)
      (proc-type () (atomic-type int))
      tree)))
 (a-static-class tree object (abstract-specifier)
   () ()
   ((a-static-method-struct
      initialize
      (concrete-specifier)
      (proc-type () (atomic-type int))
      object)
    (a-static-method-struct
      sum
      (abstract-specifier)
      (proc-type () (atomic-type int))
      object)))))
```

Figure 6.10 Static class environment built for the sample program

```
(define type-of-application
  (lambda (rator-type rand-types rator rands exp)
    (cases type rator-type
      (proc-type (arg-types result-type)
        (if (= (length arg-types) (length rand-types))
          (begin
            (for-each
              check-is-subtype!
              rand-types arg-types rands)
            result-type)
          (eopl:error 'type-of-expression
            (string-append
              "Wrong number of arguments in expression ~s:"
              " ~%expected ~s~%got ~s")
            exp
            (map type-to-external-form arg-types)
            (map type-to-external-form rand-types)))))
      (else
        (eopl:error 'type-of-expression
          "Rator not a proc type:~%~s~%had rator type ~s"
          rator (type-to-external-form rator-type)))))))
```

We may now proceed to include a new clause in type-of-expression for each additional kind of expression in our language. In each case, we find the type of each subexpression and pass this information to an auxiliary procedure; we also pass the original expression for error reporting. See figure 6.11.

We consider each expression (figure 6.12) in turn. For a new expression, we first retrieve the class information for the class name. If there is no class associated with the name, a type error is reported. We then check to see if the class is abstract. If it is, a type error is reported. Last, we call type-of-method-app-exp with the types of the operands to see if the call to initialize is safe. If these checks succeed, then the execution of the expression is safe. Since the new expression returns a new object of the specified class, the type of the result is the type corresponding to the specified class.

Method applications and super calls have much in common, so we deal with them together. For a method application, we verify that the expression denoting the target of the application is in fact an object by checking that its type is a class-type. If it is, we retrieve the class information associated with the class name. If either of these type checks fail, a type error is reported. For a super call, we need to find the parent of the class in which the current method was declared. This is bound in the type environment by typecheck-method-decl!, and is retrieved by looking up %super. We also pass a boolean value to indicate whether or not this was a super call.

```
(new-object-exp (class-name rands)
  (type-of-new-obj-exp
    class-name
    (types-of-expressions rands tenv)
    rands
    exp))
(method-app-exp (obj-exp msg rands)
  (type-of-method-app-exp
    (type-of-expression obj-exp tenv)
    msg
    (types-of-expressions rands tenv)
    rands
    exp))
(super-call-exp (msg rands)
  (type-of-super-call-exp
    (class-type->name (apply-tenv tenv '%super))
    msg
    (types-of-expressions rands tenv)
    rands
    exp))
(cast-exp (exp1 class-name)
  (type-of-cast-exp
    (type-of-expression exp1 tenv)
    class-name
    exp))
(instanceof-exp (exp1 class-name)
  (type-of-instanceof-exp
    (type-of-expression exp1 tenv)
    class-name
    exp))
```

Figure 6.11   `type-of-expression` clauses for object-oriented expressions

Once this information is collected, `type-of-method-app-or-super-call`, shown in figure 6.13, obtains the type of the method from the static class structure. If there is no method with the specified name in the class, then a "missing method" type error is reported. It then calls `type-of-application` to see whether these arguments are legal for the method. Last, it checks to see whether the call is a super call or not. If the call was a super call, then the method must be concrete. If the call was an ordinary call, then

```
(define type-of-new-obj-exp
  (lambda (class-name rand-types rands exp)
    (cases static-class (statically-lookup-class class-name)
      (a-static-class
        (class-name super-name specifier field-ids
          field-types methods)
        (cases abstraction-specifier specifier
          (abstract-specifier ()
            (eopl:error 'type-of-new-obj-exp
              "Can't instantiate abstract class ~s"
              class-name))
          (concrete-specifier ()
            (begin
              (type-of-method-app-exp
                (class-type class-name)
                'initialize
                rand-types
                rands
                exp)
              (class-type class-name))))))))

(define type-of-method-app-exp
  (lambda (obj-type msg rand-types rands exp)
    (cases type obj-type
      (class-type (class-name)
        (type-of-method-app-or-super-call
          #f class-name msg rand-types rands exp))
      (else
        (eopl:error 'type-of-method-app-exp
          "~%Can't send message to non-object ~s in ~%~s"
          obj-type exp)))))

(define type-of-super-call-exp
  (lambda (super-name msg rand-types rands exp)
    (type-of-method-app-or-super-call
      #t super-name msg rand-types rands exp)))
```

Figure 6.12   Checking the chapter 5 expressions

the method may be either concrete or abstract; when an actual object is supplied, we know the method will be concrete because of the check in `check-for-abstract-methods!`. To see this, consider the following example:

```
abstract class c1 extends object
  abstractmethod int m1 ()
class c2 extends c1
  method int m1 () 2
  method int m2 () super m1()
class c3 extends c1
  method int m1 () 3
let f = proc (c1 x) send x m1()
    o2 = new c2()
    o3 = new c3()
in list((f o2), (f o3), send o2 m2())
```

Here the `send x m1()` is legal, even though `m1` is abstract in `c1`, because `m1` will be concrete in both of `c1`'s concrete subclasses. But the `super m1()` will cause an error, because it specifies that `c1`'s method for `m1` should be used, and `c1` has no concrete method for `m1`.

An `instanceof` expression executes without an error so long as its argument is an object. So `type-of-instanceof-exp` returns `bool` so long as its argument is any object type and the class name is that of a class:

```
(define type-of-instanceof-exp
  (lambda (ty class-name exp)
    (cases type ty
      (class-type (name)
        (if (statically-is-subclass? class-name 'object)
          bool-type
          (eopl:error 'type-of-instanceof-exp
            "~%Unknown class ~s in ~%~s" name exp)))
      (else
        (eopl:error 'type-of-expression
          "~%~s not an object type in ~%~s" ty exp)))))
```

For a `cast` expression, the situation is a little more complicated. Some `cast` expressions may fail at run-time. In general, it is impossible to guarantee statically that a `cast` expression will succeed. Hence the best the checker can do is to reject any `cast` expression that will always fail. At run-time, every `cast` operation should be guarded by a corresponding `instanceof`.

The expression `cast x c1` will succeed if the class of x is either the class `c1` or one of `c1`'s subclasses. If the type of x is `c2`, then the potential values of

```
(define type-of-method-app-or-super-call
  (lambda (super-call? host-name msg rand-types rands exp)
    (let ((method
            (statically-lookup-method msg
              (static-class->methods
                (statically-lookup-class host-name)))))
      (if (static-method-struct? method)
        (cases static-method-struct method
          (a-static-method-struct (method-name specifier
                                    method-type super-name)
            (let ((result-type
                    (type-of-application
                      method-type rand-types '() rands exp)))
              (if super-call?
                (cases abstraction-specifier specifier
                  (concrete-specifier () result-type)
                  (abstract-specifier ()
                    (eopl:error 'type-of-method-or-super-call
                      (string-append
                        "~%Super call on abstract method ~s"
                        "in class ~s in~%~s")
                      msg host-name exp)))
                result-type))))
        (eopl:error 'type-of-method-app-exp
          "~%Class ~s has no method for ~s in ~%~s"
          host-name msg exp)))))
```

Figure 6.13   `type-of-method-app-or-super-call`

x may have classes that are any subclass of c2. So the cast can succeed only if the subclasses of c1 and the subclasses of c2 have a non-empty intersection. If either c1 is a subclass of c2 or c2 is a subclass of c1, or they are the same, this intersection will be non-empty. Otherwise c1 and c2 are incomparable in the inheritance hierarchy, and their descendants will be disjoint. This leads to the definition of `type-of-cast-exp`, below.

```
(define type-of-cast-exp
  (lambda (ty name2 exp)
    (cases type ty
      (class-type (name1)
        (if (or
               (statically-is-subclass? name1 name2)
               (statically-is-subclass? name2 name1))
          (class-type name2)
          (eopl:error 'type-of-expression
            "~%~s incomparable with ~s in ~%~s"
            ty name1 exp)))
      (else
        (eopl:error 'type-of-expression
          "~%~s not an object type in ~%~s"
          ty exp)))))
```

This completes the presentation of the checker.

Exercise 6.7 [⋆] Complete the implementation of the checker.

Exercise 6.8 [⋆] Modify the design of the language so that every field declaration contains an expression that is used to initialize the field. Such a design has the advantage that a checked program will never refer to an uninitialized value.

Exercise 6.9 [⋆⋆] Extend the checker to handle `fieldref` and `fieldset`, as in exercise 5.14.

Exercise 6.10 [⋆⋆] Extend the checker of this section to handle `lettype`. Hint: treat type identifiers in the same manner as in section 4.3, and initialize the type environment to bind each class name to a corresponding class type.

Exercise 6.11 [⋆⋆⋆] Our definition of `is-subtype?` is unnecessarily restrictive when dealing with procedure types. For example, if `c2` extends `c1`, then a procedure of type `(int -> c2)` could be used whenever a procedure of type `(int -> c1)` is expected, since the result of the first procedure (a value of type `c2`) can always be used where the result of the second procedure is expected. Hence we should count `(int -> c2)` as a subtype of `(int -> c1)`. Similarly, a procedure of type `(c1 -> int)` can be used in place of a procedure of type `(c2 -> int)`, since the first procedure will accept all the arguments that the second would. Hence `(c1 -> int)` should be a subtype of `(c2 -> int)`. Of course, the same reasoning works for any pair types such that $t_2 < t_1$. Modify `is-subtype?` to accept these possibilities (called *deep subtyping*).

Exercise 6.12 [⋆⋆⋆] An *interface* is a collection of method names and their types. We say that a class *implements* an interface if it supplies methods of the correct type for each of the names in the interface. We can make an interface into a type: if `i1` is an interface, an object is of type `i1` if it is an instance of a class that implements `i1`. Interfaces provide a cheap way of achieving most of the benefits of multiple inheritance (exercise 5.31).

For example, we could write

```
interface summable
  int sum ()

interface printable
  void print ()

class interior_node
  extends tree
  implements summable
  implements printable
  method void print () ...
  ...

let p = proc (summable o) add1(send o sum())
    q = proc (printable o) send o print()
in ...
```

and we could apply p to any object of a class that implemented summable, and q to any object of a class that implemented printable, regardless of where those classes lay in the inheritance hierarchy.

Extend the checker to handle interfaces. Rewrite the example of figure 6.1 to make tree an interface rather than an abstract class.

Exercise 6.13 [⋆ ⋆ ⋆] With the extensions in the preceding exercise, our language handles single inheritance of implementation and multiple inheritance of interfaces into classes. We could also define interfaces by inheritance. Extend the language and the checker to allow interfaces to inherit from other interfaces.

6.3   The Translator

In this section we show how the information generated by the checker can be used to optimize the programs in our typed object-oriented language. We write a translator that processes our language to a slightly extended language, performing three optimizations:

1. Method lookups are replaced by direct access to the slot in which the method is stored (exercise 5.18),

2. Calls to instanceof whose result is predictable are replaced by boolean literals, and

3. Casts that are guaranteed to succeed are eliminated.

Method lookups are replaced because if we know the type of an object, we can predict where each method can be found in the object's method vector. Consider the following example:

```
abstract class c1 extends object
  method int initialize () 1
  method int m1 () 11
  abstractmethod int m2 ()
class c2 extends c1
  method int m1 () 21
  method int m2 () 22
  method int m3 () 23
class c3 extends c2
  method int m4 () 34
class c4 extends c3
  method int m2 () 42
  method int m5 () 45
proc (c3 o) send o m2()
```

In an object of class c3, the methods are laid out in the method table in the following order: m1 m2 m3 m4. Even though m1 and m2 are overridden, they keep their place in the list. Furthermore, if class c3 is extended, as it is by c4, any additional methods will be added to the right of these four, and these four methods will be stored in the first four positions in the vector. Hence, if variable x is of type c3, then we know that x will be bound to an object whose class is either c3 or one of its subclasses, and hence the m1 method of the object will be in position 0 of the table, the m2 method will be in position 1, the m3 method will be in position 2, and the m4 method will be in position 3. In particular, in the method application in the last line of the program, we know that m2 will always be found in position 1.

To take advantage of this fact, let us add to our language a new expression apply-method-indexed, with syntax given by the production

⟨expression⟩ ::= apply-method-indexed ⟨expression⟩ ⟨number⟩
                   ({⟨expression⟩}*⁽ʼ⁾)

> apply-method-indexed-exp (obj-exp index rands)

We assume that this construct will not appear in our source programs. The goal of our translator will be to analyze the source program and convert all ordinary method applications to indexed method applications. For instance, in the preceding example, the method application with abstract syntax tree `(method-app-exp (var-exp o) m2 ())` should be replaced by the abstract syntax tree `(apply-method-indexed-exp (var-exp o) 1 ())`. Similarly, in the sample program of figure 6.1, `send left sum()` should be converted to the abstract sytnax tree `(apply-method-indexed-exp (var-exp left) 1 ())`.

The translator begins by type-checking the program. We do not use the resulting type, but this sets up the static class environment and checks the entire program for type errors. It then translates the program by doing a simple, grammar-directed traversal of the program:

```
(define translation-of-program
  (lambda (pgm)
    (let ((pgm-type (type-of-program pgm)))
      (cases program pgm
        (a-program (c-decls exp)
          (a-program
            (translation-of-class-decls c-decls)
            (translation-of-expression exp (empty-tenv)))))))))
```

We first consider `translation-of-expression`. This procedure takes two arguments, an expression and a type environment. It recurs through the expression, passing along a type environment. For expressions involving binding, it recurs on the subexpressions using the same type environment that `type-of-expression` would have used. Generally it simply recursively copies the expression. The exceptions are method applications, `instanceof` expressions, and `cast` expressions, where it performs optimizations based on the types of the subexpressions. See figure 6.14. Figure 6.15 shows how the type environments are built (cf. figure 4.8).

Next we consider the translation of the expressions dealing with objects. A `new` expression is translated by recursion. For a method application, we wish to produce an `apply-method-indexed` expression. To find the proper index, we first call `type-of-expression` to find the type `obj-type` of the object on which the method is being invoked. We then find the position `pos` of the given method in the static method table. Because methods are always laid out in the order they are declared, we know that at execution time this method will always be at position `pos`, even if the actual object is of a subclass of `class-name`. Hence we may safely translate the method application as an `apply-method-indexed`. See figure 6.16. The code must specify an action in the case that `obj-type` is not a class type, or that the method is missing, but these cases are impossible, since they will already have been detected by `type-of-expression`.

```
(define translation-of-expression
  (lambda (exp tenv)
    (cases expression exp
      (lit-exp (number) exp)
      (true-exp () exp)
      (false-exp () exp)
      (var-exp (id) exp)
      (primapp-exp (prim rands)
        (primapp-exp prim
          (translations-of-expressions rands tenv)))
      (if-exp (test-exp true-exp false-exp)
        (if-exp (translation-of-expression test-exp tenv)
          (translation-of-expression true-exp tenv)
          (translation-of-expression false-exp tenv)))
      (app-exp (rator rands)
        (app-exp
          (translation-of-expression rator tenv)
          (translations-of-expressions rands tenv)))
      (let-exp (ids rands body)
        (translation-of-let-exp ids rands body tenv))
      (proc-exp (id-texps ids body)
        (translation-of-proc-exp id-texps ids  body tenv))
      (letrec-exp (result-texps proc-names id-texpss idss
                    bodies letrec-body)
        (translation-of-letrec-exp
          result-texps proc-names id-texpss idss bodies
          letrec-body tenv))
      ...
      (new-object-exp (class-name rands)
        (new-object-exp class-name
          (translations-of-expressions rands tenv)))
      (super-call-exp (msg rands)
        (super-call-exp msg
          (translations-of-expressions rands tenv)))
      (method-app-exp (obj-exp msg rands)
        (translation-of-method-app-exp
          obj-exp msg rands tenv))
      (instanceof-exp (obj-exp name)
        (translation-of-instanceof-exp obj-exp name tenv))
      (cast-exp (obj-exp name)
        (translation-of-cast-exp obj-exp name tenv))
      )))
```

Figure 6.14 Excerpts from `translation-of-expression`

```
(define translation-of-proc-exp
  (lambda (id-texps ids body tenv)
    (let ((id-types (expand-type-expressions id-texps)))
      (proc-exp
        id-texps
        ids
        (translation-of-expression body
          (extend-tenv ids id-types tenv)))))))

(define translation-of-let-exp
  (lambda (ids rands body tenv)
    (let ((tenv-for-body
            (extend-tenv
              ids
              (types-of-expressions rands tenv)
              tenv)))
      (let-exp
        ids
        (translations-of-expressions rands tenv)
        (translation-of-expression body tenv-for-body)))))

(define translation-of-letrec-exp
  (lambda (result-texps proc-names id-texpss idss bodies
            letrec-body tenv)
    (let ((id-typess (map expand-type-expressions id-texpss))
          (result-types
            (expand-type-expressions result-texps)))
      (let ((the-proc-types
              (map proc-type id-typess result-types)))
        (let ((tenv-for-body
                (extend-tenv proc-names the-proc-types tenv)))
          (letrec-exp result-texps proc-names id-texpss idss
            (map
              (lambda (id-types ids body)
                (translation-of-expression body
                  (extend-tenv ids id-types tenv-for-body)))
              id-typess idss bodies)
            (translation-of-expression
              letrec-body
              tenv-for-body)))))))
```

Figure 6.15   Translating proc, let, and letrec

```
(define translation-of-method-app-exp
  (lambda (obj-exp msg rands tenv)
    (let ((obj-type (type-of-expression obj-exp tenv)))
      (cases type obj-type
        (class-type (class-name)
          (let ((class (statically-lookup-class class-name)))
            (let ((pos
                    (list-index
                      (lambda (method)
                        (eqv?
                          msg
                          (static-method->method-name
                            method)))
                      (static-class->methods class))))
              (if (number? pos)
                (apply-method-indexed-exp
                  (translation-of-expression obj-exp tenv)
                  pos
                  (translations-of-expressions rands tenv))
                (eopl:error 'translation-of-method-app-exp
                  (string-append
                    "~%Shouldn't have gotten here: Class"
                    "~s has no method for ~s in ~%~s")
                  class-name
                  msg
                  (method-app-exp obj-exp msg rands))))))
        (else
          (eopl:error 'translation-of-method-app-exp
            (string-append
              "~%Shouldn't have gotten here:"
              " Can't send message to non-object"
              "~s in ~%~s")
            obj-type
            (method-app-exp obj-exp msg rands)))))))
```

Figure 6.16   Translating object-oriented constructs

For an expression `instanceof e c`, we compare the type of the object with the target class for which it is being tested. If the type of the object is a subclass of the target class, then `instanceof` will always succeed. We would like to simply emit `true`, but it is possible that evaluation of the expression e will cause a side-effect. Hence we emit `begin e'; true end`, where e' is the translation of e. If the type of the target is a subclass of the type of the object, then we need to generate a test. On the other hand, if the type of the object and type of the target class are incomparable, we know that the `instanceof` should always be false, so we can emit `begin e'; false end`. Since all the types here are class types, we use `statically-is-subclass?` to compare the classes and hence the types.

For a `cast` expression, we similarly compare the type of the object and the type of the target class to which it is being cast. If the object type is known to be a subclass of the target class, then this is an up-cast, which always succeeds, and we merely emit the code that produces the object. If the target class is a subtype of the object type, then we must emit the `cast` expression to perform the check at run time. Otherwise, the types are incomparable, and the cast will always fail. This case is already detected by `type-of-cast-exp`, so it should not arise here. See figures 6.17 and 6.18.

The three procedures `translation-of-method-app-exp`, `translation-of-instanceof-exp`, and `translation-of-cast-exp` constitute the heart of this example. They show how type information can be used to eliminate run-time testing and searching.

All that remains is to consider the translation of the class declarations. This is for the most part straightforward recursive copying. The exception is that in order to translate the method bodies, we must collect enough information to build the same type environment as that used to check the body in `typecheck-method-decl!`. To do this, we pass the name of the class to `translation-of-method-decl`, which statically looks up the class and extracts the needed information. See figure 6.19.

This completes the discussion of the translator.

Exercise 6.14 [★★] Complete the implementation of the translator.

Exercise 6.15 [★★] Because the type environment is always laid out in exactly the same way as the run-time environment, we can use it to predict the lexical address of each lexical variable reference. Extend the translator so that it produces a lexical address for each variable reference, in the style of exercise 3.25. Do something similar for variable assignments as well. Modify the interpreter to test this translator's output.

```
(define translation-of-instanceof-exp
  (lambda (obj-exp name tenv)
    (let ((obj-type (type-of-expression obj-exp tenv))
          (obj-code (translation-of-expression obj-exp tenv)))
      (cases type obj-type
        (class-type (obj-class-name)
          (cond
            ((statically-is-subclass? obj-class-name name)
             (begin-exp obj-code (list (true-exp))))
            ((statically-is-subclass? name obj-class-name)
             (instanceof-exp obj-code name))
            (else
              (begin-exp obj-code (list (false-exp))))))
        (else
          (eopl:error 'translation-of-instanceof-expression
            (string-append
              "~%Shouldn't have gotten here:"
              " ~s not an object type in ~%~s")
            obj-type
            (instanceof-exp obj-exp name)))))))
```

Figure 6.17   Translating `instanceof`

Exercise 6.16 [★★] Modify the translator so that it also predicts the position of a method in a super call.

Exercise 6.17 [★] For a super call, we can do even better: we can predict at translation time not only the position of the method but the method itself. Add to the grammar a new kind of expression, `apply-method-immediate`, containing a method and a list of operands. Then modify the translator so that for a super call it produces an `apply-method-immediate` expression containing the actual method to be applied. Modify the interpreter to test this translator's output.

Exercise 6.18 [★★★] Extend the translator to handle interfaces (exercise 6.12). Construct an example to show that if i is an interface, objects of type i may have their methods arranged in different orders. What can be done to optimize method application when all that is known about the target object is an interface that it implements?

Exercise 6.19 [★★] Extend `translation-of-instanceof-exp` so that it emits `true` instead of `begin` e'; `true end` (and similarly for `false`) when it can guarantee that the execution of e' will have no side effects.

```
(define translation-of-cast-exp
  (lambda (obj-exp name tenv)
    (let ((obj-type (type-of-expression obj-exp tenv))
          (obj-code (translation-of-expression obj-exp tenv)))
      (cases type obj-type
        (class-type (obj-class-name)
          (cond
            ((statically-is-subclass? obj-class-name name)
             obj-code)
            ((statically-is-subclass? name obj-class-name)
             (cast-exp obj-code name))
            (else
              (eopl:error 'translation-of-cast-exp
                (string-append
                  "~%Shouldn't have gotten here:"
                  " ~s incomparable with ~s in ~%~s")
                obj-class-name
                name
                (cast-exp obj-exp name)))))
        (else
          (eopl:error 'translation-of-cast-expression
            (string-append
              "~%Shouldn't have gotten here:"
              "~s not an object type in ~%~s")
            obj-type
            (cast-exp obj-exp name)))))))
```

Figure 6.18   Translating of cast

Exercise 6.20 [⋆ ⋆] The translator, as we have organized it, has the potential to recalculate the type of any subexpression many times. Reorganize the translator so that the type checker produces not just a type, but an annotated syntax tree for the entire program. The annotated tree should contain all the information in the original syntax tree, along with the type of each expression and the type environment in which that expression was checked. Then the translator can do a recursive walk over the annotated tree, retrieving the type information and the type environment from the tree rather than reconstructing them.

Exercise 6.21 [⋆ ⋆ ⋆] Another way to organize the translator is to modify the checker so it produces not just the type, but the type and the translation of each expression in a single recursive pass over the input tree. Rewrite the translator following this organization.

```
(define translation-of-class-decls
  (lambda (c-decls)
    (map translation-of-class-decl c-decls)))


(define translation-of-class-decl
  (lambda (c-decl)
    (cases class-decl c-decl
      (a-class-decl (specifier class-name super-name
                       local-field-texps local-field-ids
                       m-decls)
        (a-class-decl specifier class-name super-name
          local-field-texps local-field-ids
          (map
            (lambda (method-decl)
              (translation-of-method-decl method-decl
                class-name))
            m-decls))))))


(define translation-of-method-decl
  (lambda (m-decl class-name)
    (let ((class (statically-lookup-class class-name)))
      (let ((super-name (static-class->super-name class))
            (field-ids  (static-class->field-ids class))
            (field-types (static-class->field-types class)))
        (cases method-decl m-decl
          (a-method-decl (result-texp name id-texps ids body)
            (let ((id-types
                    (expand-type-expressions id-texps)))
              (let ((tenv
                      (extend-tenv
                        (cons '%super (cons 'self ids))
                        (cons (class-type super-name)
                          (cons (class-type class-name)
                            id-types))
                        (extend-tenv field-ids field-types
                        (empty-tenv)))))
                (a-method-decl
                  result-texp name id-texps ids
                  (translation-of-expression body tenv)))))
          (an-abstract-method-decl (result-texp name id-texps
                                      ids)
            m-decl))))))
```

Figure 6.19   Translating class and method declarations

In chapter 5, we discussed dynamic versus static method dispatch. In static method dispatch, the choice of method depends on an object's type rather than its class. Consider the example

```
class c1 extends object
  method int initialize () 1
  method int m1 () 11
  staticmethod int m2 () 21
class c2 extends c1
  method void m1 () 12
  staticmethod int m2 () 22
let f = proc (c1 x) send x m1()
    g = proc (c1 x) send x m2()
    o = new c2()
in list((f o),(g o))
```

When `f` and `g` are called, `x` will have type `c1`, but it is bound to an object of class `c2`. The method `m1` uses dynamic dispatch, so `c2`'s method for `m1` is invoked, returning 12. The method `m2` uses static dispatch, so sending an `m2` message to `x` invokes the method associated with the type of `x`, in this case `c1`, so 21 is returned.

Exercise 6.22 [⋆⋆] Modify the interpreter of section 6.1 to handle static methods. Hint: keep type information in the environment so that the interpreter can figure out the type of the target expression in a `send`.

Exercise 6.23 [⋆⋆] In the type checker, static methods are treated in the same way as ordinary methods, except that a static method may not be overridden by a dynamic one, or vice versa. Extend the checker to handle static methods.

Exercise 6.24 [⋆⋆] Extend the translator to handle static methods. A `send` with a static method is translated into an `apply-method-immediate`, as in exercise 6.17.

Further Reading

The language in this chapter is loosely based on Java, but with far less syntax. (Arnold & Gosling, 1998) is the standard reference, but (Gosling, Joy, & Steele, 1996) is the specification for the serious reader. (Flatt, Krishnamurthi, & Felleisen, 1998) formalizes a subset of Java. (Gamma, Helm, Johnson, & Vlissides, 1995) is a fascinating handbook of useful organizational principles for writing object-oriented programs. The principles of abstract interpretation, along with other methods of program analysis, are presented in (Nielson, Nielson, & Hankin, 1999). (Abadi & Cardelli, 1996) defines a very simple object calculus, which is a useful foundation for the study of types in object-oriented systems.

7 Continuation-Passing Interpreters

In chapter 3, we used the concept of environments to explore the behavior of bindings, which establish the data context in which each portion of a program is executed. Here we will do the same for the *control context* in which each portion of a program is executed. We will introduce the concept of a *continuation* as an abstraction of the control context, and we will write interpreters that take a continuation as an argument, thus making the control context explicit.

Consider the following definition of the factorial function in Scheme.

```
(define fact
  (lambda (n)
    (if (zero? n) 1 (* n (fact (- n 1))))))
```

We can use a derivation to model a calculation with `fact`:

```
  (fact 4)
= (* 4 (fact 3))
= (* 4 (* 3 (fact 2)))
= (* 4 (* 3 (* 2 (fact 1))))
= (* 4 (* 3 (* 2 (* 1 (fact 0)))))
= (* 4 (* 3 (* 2 (* 1 1))))
= (* 4 (* 3 (* 2 1)))
= (* 4 (* 3 2))
= (* 4 6)
= 24
```

This is the natural recursive definition of factorial. Each call of `fact` is made with a promise that the value returned will be multiplied by the value of n at the time of the call. Thus `fact` is invoked in larger and larger *control contexts* as the calculation proceeds.

Compare this behavior to that of the following procedures.

```
(define fact-iter
  (lambda (n)
    (fact-iter-acc n 1)))

(define fact-iter-acc
  (lambda (n a)
    (if (zero? n) a (fact-iter-acc (- n 1) (* n a)))))
```

With these definitions, we calculate:

```
  (fact-iter 4)
= (fact-iter-acc 4 1)
= (fact-iter-acc 3 4)
= (fact-iter-acc 2 12)
= (fact-iter-acc 1 24)
= (fact-iter-acc 0 24)
= 24
```

Here, fact-iter-acc is always invoked in the same context: in this case, no context at all. When fact-iter-acc calls itself, it does so at the "tail end" of a call to fact-iter-acc. We call this a *tail call*. No promise is made to do anything with the returned value other than to return it as the result of the call to fact-iter-acc. Thus each step in the derivation above has the form (fact-iter-acc *n a*).

When a procedure such as fact executes, additional control information must be recorded with each recursive call, and this information must be retained until the call returns. This reflects growth of the control context in the first derivation above. Such a process is said to exhibit *recursive control behavior*.

By contrast, no additional control information need be recorded when fact-iter-acc calls itself. This is reflected in the derivation by recursive calls occurring at the same level within the expression (on the outside in the derivation above). In such cases the system does not need an ever-increasing amount of memory for control contexts as the depth of recursion (the number of recursive calls without corresponding returns) increases. A process that uses a bounded amount of memory for control information is said to exhibit *iterative control behavior*.

Why do these programs exhibit different control behavior? In the recursive definition of factorial, the procedure fact is called *in an operand position*. We need to save context around this call because we need to remember that after the evaluation of the procedure call, we still need to finish evaluating the operands and executing the outer call, in this case to the waiting multiplication. This leads us to an important principle:

It is evaluation of actual parameters, not the calling of procedures, that requires creating a control context.

In this chapter we will learn how to track and manipulate control contexts. Our central tool will be the data type of *continuations*. Continuations are an abstraction of the notion of control context, much as environments are an abstraction of data contexts. We will explore continuations by writing an interpreter that explicitly passes a continuation parameter, just as our previous interpreters explicitly passed an environment parameter. Once we do this for the simple cases, we can see how to add to our language facilities that manipulate control contexts in more complicated ways, such as exceptions and threads. We conclude by showing how these ideas can be applied to a very different programming paradigm, called *logic programming*.

In chapter 8 we shall see that the technique of converting to continuation-passing style is very general and can be applied to many programs. The experience with continuations gained in this chapter will greatly assist in understanding the general technique to come. Also, the additional experience provided by the next chapter is necessary to obtain a general working knowledge of continuations. It is a deep and subtle concept that can be mastered only by working with it from several angles.

7.1 A Continuation-Passing Interpreter

In our new interpreter, the major procedures such as `eval-expression` will take a third parameter. This new parameter, the *continuation*, is intended to be an abstraction of the control context in which each expression is evaluated. We begin with an interpreter in figure 7.1 of the language of section 3.7.

Our goal is to rewrite the interpreter so that no call to `eval-expression` builds control context: all of the control context will be contained in the continuation parameter.

Now, we know that an environment is a representation of a function from symbols to locations. What does a continuation represent? The continuation of an expression represents a procedure that takes the result of the expression and completes the computation. So our interface must include a procedure, `apply-cont`, that takes a continuation `cont` and an expressed value `val` and finishes the computation as specified by `cont`.

```
(define eval-program
  (lambda (pgm)
    (cases program pgm
      (a-program (body)
        (eval-expression body (init-env))))))

(define eval-expression
  (lambda (exp env)
    (cases expression exp
      (lit-exp (datum) datum)
      (var-exp (id) (apply-env env id))
      (proc-exp (ids body) (closure ids body env))
      (letrec-exp (proc-names idss bodies letrec-body)
        (eval-expression letrec-body
          (extend-env-recursively
            proc-names idss bodies env)))
      (if-exp (test-exp true-exp false-exp)
        (if (true-value? (eval-expression test-exp env))
          (eval-expression true-exp env)
          (eval-expression false-exp env)))
      (primapp-exp (prim rands)
        (let ((args (eval-rands rands env)))
          (apply-primitive prim args)))
      (app-exp (rator rands)
        (let ((proc (eval-expression rator env))
              (args (eval-rands rands env)))
          (if (procval? proc)
            (apply-procval proc args)
            (eopl:error 'eval-expression
              "Attempt to apply non-procedure ~s" proc))))
      (let-exp (ids rands body)
        (let ((args (eval-rands rands env)))
          (eval-expression body (extend-env ids args env))))
      (varassign-exp (id rhs-exp)
        (begin
          (setref!
            (apply-env-ref env id)
            (eval-expression rhs-exp env))
          1))
      )))
```

Figure 7.1 Environment-passing Interpreter

What kind of continuation-builders will be included in the interface? We will discover these continuation-builders as we analyze the interpreter. To begin, we will need a continuation-builder for the context that says there is nothing more to do with the value of the computation. We call this continuation `(halt-cont)`, and we will specify it by

```
(apply-cont (halt-cont) val)
= (begin (write val) (newline))
```

assuming that we want to end the computation by writing the value of the entire expression passed to the interpreter and then end the output line.

We rewrite `eval-program` as:

```
(define eval-program
  (lambda (pgm)
    (cases program pgm
      (a-program (exp)
        (eval-expression exp (init-env) (halt-cont))))))
```

We can now begin to rewrite `eval-expression`. The first few lines of `eval-expression` simply calculate a value and return it, without calling `eval-expression` again. In the continuation-passing interpreter, these same lines send the same value to the continuation by calling `apply-cont`:

```
(define eval-expression
  (lambda (exp env cont)
    (cases expression exp
      (lit-exp (datum)
        (apply-cont cont datum))
      (var-exp (id)
        (apply-cont cont (apply-env env id)))
      (proc-exp (ids body)
        (apply-cont cont (closure ids body env)))
      ...)))
```

Right now the only possible value of `cont` is the halt continuation, but that will change momentarily. It is easy to check that if the program consists of an expression of one of these forms, the value of the expression will be applied to `halt-cont`, which will cause the value to be printed.

The behavior of `letrec` is almost as simple: it creates a new environment without calling `eval-expression`, and then evaluates the body in the new environment. The value of the body becomes the value of the entire expression. That means that the body is performed in the same control context as the entire expression. The resulting code is unchanged from the original, except for the addition of `cont`.

```
(letrec-exp (proc-names idss bodies letrec-body)
  (eval-expression letrec-body
    (extend-env-recursively proc-names idss bodies env)
    cont))
```

We cannot say

```
(letrec-exp (proc-names idss bodies letrec-body)
  (apply-cont cont
    (eval-expression letrec-body
      (extend-env-recursively proc-names idss bodies env)
      (halt-cont))))
```

because using the continuation (halt-cont) causes the value to be printed. This would also defeat our purpose of making the control context explicit, because the call to eval-expression is in an operand position.

Let us next consider an if expression. In an if expression, the first thing evaluated is the test, but the result of the test is not the value of the entire expression. We need to build a new context that will see if the result of the test expression is a true value, and evaluate either the true expression or the false expression. So in eval-expression we write

```
(if-exp (test-exp true-exp false-exp)
  (eval-expression test-exp env
    (test-cont true-exp false-exp env cont)))
```

where test-cont is a new continuation-builder subject to the specification

```
(apply-cont (test-cont true-exp false-exp env cont) val)
= (if (true-value? val)
    (eval-expression true-exp env cont)
    (eval-expression false-exp env cont))
```

We now have two continuation-builders, so we can implement them either using a procedural representation or a data structure representation. The procedural representation is in figure 7.2 and the data structure representation, using define-datatype, is in figure 7.3.

Here is a sample calculation to show how these pieces fit together. As we did in section 3.5, we write «*exp*» to denote the abstract syntax tree associated with the expression *exp*. Assume e0 is an environment in which b is bound to true and assume k0 is the initial continuation, which is the value of (halt-cont). The commentary is informal and should be checked against the definition of eval-expression and the specification of apply-cont. This example is contrived because we have letrec to introduce procedures but we do not yet have a way to invoke them.

```
(define halt-cont
  (lambda ()
    (lambda (val)
      (begin (write val) (newline)))))

(define test-cont
  (lambda (true-exp false-exp env cont)
    (lambda (val)
      (if (true-value? val)
        (eval-expression true-exp env cont)
        (eval-expression false-exp env cont)))))

(define apply-cont
  (lambda (cont v)
    (cont v)))
```

Figure 7.2   Procedural representation of continuations

```
(define-datatype continuation continuation?
  (halt-cont)
  (test-cont
    (true-exp expression?)
    (false-exp expression?)
    (env environment?)
    (cont continuation?)))

(define apply-cont
  (lambda (cont val)
    (cases continuation cont
      (halt-cont ()
        (begin (write val) (newline)))
      (test-cont (true-exp false-exp env cont)
        (if (true-value? val)
          (eval-expression true-exp env cont)
          (eval-expression false-exp env cont))))))
```

Figure 7.3   Data structure representation of continuations

```
(eval-expression <<letrec p(x) = x in if b then 3 else 4>> e0
  k0)
= where e1 is (extend-env-recursively ... e0)
(eval-expression <<if b then 3 else 4>> e1 k0)
= evaluate the test expression
(eval-expression <<b>> e1 (test-cont <<3>> <<4>> e1 k0))
= send the value of b to the continuation
(apply-cont (test-cont <<3>> <<4>> e1 k0) true)
= evaluate the true expression
(eval-expression <<3>> e1 k0)
= send the value of the literal expression to the continuation
(apply-cont k0 3)
= invoke the final continuation with the final answer
(begin (write 3) (newline))
```

Next we consider primitive applications. We will need to supply a continuation argument to `eval-rands`. This continuation will accept the arguments to the primitive and call `apply-primitive` to perform the primitive operation. So in `eval-expression` we write

```
(primapp-exp (prim rands)
   (eval-rands rands env (prim-args-cont prim cont)))
```

where `prim-args-cont` is the new continuation-builder, subject to

```
(apply-cont (prim-args-cont prim cont) val)
= (let ((args val))
     (apply-cont cont (apply-primitive prim args)))
```

In the right-hand side, we bind `args` to the value of `val` to connect this specification to code of figure 7.1, which says `(apply-primitive prim args)`.

Before finishing `eval-expression`, we turn our attention to the procedure `eval-rands`, so we will have a self-contained language we can test. It will be easier to analyze `eval-rands` if we expand the use of `map` and give a name to each intermediate value as in figure 7.4(top). The continuation-passing version of `eval-rands` is in figure 7.4(bottom).

If `rands` is empty, we return the empty list to the context. If `rands` is nonempty, we evaluate the first expression in a control context that will finish the computation. What should the specification for `eval-first-cont` be? We want it to evaluate the rest of the expressions, create the list of all the values, and return it by sending it to the continuation `cont`. Therefore we expect it to be something like:

```
(define eval-rands
  (lambda (rands env)
    (if (null? rands)
      '()
      (let ((first (eval-expression (car rands) env))
            (rest (eval-rands (cdr rands) env)))
        (cons first rest)))))

(define eval-rands
  (lambda (rands env cont)
    (if (null? rands)
      (apply-cont cont '())
      (eval-expression (car rands) env
        (eval-first-cont rands env cont)))))
```

Figure 7.4   Direct and continuation-passing versions of `eval-rand`

```
  (apply-cont (eval-first-cont rands env cont) val)
= (let ((first val)
        (rest (eval-rands (cdr rands) env)))
    (apply-cont cont (cons first rest)))
```

But this is not right. Recall that in Scheme `(let ((x $e_0$)) $e_1$)` is the same as `((lambda (x) $e_1$) $e_0$)`, so the `let`'s right-hand sides count as operand positions. Therefore the call to `eval-rands` is in an operand position, and that would require a control context. So we need to analyze this bit of code in the same way we analyzed the bodies of `eval-expression` and `eval-rands`. In this expression, we need to evaluate the call to `eval-rands` in a new context that will finish the computation. So we have

```
  (apply-cont (eval-first-cont rands env cont) val)
= (eval-rands (cdr rands) env (eval-rest-cont val cont))

  (apply-cont (eval-rest-cont first-val cont) val)
= (let ((first first-val)
        (rest val))
    (apply-cont cont (cons first rest)))
```

The following calculation shows how continuations are used in operand evaluation. As before, it is helpful to check the commentary against the definitions of `eval-expression`, and now `eval-rands`, and against the specifi-

cation of `apply-cont`. Assume `e0` is an environment in which `x` is bound to
3, `y` is bound to 4, and `z` is bound to 5. We also assume, for the sake of this
example, that the addition primitive can take more than two arguments.

```
(eval-expression <<+(x,y,z)>> e0 k0)
= begin evaluating actuals in new continuation
(eval-rands <<(x,y,z)>> e0
  (prim-args-cont <<+>> k0))
= evaluate first actual in a new continuation
(eval-expression <<x>> e0
  (eval-first-cont <<(x,y,z)>> e0
    (prim-args-cont <<+>> k0)))
= x is bound to 3, so apply the continuation to 3
(apply-cont
  (eval-first-cont <<(x,y,z)>> e0
    (prim-args-cont <<+>> k0))
  3)
= continue evaluating actuals
(eval-rands <<(y,z)>> e0
  (eval-rest-cont 3
    (prim-args-cont <<+>> k0)))
= evaluate second actual
(eval-expression <<y>> e0
  (eval-first-cont <<y,z>> e0
    (eval-rest-cont 3
      (prim-args-cont <<+>> k0))))
= y is bound to 4, so send it to the continuation
(apply-cont
  (eval-first-cont <<(y,z)>> e0
    (eval-rest-cont 3
      (prim-args-cont <<+>> k0)))
  4)
= continue evaluating actuals
(eval-rands <<(z)>> e0
  (eval-rest-cont 4
    (eval-rest-cont 3
      (prim-args-cont <<+>> k0))))
= evaluate third actual
(eval-expression <<z>> e0
  (eval-first-cont <<(z)>> e0
    (eval-rest-cont 4
      (eval-rest-cont 3
        (prim-args-cont <<+>> k0)))))
```

```
=   z is bound to 5, so send it to the continuation
(apply-cont
  (eval-first-cont <<(z)>> e0
    (eval-rest-cont 4
      (eval-rest-cont 3
        (prim-args-cont <<+>> k0))))
  5)
=   continue evaluating actuals
(eval-rands <<()>> e0
  (eval-rest-cont 5
    (eval-rest-cont 4
      (eval-rest-cont 3
        (prim-args-cont <<+>> k0)))))
=   no more actuals, so apply continuation to empty list
(apply-cont
  (eval-rest-cont 5
    (eval-rest-cont 4
      (eval-rest-cont 3
        (prim-args-cont <<+>> k0))))
  '())
=   cons value onto list
(apply-cont
  (eval-rest-cont 4
    (eval-rest-cont 3
      (prim-args-cont <<+>> k0)))
  '(5))
=   cons value onto list
(apply-cont
  (eval-rest-cont 3
    (prim-args-cont <<+>> k0))
  '(4 5))
=   cons value onto list
(apply-cont
  (prim-args-cont <<+>> k0)
  '(3 4 5))
=   invoke the primitive
(apply-cont
  k0
  (apply-primitive <<+>> '(3 4 5)))
=   send the result to the original continuation k0
(apply-cont k0 12)
```

We now have a working interpreter, which we display in figure 7.5. Figure 7.6 shows the implementation of continuations using define-datatype.

```
(define eval-program
  (lambda (pgm)
    (cases program pgm
      (a-program (body)
        (eval-expression body (init-env) (halt-cont))))))

(define eval-expression
  (lambda (exp env cont)
    (cases expression exp
      (lit-exp (datum) (apply-cont cont datum))
      (var-exp (id) (apply-cont cont (apply-env env id)))
      (proc-exp (ids body)
        (apply-cont cont (closure ids body env)))
      (letrec-exp (proc-names idss bodies letrec-body)
        (eval-expression letrec-body
          (extend-env-recursively proc-names idss bodies env)
          cont))
      (if-exp (test-exp true-exp false-exp)
        (eval-expression test-exp env
          (test-cont true-exp false-exp env cont)))
      (primapp-exp (prim rands)
        (eval-rands rands env (prim-args-cont prim cont)))
      )))

(define eval-rands
  (lambda (rands env cont)
    (if (null? rands)
      (apply-cont cont '())
      (eval-expression (car rands) env
        (eval-first-cont rands env cont)))))
```

Figure 7.5   First continuation-passing interpreter

Exercise 7.1 [⋆] Implement this data type of continuations using procedural representation.

Exercise 7.2 [⋆] In the example above, each eval-first-cont continuation keeps one more expression than it needs to. Modify the constructor eval-first-cont so that it keeps only the expressions remaining to be evaluated.

Exercise 7.3 [⋆] Rewrite apply-cont in figure 7.6 to eliminate the use of Scheme let-expressions.

```
(define-datatype continuation continuation?
  (halt-cont)
  (test-cont
    (true-exp expression?)
    (false-exp expression?)
    (env environment?)
    (cont continuation?))
  (prim-args-cont
    (prim primitive?)
    (cont continuation?))
  (eval-first-cont
    (exps (list-of expression?))
    (env environment?)
    (cont continuation?))
  (eval-rest-cont
    (first-value expval?)
    (cont continuation?))
  )

(define apply-cont
  (lambda (cont val)
    (cases continuation cont
      (halt-cont ()
        (begin (write val) (newline)))
      (test-cont (true-exp false-exp env cont)
        (if (true-value? val)
            (eval-expression true-exp env cont)
            (eval-expression false-exp env cont)))
      (prim-args-cont (prim cont)
        (let ((args val))
          (apply-cont cont (apply-primitive prim args))))
      (eval-first-cont (exps env cont)
        (eval-rands (cdr exps) env
          (eval-rest-cont val cont)))
      (eval-rest-cont (first cont)
        (let ((rest val))
          (apply-cont cont (cons first rest))))
      )))
```

Figure 7.6 Continuations for figure 7.5

Exercise 7.4 [★★] Add variable assignment to this interpreter by including a new continuation-builder (varassign-cont env id cont).

Exercise 7.5 [★★] Modify the solution to the previous exercise so that the environment is not kept in the continuation.

Exercise 7.6 [★★] Our translation of eval-rands evaluated the expressions in left-to-right order. Write a new translation of eval-rands that evaluates the expressions in right-to-left order. Write out a derivation of eval-expression using the expression «+(x,y,z)», the environment e0, and the continuation k0 like the one above for this translation.

Exercise 7.7 [★★] When we said that apply-cont took a continuation and an expressed value as arguments, we were not quite accurate: a continuation built by prim-args-cont, for example, expects to be passed not an expressed value but a *list* of expressed values. Which continuation-builders build continuations that expect to be passed a list of expressed values? Make this distinction explicit in the interpreter by splitting the data type continuation into two data types: expval-continuation and expval-list-continuation, with application procedures apply-expval-cont and apply-expval-list-cont, so that the arguments of apply-expval-cont are an expval-continuation and an expressed value, while the arguments of apply-expval-list-cont are an expval-list-continuation and a list of expressed values.

We've now done most of the language of figure 7.1. Let us next consider let expressions. The original code for let was

```
(let-exp (ids rands body)
  (let ((args (eval-rands rands env)))
    (eval-expression body (extend-env ids args env)))))
```

In the continuation-passing interpreter, we need to call eval-rands in a context that will finish the computation. So in the continuation-passing version of eval-expression we write

```
(let-exp (ids rands body)
  (eval-rands rands env
    (let-exp-cont ids env body cont)))
```

and we add to our continuations interface the specification

```
(apply-cont (let-exp-cont ids env body cont) val)
= (let ((new-env (extend-env ids val env)))
    (eval-expression body new-env cont))
```

The last thing in our language is procedure application. In the environment-passing interpreter, we wrote

```
(app-exp (rator rands)
  (let ((proc (eval-expression rator env))
        (args (eval-rands rands env)))
    (if (procval? proc)
      (apply-procval proc args)
      (eopl:error 'eval-expression
        "Attempt to apply non-procedure ~s" proc))))
```

Here we have two calls to consider, as we did in eval-rands. So we must choose one of them to be first, and then we must transform the remainder to handle the second. Furthermore, we will have to pass the continuation to apply-procval, because apply-procval contains a call to eval-expression.

We choose the evaluation of the operator to be first, so in eval-expression we write

```
(app-exp (rator rands)
  (eval-expression rator env
    (eval-rator-cont rands env cont)))
```

with the untransformed continuation specified by

```
(apply-cont (eval-rator-cont rands env cont) val)
= (let ((proc val)
        (args (eval-rands rands env)))
    (if (procval? proc)
      (apply-procval proc args cont)
      (eopl:error 'eval-expression
        "attempt to apply non-procedure ~s"
        proc)))
```

As with eval-rands, we will need another continuation-builder to represent the context around the call to apply-procval. This yields the specification

```
(apply-cont (eval-rator-cont rands env cont) val)
= (let ((proc val))
    (eval-rands rands env (eval-rands-cont proc cont)))

(apply-cont (eval-rands-cont proc cont) val)
= (let ((args val))
    (if (procval? proc)
      (apply-procval proc args cont)
      (eopl:error 'eval-expression
        "Attempt to apply non-procedure ~s"
        proc)))
```

Last, we must modify `apply-procval` to fit in this continuation-passing style:

```
(define apply-procval
  (lambda (proc args cont)
    (cases procval proc
      (closure (ids body env)
        (eval-expression body
          (extend-env ids args env)
          cont)))))
```

This completes the presentation of the continuation-passing interpreter. The complete interpreter is shown in figures 7.7–7.8. The complete specification of the continuations is shown in figure 7.9.

Now we can check the assertion that it is evaluation of actual parameters, not the calling of procedures, that requires creating a control context. What expressions require the building of new continuations? Continuations are built for:

- Evaluation of the test in a conditional (the `test-cont` continuation).

- Evaluation of the operands to a primitive (the `prim-args-cont` continuation).

- Evaluation of the operator and operands of a procedure call (the `eval-rator-cont` and `eval-rands-cont` continuations).

- Evaluation of the right-hand-sides of a `let` expression (the `let-exp-cont` continuation).

Each of these is like the evaluation of an operand. The other continuation-builders, `eval-first-cont` and `eval-rest-cont`, are triggered only from these continuations.

But procedure calls do not themselves grow control contexts. Consider the evaluation of `(f x y z)`, where `f` is bound to some closure `cloo`.

```
(eval-expression <<(f x y z)>> e0 k0)
= evaluate operator
(eval-expression <<f>> e0
  (eval-rator-cont <<(x,y,z)>> e0 k0))
= send the closure to the continuation
(apply-cont
  (eval-rator-cont <<(x,y,z)>> e0 k0)
  cloo)
```

```
=  evaluate the operands
(eval-rands <<(x,y,z)>> e0
   (eval-rands-cont clo0 k0))
=  evaluate expressions as on page 250
(apply-cont
   (eval-rands-cont clo0 k0)
   '(3 4 5))
=  receive the arguments and apply the closure
(apply-procval clo0 '(3 4 5) k0)
```

So the closure is applied, and its body is evaluated, in the same continuation in which it was called. It is the evaluation of operands, not the entry into a procedure body, that requires control context.

Exercise 7.8 [★★] Add the `begin` expression of exercise 3.39 to the continuation-passing interpreter. Be sure that no call to `eval-expression` or `eval-rands` occurs in a position that would build control context.

Exercise 7.9 [★] Instrument the interpreter of figures 7.7–7.9 to produce output similar to that of the calculation on page 250. Watch out for the circular links in environments built by `letrec`.

Exercise 7.10 [★] Translate the definitions of `fact` and `fact-iter` into the defined language. Then, using the instrumented interpreter of the previous exercise, compute `(fact 4)` and `(fact-iter 4)`. Compare them to the calculations at the beginning of this chapter. Find `(* 4 (* 3 (* 2 (fact 1))))` in the trace of `(fact 4)`. What is the continuation of `apply-procval` for this call of `(fact 1)`?

Exercise 7.11 [★] The instrumentation of the preceding exercise produces voluminous output. Modify the instrumentation to track instead only the *size* of the largest continuation used during the calculation. We measure the size of a continuation by the number of continuation-builders employed in its construction, so the size of the largest continuation in the calculation on page 250 is 4. Then calculate the values of `fact` and `fact-iter` applied to several operands. Confirm that the size of the largest continuation used by `fact` grows linearly with its argument, but the size of the largest continuation used by `fact-iter` is a constant.

Exercise 7.12 [★] Our continuation data type contains just the single constant, `halt-cont`, and all the other continuation-builders have a single continuation argument. Implement continuations by representing them as lists, where `(halt-cont)` is represented by the empty list, and each other continuation is represented by a nonempty list whose car contains a distinctive data structure (called *frame* or *activation record*) and whose cdr contains the embedded continuation. Observe that the interpreter treats these lists like a stack (of frames).

Exercise 7.13 [★★] Extend the continuation-passing interpreter to the language of figure 3.24. Pass a continuation argument to `execute-statement`, and make sure that no call to `execute-statement` occurs in a position that grows a control context.

```
(define eval-program
  (lambda (pgm)
    (cases program pgm
      (a-program (body)
        (eval-expression body (init-env) (halt-cont))))))

(define eval-expression
  (lambda (exp env cont)
    (cases expression exp
      (lit-exp (datum) (apply-cont cont datum))
      (var-exp (id) (apply-cont cont (apply-env env id)))
      (proc-exp (ids body)
        (apply-cont cont (closure ids body env)))
      (letrec-exp (proc-names idss bodies letrec-body)
        (eval-expression letrec-body
          (extend-env-recursively proc-names idss bodies env)
          cont))
      (if-exp (test-exp true-exp false-exp)
        (eval-expression test-exp env
          (test-cont true-exp false-exp env cont)))
      (primapp-exp (prim rands)
        (eval-rands rands env (prim-args-cont prim cont)))
      (let-exp (ids rands body)
        (eval-rands rands env
          (let-exp-cont ids env body cont)))
      (app-exp (rator rands)
        (eval-expression rator env
          (eval-rator-cont rands env cont)))
      )))
```

Figure 7.7   Continuation-passing interpreter (part 1)

Since a statement does not return a value, distinguish between ordinary continuations and continuations for statements; the latter are usually called *command continuations*. The interface should include a procedure apply-command-cont that takes a command continuation and invokes it. Implement command continuations both as data structures and as 0-argument procedures.

One might now be tempted to transcribe the interpreter into an ordinary procedural language, using a data structure representation of continuations to avoid the need for higher-order procedures. Most procedural languages,

```
(define eval-rands
  (lambda (rands env cont)
    (if (null? rands)
      (apply-cont cont '())
      (eval-expression (car rands) env
        (eval-first-cont rands env cont)))))

(define apply-procval
  (lambda (proc args cont)
    (cases procval proc
      (closure (ids body env)
        (eval-expression body
          (extend-env ids args env)
          cont)))))
```

Figure 7.8   Continuation-passing interpreter (part 2)

however, make it difficult to do this translation: instead of growing control context only when necessary, they add to the control context (the stack!) on every procedure call. Since the procedure calls in our system never return until the very end of the computation, the stack in these systems continues to grow until that time.

This behavior is not entirely irrational: in such languages almost every procedure call occurs on the right-hand side of an assignment statement, so that almost every procedure call must grow the control context already. Hence the architecture is optimized for this most common case. Furthermore, most languages store environment information on the stack, so every procedure call must generate a control context that remembers to remove the environment information from the stack.

In such languages, one solution is to use a technique called *trampolining*. To avoid having an unbounded chain of procedure calls, we break the chain by having one of the procedures in the interpreter actually return a 0-argument procedure. This procedure, when called, will continue the computation. The entire computation is driven by a procedure called a *trampoline* that bounces from one procedure to the next. (See figure 7.10.)

Each 0-argument procedure returned by `apply-cont` represents a *thread* of the computation; we shall see in section 7.5 how this idea can be used to simulate multithreaded programs.

```
(apply-cont (test-cont true-exp false-exp env cont) val)
= (if (true-value? val)
      (eval-expression true-exp env cont)
      (eval-expression false-exp env cont))

(apply-cont (prim-args-cont prim cont) val)
= (let ((args val))
      (apply-cont cont (apply-primitive prim args cont)))

(apply-cont (let-exp-cont ids env body cont) val)
= (let ((new-env (extend-env ids val env)))
      (eval-expression body new-env cont))

(apply-cont (eval-rator-cont rands env cont) val)
= (let ((proc val))
      (eval-rands rands env (eval-rands-cont proc cont)))

(apply-cont (eval-rands-cont proc cont) val)
= (let ((args val))
      (if (procval? proc)
        (apply-procval proc args cont)
        (eopl:error 'eval-expression
          "Attempt to apply non-procedure ~s"
          proc))))

(apply-cont (eval-first-cont rands env cont) val)
= (eval-rands (cdr rands) env
      (eval-rest-cont val cont))

(apply-cont (eval-rest-cont first-val cont) val)
= (apply-cont cont (cons first-val val))
```

Figure 7.9   Specification of continuations for figure 7.7

Exercise 7.14 [★★★] Finish implementing the trampolining interpreter. How does this computation terminate? Devise a way for the interpreter to finish cleanly.

Exercise 7.15 [★]   The (lambda () (cases ...)) in apply-cont and the (proc) in trampoline constitute a procedural representation of threads. Replace this by a data structure representation.

```
(define trampoline
  (lambda (proc)
    (trampoline (proc))))

(define apply-cont
  (lambda (cont val)
|    (lambda ()
      (cases continuation cont
        ...)))))
```

Figure 7.10   Procedural representation of trampolining

Exercise 7.16 [★★] Implement a trampolining interpreter in an ordinary procedural language. Use a data structure representation of threads, as in the preceding exercise, and replace the recursive call to `trampoline` in its own body by an ordinary `while` or other looping construct.

Exercise 7.17 [★★★] One could also attempt to transcribe the environment-passing interpreters of chapter 3 in an ordinary procedural language. Such a transcription would fail in all but the simplest cases, for the same reasons as suggested above. Can the technique of trampolining be used in this situation as well?

7.2   Procedural Representation of Continuations

It can be difficult to follow the workings of the continuation-passing interpreter because the specification of the continuations is separate from the clauses of the interpreter to which they are associated. This difficulty can be alleviated by using a procedural representation of continuations, and expanding the continuation-builders and `apply-cont` where they occur.

A procedural implementation of the continuation interface is shown in figures 7.11–7.12. Here we have implemented the interface in a most straightforward way, so that every continuation uses `val` as its bound variable.

Now we can substitute these definitions into the interpreter of figures 7.7–7.8. When we do this, we will also replace expressions like `(lambda (val) (let ((args val)) ...))` by `(lambda (args) ...)`. The result is shown in figures 7.13–7.14. This interpreter is more readable than the preceding ones: we can read the final lines of `eval-program` as: "Apply `eval-expression` to `exp` with the initial environment, call the result `val`,

```
(define apply-cont
  (lambda (cont v)
    (cont v)))

(define halt-cont
  (lambda ()
    (lambda (val)
      (begin (write val) (newline)))))

(define test-cont
  (lambda (true-exp false-exp env cont)
    (lambda (val)
      (if (true-value? val)
          (eval-expression true-exp env cont)
          (eval-expression false-exp env cont)))))

(define varassign-cont
  (lambda (env id cont)
    (lambda (val)
      (begin
        (setref! (apply-env-ref env id) val)
        (apply-cont cont 1)))))

(define prim-args-cont
  (lambda (prim cont)
    (lambda (val)
      (let ((args val))
        (apply-cont cont (apply-primitive prim args))))))

(define let-exp-cont
  (lambda (ids env body cont)
    (lambda (val)
      (let ((new-env (extend-env ids val env)))
        (eval-expression body new-env cont)))))
```

Figure 7.11   Procedural implementation of continuations (part 1)

```
(define eval-rator-cont
  (lambda (rands env cont)
    (lambda (val)
      (let ((proc val))
        (eval-rands rands env
          (eval-rands-cont proc cont))))))

(define eval-rands-cont
  (lambda (proc cont)
    (lambda (val)
      (let ((args val))
        (if (procval? proc)
          (apply-procval proc args cont)
          (eopl:error 'eval-expression
            "Attempt to apply non-procedure ~s" proc))))))

(define eval-first-cont
  (lambda (rands env cont)
    (lambda (val)
      (eval-rands (cdr rands) env
        (eval-rest-cont val cont)))))

(define eval-rest-cont
  (lambda (first-val cont)
    (lambda (val)
      (let ((rest val))
        (apply-cont cont (cons first-val rest))))))
```

Figure 7.12   Procedural implementation of continuations (part 2)

and then print it." Similarly, the code for eval-rands,

```
(define eval-rands
  (lambda (rands env cont)
    (if (null? rands)
      (cont '())
      (eval-expression (car rands) env
        (lambda (first-val)
          (eval-rands (cdr rands) env
            (lambda (rest)
              (cont (cons first-val rest)))))))))
```

can be read as: "if `rands` is empty, return the empty list. Otherwise, evaluate the first expression and call the result `first-val`. Then evaluate the second expression and call the result `rest`. Then return the cons of `first-val` and `rest`."

Using a procedural representation makes the program easier to read, and also allows the programmer more freedom to include additional continuation-builders. We shall see in chapter 8 how this idea can be used to convert any program to continuation-passing style. A disadvantage of the procedural representation is that it is harder to debug, since procedures are usually unprintable.

Exercise 7.18 [⋆⋆]   Transform the state-passing interpreter of exercise 3.48 into continuation-passing style.   The continuations should take two arguments: the expressed value and the state, so one might write:

```
(define eval-expression
  (lambda (exp env store cont)
    (cases expression exp
      (var-exp (id)
        (cont (apply-store store (apply-env env id)) store))
      (varassign-exp (id rhs-exp)
        (eval-expression rhs-exp env store
          (lambda (val new-store)
            (cont 1
              (extend-store (apply-env env id) val store)))))
      (if-exp (test-exp true-exp false-exp)
        (eval-expression test-exp env store
          (lambda (val new-store)
            (if (true-value? val)
              (eval-expression true-exp  new-store cont)
              (eval-expression false-exp new-store cont)))))
      ...)))
```

7.3   An Imperative Interpreter

In section 3.7, we saw how assignment to shared variables could sometimes be used in place of binding. Consider the familiar example of `even` and `odd` at the top of figure 7.15. It could be replaced by the program below it in figure 7.15. There the shared variable x allows communication between the two procedures. In the top example, the procedure bodies look for the relevant data in the environment; in the other program, they look for it in the store.

```
(define eval-program
  (lambda (pgm)
    (cases program pgm
      (a-program (exp)
        (eval-expression exp (init-env)
          (lambda (val)
            (begin (write val) (newline))))))))

(define eval-expression
  (lambda (exp env cont)
    (cases expression exp
      (lit-exp (datum) (cont datum))
      (var-exp (id) (cont (apply-env env id)))
      (proc-exp (ids body)
        (cont (closure ids body env)))
      (letrec-exp (proc-names idss bodies letrec-body)
        (eval-expression letrec-body
          (extend-env-recursively proc-names idss bodies env)
          cont))
      (if-exp (test-exp true-exp false-exp)
        (eval-expression test-exp env
          (lambda (val)
            (if (true-value? val)
              (eval-expression true-exp env cont)
              (eval-expression false-exp env cont)))))
      (varassign-exp (id exp)
        (eval-expression exp env
          (lambda (val)
            (begin
              (setref! (apply-env-ref env id) val)
              (cont 1))))))))
```

Figure 7.13 Continuation-passing interpreter with higher-order continuations inlined (part 1)

Consider a trace of the computation at the bottom of figure 7.15. This could be a trace of either computation. It could be a trace of the first computation, in which we keep track of the procedure being called and its argument, or it could be a trace of the second, in which we keep track of the procedure being called and the contents of the register x.

```
        (primapp-exp (prim rands)
          (eval-rands rands env
            (lambda (args)
              (cont (apply-primitive prim args)))))
        (let-exp (ids rands body)
          (eval-rands rands env
            (lambda (vals)
              (let ((new-env (extend-env ids vals env)))
                (eval-expression body new-env cont)))))
        (app-exp (rator rands)
          (eval-expression rator env
            (lambda (proc)
              (eval-rands rands env
                (lambda (args)
                  (if (procval? proc)
                    (apply-procval proc args cont)
                    (eopl:error 'eval-expression
                      "Attempt to apply non-procedure ~s"
                      proc)))))))
        )))

(define eval-rands
  (lambda (rands env cont)
    (if (null? rands)
      (cont '())
      (eval-expression (car rands) env
        (lambda (first-val)
          (eval-rands (cdr rands) env
            (lambda (rest)
              (cont (cons first-val rest)))))))))

(define apply-procval
  (lambda (proc args cont)
    (cases procval proc
      (closure (ids body env)
        (eval-expression body
          (extend-env ids args env)
          cont)))))
```

Figure 7.14 Continuation-passing interpreter with higher-order continuations inlined (part 2)

```
letrec
  even(x)  = if zero?(x)
             then 1
             else (odd sub1(x))
  odd(x)   = if zero?(x)
             then 0
             else (even sub1(x))
in (odd 13)

let x = 0
in letrec
     even() = if zero?(x)
              then 1
              else let d = set x = sub1(x)
                   in (odd)
     odd()  = if zero?(x)
              then 0
              else let d = set x = sub1(x)
                   in (even)
   in let d = set x = 13 in (odd)

       x = 13;
       goto odd;
even:  if (x=0) then return(1)
               else {x = x-1;
                     goto odd;}
odd:   if (x=0) then return(0)
               else {x = x-1;
                     goto even;}

  (odd  13)
= (even 12)
= (odd  11)
...
= (odd   1)
= (even  0)
= 1
```

Figure 7.15 Three programs with a common trace

Yet a third interpretation of this trace would be as the trace of *goto*s (called a flowchart program), in which we keep track of the location of the program counter and the contents of the register x.

But this works only because in the original code the calls to even and odd do not grow any control context: they are *tail calls*. We could not carry out this transformation for fact, because the trace of fact grows unboundedly: the "program counter" appears not at the outside of the trace, as it does here, but inside a control context.

We can carry out this transformation for any procedure that does not require control context. This leads us to an important principle:

> **A procedure call that does not grow control context is the same as a jump.**

Such a procedure call is said to be a *tail call*.

If a group of procedures call each other only by tail calls, then we can translate the calls to use assignment instead of binding, and we can translate such an assignment program into a flowchart program.

In this section, we shall use this principle to translate the continuation-passing interpreter into a form suitable for transcription into a language without higher-order procedures.

We begin with the interpreter of figures 7.7–7.8, using a data structure representation of continuations. The data structure representation is shown in figures 7.16 and 7.17.

Our first task is to list the procedures that will communicate via shared registers. These procedures, with their formal parameters, are:

```
(eval-expression exp env cont)
(eval-rands rands env cont)
(apply-procval proc args cont)
(apply-cont cont val)
```

So we will need seven global registers: exp, env, cont, rands, proc, args, and val. Each of these procedures will be replaced by a 0-argument procedure, and each call to one of these procedures will be replaced by code that stores the value of each actual parameter in the corresponding register and then invokes the new 0-argument procedure. So the fragment

```
(define-datatype continuation continuation?
  (halt-cont)
  (test-cont
    (true-exp expression?)
    (false-exp expression?)
    (env environment?)
    (cont continuation?))
  (varassign-cont
    (env environment?)
    (id symbol?)
    (cont continuation?)))
  (prim-args-cont
    (prim primitive?)
    (cont continuation?))
  (let-exp-cont
    (ids (list-of symbol?))
    (env environment?)
    (body expression?)
    (cont continuation?))
  (eval-rator-cont
    (rands (list-of expression?))
    (env environment?)
    (cont continuation?))
  (eval-rands-cont
    (proc expval?)
    (cont continuation?))
  (eval-first-cont
    (exps (list-of expression?))
    (env environment?)
    (cont continuation?))
  (eval-rest-cont
    (first-value expval?)
    (cont continuation?))
  )
```

Figure 7.16 Data structure implementation of continuations (part 1)

```
(define apply-cont
  (lambda (cont val)
    (cases continuation cont
      (halt-cont () (begin (write val) (newline)))
      (test-cont (true-exp false-exp env cont)
        (if (true-value? val)
          (eval-expression true-exp env cont)
          (eval-expression false-exp env cont)))
      (varassign-cont (env id cont)
          (begin
            (setref! (apply-env-ref env id) val)
            (apply-cont cont 1)))
      (prim-args-cont (prim cont)
        (let ((args val))
          (apply-cont cont (apply-primitive prim args))))
      (let-exp-cont (ids env body cont)
        (let ((new-env (extend-env ids val env)))
          (eval-expression body new-env cont)))
      (eval-rator-cont (rands env cont)
        (let ((proc val))
          (eval-rands rands env
            (eval-rands-cont proc cont))))
      (eval-rands-cont (proc cont)
        (let ((args val))
          (if (procval? proc)
            (apply-procval proc args cont)
            (eopl:error 'eval-expression
              "Attempt to apply non-procedure ~s" proc))))
      (eval-first-cont (exps env cont)
        (eval-rands (cdr exps) env
          (eval-rest-cont val cont)))
      (eval-rest-cont (first cont)
        (let ((rest val))
          (apply-cont cont (cons first rest))))
      )))
```

Figure 7.17   Data structure implementation of continuations (part 2)

```
(define eval-expression
  (lambda (exp env cont)
    (cases expression exp
      (lit-exp (datum)
        (apply-cont cont datum))
      ...)))
```

can be replaced by

```
(define eval-expression
  (lambda ()
    (cases expression exp
      (lit-exp (datum)
        (set! cont cont)
        (set! val datum)
        (apply-cont))
      ...)))
```

We can now systematically go through each of our four procedures and perform this transformation. We will also have to transform the body of `eval-program`, since that is where `eval-expression` is initially called. There are just three complications:

1. Often a register is unchanged from one procedure invocation to another. This yields an assignment like `(set! cont cont)` in the example above. We can safely omit such assignments.

2. When a field name of a data type happens to be the same as a register name, the field shadows the register, so the register becomes inaccessible. For example, in `eval-program` we have

```
(cases program pgm
  (a-program (exp)
    (eval-expression exp (init-env) (halt-cont))))
```

Here `exp` is locally bound, so we cannot assign to the global register `exp`. The solution is to rename the local variable to avoid the conflict:

```
(cases program pgm
  (a-program (exp1)
    (eval-expression exp1 (init-env) (halt-cont))))
```

Then we can write

```
(cases program pgm
  (a-program (exp1)
    (set! exp exp1)
    (set! env (init-env))
    (set! cont (halt-cont))
    (eval-expression)))
```

These rebindings occur primarily in `apply-cont`, where we often use `env` and `cont` as field names. There are a total of 14 bound variables that need to be renamed in their scopes: 13 in `apply-cont` and one in `eval-program`.

3. There is an additional complication that might arise in such a translation, though it does not occur in our example. Consider transforming a call `(f (+ x y) x)`, where `x` and `y` are the formal parameters of `f`. A naive transformation of this call would be:

```
(begin
  (set! x (+ x y))
  (set! y x)
  (f))
```

But this is incorrect, because it loads the register `y` with the new value of `x`, when the old value of `x` was intended. The solution is either to reorder the assignments so the right values are loaded into the registers, or to use temporary variables. Sometimes temporary variables are unavoidable; consider `(f y x)` where `x` and `y` are the formal parameters of `f`.

The result of performing this translation on our interpreter is shown in figures 7.18–7.21. This process is called *registerization*. It is an easy process to translate this into an imperative language.

Exercise 7.19 [⋆] Instrument this interpreter as in exercise 7.9. Since continuations are represented the same way, reuse that code. Verify that the imperative interpreter of this section generates *exactly* the same traces as the interpreter in exercise 7.9.

Exercise 7.20 [⋆⋆] Modify the interpreter of this section so that procedures use dynamic binding, as in exercise 3.30. (Hint: do this by transforming the interpreter of exercise 3.30 as we did in this chapter; it will differ from the interpreter of this section only for those portions of the original interpreter that are different.) Instrument the interpreter as in exercise 7.19. Observe that just as there is only one continuation in

```
(define exp    'uninitialized)
(define env    'uninitialized)
(define cont   'uninitialized)
(define rands  'uninitialized)
(define val    'uninitialized)
(define proc   'uninitialized)
(define args   'uninitialized)

(define eval-program
  (lambda (pgm)
    (cases program pgm
      (a-program (exp1)
        (set! exp exp1)
        (set! env (init-env))
        (set! cont (halt-cont))
        (eval-expression)))))

(define eval-expression
  (lambda ()
    (cases expression exp
      (lit-exp (datum)
        (set! val datum)
        (apply-cont))
      (var-exp (id)
        (set! val (apply-env env id))
        (apply-cont))
      (proc-exp (ids body)
        (set! val (closure ids body env))
        (apply-cont))
      (letrec-exp (proc-names idss bodies letrec-body)
        (set! exp letrec-body)
        (set! env
          (extend-env-recursively proc-names idss bodies env))
        (eval-expression))
```

Figure 7.18   Imperative interpreter (part 1)

```
        (if-exp (test-exp true-exp false-exp)
          (set! exp test-exp)
          (set! cont (test-cont true-exp false-exp env cont))
          (eval-expression))
        (varassign-exp (id rhs-exp)
          (set! exp rhs-exp)
          (set! cont (varassign-cont env id cont))
          (eval-expression))
        (primapp-exp (prim rands1)
          (set! cont (prim-args-cont prim cont))
          (set! rands rands1)
          (eval-rands))
        (let-exp (ids rands1 body)
          (set! rands rands1)
          (set! cont (let-exp-cont ids env body cont))
          (eval-rands))
        (app-exp (rator rands)
          (set! exp rator)
          (set! cont (eval-rator-cont rands env cont))
          (eval-expression))
        )))

(define eval-rands
  (lambda ()
    (if (null? rands)
        (begin
          (set! val '())
          (apply-cont))
        (begin
          (set! exp (car rands))
          (set! cont (eval-first-cont rands env cont))
          (eval-expression)))))
```

Figure 7.19   Imperative interpreter (part 2)

the state, there is only one environment that is pushed and popped, and furthermore, it is pushed and popped in parallel with the continuation. We can conclude that dynamic bindings have *dynamic extent*: that is, a binding to a formal parameter lasts exactly until that procedure returns. This is different from lexical bindings, which can persist indefinitely if they wind up in a closure.

```
(define apply-cont
  (lambda ()
    (cases continuation cont
      (halt-cont () (begin (write val) (newline)))
      (test-cont (true-exp false-exp old-env old-cont)
        (if (true-value? val)
          (begin
            (set! exp true-exp)
            (set! env old-env)
            (set! cont old-cont)
            (eval-expression))
          (begin
            (set! exp false-exp)
            (set! env old-env)
            (set! cont old-cont)
            (eval-expression))))
      (varassign-cont (old-env id old-cont)
        (begin
          (setref! (apply-env-ref old-env id) val)
          (set! cont old-cont)
          (set! val 1)
          (apply-cont)))
      (prim-args-cont (prim old-cont)
        (let ((args val))
          (set! cont old-cont)
          (set! val (apply-primitive prim args))
          (apply-cont)))
      (let-exp-cont (ids old-env body old-cont)
        (let ((new-env (extend-env ids val old-env)))
          (set! exp body)
          (set! env new-env)
          (set! cont old-cont)
          (eval-expression)))
      (eval-rator-cont (rands1 old-env old-cont)
        (let ((proc val))
          (set! rands rands1)
          (set! env old-env)
          (set! cont (eval-rands-cont proc old-cont))
          (eval-rands)))
```

Figure 7.20 Imperative interpreter (part 3)

```
(eval-rands-cont (old-proc old-cont)
  (let ((new-args val))
    (if (procval? old-proc)
      (begin
        (set! proc old-proc)
        (set! args new-args)
        (set! cont old-cont)
        (apply-procval))
      (eopl:error 'eval-expression
        "Attempt to apply non-procedure ~s" proc))))
(eval-first-cont (old-rands old-env old-cont)
  (set! rands (cdr old-rands))
  (set! env old-env)
  (set! cont (eval-rest-cont val old-cont))
  (eval-rands))
(eval-rest-cont (first-val old-cont)
  (let ((rest val))
    (set! cont old-cont)
    (set! val (cons first-val rest))
    (apply-cont)))
)))

(define apply-procval
  (lambda ()
    (cases procval proc
      (closure (ids body old-env)
        (set! exp body)
        (set! env (extend-env ids args old-env))
        (eval-expression)))))
```

Figure 7.21   Imperative interpreter (part 4)

Exercise 7.21 [⋆] Eliminate the remaining let expressions in this code by using additional global registers.

Exercise 7.22 [⋆⋆] Translate the interpreter of this section into an imperative language. Do this twice: once using 0-argument procedure calls in the host language, and once replacing each 0-argument procedure call by a goto. How do these alternatives perform as the computation gets longer?

Exercise 7.23 [⋆⋆] As noted on page 260, most imperative languages make it difficult to do this translation, because they use the stack for all procedure calls, even tail calls. Furthermore, for large interpreters, the pieces of code linked by goto's may be too large for some compilers to handle. Translate the interpreter of this section into an imperative language, circumventing this difficulty by using the technique of trampolining, as in exercise 7.14.

7.4   Exceptions and Control Flow

So far we have used continuations only to manage the ordinary flow of control in our languages. But continuations allow us to alter the control context as well. Let us consider adding *exception handling* to our defined language. We add to the language two new productions:

⟨expression⟩ ::= try ⟨expression⟩ handle ⟨expression⟩
> try-exp (body-exp handler-exp)

⟨expression⟩ ::= raise ⟨expression⟩
> raise-exp (exp)

A try expression first evaluates its second expression (which should evaluate to a procedure of one argument). It installs this value as an exception handler and then evaluates its first expression. If this expression returns normally, its value becomes the value of the entire try expression, and the exception handler is removed.

A raise expression evaluates its single expression and raises an exception with that value. The value is sent to the most-recently installed exception handler. It is the job of the handler to determine what to do with this exceptional condition. It can either return a value, which becomes the value of the associated try expression, or it can *propagate* the exception by raising another exception; in this case the exception would be sent to the next most recently installed exception handler.

This is less complicated than it sounds. Let us consider a version of list-index written in our defined language. The defined-language procedure index is given a number and a list of numbers, and should return the position of the first occurrence of that number in the list, or -1 if it does not occur. We can write this as:

```
letrec
  index(n, l) =
    if null?(l)
    then sub1(0)
    else if equal?(n,car(l))
         then 0
         else let p = (index n cdr(l))
               in if equal?(p,sub1(0))
                   then sub1(0)
                   else add1(p)
in ...
```

This code is awkward because we need to check the value for -1 at every level. This might be manageable in this example, but would be error-prone if there had been many places where index was called. We can avoid this testing by raising an exception when the list becomes empty:

```
let index = proc (n, l)
  letrec
    loop(l) = if null?(l)
              then raise sub1(0)
              else if equal?(n,car(l))
                   then 0
                   else add1((loop cdr(l)))
  in try (loop l) handle proc (x) x
in ...
```

If the end of the list is found, an exception with value -1 is raised and is passed to the most-recently installed exception handler, in this case proc(x)x, so -1 is returned as the value of the call to index. If the call to loop returns normally, then we know that the desired element was found, so we can safely add 1 to it to find the right answer. In this way, we avoid the repetitious and error-prone manual testing for -1.

Implementing this exception-handling mechanism using the continuation-passing interpreter is straightforward. We begin with the try expression. We add two new continuation-builders:

```
(handler-cont
  (body expression?)
  (env environment?)
  (cont continuation?))
(try-cont
  (handler expval?)
  (cont continuation?))
```

and we add to `eval-expression` the following clause for `try`:

```
(try-exp (body-exp handler-exp)
  (eval-expression handler-exp env
    (handler-cont body-exp env cont)))
```

and to the specification of continuations the equation

```
(apply-cont (handler-cont body-exp env cont) handler-val)
= (if (procval? handler-val)
    (eval-expression body-exp env
      (try-cont handler-val cont))
    (eopl:error 'eval-expression
      "Error handler not a procedure: ~s" handler-val))
```

Now, what happens when the body of the `try` expression is evaluated? If the body returns normally, then that value should be sent to the continuation of the `try` expression, in this case `cont`:

```
(apply-cont (try-cont handler cont) val)
= (apply-cont cont val)
```

What happens if an exception is raised? Then we need to search through the continuation for the nearest handler, which may be found in the topmost `try-cont` continuation. So in `eval-expression` we write

```
(raise-exp (exp)
  (eval-expression exp env (raise-cont cont)))
```

and in the specification of continuations we write

```
(apply-cont (raise-cont cont) val)
= (find-handler val cont)
```

where `find-handler` is a procedure that finds the closest exception handler and applies it (figure 7.22).

To show how all this fits together, let us consider a calculation using a defined language implementation of `index`.

```
(define find-handler
  (lambda (val cont)
    (cases continuation cont
      (try-cont (handler cont)
        (apply-procval handler (list val) cont))
      (halt-cont ()
        (eopl:error 'find-handler
          "Uncaught exception ~s" val))
      (test-cont (true-exp false-exp env cont)
        (find-handler val cont))
      (prim-args-cont (prim cont)
        (find-handler val cont))
      ...)))
```

Figure 7.22 The procedure find-handler

Let exp0 denote the expression

```
let index = proc (n, l)
              letrec
                loop (l) = if null?(l)
                           then raise sub1(0)
                           else if equal?(n,car(l))
                                then 0
                                else add1((loop cdr(l)))
              in try (loop l) handle proc (x) x
in (index 1 list(2,3))
```

let exp1 denote the body of the procedure index, and let exp2 denote the
body of the local procedure loop. As we did above, we write «*exp*» to denote
the abstract syntax tree associated with the expression *exp*, and we write
[x=*a*,y=*b*] *env* in place of (extend-env ' (x y) ' (*a b*) *env*).

We start exp0 in an arbitrary environment env0 and an arbitrary continuation cont0. We will show only the highlights of the calculation, with
comments interspersed. In particular, we will not show the evaluation of
the actual parameters to procedure calls, nor will we show the evaluation of
conditionals.

```
(eval-expression exp0 env0 cont0)
```
=   *execute the body of the* let
```
(eval-expression <<(index 1 list(2, 3))>> env1 cont0)
   where env1 = [index = (closure (n l) exp1 env0)]env0
```
=   *evaluate the body of* index
```
(eval-expression exp1 [n=1,l=(2 3)]env1 cont0)
```
=   *the body of index is a* letrec-- *evaluate the body of the*
    letrec *in a suitably extended environment*
```
(eval-expression <<try (loop l) handle proc (x) x>> env2 cont0)
  where env2 = [loop=(closure (l) exp2 env2)]env1
```
=   *evaluate the handler, yielding a closure, then evaluate the body*
    of the try *in a try-cont continuation*
```
(eval-expression <<(loop l)>> env2
   (try-cont (closure (x) <<x>> env2) cont0))
```
=   *evaluate the body of* loop *with* l *bound to (2 3)*
```
(eval-expression exp2 [l=(2 3)]env2
   (try-cont (closure (x) <<x>> env2) cont0))
```
=   *evaluate the conditional, getting to the recursion line*
```
(eval-expression <<add1((loop cdr(l)))>> [l=(2 3)]env2
   (try-cont (closure (x) <<x>> env2) cont0))
```
=   *evaluate the argument to* add1
```
(eval-expression <<(loop cdr(l))>> [l=(2 3)]env2
   (prim-args-cont <<add1>>
      (try-cont (closure (x) <<x>> env2) cont0)))
```
=   *evaluate the body of* loop *with* l *bound to (3)*
```
(eval-expression exp2 [l=(3)]env2
   (prim-args-cont <<add1>>
      (try-cont (closure (x) <<x>> env2) cont0)))
```
=   *evaluate the conditional, getting to the recursion line again*
```
(eval-expression <<add1((loop cdr(l)))>> [l=(3)]env2
   (try-cont (closure (x) <<x>> env2) cont0))
```
=   *evaluate the argument to* add1
```
(eval-expression <<(loop cdr(l))>> [l=(3)]env2
   (prim-args-cont <<add1>>
      (try-cont (closure (x) <<x>> env2) cont0)))
```
=   *evaluate the body of* loop *with* l *bound to ()*
```
(eval-expression exp2 [l=()]env2
   (prim-args-cont <<add1>>
      (prim-args-cont <<add1>>
         (try-cont (closure (x) <<x>> env2) cont0))))
```

```
= evaluate the raise expression
(eval-expression <<raise sub1(0)>> [l=()]env2
  (prim-args-cont <<add1>>
    (prim-args-cont <<add1>>
      (try-cont (closure (x) <<x>> env2) cont0)))))
= use find-handler to unwind the continuation until we find a handler
(find-handler -1
  (prim-args-cont <<add1>>
    (prim-args-cont <<add1>>
      (try-cont (closure (x) <<x>> env2) cont0)))))
=
(find-handler -1
  (prim-args-cont <<add1>>
    (try-cont (closure (x) <<x>> env2) cont0)))
=
(find-handler -1
  (try-cont (closure (x) <<x>> env2) cont0))
= we've found a handler, now apply it
(apply-procval (closure (x) <<x>> env2) '(-1) cont0)
= run the body of the procedure
(eval-expression <<x>> [x=-1]env2 cont0)
= send the value of x to the continuation
(apply-cont cont0 -1)
```

If the list had contained the desired element, then we would have called `apply-cont` instead of `find-handler`, and we would have executed all the «add1»'s in the continuation.

Exercise 7.24 [⋆⋆] This implementation is inefficient, because when an exception is raised, `find-handler` must search linearly through the continuation to find a handler. Avoid this search by representing the continuation as a pair, consisting of a normal continuation and an exception continuation. Then `apply-cont` invokes the normal continuation, and `find-handler` invokes the exception continuation.

Exercise 7.25 [⋆] An alternative design that also avoids the linear search in `find-handler` is to use two continuations, a normal continuation and an exception continuation. Achieve this goal by modifying the interpreter of this section to take two continuations instead of one.

Exercise 7.26 [⋆] Modify the defined language to raise an exception when a procedure is called with the wrong number of arguments.

Exercise 7.27 [⋆] Modify the defined language to add division as a primitive. Raise an exception on division by zero.

Exercise 7.28 [⋆] The interpreter of this section seems to depend on the data structure representation, since we have two observers that examine the structure of the continuation. Re-implement the interpreter of this section using a procedural representation of continuations.

Exercise 7.29 [⋆⋆] So far, an exception handler can propagate the exception by re-raising it, or it can return a value that becomes the value of the `try` expression. One might instead design the language to allow the computation to resume from the point at which the exception was raised. Modify the interpreter of this section to accomplish this by running the body of the handler in the continuation from the point at which the `raise` was invoked.

Exercise 7.30 [⋆⋆⋆] Give the exception handlers in the defined language the ability to either return or resume. Do this by passing the continuation from the `raise` exception as a second argument. This may require adding continuations as a new kind of expressed value. Devise suitable syntax for invoking a continuation on a value.

Exercise 7.31 [⋆⋆] The preceding exercise captures the continuation only when an exception is raised. Add to the language the ability to capture a continuation anywhere by adding the form `letcc` ⟨identifier⟩ in ⟨expression⟩ with the specification

```
(eval-expression (letcc id exp) env cont)
= (eval-expression exp
     (extend-env (list id) (list cont) env)
     cont)
```

Such a captured continuation may be invoked with `throw`: the expression `throw` ⟨expression⟩ to ⟨expression⟩ evaluates the two subexpressions. The second expression should return a continuation, which is applied to the value of the first expression. The current continuation of the `throw` expression is ignored.

Devise a suitable method to invoke such a captured continuation.

Exercise 7.32 [⋆⋆] An alternative to `letcc` and `throw` of the preceding exercise is to add a single primitive procedure to the language. This procedure, which in Scheme is called `call-with-current-continuation`, takes a 1-argument procedure, `p`, and passes to `p` a procedure that when invoked with one argument, passes that argument to the current continuation, `cont`. We could define `call-with-current-continuation` in terms of `letcc` and `throw` as follows:

```
let call-with-current-continuation
      = proc (p)
          letcc cont
          in (p proc (v) throw v to cont)
in ...
```

Add `call-with-current-continuation` as a primitive. Then write a translator that takes the language with `letcc` and `throw` and translates it into the language without `letcc` and `throw`, but with `call-with-current-continuation`.

7.5   Multithreading

In many programming tasks, one may wish to have multiple computations proceeding at once. When these computations are run in the same address space as part of the same process, they are usually called *threads*. Threads are sometimes called *lightweight processes*. In this section, we will see how to modify our interpreter to simulate multi-threaded programs by interleaving the steps of their executions.

To do this, we build on the trampolining interpreter of section 7.1. Rather than having a single thread of computation, our multi-threaded interpreter will maintain several threads. The threads that are not currently running will be kept on a queue called the *ready queue*.

A thread is a computation in progress. There will be two kinds of threads: runnable threads and completed threads. We choose to represent runnable threads as 0-argument procedures, and completed threads as symbols. The basic constructor on threads is `make-thread`, which builds a runnable thread. Since we are using a procedural representation, `make-thread` is the identity procedure. There are two observers on threads. The procedure `run-thread` takes a nonnegative integer and a thread; it runs the thread for that number of steps, and returns the resulting thread. If the thread becomes non-runnable before the clock runs out, then the resulting non-runnable thread is returned. We will count each bounce of the trampoline as one step. The procedure `run-thread` is much like `trampoline`, except that it maintains a counter. We will also need the tester `runnable?` that checks to see if a thread is runnable.

```
(define make-thread (lambda (proc) proc))

(define run-thread
  (lambda (ticks thread)
    (if (runnable? thread)
      (if (zero? ticks)
        thread
        (run-thread (- ticks 1) (thread)))
      thread)))

(define runnable? procedure?)
```

Threads are scheduled for execution by a *scheduler*. The scheduler takes a number and a thread. The number specifies the number of steps in a time slice. If the thread is runnable, it is placed on the ready queue. A thread is then fetched from the ready queue and run, using `run-thread`, for a full time slice. The resulting thread is then scheduled. The procedure `schedule` is called with a non-runnable thread only when there are no more threads to run. In this case, the scheduler halts:

```
(define schedule
  (lambda (quantum thread)
    (if (runnable? thread)
      (begin
        (place-on-ready-queue thread)
        (schedule quantum
          (run-thread quantum (get-next-from-ready-queue))))
      thread)))
```

The ready queue is a global data structure with three operations:

- The procedure `initialize-ready-queue`, which initializes the queue to empty.

- The procedure `place-on-ready-queue`, which places a runnable thread on the ready queue.

- The procedure `get-next-from-ready-queue`, a 0-argument procedure that removes a thread from the ready queue and returns it. If the ready queue is empty, then the symbol `done!`, a non-runnable thread, is returned.

We create the ready queue using the queue interface of section 2.4.

```
(define the-ready-queue (create-queue))

(define initialize-ready-queue
  (queue-get-reset-operation the-ready-queue))

(define place-on-ready-queue
  (queue-get-enqueue-operation the-ready-queue))

(define get-next-from-ready-queue
  (let ((empty? (queue-get-empty?-operation the-ready-queue))
        (dequeue
          (queue-get-dequeue-operation the-ready-queue)))
    (lambda ()
      (if (empty?) the-final-answer (dequeue)))))
```

Now, how do we use this scheduler with our defined language?

- We need to start the program by creating and scheduling an initial thread:

```
(define eval-program
  (lambda (quantum pgm)
    (initialize-ready-queue)
    (cases program pgm
      (a-program (exp)
        (schedule quantum
          (make-thread
            (lambda ()
              (eval-expression exp
                (init-env)
                (halt-cont)))))))))))
```

We start programs by using the procedure run-with-quantum:

```
(define run-with-quantum
  (lambda (quantum string)
    (eval-program quantum (scan&parse string)))))
```

- As in the trampolining interpreter, we modify apply-cont to return a thread rather than actually applying the continuation:

```
(define apply-cont
  (lambda (cont val)
    (make-thread
      (lambda ()
        (cases continuation cont
          ...)))))
```

- We add a new production,

$$\langle expression \rangle ::= \text{spawn } \langle expression \rangle$$

to our grammar. Executing a spawn expression causes a new thread to be created and placed on the ready queue, so its evaluation proceeds concurrently with the current thread. The new thread evaluates the subexpression in the current environment. But in what continuation should this subexpression be evaluated? We choose to evaluate the subexpression in a continuation that when executed simply allows its thread to die. Even though the new thread cannot return a value to its parent, it can communicate with its parent via shared variables. Hence we write in eval-expression:

```
(spawn-exp (exp)
  (begin
    (place-on-ready-queue
      (make-thread
        (lambda ()
          (eval-expression exp env (die-cont)))))
    (apply-cont cont 1)))
```

A `spawn` expression returns immediately with 1 as its value, signifying successful creation of the thread.

The continuation `(die-cont)` should ignore the value sent to it and allow its thread to die by simply getting the next thread from the ready queue and returning it:

```
(apply-cont (die-cont) val)
= (get-next-from-ready-queue)
```

This thread is returned to the trampoline, so it takes over the remainder of the current thread's time slice. In this specification, we have ignored the `(make-thread (lambda () ...))` that is wrapped around the body of `apply-cont`.

* What should happen when the initial continuation `(halt-cont)` is executed? Unlike `(die-cont)`, `(halt-cont)` should print an answer, as it did before. But there may be other threads waiting to execute afterwards. So `(halt-cont)` should print out its answer and then die, allowing the remaining threads to execute by calling `(get-next-from-ready-queue)`. This leads to the following specification:

```
(apply-cont (halt-cont) val)
= (begin
    (eopl:printf "final answer is: ~a~%" val)
    (get-next-from-ready-queue))
```

Here we have added a distinctive label to this outcome to help distinguish it from the output of other threads.

Figure 7.23 shows some programs using threads in our defined language. The first two programs illustrate how threads can communicate via shared variables. The program `pgm5-1` spawns a thread that sets the variable `acc` to 20. The main thread then enters a busy-waiting loop that waits for `acc` to become non-zero, and returns its value. The program pgm5-2 sets up a three-stage pipeline, in which the first thread puts 20 in buf1, the second waits for buf1 to fill, adds 2 to the result, and puts the resulting value in buf2. The third thread similarly waits for buf2 to fill, adds 2 to the result, and puts the resulting value in buf3. The body of the program waits for buf3 to fill and reports the answer. Last, the program pgm5-3 illustrates the interleaving of different threads. The procedure noisy recurs linearly down a list, printing out the list at each step. The output of running these programs is shown in figure 7.24. In the final example, why does the computation continue well after the main thread has finished?

Exercise 7.33 [⋆] How does the behavior of pgm5-3 change as the time slice changes?

Exercise 7.34 [⋆] Add to the defined language a construction die that kills the current thread.

Exercise 7.35 [⋆⋆] Add to the defined language a construction yield that causes the current thread to yield the remainder of its time slice.

Exercise 7.36 [⋆] Instead of representing a thread as a 0-argument procedure, represent it as a data structure containing the same 0-argument procedure. Then modify run-thread to check to see that its argument is a legal thread.

Exercise 7.37 [⋆⋆] Replace the procedural representation of threads with a data structure representation.

Exercise 7.38 [⋆⋆⋆] In apply-cont, move (make-thread (lambda () ...)) inside the cases and replace the procedural representation with a data structure representation with a separate constructor for each instance of make-thread. What are the trade-offs between this representation and the one in the preceding exercise?

Exercise 7.39 [⋆⋆⋆] Modify the thread package to include *thread identifiers*. To do this, change the grammar of spawn expressions to be

$$\langle\text{expression}\rangle ::= \text{spawn} \ (\langle\text{identifier}\rangle) \ \langle\text{expression}\rangle$$

Each new thread gets a fresh number (its thread identifier). When the child thread is spawned, it receives its number as the binding of the identifier. The child's number is returned to the parent as the value of the spawn expression. Instrument the interpreter to trace the creation of thread identifiers. Check to see that the ready queue contains at most one thread for each thread identifier. What should be done about the thread identifier of the original program?

Exercise 7.40 [⋆⋆] Add to the interpreter of the preceding exercise a kill facility. The kill construct, when given a thread number, finds the corresponding thread on the ready queue and removes it. In addition, kill should return 1 if the target thread is found and 0 if the thread number is not found on the ready queue.

```
let acc = 0 done = 0
in let d = spawn set acc = 20
   in letrec
        loop () = if acc
                  then let d = set done = 1
                       in acc
                  else (loop)
      in (loop)
```

Program pgm5-1

```
let buf1 = 0 buf2 = 0 buf3 = 0
in let d1 = spawn set buf1 = 20
      d2 = spawn letrec
                   loop () = if buf1
                             then set buf2 = +(buf1,2)
                             else (loop)
                 in (loop)
      d3 = spawn letrec
                   loop () = if buf2
                             then set buf3 = +(buf2,2)
                             else (loop)
                 in (loop)
   in letrec
        loop () = if buf3 then buf3 else (loop)
      in (loop)
```

Program pgm5-2

```
letrec
  noisy (l) = let d = print(l)
              in if null?(l)
                 then 0
                 else (noisy cdr(l))
in let d1 = spawn (noisy list(1,2,3,4,5))
      d2 = spawn (noisy list(6,7,8,9,10))
      d3 = spawn (noisy list(11,12,13,14,15,16,17))
   in 33
```

Program pgm5-3

Figure 7.23 Some programs using threads

```
> (run-with-quantum 50 pgm5-1)
final answer is: 20
done!
> (run-with-quantum 50 pgm5-2)
final answer is: 24
done!
> (run-with-quantum 50 pgm5-3)
final answer is: 33
(1 2 3 4 5)
(2 3 4 5)
(6 7 8 9 10)
(7 8 9 10)
(11 12 13 14 15 16 17)
(12 13 14 15 16 17)
(3 4 5)
(4 5)
(5)
(8 9 10)
(9 10)
(10)
(13 14 15 16 17)
(14 15 16 17)
(15 16 17)
()
()
(16 17)
(17)
()
done!
```

Figure 7.24 Sample output from thread programs

Shared variables are an unreliable method of communication if several threads try to write to the same variable. Consider the program in figure 7.25. Two threads each try to increment the same variable twice. The main loop waits for both of the threads d1 and d2 to finish. But if a thread switch occurs between reading and writing the variable, unpredictable behavior can result.

Exercise 7.41 [⋆] If we vary the size of the time slice, how many different results can this program produce?

```
let x = list(0) done1 = 0 done2 = 0
in let d1 = spawn begin
                    setcar(x,add1(car(x)));
                    setcar(x,add1(car(x)));
                    print(list(1,car(x)));
                    set done1 = 1
                  end
        d2 = spawn begin
                    setcar(x,add1(car(x)));
                    setcar(x,add1(car(x)));
                    print(list(2,car(x)));
                    set done2 = 1
                  end
    in letrec
        loop () = if equal?(done1,1)
                  then if equal?(done2,1)
                       then print(list(0,car(x)))
                       else (loop)
                  else (loop)
      in (loop)
```

Figure 7.25 Shared variable example with two threads: unreliable

There are many ways to design a better synchronization facility for threads. A simple one is *locks*, which has the following interface.

- `lock` ⟨expression⟩: evaluates the expression and creates a lock containing the resulting value. The value of the expression is the lock.

- `acquire` ⟨expression⟩: evaluates the expression, which should return a lock. If no other thread has acquired the lock, then the current thread acquires the lock and the expression returns the value held in the lock. Otherwise, the thread waits until the lock is free.

- `release` ⟨expression⟩: evaluates the expression, which should return a lock. It releases the lock and returns 1.

We implement the lock as a data structure containing an integer-valued cell (as in exercise 2.26), indicating whether the lock is occupied, and a value:

```
(define-datatype lock lock?
  (a-lock
    (occupied
      (lambda (x)
        (and (cell? x) (integer? (contents x)))))
    (value expval?)))
```

We add three clauses to `eval-expression`, while extending the set of expressed values to include locks.

```
(lock-exp (exp)
  (eval-expression exp env
    (lock-cont cont)))
(acquire-exp (exp)
  (eval-expression exp env
    (acquire-cont cont)))
(release-exp (exp)
  (eval-expression exp env
    (release-cont cont)))
```

In addition, we add three clauses to `apply-cont` and we extend the associated data type of continuations accordingly. (See figure 7.26.)

For `lock`, we construct a new lock containing a cell initialized to zero, indicating that the lock is unoccupied, and the locked value.

For `acquire`, we check that the value passed to it is a lock; if it is, we check to see whether it is already occupied. If it is unoccupied, then we mark it as occupied by setting its `occupied` cell to 1, and we return its value to the continuation `cont1` of the `acquire`. If it is occupied, we place the current thread on the ready queue (by calling `(apply-cont cont val)`, which returns a thread), and call `get-next-from-ready-queue` to get the next runnable thread. In this way the current thread will repeatedly try the lock until it is unoccupied. Since this code is within a single call to `apply-cont`, it will be executed without interruption, so no race condition can occur.

Last, for a `release`, we check to see whether the lock is occupied; if it is, we release it by setting its `occupied` cell to 0. It is an error to attempt to release a lock that is not occupied.

Figure 7.27 is the same program as figure 7.25, using a lock to synchronize access to the shared list cell. This time the final value of the list is `(4)`, regardless of the length of the time slice.

Exercise 7.42 [★★] The algorithm used for `acquire` is called a *spin lock*. This can be wasteful if the lock may be held for a long time, because the waiting thread will continually retry the lock. Avoid this by associating a queue of waiting threads with

```
(define apply-cont
  (lambda (cont val)
    (make-thread
      (lambda ()
        (cases continuation cont
          (lock-cont (cont)
            (let ((c (cell 0)))
              (apply-cont cont (a-lock c val))))
          (acquire-cont (cont1)
            (if (lock? val)
              (cases lock val
                (a-lock (occupied value)
                  (if (= (contents occupied) 0)
                    (begin
                      (setcell occupied 1)
                      (apply-cont cont1 value))
                    (begin
                      (place-on-ready-queue
                        (apply-cont cont val))
                      (get-next-from-ready-queue)))))
              (eopl:error 'acquire-cont
                "Non-lock to acquire: ~s~%" v)))
          (release-cont (cont)
            (if (lock? val)
              (cases lock val
                (a-lock (occupied value)
                  (if (= (contents occupied) 1)
                    (begin
                      (setcell occupied 0)
                      (apply-cont cont 1))
                    (eopl:error 'release-cont
                      "Must acquire lock before releasing"))))
              (eopl:error 'release-cont
                "Non-lock to release: ~s~%" v)))
          ...)))))
```

Figure 7.26 `lock`, `release`, and `acquire`

```
let l = lock list(0)
    done = 0
in let t1 = spawn let c = acquire l
                  in begin
                         setcar(c,add1(car(c)));
                         setcar(c,add1(car(c)));
                         print(list(1,car(c)));
                         set done = add1(done);
                         release l
                     end
       t2 = spawn let c = acquire l
                  in begin
                         setcar(c,add1(car(c)));
                         setcar(c,add1(car(c)));
                         print(list(2,car(c)));
                         set done = add1(done);
                         release l
                     end
   in let v = 0
      in letrec loop() = if equal?(done,2)
                         then let c = acquire l
                              in begin
                                     set v = car(c);
                                     release l;
                                     v
                                 end
                         else (loop)
         in (loop)
```

Figure 7.27   Shared variable example with two threads: reliable

each lock. (This is sometimes called a *sleep queue*). If a thread attempts to acquire an occupied lock, it places itself on the queue for that lock. When a lock is released, it wakes up the first thread on its queue.

Exercise 7.43 [⋆⋆⋆]   Our code for release is insecure, because a thread could release a lock owned by another thread. Use the mechanism of thread identifiers to guarantee that release can only release a lock held by the current thread.

Exercise 7.44 [⋆]   In most languages, constructions like lock, acquire, and release take the form of operating system calls. Rewrite the interpreter to make these constructions primitives, rather than syntactic constructions.

Exercise 7.45 [⋆] Before threads came into widespread use, some programming languages had *coroutines* to accomplish similar goals on a single processor. A coroutine is like a procedure, except that when it transfers control to another coroutine, it keeps track of its current continuation. Control leaves one continuation and enters another using the operation `resume`, which takes two arguments: a coroutine, to which it transfers control, and a value to be passed to that coroutine.

A coroutine may be implemented as a cell that contains a continuation. Initially, that continuation should execute the body of the coroutine (in some suitable initial continuation, as we did for threads). In this model, after the `resume` operation evaluates its arguments, it saves the current continuation in its own coroutine's cell. It then extracts the continuation from the target coroutine's cell, and sends the value to that continuation. The effect is that the value appears as the result of the `resume` by which the target coroutine relinquished control.

Implement this model of coroutines.

7.6   Logic Programming

We normally think of `append` as a procedure that takes two lists and returns the concatenation of the two lists. But, we can also think about the problem this way: given the resultant list and the first list, what should the second list be? If we are also not given the first list, what two lists could be passed to `append` to make the resultant list? Problems like this are some of the motivations for *logic programming*. In this section, we explore a rudimentary implementation of logic programming. Our implementation uses continuation-passing style to organize the control structure of the program.

In logic programming, we start with a list of *goals* to be solved. The goals are solved by reducing them using a global set of *rules*. A *rule* is defined to be a list of the form $(h \;\text{<--}\; t_1 \;\ldots\; t_n)$, where $h, t_1, \ldots, t_n$ are terms (exercise 2.13). The h is called the *head* term and the $t_1 \ldots t_n$ are called the *subgoal* terms. The rule says that one way to find a solution of the head h is to find a solution for the subgoals $t_1, \ldots, t_n$.

For example, here are the rules for `append`.

```
(("append" "empty" x x) <--)

(("append" ("cons" w x) y ("cons" w z))
 <-- ("append" x y z))
```

The first rule may be read as saying that `"append"` applied to `"empty"` and any value x returns that value x. The second rule says that if `"append"` applied to some values x and y returns z, then `"append"` applied to (`"cons"` w x) and y returns (`"cons"` w z). Using the terminology of

subgoals, we can read these rules as saying that any goal of the form
(`"append"` `"empty"` x x) is immediately solved, and that any goal of the
form (`"append"` (`"cons"` w x) y (`"cons"` w z)) may be solved by solving (`"append"` x y z).

For these rules, some sample goal terms might be

```
("append" ("cons" 1 ("cons" 2 "empty")) y
  ("cons" 1 ("cons" 2 ("cons" 3 ("cons" 4 "empty"))))))
```

and

```
("append" x y
  ("cons" 1 ("cons" 2 ("cons" 3 ("cons" 4 "empty"))))))
```

The first goal determines that y must be (`"cons"` 3 (`"cons"` 4 `"empty"`)),
but the second goal is satisfied by five different sets of values for x and y.

The interpreter evaluates a goal term by comparing it to the head of each
rule. If the goal unifies (exercise 2.25) with the head term of a rule, then the
unifying substitution is applied to each of the subgoals (if any) of the rule,
and the resulting terms are added as goals to be evaluated. We keep track
of the substitutions as they are applied; if eventually all the subgoals are
satisfied, then the resulting substitution is said to be a *solution* of the original
goal.

When we try to evaluate a subgoal that does not match the head of any
rule, we say that the subgoal has *failed*. In this situation, the interpreter
backtracks to the last application of a rule, and tries the next applicable rule
instead. Backtracking is done in a stack-like fashion: the last rule applied is
always the first to be undone. Upon backtracking, the computation reverts
to an earlier substitution.

For example, consider the following set of rules:

```
(("p" x) <-- ("q" x) ("r" x))
(("p" x) <-- ("s" x))
(("q" 1) <--)
(("r" 2) <--)
(("s" 3) <--)
```

and the goal term (`"p"` x). The interpreter would try the first rule, giving
the subgoals (`"q"` x) and (`"r"` x). The first of these would succeed, yielding the value 1 for x. The second subgoal would then fail, since there is no
rule applicable to (`"r"` 1). Hence the system must backtrack to the application of the first rule, and try the second rule instead. The second rule would

find the subgoal (`"s"` x), which would then succeed, yielding a substitution that associates the x in the goal term to 3.

In order to organize this control structure, we use two continuations: a *success continuation* that records what to do when a unification step succeeds, and a *failure continuation* that keeps track of what to try next at each potential backtrack point. Each new failure continuation represents a new backtrack point and closes over the substitution with which to continue the computation.

A failure does not return anything to its failure continuation, so we model failure continuations as 0-argument procedures. A success continuation takes two arguments: a solution (a substitution) and a failure continuation that gives access to more results.

The procedure `solve-terms` takes as its argument a list of goals (with possibly one element, as in our examples). It calls `match-terms` with the list of goals, an empty substitution, an initial success continuation, and an initial failure continuation. If it succeeds, the success continuation applies the substitution to the initial list of goals and unparses the result for readability.

```
(define solve-terms
  (lambda (goals)
    (match-terms goals (empty-subst)
      (lambda (subst failure-fk)
        (unparse-terms (subst-in-terms goals subst)))
      (lambda () #f))))
```

The procedure `match-terms` and its auxiliary procedures are in figure 7.28. Its arguments are a list of goals to be satisfied, a substitution, a success continuation, and a failure continuation. It attempts to satisfy each of the goals. If there are no goals to satisfy, then it passes to its success continuation the current substitution and the current failure continuation. Otherwise, it calls `match-term` to try to solve the first goal. It passes to `match-term` a continuation that specifies that if the first goal can be solved with a substitution `new-subst`, then the computation should continue by solving the rest of the goals, using the new substitution. This sequence of goals corresponds to a logical *conjunction* ("and") of the goals. The continued computation uses the failure continuation `new-fk` so that the next failure will backtrack to the chronologically last backtrack point.

The procedure `match-term` attempts to solve a single term by invoking `match-term-against-rule` for each rule. The failure continuation passed along to it ensures that on failure, we continue searching the rest of the rules. The rules are kept in the global variable `the-rules`. If no matching rule is

```
(define match-terms
  (lambda (goals subst sk fk)
    (if (null? goals)
      (sk subst fk)
      (match-term (car goals) subst
        (lambda (new-subst new-fk)
          (match-terms (cdr goals) new-subst sk new-fk))
        fk))))

(define match-term
  (lambda (goal subst sk fk)
    (let loop ((rules the-rules))
      (if (null? rules)
        (fk)
        (match-term-against-rule goal (car rules) subst sk
          (lambda ()
            (loop (cdr rules)))))))))

(define match-term-against-rule
  (lambda (goal rule subst sk fk)
    (let ((instantiated-rule (instantiate rule)))
      (let ((head (rule->head instantiated-rule))
            (subgoals (rule->subgoals instantiated-rule)))
        (let ((new-subst
                (unify-term
                  (subst-in-term head subst)
                  (subst-in-term goal subst))))
          (if (not new-subst)
            (fk)
            (match-terms subgoals
              (compose-substs subst new-subst)
              sk fk)))))))
```

Figure 7.28   Procedures for logic programming

found, we report failure by invoking the failure continuation. Such a loop
in the failure continuation represents a logical *disjunction* ("or"): if one thing
doesn't work, we try the next one.

Finally, match-term-against-rule matches a term against a single rule.
It first creates a fresh instance of the rule, renaming all of the variables in
the rule with fresh variables. It then applies the current substitution to the

goal term and the head of the freshly instantiated rule, and attempts to unify them. If this fails, then the failure continuation is invoked, which will try the next rule. Otherwise, the resulting substitution is added to the current substitution, and the procedure calls `match-terms` to solve the subgoals.

We see that `match-terms` is called from two places: `solve-terms` and `match-term-against-rule`. Since the first argument to `match-terms` from within `match-term-against-rule` is a list of instantiated subgoals, we treat the argument to `solve-terms` in the same fashion.

Exercise 7.46 [⋆] Implement the procedure `instantiate`, which takes a rule as an argument and replaces each variable's identifier by a unique identifier. If two identifiers are the same, they should be replaced by the same unique identifier. Each time a rule is instantiated, its unique identifiers *must* change. Why? One way to create unique identifiers is to define a variant of `fresh-id` (exercise 2.11) for terms that keeps track of every unique identifier generated. Another way would be to use `gensym`, which is available on most Scheme implementations.

Exercise 7.47 [⋆] Implement a set of rules for `even-length` such that (`"even-length"` x) succeeds if and only if x is a list of even length. Represent lists as in the append example of this section. Hint: consider the mutually-recursive definition of even and odd of section 3.6.

Exercise 7.48 [⋆ ⋆] Implement a version of `solve-terms` that produces a finite list of results, not just the first one. Then, test `solve-terms` with the append rules on each of the two sample goal terms. Finally, implement and test an improvement to this interface when the number of results is unbounded.

Exercise 7.49 [⋆] Design a concrete syntax for logic programming, and modify this interpreter to use it.

Exercise 7.50 [⋆] Include (`fails` t) as a new kind of subgoal term. If t succeeds, then the term fails. If t fails, then the term succeeds and continues with the substitution that existed prior to the interpretation of the `fails` term.

Exercise 7.51 [⋆] One modification that is often used in logic programming languages is to require each rule head to be an `app` term whose first term is a string constant, called a *functor*. Redefine an `app-term` to be a symbol (corresponding to the functor) and a list of terms (corresponding to the rest of the terms), to take advantage of this modification. This improves `match-term`, since the functor symbol can also be used as a key to find the appropriate set of rules in a global table. Implement these ideas.

Exercise 7.52 [⋆ ⋆] The `cut` operator in logic programming is a mechanism for reducing the amount of search that occurs. In a language that supports `cut` and the modification of the preceding exercise, the global set of rules is divided into subsets, whose heads all have the same functor symbol and the same number of subterms. For example, the rules for `"append"` might be one such subset. A cut is a special subgoal that always succeeds. If it is backtracked into, however, it abandons not just the rule in which it occurs, but the entire subset in which the rule appears. Consider the example above, with the two "p" rules in the same subset. Then if there is a cut between ("q" x) and ("r" x), the goal term fails, since (("p" x) <-- ("s" x)) would not be tried. Treat the argument to solve-terms as an already instantiated headless rule, thus placing it into its own subset. Extend the term data type to include cut-term and implement cut.

Exercise 7.53 [⋆] It is possible to remove the occurs check in unify-term Doing this requires the programmer to ensure that no unsound unifying substitutions will occur, but it has been the standard in most logic languages. Implement this modification.

Exercise 7.54 [⋆ ⋆ ⋆] Consider the modifications made in exercises 7.51 and 7.53. Give some example programs that can be written with the unmodified version that cannot be written with the modified version?

Exercise 7.55 [⋆ ⋆] Add terms of the form (istrue e) and (is t e), where t is any term and e is an expression consisting of constants, variable references and primitive applications. Include numeric valued primitives as in section 3.1 and exercise 3.11. The expressions must be evaluated in the substitution (treated as an environment) by a separate interpreter. An istrue term succeeds if its expression's value is true and fails otherwise. An is term unifies its subterm with the value of its expression.

Exercise 7.56 [⋆ ⋆ ⋆] A substitution that fails the occurs check could be regarded as introducing a recursive association, somewhat like the way bindings are built to implement letrec expressions. Implement an extension of unification that takes advantage of this observation and as such does not include the occurs check.

Further Reading

(Reynolds, 1993) gives a fascinating history of the several independent discoveries of continuations and the CPS transform. (Strachey & Wadsworth, 1974; 2000) is probably the most influential of these. (Reynolds, 1972; 1998) transforms a metacircular interpreter into CPS and shows how this avoids some of the problems of metacircularity. The translation of programs in tail form to imperative form dates back to (McCarthy, 1962).

(Wand, 1980a; 1999) introduces the use of continuations as a model for lightweight processes or threads. Continuations may also be used for a variety of purposes beyond those discussed in the text, such as coroutines (Haynes, Friedman, & Wand, 1986) and program transformations (Wand, 1980b). (Clocksin & Mellish, 1994) is a standard text on logic programming. The two-continuation model used here was introduced in (Federhen, 1980).

The efficient implementation of continuations is treated in (Hieb, Dybvig, & Bruggeman, 1990) and (Clinger, Hartheimer, & Ost, 1999). (Clinger, 1998) discusses some of the subtleties of tail recursion.

8 *Continuation-Passing Style*

In chapter 7, we took an interpreter and rewrote it so that all of the major procedure calls were *tail calls*. By doing so, we guaranteed that the interpreter built up at most a bounded amount of control context, no matter how large or complex a program it was called upon to interpret. This property is called *iterative control behavior*.

We achieved this goal by passing an extra parameter, the *continuation*, to each procedure. This style of programming is called *continuation-passing style*, and it is not restricted to interpreters.

Of course, there is no completely general way of determining whether the control behavior of a procedure is iterative or not. Consider

```
(lambda (n)
  (if (strange-predicate? n)
    (fact n)
    (fact-iter n)))
```

This procedure is iterative only if `strange-predicate?` returns false for all sufficiently large values of n. But it is not always possible to determine the truth or falsity of this condition, even if it were possible to examine the code of `strange-predicate?`. Therefore the best we can hope for is to make sure that no procedure call in the program will build up control context, whether or not it is actually executed.

In this chapter we develop a systematic method for transforming any procedure into an equivalent procedure that has iterative control behavior. This is accomplished by converting it into continuation-passing style.

8.1   Tail Form

Our goal is to identify the class of expressions in which no procedure call is in a position that requires control context to be built. We will say that such expressions are in *tail form*.

Recall our principle from chapter 7:

> **It is evaluation of actual parameters, not the calling of procedures, that requires creating a control context.**

Thus in

```
(define fact
  (lambda (n)
    (if (zero? n) 1 (* n (fact (- n 1)))))))
```

it is the position of the call to fact *as an operand* that requires the creation of a control context. By contrast, in

```
(define fact-iter
  (lambda (n)
    (fact-iter-acc n 1)))

(define fact-iter-acc
  (lambda (n a)
    (if (zero? n) a (fact-iter-acc (- n 1) (* n a)))))
```

none of the procedure calls are in operand position. We say these calls are *tail calls* because their value is the result of the whole call.

Our goal in this section is to define formally the notion of a tail-form expression. In order to do this we need to identify two things:

- We identify those places where evaluation of an expression would not require a control context to be generated. We call these the *tail positions* of the language, and we say that procedure calls in these positions are *tail calls*.

- We identify a syntactic class of expressions that are guaranteed not to execute any procedure calls. We say such expressions are *simple*.

We will eventually say that an expression is in tail form if every subexpression in *non-tail position* is simple. Since simple expressions contain no procedure calls, this means that procedure calls can occur only in tail position, and therefore do not build any control context.

⟨program⟩   ::= ⟨expression⟩
⟨expression⟩ ::= ⟨number⟩
⟨expression⟩ ::= ⟨identifier⟩
⟨expression⟩ ::= ⟨primop⟩ ({⟨expression⟩}*⁽ʼ⁾)
⟨expression⟩ ::= if ⟨expression⟩ then ⟨expression⟩ else ⟨expression⟩
⟨expression⟩ ::= let {⟨identifier⟩ = ⟨expression⟩}* in ⟨expression⟩
⟨expression⟩ ::= proc ({⟨identifier⟩}*⁽ʼ⁾) ⟨expression⟩
⟨expression⟩ ::= (⟨expression⟩ {⟨expression⟩}*)
⟨expression⟩ ::= letrec {⟨identifier⟩ ({⟨identifier⟩}*⁽ʼ⁾) = ⟨expression⟩}*
                in ⟨expression⟩

Figure 8.1   Grammar for source language

But first we need to make all of this precise. We use the language of section 3.6, whose grammar is summarized in figure 8.1.

For each expression of this language, we can classify its immediate subexpressions into two classes:

- A subexpression in *head position* is one that must be evaluated, could be evaluated first, and is evaluated in the environment of the entire expression. An expression may have more than one head position because our interpreter does not, for example, specify the order of evaluation of the actual parameters of a procedure.

- A subexpression in *tail position* has the property that if it is evaluated, its value immediately becomes the value of the entire expression. For procedures defined by proc or letrec, the meaning of this criterion is explained below. For a subexpression in tail position, no information need be saved, and therefore no control context need be built. An expression may have more than one tail position because, for example, our if expressions may choose either the true or the false branch.

We show these positions for the language of figure 8.1 in figure 8.2. Head positions are indicated by H and tail positions by T.

We justify the entries in this figure as follows. Literals and variables are not listed, because they have no subexpressions. In a conditional, the test is

$\langle$primop$\rangle$ $(H, \dots, H)$
if H then T else T
let $\{\langle$identifier$\rangle = H\}^*$ in T
proc $(\{\langle$identifier$\rangle\}^{*(,)})$ T
$(H\,H\,\dots\,H\,)$
letrec $\{\langle$identifier$\rangle\,(\{\langle$identifier$\rangle\}^{*(,)}) = T\}^*$ in T

Figure 8.2   Head (H) and tail (T) positions in the source language

always evaluated first, so it is in head position. When one of the branches of a conditional is evaluated, its value becomes the value of the entire conditional, so the branches are both in tail position. In a let expression, each of the right-hand sides must be evaluated, so they are all in head position; the value of the body becomes the value of the entire expression, so it is in tail position. In a proc, the body is in tail position because its value will become the value of the application when it is invoked. In a procedure application, all of the subexpressions must be evaluated, so they are in head position. None of them is in tail position, because after they are all evaluated the procedure body is executed. In letrec declarations, the bodies are in tail position as they are for a proc expression, and the letrec body is in tail position.

In an expression, every subexpression except the entire expression appears as an immediate subexpression of some other subexpression. We can therefore classify every subexpression by whether it appears in a head position or a tail position of its immediate parent expression. For example, consider if zero?(x) then (f x) else (g (h y)). Here zero?(x) appears in head position, and (f x) and (g (h y)) appear in tail position. The expressions f, g, (h y), and both occurrences of x occur in head position. The expressions h and y also occur in head position.

Exercise 8.1 [⋆] For each expression, underline all of the subexpressions that appear in head position.

1. if (g x) then (f add1(b)) else (b (c x))
2. proc(u)(f if (g x) then (g (h y)) else u)
3. (f if zero?(x) then (g (h 3)) else (g 4))
4. (f if zero?(x) then 3 else 4 if (p x) then 3 else 4)
5. let x = 3 y = (fact 4) in (p x b)

Exercise 8.2 [⋆] Write a table like the one above showing head and tail positions for the fragment of the Scheme language used in the interpreter of section 3.6. Treat the `cases` form as a nested `if`. Now, when a subexpression in tail position of the defined language is evaluated, the corresponding call to `eval-expression` will also be in tail position.

Exercise 8.3 [⋆ ⋆] If the language included `set`, would the right-hand side of the assignment be in head position, tail position, both, or neither?

Exercise 8.4 [⋆ ⋆] Add to the language a construct that has some subexpressions that are in neither head nor tail position according to our criteria. Invent a construct with a subexpression that is in both head and tail position.

Exercise 8.5 [⋆ ⋆] Extend the CPS transformation to handle `letinorder` $x1 = e1$ $x2 = e2$ in $e3$. Here the scope of $x1$ is $e2$ and $e3$, and the scope of $x2$ is $e3$, like the `let*` of Scheme. Observe that $e2$ is neither in head nor tail position. This will require a new rule.

We now turn to the definition of those expressions that can never cause a procedure call. These are the *simple* expressions. We define these inductively:

Definition 8.1.1 *The simple expressions are defined as follows:*

- *A literal or a variable reference is always simple.*

- *A primitive application is simple if and only if all of its operands are simple.*

- *A conditional expression is simple if and only if all three of its subexpressions are simple.*

- *A* `let` *expression is simple if and only if all of its subexpressions are simple.*

- *A* `proc` *expression is always simple.*

- *A* `letrec` *expression is simple if and only if its body is simple.*

- *A procedure application is never simple.*

The intent of this definition is that the evaluation of a simple expression is just a short sequence of primitive operations, possibly with some closure creations and tests. Closure creation and `letrec` are treated in this category because they are simple data structure operations. Because the body of a closure is not evaluated when the closure is constructed, its body need not be simple, but all other subexpressions of a simple expression must be simple.

Exercise 8.6 [⋆] Draw a rectangle around every non-simple expression in exercise 8.1 that occurs in head position.

Exercise 8.7 [⋆] Write a Scheme procedure `simple?` that takes an abstract syntax tree for the defined language and tests whether it is simple.

Exercise 8.8 [⋆] Write `simple?` (see previous exercise) for the language of Scheme expressions of exercise 8.2.

We can now give the key definition:

Definition 8.1.2 *A tail-form expression is one in which every subexpression in non-tail position is simple.*

In this definition, the phrase "every subexpression" means not just the immediate subexpressions, but all subexpressions. So in a tail-form expression, the non-tail positions contain simple expressions that are also in tail form, and the tail positions contain tail-form expressions. This leads us to the grammar for tail-form expressions shown in figure 8.3. We say "non-tail position" because in some languages there may be subexpressions that are in neither head nor tail position.

Expressions may be in tail form but not simple, or simple but not in tail form. For example,

`add1(x)`	simple	tail form
`if p then x else add1(add1(x))`	simple	tail form
`(f +(x,y))`	not simple	tail form
`add1((f x))`	not simple	not tail form
`if p then x else (f sub1(x))`	not simple	tail form
`if (f x) then x else (f sub1(x))`	not simple	not tail form
`proc(x)(f x)`	simple	tail form
`proc(x)add1((f x)))`	simple	not tail form

These examples also demonstrate that not every tail-form expression is in continuation-passing style: the tail-form expressions in this table have no obvious continuations, nor could they be generated by the CPS algorithm in this chapter, but they are nevertheless in tail form.

Because we know that when an application in tail position is evaluated, no control information need be stored, and because in a tail-form expression all procedure applications are in tail position, we conclude:

Tail form implies iterative control behavior.

If an expression is in tail form, and any procedures accessible through variable bindings are also in tail form, then the expression will execute with iterative control behavior.

⟨tf-program⟩   ::= ⟨tf-exp⟩
⟨tf-exp⟩   ::= ⟨tf-simple-exp⟩
⟨tf-exp⟩   ::= if ⟨tf-simple-exp⟩ then ⟨tf-exp⟩ else ⟨tf-exp⟩
⟨tf-exp⟩   ::= let {⟨identifier⟩ = ⟨tf-simple-exp⟩}* in ⟨tf-exp⟩
⟨tf-exp⟩   ::= (⟨tf-simple-exp⟩ {⟨tf-simple-exp⟩}*)
⟨tf-exp⟩   ::= letrec {⟨identifier⟩ ({⟨identifier⟩}*⁽ʼ⁾) = ⟨tf-exp⟩}*
                       in ⟨tf-exp⟩
⟨tf-simple-exp⟩ ::= ⟨number⟩
⟨tf-simple-exp⟩ ::= ⟨identifier⟩
⟨tf-simple-exp⟩ ::= ⟨primop⟩ ({⟨tf-simple-exp⟩}*⁽ʼ⁾)
⟨tf-simple-exp⟩ ::= if ⟨tf-simple-exp⟩
                       then ⟨tf-simple-exp⟩
                       else ⟨tf-simple-exp⟩
⟨tf-simple-exp⟩ ::= let {⟨identifier⟩ = ⟨tf-simple-exp⟩}*
                       in ⟨tf-simple-exp⟩
⟨tf-simple-exp⟩ ::= proc ({⟨identifier⟩}*⁽ʼ⁾) ⟨tf-exp⟩
⟨tf-simple-exp⟩ ::= letrec {⟨identifier⟩ ({⟨identifier⟩}*⁽ʼ⁾) = ⟨tf-exp⟩}*
                       in ⟨tf-simple-exp⟩

but NOT:
⟨tf-simple-exp⟩ ::= (⟨tf-exp⟩ {⟨tf-exp⟩}*)
because an application is never simple.

Figure 8.3   Grammar for tail-form expressions

As an example, consider an instance of the factorial procedure in our
defined language:

```
letrec
  fact(n) =
    if zero?(n)
    then 1
    else *(n,(fact sub1(n)))
in (fact 4)
```

This is not in tail form, because the recursive call to fact occurs in an
operand position. If we give fact an additional continuation argument, then
we can rewrite this program in tail form as

```
letrec
  fact(n, k) =
    if zero?(n)
    then (k 1)
    else (fact sub1(n) proc(val)(k *(n,val)))
in (fact 4 proc(val)val)
```

Here we have used a procedural representation of continuations. If n is 0, then (fact n k) sends 1, the value of 0!, to k. If n is nonzero, then (fact n k) computes $(n-1)!$, calls the value val, and sends the value of *(n,val), namely $n \times (n-1)! = n!$ to k, as desired.

In the next section, we shall see how to convert any program in our defined language into tail form by using continuation-passing style.

Exercise 8.9 [⋆] Determine whether each of the following expressions is simple and whether it is in tail form.

1. add1((f sub1(x)))
2. (f add1(*(x,y)))
3. if zero?(x) then +(x,y) else add1(-(x,y))
4. let x = proc(y)(y x) in +(x,3)
5. let f = proc(x)x in (f 3)

Exercise 8.10 [⋆⋆] Write a Scheme procedure tail-form? that takes a program in the language of figure 8.1 and determines whether or not it is in tail form, by checking the abstract syntax tree of the program against the grammar of figure 8.3.

Exercise 8.11 [⋆⋆] Write a grammar similar to that of figure 8.3 for the subset of Scheme consisting of the following forms: variable, literal, primitive application, application, if, cond, lambda, let, and letrec. Make reasonable assumptions about what constitutes a primitive application. Write a procedure to test whether an expression in Scheme, according to this grammar, is in tail form.

8.2   Converting to Continuation-Passing Style

In this section we develop a set of rules for transforming any program in our defined language into an equivalent program in tail form. We do this by transforming the program into continuation-passing style.

The continuation-passing interpreter of chapter 7 suggests how a CPS transformation might be accomplished. The CPS transformation changes the procedure-calling convention so that every procedure takes an extra argument: the continuation to which the answer should be passed. It is then possible to transform every expression so that only simple expressions occur in non-tail positions.

Since our defined language does not have data structures like those built by `define-datatype`, we will use the procedural representation of continuations throughout.

The transformation is accomplished by three operations:

1. The first operation, denoted $\{\!\!\{-\}\!\!\}$, transforms a whole program into a procedure that accepts a continuation and then performs a calculation. The intention is that if P is the whole program, then $(\{\!\!\{P\}\!\!\}$ `proc(val)val`) should return the same answer as P.

2. The second operation, denoted $\langle\!\langle-\rangle\!\rangle$, takes a simple expression and transforms it by modifying each procedure occurring in the expression. Each procedure is transformed by adding an extra formal parameter k and by transforming the body so that instead of simply returning a value, it passes the same value to the continuation k. The transformation of the body is accomplished by the third operation.

3. The third operation is denoted $[\![-]\!]\bullet[\![-]\!]$. If E is an expression and K is a simple expression, then $[\![E]\!]\bullet[\![K]\!]$ will be a tail-form expression that sends the value of E to the continuation K. This operation is the heart of the CPS transformation.

Starting with these informal specifications, we can now describe these operations in more detail.

1. The transformation on programs can be written as

$$\{\!\!\{E\}\!\!\} = \texttt{proc(k)} \ [\![E]\!]\bullet[\![\texttt{k}]\!] \qquad\qquad (C_{pgm})$$

where k is a fresh variable that does not appear in E. $[\![E]\!]\bullet[\![\texttt{k}]\!]$ is a tail-form expression that sends the value of E to k, so $\{\!\!\{E\}\!\!\}$ will be a tail-form expression that, given a continuation, sends the value of E to that continuation, as desired.

2. The transformation rule for procedures is

$$\langle\!\langle\texttt{proc}\ (x_1,\ldots,x_n)\ E\rangle\!\rangle = \texttt{proc}\ (x_1,\ldots,x_n,\texttt{k})\ [\![E]\!]\bullet[\![\texttt{k}]\!] \qquad (C_{proc})$$

where k is a fresh variable. The transformed procedure takes an extra continuation argument, and its body is a tail-form expression that sends the value of E to the continuation k.

3. Any simple expression other than a procedure is transformed by applying the preceding rule to each procedure that occurs within it, including those that appear in `letrec` expressions.

Now all we need to do is to define $[\![E]\!] \bullet [\![K]\!]$. Overall this will be done by a case analysis on whether E and its subexpressions are simple. A subsidiary analysis is sometimes done on the form of K. There are five rules that define $[\![E]\!] \bullet [\![K]\!]$. We will state these rules as clearly as we can in prose; we make them more precise when we get to the implementation of the transformation in section 8.4. The algorithm $[\![-]\!] \bullet [\![-]\!]$ always terminates, because whenever $[\![E]\!] \bullet [\![K]\!]$ recursively invokes the algorithm, the left-hand argument is smaller than E.

1. If the expression E is simple and the continuation K is a variable k, then

$$[\![E]\!] \bullet [\![k]\!] = (k \; \langle\!\langle E \rangle\!\rangle) \qquad\qquad (C_{simple\text{-}var})$$

This rule is reasonable, because instead of returning the value of the expression E, it passes that value to k, as desired. For example,

$$
\begin{aligned}
[\![\texttt{x}]\!] \bullet [\![\texttt{k}]\!] &= \quad (\texttt{k} \; \langle\!\langle \texttt{x} \rangle\!\rangle) \\
&= \quad (\texttt{k} \; \texttt{x}) \\
[\![\texttt{+(x,y)}]\!] \bullet [\![\texttt{k}]\!] &= \quad (\texttt{k} \; \langle\!\langle \texttt{+(x,y)} \rangle\!\rangle) \\
&= \quad (\texttt{k} \; \texttt{+(x,y)}) \\
[\![\texttt{proc(x,y) (f x y)}]\!] \bullet [\![\texttt{k}]\!] &= \quad (\texttt{k} \; \langle\!\langle \texttt{proc(x,y) (f x y)} \rangle\!\rangle) \\
&= \quad (\texttt{k} \; \texttt{proc(x,y,k)} [\![\texttt{(f x y)}]\!] \bullet [\![\texttt{k}]\!])
\end{aligned}
$$

In the first example, the value of $\texttt{x}$ is returned to $\texttt{k}$. In the second example, the sum of $\texttt{x}$ and $\texttt{y}$ is computed and returned to $\texttt{k}$. In the last example, we are asked to return a procedure, so the procedure is transformed using $\langle\!\langle - \rangle\!\rangle$ and returned to $\texttt{k}$. Of course, the last example isn't finished yet, because we have not yet written down enough rules to figure out what expression is denoted by $[\![\texttt{(f x y)}]\!] \bullet [\![\texttt{k}]\!]$.

2. If the expression E is simple and the continuation K is a `proc` expression, then applying $C_{simple\text{-}var}$ would lead to an expression in which the procedure is applied to an argument. In this case we use the rule

$$[\![E]\!] \bullet [\![\texttt{proc} \, (v) \, T]\!] = \texttt{let} \; v \; = \; \langle\!\langle E \rangle\!\rangle \; \texttt{in} \; T \qquad (C_{simple\text{-}proc})$$

The `let` expression is equivalent to the expression that would have been generated by $C_{simple\text{-}var}$ but is easier to read. For example,

$$\llbracket \texttt{add1(x)} \rrbracket \bullet \llbracket \texttt{proc(v) (k v)} \rrbracket \quad = \quad \texttt{let v = add1(x) in (k v)}$$

which is in tail form. This rule will only be needed when processing expressions such as `if` or `let`.

3. It may be that E is non-simple, but has no non-simple subexpressions. In our language, the only way this can happen is when E is a procedure application $(S_0 \dots S_n)$, where each of the S_i is simple. In that case, what should happen? S_0 in the original program denoted a procedure of n arguments; in the transformed program it denotes a procedure of $n + 1$ arguments that computes the same thing the old procedure did, but sends the result to the last argument. Hence we write

$$\llbracket (S_0 \ \dots \ S_n) \rrbracket \bullet \llbracket K \rrbracket = (\langle\!\langle S_0 \rangle\!\rangle \ \dots \ \langle\!\langle S_n \rangle\!\rangle \ K) \qquad (C_{app})$$

where as before $\langle\!\langle S_i \rangle\!\rangle$ is obtained by performing the transformation $\langle\!\langle - \rangle\!\rangle$ on each procedure that appears in S_i. For example,

$$\llbracket \texttt{(f x)} \rrbracket \bullet \llbracket K \rrbracket = \texttt{(f x } K\texttt{)}$$

$$\llbracket \texttt{(fact sub1(n))} \rrbracket \bullet \llbracket K \rrbracket = \texttt{(fact sub1(n) } K\texttt{)}$$

$$\llbracket \texttt{(proc(x)} E \ \texttt{*(x,y))} \rrbracket \bullet \llbracket K \rrbracket = (\langle\!\langle \texttt{proc(x)} E \rangle\!\rangle \ \langle\!\langle \texttt{*(x,y)} \rangle\!\rangle \ K)$$

$$= \texttt{(proc(x,k)} \llbracket E \rrbracket \bullet \llbracket \texttt{k} \rrbracket \ \texttt{*(x,y)} \ K\texttt{)}$$

$$\llbracket \texttt{(g proc(a) (f a b))} \rrbracket \bullet \llbracket K \rrbracket = \texttt{(g } \langle\!\langle \texttt{proc(a) (f a b)} \rangle\!\rangle \ K\texttt{)}$$

$$= \texttt{(g proc(a,k)} \llbracket \texttt{(f a b)} \rrbracket \bullet \llbracket \texttt{k} \rrbracket \ K\texttt{)}$$

$$= \texttt{(g proc(a,k) (f a b k)} \ K\texttt{)}$$

$$\llbracket \texttt{proc(x,y) (f x y)} \rrbracket \bullet \llbracket \texttt{k} \rrbracket = \texttt{(k } \langle\!\langle \texttt{proc(x,y) (f x y)} \rangle\!\rangle \texttt{)}$$

$$= \texttt{(k proc(x,y,k)} \llbracket \texttt{(f x y)} \rrbracket \bullet \llbracket \texttt{k} \rrbracket \texttt{)}$$

$$= \texttt{(k proc(x,y,k) (f x y k))}$$

In the second example, `fact` was a 1-argument procedure in the original program, but is a 2-argument procedure in the transformed program. Similarly, in the fourth example, the original `g` took a 1-argument procedure as its sole argument; in the transformed program `g` takes two arguments: a procedure and a continuation. Since the procedure passed to `g` will likewise be applied to an argument and a continuation, it must be transformed as well, even though its body happens to be in tail form. The fourth example completes the last example from the first rule.

4. It may be that one of the head positions of E is non-simple. For example, E might be `*(n,(fact sub1(n)))`. In that case, we would like to evaluate the non-simple head expression, and send the result to a new continuation that performs the rest of the computation. Let E be $(\ldots H \ldots)$, where H is a non-simple immediate subexpression of E in a head position. E need not be an application, but we show parentheses for readability. We can write this rule as

$$[\![(\ldots H \ldots)]\!] \bullet [\![K]\!] = [\![H]\!] \bullet [\![\texttt{proc}\,(v)\,[\![(\ldots v \ldots)]\!] \bullet [\![K]\!]]\!] \qquad (C_{head})$$

where v is a fresh variable. Why does this work? When

$$[\![H]\!] \bullet [\![\texttt{proc}\,(v)\,[\![(\ldots v \ldots)]\!] \bullet [\![K]\!]]\!]$$

is evaluated, the value of H is sent to the procedure

$$\texttt{proc}\,(v)\,[\![(\ldots v \ldots)]\!] \bullet [\![K]\!]$$

whose bound variable is v and whose body is $[\![(\ldots v \ldots)]\!] \bullet [\![K]\!]$. This procedure computes the value of $(\ldots\ v \ldots)$ in an environment where v is bound to the value of H, and sends the result to the continuation K. This is the same as computing the value of $(\ldots H \ldots)$ and sending the result to K, as desired.

This may be clearer if we look at some examples.

$$
\begin{aligned}
&[\![+((\texttt{f x}),\texttt{y})]\!] \bullet [\![\texttt{k}]\!] \\
&= \textit{create a continuation for } (\texttt{f x}) \qquad (C_{head}) \\
&[\![(\texttt{f x})]\!] \bullet [\![\texttt{proc}\,(\texttt{v})\,[\![+(\texttt{v},\texttt{y})]\!] \bullet [\![\texttt{k}]\!]]\!] \\
&= \textit{send } +(\texttt{v},\texttt{y}) \textit{ to } \texttt{k} \qquad (C_{simple\text{-}var}) \\
&[\![(\texttt{f x})]\!] \bullet [\![\texttt{proc}\,(\texttt{v})\,(\texttt{k }+(\texttt{v},\texttt{y}))]\!] \\
&= \textit{transform the call to } \texttt{f} \qquad (C_{app}) \\
&(\texttt{f x proc}\,(\texttt{v})\,(\texttt{k }+(\texttt{v},\texttt{y})))
\end{aligned}
$$

The expression to be transformed computes the value of `(f x)` (let us call that value v) and returns the sum of v and the value of `y`. In the transformed expression, the transformed procedure `f` sends the value v to its continuation argument, `proc (v) (k +(v,y))`. Hence `v` is bound to v, so the sum of v and the value of `y` is sent to `k`, as desired.

Here is a nested procedure call:

$[\![+((\mathtt{f}\ (\mathtt{g}\ \mathtt{x})),\mathtt{y})]\!]\bullet[\![\mathtt{k}]\!]$
$=$ *create a continuation for* $(\mathtt{f}\ (\mathtt{g}\ \mathtt{x}))$ $\hspace{3em}(C_{head})$
$[\![(\mathtt{f}\ (\mathtt{g}\ \mathtt{x}))]\!]\bullet[\![\mathtt{proc}(\mathtt{v})[\![+(\mathtt{v},\mathtt{y})]\!]\bullet[\![\mathtt{k}]\!]]\!]$
$=$ *send* $+(\mathtt{v},\mathtt{y})$ *to* $\mathtt{k}$ $\hspace{3em}(C_{simple\text{-}var})$
$[\![(\mathtt{f}\ (\mathtt{g}\ \mathtt{x}))]\!]\bullet[\![\mathtt{proc}(\mathtt{v})(\mathtt{k}\ +(\mathtt{v},\mathtt{y}))]\!]$
$=$ *create a continuation for* $(\mathtt{g}\ \mathtt{x})$ $\hspace{3em}(C_{head})$
$[\![(\mathtt{g}\ \mathtt{x})]\!]\bullet[\![\mathtt{proc}(\mathtt{w})[\![(\mathtt{f}\ \mathtt{w})]\!]\bullet[\![\mathtt{proc}(\mathtt{v})(\mathtt{k}\ +(\mathtt{v},\mathtt{y}))]\!]]\!]$
$=$ *transform the call to* $\mathtt{f}$ $\hspace{3em}(C_{app})$
$[\![(\mathtt{g}\ \mathtt{x})]\!]\bullet[\![\mathtt{proc}(\mathtt{w})(\mathtt{f}\ \mathtt{w}\ \mathtt{proc}(\mathtt{v})(\mathtt{k}\ +(\mathtt{v},\mathtt{y})))]\!]$
$=$ *transform the call to* $\mathtt{g}$ $\hspace{3em}(C_{app})$
$(\mathtt{g}\ \mathtt{x}\ \mathtt{proc}(\mathtt{w})(\mathtt{f}\ \mathtt{w}\ \mathtt{proc}(\mathtt{v})(\mathtt{k}\ +(\mathtt{v},\mathtt{y}))))$

The expression to be transformed computes the value of $(\mathtt{g}\ \mathtt{x})$ (let us call that value w). Then it computes the value of $\mathtt{f}$ applied to w (let us call that v), and returns the sum of v and the value of $\mathtt{y}$. In the transformed expression, the procedure $\mathtt{g}$ sends the value w to its continuation argument, $\mathtt{proc}(\mathtt{w})(\mathtt{f}\ \mathtt{w}\ \mathtt{proc}(\mathtt{v})(\mathtt{k}\ +(\mathtt{v},\mathtt{y})))$, which binds the identifier $\mathtt{w}$ to w. Then the procedure $\mathtt{f}$ receives the value w, so it sends the value v to its continuation $\mathtt{proc}(\mathtt{v})(\mathtt{k}\ +(\mathtt{v},\mathtt{y}))$, which sends the sum of v and the value of $\mathtt{y}$ to $\mathtt{k}$, as desired.

Below is an example of two procedure calls in operand position.

$[\![+((\mathtt{f}\ \mathtt{x}),(\mathtt{g}\ \mathtt{y}))]\!]\bullet[\![\mathtt{k}]\!]$
$=$ *create a continuation for* $(\mathtt{f}\ \mathtt{x})$ $\hspace{3em}(C_{head})$
$[\![(\mathtt{f}\ \mathtt{x})]\!]\bullet[\![\mathtt{proc}(\mathtt{v})[\![+(\mathtt{v},(\mathtt{g}\ \mathtt{y}))]\!]\bullet[\![\mathtt{k}]\!]]\!]$
$=$ $\hspace{3em}(C_{head})$
$[\![(\mathtt{f}\ \mathtt{x})]\!]\bullet[\![\mathtt{proc}(\mathtt{v})[\![(\mathtt{g}\ \mathtt{y})]\!]\bullet[\![\mathtt{proc}(\mathtt{w})[\![+(\mathtt{v},\mathtt{w})]\!]\bullet[\![\mathtt{k}]\!]]\!]]\!]$
$=$ $\hspace{3em}(C_{simple\text{-}var})$
$[\![(\mathtt{f}\ \mathtt{x})]\!]\bullet[\![\mathtt{proc}(\mathtt{v})[\![(\mathtt{g}\ \mathtt{y})]\!]\bullet[\![\mathtt{proc}(\mathtt{w})(\mathtt{k}\ +(\mathtt{v},\mathtt{w}))]\!]]\!]$
$=$ $\hspace{3em}(C_{app})$
$(\mathtt{f}\ \mathtt{x}\ \mathtt{proc}(\mathtt{v})[\![(\mathtt{g}\ \mathtt{y})]\!]\bullet[\![\mathtt{proc}(\mathtt{w})(\mathtt{k}\ +(\mathtt{v},\mathtt{w}))]\!])$
$=$ $\hspace{3em}(C_{app})$
$(\mathtt{f}\ \mathtt{x}\ \mathtt{proc}(\mathtt{v})(\mathtt{g}\ \mathtt{y}\ \mathtt{proc}(\mathtt{w})(\mathtt{k}\ +(\mathtt{v},\mathtt{w}))))$

Here $(\mathtt{f}\ \mathtt{x})$ is the first non-simple expression in head position in $+((\mathtt{f}\ \mathtt{x}),(\mathtt{g}\ \mathtt{y}))$, and $(\mathtt{g}\ \mathtt{y})$ is the first non-simple expression in head position in $+(\mathtt{v},(\mathtt{g}\ \mathtt{y}))$. The original expression computed $(\mathtt{f}\ \mathtt{x})$ (let us call that value v) and $(\mathtt{g}\ \mathtt{y})$ (let us call that value w), and returned the sum of v and w. If `f` and `g` have also been transformed, then the call to `f` in the transformed expression will send v to the continuation `proc(v)(g y proc(w)(k +(v,w)))`, thus binding `v` to v. Similarly, the call to `g` will bind `w` to w, so the sum of v and w will be sent to `k`, as desired.

Next, we show an example with a procedure passed to `g`, so we transform that procedure as well.

$$
\begin{aligned}
&[\![+((\texttt{f a b}),(\texttt{g proc(a)(f a b)}))]\!] \bullet [\![\texttt{k}]\!] \\
&= \qquad\qquad\qquad\qquad\qquad\qquad\qquad\qquad\qquad (C_{head}) \\
&[\![(\texttt{f a b})]\!] \bullet [\![\texttt{proc(v)} [\![+(\texttt{v},(\texttt{g proc(a)(f a b)}))]\!] \bullet [\![\texttt{k}]\!]]\!] \\
&= \qquad\qquad\qquad\qquad\qquad\qquad\qquad\qquad\qquad (C_{head}) \\
&[\![(\texttt{f a b})]\!] \bullet [\![\texttt{proc(v)} \ [\![(\texttt{g proc(a)(f a b)})]\!] \\
&\qquad\qquad\qquad\qquad\quad \bullet [\![\texttt{proc(w)} [\![+(\texttt{v,w})]\!] \bullet [\![\texttt{k}]\!]]\!]]\!] \\
&= \qquad\qquad\qquad\qquad\qquad\qquad\qquad\qquad\qquad (C_{simple\text{-}var}) \\
&[\![(\texttt{f a b})]\!] \bullet [\![\texttt{proc(v)} \ [\![(\texttt{g proc(a)(f a b)})]\!] \\
&\qquad\qquad\qquad\qquad\quad \bullet [\![\texttt{proc(w)(k +(v,w))}]\!]]\!] \\
&= \qquad\qquad\qquad\qquad\qquad\qquad\qquad\qquad\qquad (C_{app}) \\
&[\![(\texttt{f a b})]\!] \bullet [\![\texttt{proc(v)(g} \ \langle\!\langle \texttt{proc(a)(f a b)} \rangle\!\rangle \\
&\qquad\qquad\qquad\qquad\quad \texttt{proc(w)(k +(v,w)))}]\!] \\
&= \qquad\qquad\qquad\qquad\qquad\qquad\qquad\qquad\qquad (C_{proc}) \\
&[\![(\texttt{f a b})]\!] \bullet [\![\texttt{proc(v)(g proc(a,k)} [\![(\texttt{f a b})]\!] \bullet [\![\texttt{k}]\!] \\
&\qquad\qquad\qquad\qquad\quad \texttt{proc(w)(k +(v,w)))}]\!] \\
&= \qquad\qquad\qquad\qquad\qquad\qquad\qquad\qquad\qquad (C_{app}) \\
&[\![(\texttt{f a b})]\!] \bullet [\![\texttt{proc(v)(g proc(a,k)(f a b k)} \\
&\qquad\qquad\qquad\qquad\quad \texttt{proc(w)(k +(v,w)))}]\!] \\
&= \qquad\qquad\qquad\qquad\qquad\qquad\qquad\qquad\qquad (C_{app}) \\
&(\texttt{f a b proc(v)(g proc(a,k)(f a b k)} \\
&\qquad\qquad\qquad\qquad\quad \texttt{proc(w)(k +(v,w))))}
\end{aligned}
$$

Because the C_{head} rule is applicable to any expression that has a non-simple subexpression in head position, we can also consider `let` expressions:

$$
\begin{aligned}
&[\![\texttt{let z = (f x) u = z in (g z u)}]\!] \bullet [\![\texttt{k}]\!] \\
&= \qquad\qquad\qquad\qquad\qquad\qquad\qquad\qquad\qquad (C_{head}) \\
&[\![(\texttt{f x})]\!] \bullet [\![\texttt{proc(v)} [\![\texttt{let z = v u = z in (g z u)}]\!] \bullet [\![\texttt{k}]\!]]\!] \\
&= \qquad\qquad\qquad\qquad\qquad\qquad\qquad\qquad\qquad (C_{app}) \\
&(\texttt{f x proc(v)} [\![\texttt{let z = v u = z in (g z u)}]\!] \bullet [\![\texttt{k}]\!])
\end{aligned}
$$

Here we have taken the (f x) that appears in head position in the let and promoted it to be evaluated first, in a continuation that binds v to the resulting value and continues with the evaluation of the let. We will present the rule for transforming the let next.

5. Finally, E is non-simple, and contains some non-simple subexpressions, but all the head positions in E contain simple expressions. Since in our language, every position is either a head position or a tail position, it follows that E contains some non-simple subexpressions in tail position in E. Consulting figure 8.2, we see that E must be either an if, a let, or a letrec expression. In this case, we can move the continuation K into the tail position. These three rules are called C_{if}, C_{let}, and C_{letrec}:

$$
\begin{aligned}
&[\![\text{if } S \text{ then } E_1 \text{ else } E_2]\!] \bullet [\![K]\!] \\
&= \text{if } \langle\!\langle S \rangle\!\rangle \text{ then } [\![E_1]\!] \bullet [\![K]\!] \text{ else } [\![E_2]\!] \bullet [\![K]\!]
\end{aligned}
\qquad (C_{if})
$$

$$
\begin{aligned}
&[\![\text{let } v_1 = S_1 \ldots v_n = S_n \text{ in } E]\!] \bullet [\![K]\!] \\
&= \ \text{let } v_1 = \langle\!\langle S_1 \rangle\!\rangle \ldots v_n = \langle\!\langle S_n \rangle\!\rangle \text{ in } [\![E]\!] \bullet [\![K]\!]
\end{aligned}
\qquad (C_{let})
$$

$$
\begin{aligned}
&[\![\text{letrec} \\
&\quad p_1(x_1, \ldots, x_{n_1}) \ = E_1 \\
&\quad \ldots \\
&\quad p_m(z_1, \ldots, z_{n_m}) = E_m \\
&\quad \text{in } E]\!] \bullet [\![K]\!] \\
&= \\
&\text{letrec} \\
&\quad p_1(x_1, \ldots, x_{n_1}, \text{k}) \ = [\![E_1]\!] \bullet [\![\text{k}]\!] \\
&\quad \ldots \\
&\quad p_m(z_1, \ldots, z_{n_m}, \text{k}) = [\![E_m]\!] \bullet [\![\text{k}]\!] \\
&\text{in } [\![E]\!] \bullet [\![K]\!]
\end{aligned}
\qquad (C_{letrec})
$$

In the rule for letrec, we transform each of the procedures, and then we transform the body in the given continuation K.

In the transformations for let and letrec, we bring the continuation K into the scope of the declarations. Therefore, if any variable declared in the expression happens to occur free in K, it must be renamed or otherwise rearranged in the expression so that it will not capture the variable in K. This is among the details we will deal with in section 8.4.

$[\![\text{if add1}((\text{f x}))\text{ then y else z}]\!] \bullet [\![\text{k}]\!]$

$= \textit{create a continuation for } \text{add1}((\text{f x}))$ \hfill $(C_{\textit{head}})$

$[\![\text{add1}((\text{f x}))]\!] \bullet [\![\text{proc}(\text{v})[\![\text{if v then y else z}]\!] \bullet [\![\text{k}]\!]]\!]$

$= \textit{move continuation } \text{k} \textit{ inside the } \text{if}$ \hfill $(C_{\textit{if}})$

$[\![\text{add1}((\text{f x}))]\!] \bullet [\![\text{proc}(\text{v})\text{if v then } [\![\text{y}]\!] \bullet [\![\text{k}]\!] \text{ else } [\![\text{z}]\!] \bullet [\![\text{k}]\!]]\!]$

$= \textit{transform } \text{y} \textit{ and } \text{z}$ \hfill $(C_{\textit{simple-var}})$

$[\![\text{add1}((\text{f x}))]\!] \bullet [\![\text{proc}(\text{v})\text{if v then }(\text{k y})\text{ else }(\text{k z})]\!]$

$= \textit{create a continuation for } (\text{f x})$ \hfill $(C_{\textit{head}})$

$[\![(\text{f x})]\!] \bullet [\![\text{proc}(\text{w})$

$\qquad\qquad [\![\text{add1}(\text{w})]\!] \bullet [\![\text{proc}(\text{v})\text{if v then }(\text{k y})\text{ else }(\text{k z})]\!]]\!]$

$= \textit{bind } \text{v} \textit{ to } \text{add1}(\text{w})$ \hfill $(C_{\textit{simple-proc}})$

$[\![(\text{f x})]\!] \bullet [\![\text{proc}(\text{w})$

$\qquad\qquad \text{let v = add1}(\text{w})\text{ in if v then }(\text{k y})\text{ else }(\text{k z})]\!]$

$= \textit{transform call to } \text{f}$ \hfill $(C_{\textit{app}})$

$(\text{f x proc}(\text{w})\text{let v = add1}(\text{w})\text{ in if v then }(\text{k y})\text{ else }(\text{k z}))$

Figure 8.4   Transforming with procedural continuations

The rule $C_{\textit{simple-proc}}$ is often used when processing these expressions, as illustrated in figure 8.4.

Exercise 8.12 [$\star$] For each expression E, below, find the expression $[\![E]\!] \bullet [\![\text{k}]\!]$.

1. `(p +(8,x) (q y))`.
2. `add1((f (g x y) +(u,v)))`
3. `add1((f (g x y) +(u,(h v))))`
4. `zero?(if a then (p x) else (p y))`
5. `zero?(if (f a) then (p x) else (p y))`
6. `let x = let y = 8 in (p y) in x`
7. `let x = if a then (p x) else (p y) in x`

Exercise 8.13 [$\star$] Our transformation of `+((f x),(g y))` evaluated `(f x)` first. CPS-transform this expression so that it evaluates `(g y)` first by choosing `(g y)` first in rule $C_{\textit{head}}$.

Exercise 8.14 [$\star$] Find the transformations of `+((f x),(g (h y)))` corresponding to each possible order of evaluation.

Exercise 8.15 [⋆⋆] When an `if` expression such as `if zero?(n) then 0 else (f sub1(n))` appears inside a large expression, then the CPS-transformed expression will look like `if zero?(n) then (K 0) else (f sub1(n)K)` where K represents the continuation that abstracts the context of the large expression. This reveals a shortcoming of the CPS transformation. Since the program text of K appears in two places, the size of the transformed program can grow exponentially. Show how this may be avoided by binding a fresh variable to K.

Exercise 8.16 [⋆⋆] The rule $C_{simple\text{-}proc}$ can be simplified further. We can tell by examining C_{head}, that in any continuation `proc (v) T`, v occurs only once in T. Furthermore, v never occurs inside any binding occurrence of a variable from the original program. Therefore the rule $C_{simple\text{-}proc}$ could be replaced by

$$\llbracket E \rrbracket \bullet \llbracket \texttt{proc } (v) \ T \rrbracket = T[\langle\!\langle E \rangle\!\rangle / v] \qquad\qquad (C_{simple\text{-}proc'})$$

where the notation $E_1[E_2/x]$ means expression E_1 with every free occurrence of the variable x replaced by E_2, being certain to avoid any unintended variable capture (exercise 2.11). How would the examples of $C_{simple\text{-}proc}$ shown in this section change if this version of the rule were applied? Redo figure 8.4 using this version of the rule.

8.3   Examples of the CPS Transformation

We next work through a few examples, starting with the factorial function.

```
{letrec
   fact(n) =
     if zero?(n)
     then 1
     else *(n,(fact sub1(n)))
 in (fact 4)}
```
$=$ *the program will accept a continuation* (C_{pgm})
```
proc(k)
  ⟦letrec
     fact(n)  =
       if zero?(n)
       then 1
       else *(n,(fact sub1(n)))
   in (fact 4)⟧ • ⟦k⟧
```
$=$ *transform the* `letrec` (C_{letrec})
```
proc(k)
  letrec
    fact(n, k) =
      ⟦if zero?(n)
        then 1
        else *(n,(fact sub1(n)))⟧ • ⟦k⟧
  in ⟦(fact 4)⟧ • ⟦k⟧
```

```
    =  transform the body                                 (C_simple-var)
proc(k)
    letrec
      fact(n, k) =
        [[if zero?(n)
          then 1
          else *(n,(fact sub1(n)))]] • [[k]]
    in (fact 4 k)
    =  take the continuation inside the if                (C_if)
proc(k)
    letrec
      fact(n, k) =
        if zero?(n)
        then [[1]] • [[k]]
        else [[*(n,(fact sub1(n)))]] • [[k]]
    in (fact 4 k)
    =  transform the then                                 (C_simple-var)
proc(k)
    letrec
      fact(n, k) =
        if zero?(n)
        then (k 1)
        else [[*(n,(fact sub1(n)))]] • [[k]]
    in (fact 4 k)
    =  transform the else: compute (fact sub1(n)) in a
       continuation that will finish the calculation      (C_head)
proc(k)
    letrec
      fact(n, k) =
        if zero?(n)
        then (k 1)
        else [[(fact sub1(n))]] • [[proc(v) [[*(n,v)]] • [[k]]]]
    in (fact 4 k)
    =  send *(n,v) to k                                   (C_simple-var)
proc(k)
    letrec
      fact(n, k) =
        if zero?(n)
        then (k 1)
        else [[(fact sub1(n))]] • [[proc(v) (k *(n,v))]]
    in (fact 4 k)
```

```
=  last, transform the recursive call to fact                    (C_app)
proc(k)
  letrec
    fact(n, k) =
      if zero?(n)
      then (k 1)
      else (fact sub1(n) proc(v)(k *(n,v)))
  in (fact 4 k)
```

which, when applied to `proc(val)val` *is* what we had on page 307.

For our examples, we will be primarily concerned with the transformation of procedures defined in a `letrec` expression. So we will just look at the declaration part of the `letrec` and use the ⟨⟨−⟩⟩ notation for this purpose.

For our next example, we transform `remove` from section 1.2.2. Since we do not have symbols in our language, we will remove numbers instead. We assume we have `cons`, `car`, `cdr`, `emptylist`, `null?` and `equal?` from the earlier exercises 3.7 and 3.11. In our defined language, this becomes

```
letrec
  remove(n, lon) =
    if null?(lon)
    then emptylist
    else if equal?(s,car(lon))
         then (remove n cdr(lon))
         else cons(car(lon),(remove n cdr(lon)))
in ...
```

which we transform as follows:

```
⟨⟨letrec
    remove(n, lon) =
      if null?(lon)
      then emptylist
      else if equal?(s,car(lon))
           then (remove n cdr(lon))
           else cons(car(lon),(remove n cdr(lon)))⟩⟩
=  transform the procedures in the letrec
letrec
  remove(n, lon, k) =
    ⟦if null?(lon)
      then emptylist
      else if equal?(s,car(lon))
           then (remove n cdr(lon))
           else cons(car(lon),(remove n cdr(lon)))⟧ • ⟦k⟧
```

```
=  take the continuation inside the if                        (C_if    (twice))
letrec
  remove(n, lon, k) =
    if null?(lon)
    then [[emptylist]]•[[k]]
    else if equal?(s,car(lon))
            then [[(remove n cdr(lon))]]•[[k]]
            else [[cons(car(lon),(remove n cdr(lon)))]]•[[k]]
=  send emptylist to k                                         (C_simple-var)
letrec
  remove(n, lon, k) =
    if null?(lon)
    then (k emptylist)
    else if equal?(s,car(lon))
            then [[(remove n cdr(lon))]]•[[k]]
            else [[cons(car(lon),(remove n cdr(lon)))]]•[[k]]
=  the first call to remove is already in tail position        (C_app)
letrec
  remove(n, lon, k) =
    if null?(lon)
    then (k emptylist)
    else if equal?(s,car(lon))
            then (remove n cdr(lon) k)
            else [[cons(car(lon),(remove n cdr(lon)))]]•[[k]]
=  create a continuation for the context of the second         (C_head)
   call to remove
letrec
  remove(n, lon, k) =
    if null?(lon)
    then (k emptylist)
     else if equal?(s,car(lon))
            then (remove n cdr(lon) k)
            else [[(remove n cdr(lon))]]
                   •[[proc(v)[[cons(car(lon),v)]]•[[k]]]]
=  send cons(car(lon),v) to k                                  (C_simple-var)
letrec
  remove(n, lon, k) =
    if null?(lon)
    then (k emptylist)
    else if equal?(s,car(lon))
            then (remove n cdr(lon) k)
            else [[(remove n cdr(lon))]]
                  •[[proc(v)(k cons(car(lon),v))]]
```

= *transform the call to* remove   (C_{app})
```
letrec
  remove(n, lon, k) =
    if null?(lon)
    then (k emptylist)
    else if equal?(s,car(lon))
         then (remove n cdr(lon) k)
         else (remove n cdr(lon)
                 proc(v)(k cons(car(lon),v)))
```

and we are done.

Finally, we transform subst (with number?) from section 1.2.2.

```
⟨⟨letrec
   subst(new, old, nlist) =
     if null?(nlist)
     then emptylist
     else cons((subst-in-num-exp new old car(nlist)),
               (subst new old cdr(nlist)))
   subst-in-num-exp(new, old, ne) =
     if number?(ne)
     then if equal?(ne,old) then new else ne
     else (subst new old ne)⟩⟩
```
= *transform the procedures in the* letrec
```
letrec
  subst(new, old, nlist, k) =
    ⟦if null?(nlist)
     then emptylist
     else cons((subst-in-num-exp new old (car nlist)),
               (subst new old cdr(nlist)))⟧ • ⟦k⟧
  subst-in-num-exp(new, old, ne, k) =
    ⟦if number?(ne)
     then if equal?(ne,old) then new else ne
     else (subst new old ne)⟧ • ⟦k⟧
```
= *move the continuations inside the* if *expressions* (C_{if} (several times))
```
letrec
  subst(new, old, nlist, k) =
    if null?(nlist)
    then ⟦emptylist⟧ • ⟦k⟧
    else ⟦cons((subst-in-num-exp new old car(nlist)),
               (subst new old cdr(nlist)))⟧ • ⟦k⟧
  subst-in-num-exp(new, old, ne, k) =
    if number?(ne)
    then ⟦if equal?(ne,old) then new else ne⟧ • ⟦k⟧
    else ⟦(subst new old ne)⟧ • ⟦k⟧
```

```
= send simple values to k                              (C_simple-var   (twice))
letrec
  subst(new, old, nlist, k) =
    if null?(nlist)
    then (k emptylist)
    else [[cons((subst-in-num-exp new old car(nlist)),
             (subst new old cdr(nlist)))]] • [[k]]
  subst-in-num-exp(new, old, ne, k) =
    if number?(ne)
    then (k if equal?(ne,old) then new else ne)
    else [[(subst new old ne)]] • [[k]]
= create continuation for call to subst-in-num-exp              (C_head)
letrec
  subst(new, old, nlist, k) =
    if null?(nlist)
    then (k emptylist)
    else [[(subst-in-num-exp new old car(nlist))]]
          • [[proc(v)
              [[cons(v,(subst new old cdr(nlist)))]]
               • [[k]]]]
  subst-in-num-exp(new, old, ne, k) =
    if number?(ne)
    then (k if equal?(ne,old) then new else ne)
    else [[(subst new old ne)]] • [[k]]
= create continuation for call to subst                          (C_head)
letrec
  subst(new, old, nlist, k) =
    if null?(nlist)
    then (k emptylist)
    else [[(subst-in-num-exp new old car(nlist))]]
          • [[proc(v)
              [[(subst new old cdr(nlist))]]
               • [[proc(w)
                   [[cons(v,w)]] • [[k]]]]]]
  subst-in-num-exp(new, old, ne, k) =
    if number?(ne)
    then (k if equal?(ne,old) then new else ne)
    else [[(subst new old ne)]] • [[k]]
```

```
=  send cons(v,w) to k                                        (C_simple-var)
letrec
   subst(new, old, nlist, k) =
      if null?(nlist)
      then (k emptylist)
      else [[(subst-in-num-exp new old car(nlist))]]
            •[[proc(v)
                [[(subst new old cdr(nlist))]]
               •[[proc(w)
                  (k cons(v,w))]]]]]
   subst-in-num-exp(new, old, ne, k) =
      if number?(ne)
      then (k if equal?(ne,old) then new else ne)
      else [[(subst new old ne)]]•[[k]]
=  transform the call to subst                                   (C_app)
letrec
   subst(new, old, nlist, k) =
      if null?(nlist)
      then (k emptylist)
      else [[(subst-in-num-exp new old car(nlist))]]
            •[[proc(v)
                (subst new old cdr(nlist)
                   proc(w)
                    (k cons(v,w)))]]
   subst-in-num-exp(new, old, ne, k) =
      if number?(ne)
      then (k if equal?(ne,old) then new else ne)
      else [[(subst new old ne)]]•[[k]]
=  transform the call to subst-in-num-exp                        (C_app)
letrec
   subst(new, old, nlist, k) =
      if null?(nlist)
      then (k emptylist)
      else (subst-in-num-exp new old car(nlist)
              proc(v)
                (subst new old cdr(nlist)
                   proc(w)
                    (k cons(v,w))))
   subst-in-num-exp(new, old, ne, k) =
      if number?(ne)
      then (k if equal?(ne,old) then new else ne)
      else [[(subst new old ne)]]•[[k]]
```

= *transform the call to* subst   (C_{app})
```
letrec
  subst(new, old, nlist, k) =
    if null?(nlist)
    then (k emptylist)
    else (subst-in-num-exp new old car(nlist)
           proc(v)
             (subst new old cdr(nlist)
               proc(w)
               (k cons(v,w))))
  subst-in-num-exp(new, old, ne, k) =
    if number?(ne)
    then (k if equal?(ne,old) then new else ne)
    else (subst new old ne k)
```

which is in tail form, as desired.

Exercise 8.17 [⋆] In this example, we chose to evaluate the two operands to cons in left-to-right order. Transform this example to CPS again, evaluating the two operands to cons from right to left.

Exercise 8.18 [⋆] For each of the definitions in this exercise, do the following: first, test the definition with the procedure tail-form? of exercise 8.10. Include a sample call to the procedure as the body of the letrec. Then transform the definition to continuation-passing style using the rules of this section. Verify that the transformed definition is in tail form by using tail-form?. Then test the transformed definition using the continuation proc(val)val. Be sure that the original and transformed versions give the same answer on each input.

1. removeall.

```
letrec
  removeall(n, s) =
    if null?(s)
    then emptylist
    else if number?(car(s))
          then if equal?(n,car(s))
                then (removeall n cdr(s))
                else cons(car(s),
                         (removeall n cdr(s)))
          else cons((removeall n car(s)),
                   (removeall n cdr(s)))
```

2. `occurs-in?`.

```
letrec
  occurs-in?(n, s) =
    if null?(s)
    then 0
    else if number?(car(s))
         then if equal?(n,car(s))
              then 1
              else (occurs-in? n cdr(s))
         else if (occurs-in? n car(s))
              then 1
              else (occurs-in? n cdr(s))
```

3. `remfirst`. This uses `occurs-in?` from the preceding example.

```
letrec
  remfirst(n, s) =
    letrec
      loop(s) =
        if null?(s)
        then emptylist
        else if number?(car(s))
             then if equal?(n,car(s))
                  then cdr(s)
                  else cons(car(s),(loop cdr(s)))
             else if (occurs-in? n car(s))
                  then cons((remfirst n car(s)),
                            cdr(s))
                  else cons(car(s),
                            (remfirst n cdr(s)))
    in (loop s)
```

4. `depth`.

```
letrec
  depth(s) =
    if null?(s)
    then 1
    else if number?(car(s))
         then (depth cdr(s))
         else if less?(add1((depth car(s))),
                       (depth cdr(s)))
              then (depth cdr(s))
              else add1((depth car(s)))
```

5. depth-with-let.

```
letrec
  depth(s) =
    if null?(s)
    then 1
    else if number?(car(s))
         then (depth cdr(s))
         else let dfirst = add1((depth car(s)))
                  drest  = add1((depth cdr(s)))
              in if less?(dfirst,drest)
                 then drest
                 else dfirst
```

Exercise 8.19 [⋆] Transform the following procedures into CPS.

1. map.

```
letrec
  map(f, l) =
    if null?(l)
    then emptylist
    else cons((f car(l)),
              (map f cdr(l)))
  square(n) = *(n,n)
in (map square list(1,2,3,4,5))
```

2. fnlrgtn. This procedure takes a list of numbers lon and a number n and returns the first number in the list (in left-to-right order) that is greater than n. Once the result is found, no further elements in the list are examined. For example,

```
> (fnlrgtn list(1,list(3,list(2),7,list(9))) 6)
```

finds 7.

3. addgtn. This procedure takes a list of numbers and a number n as arguments. It returns the sum of all numbers in the list that are greater than n.

```
letrec
  addgtn(l,n) =
    if null?(l)
    then 0
    else if greater?(car(l),n)
         then +(car(l),(addgtn cdr(l) n))
         else (addgtn cdr(l) n)
in (addgtn list(1,5,10,50) 5)
```

4. `every`. This procedure takes a predicate and a list and returns a true value if and only if the predicate holds for each list element.

```
letrec
  every(pred, l) =
    if null?(l)
    then 1
    else if (pred car(l))
         then (every pred cdr(l))
         else 0
in (every proc(n)greater?(n,5) list(6,7,8,9))
```

8.4 Implementing the CPS Transformation

Our next task is to implement the transformation described in section 8.2. We will have three main procedures, one for each of the main operations in the transformation: `cps-of-program` ($\{\!\{-\}\!\}$), `cps-of-simple-exp` ($\langle\!\langle - \rangle\!\rangle$), and `cps-of-expression` ($[\![-]\!] \bullet [\![-]\!]$).

The procedure `cps-of-simple-exp`, shown in figure 8.5, takes a simple expression. If the argument is a `proc` expression, then `cps-of-simple-exp` returns another `proc` expression with an additional continuation formal parameter and with a body transformed by `cps-of-expression`. If the argument is not a `proc` expression, then `cps-of-simple-exp` creates an expression like the original, but in which every `proc` expression contained in the original is similarly transformed. Procedures declared in a `letrec` are also transformed in this way, as described in section 8.2.

The definitions of `cps-of-program` and `cps-of-expression` are presented in figure 8.6. The procedure `cps-of-program` takes a program and builds a `proc` expression with a continuation formal parameter and a body that contains the transformed expression, as described in section 8.2.

The procedure `cps-of-expression` implements the rules of section 8.2. It first tests to see whether the expression is simple; if so, then it calls the procedure `csimple`, which applies either $C_{simple\text{-}var}$ or $C_{simple\text{-}proc}$. Otherwise, it sends the information to an auxiliary procedure that performs the rest of the transformation. In the `letrec` and the `let` clauses, we make a test to determine if the continuation is a variable and invoke the appropriate auxiliary procedure. If the continuation is not a variable, then it is a `proc-exp`, and it may therefore contain variables that may be captured by the `let` or `letrec`, as on page 315. We defer the discussion of this capturing case until later.

The variable `k-id` is bound to a fresh identifier that we use as our bound variable for continuations throughout the transformed program. We use

```
(define cps-of-simple-exp
  (lambda (exp)
    (cases expression exp
      (proc-exp (ids body)
        (proc-exp
          (append ids (list k-id))
          (cps-of-expression body k-var-exp)))
      (lit-exp (datum) (lit-exp datum))
      (var-exp (id) (var-exp id))
      (primapp-exp (prim rands)
        (primapp-exp prim (map cps-of-simple-exp rands)))
      (if-exp (test-exp true-exp false-exp)
        (if-exp
          (cps-of-simple-exp test-exp)
          (cps-of-simple-exp true-exp)
          (cps-of-simple-exp false-exp)))
      (let-exp (ids rands body)
        (let-exp ids
          (map cps-of-simple-exp rands)
          (cps-of-simple-exp body)))
      (letrec-exp (proc-names idss bodies letrec-body)
        (letrec-exp proc-names
          (map
            (lambda (ids)
              (append ids (list k-id)))
            idss)
          (map
            (lambda (body)
              (cps-of-expression body k-var-exp))
            bodies)
          (cps-of-simple-exp letrec-body)))
      (app-exp (rator rands)
        (eopl:error 'cps-of-simple-exp
          "Can't call on application ~s" exp))
      )))
```

Figure 8.5 cps-of-simple-exp

k-var-exp to denote an expression containing the identifier k-id. We generate k-id and other new identifiers using gensymbol, which takes an argument that becomes the beginning of the resulting unique name. We use var-exp? to test whether an expression is a variable. See figure 8.7.

Now we describe each of the auxiliary procedures in turn, in increasing order of difficulty. Each auxiliary procedure finds the non-simple subexpressions, if any, of the expression, and applies the appropriate rule: either C_{app}, C_{head}, or one of C_{if}, C_{let}, or C_{letrec}.

Let us first consider if expressions. The C_{app} rule is not applicable, so the only two possible rules are C_{head} and C_{if}. C_{head} applies if there is a non-simple subexpression in head position. For an if-expression, the only head position is the test. So if the test expression is non-simple, then the transformation should be:

$$\llbracket \texttt{if } H \texttt{ then } E_1 \texttt{ else } E_2 \rrbracket \bullet \llbracket K \rrbracket \qquad\qquad (C_{head})$$
$$= \llbracket H \rrbracket \bullet \llbracket \texttt{proc}\,(v)\, \llbracket \texttt{if } v \texttt{ then } E_1 \texttt{ else } E_2 \rrbracket \bullet \llbracket K \rrbracket \rrbracket$$

If the test expression is simple, then the transformation is given by C_{if}

$$\llbracket \texttt{if } S \texttt{ then } E_1 \texttt{ else } E_2 \rrbracket \bullet \llbracket K \rrbracket \qquad\qquad (C_{if})$$
$$= \texttt{if } \langle\!\langle S \rangle\!\rangle \texttt{ then } \llbracket E_1 \rrbracket \bullet \llbracket K \rrbracket \texttt{ else } \llbracket E_2 \rrbracket \bullet \llbracket K \rrbracket$$

We can code this transformation as follows:

```
(define cps-of-if-exp
  (lambda (test-exp true-exp false-exp k)
    (if (non-simple? test-exp)
      (let ((v-id (gensymbol "v")))
        (cps-of-expression test-exp
          (proc-exp (list v-id)
            (cps-of-expression
              (if-exp (var-exp v-id) true-exp false-exp)
              k))))
      (if-exp (cps-of-simple-exp test-exp)
        (cps-of-expression true-exp k)
        (cps-of-expression false-exp k)))))
```

Let us next consider non-simple primitive applications. A primitive application $p(E_1, \ldots, E_n)$ is non-simple if and only if at least one of E_1, ..., E_n is non-simple. Therefore the expression must be of the form $p(S_1, \ldots, S_{i-1}, E_i, E_{i+1}, \ldots, E_n,)$, where E_i is the first non-simple subexpression. We therefore apply the C_{head} rule to get

$$\llbracket p(S_1, \ldots, S_{i-1}, E_i, E_{i+1}, \ldots, E_n) \rrbracket \bullet \llbracket K \rrbracket \qquad (C_{head})$$
$$= \llbracket E_i \rrbracket \bullet \llbracket \texttt{proc}\,(v)\, \llbracket p(S_1, \ldots, S_{i-1}, v, E_{i+1}, \ldots, E_n) \rrbracket \bullet \llbracket K \rrbracket \rrbracket$$

```
(define k-id (gensymbol "k"))

(define k-var-exp (var-exp k-id))

(define cps-of-program
  (lambda (pgm)
    (cases program pgm
      (a-program (exp)
        (proc-exp (list k-id)
          (cps-of-expression exp k-var-exp))))))

(define cps-of-expression
  (lambda (exp k)
    (if (non-simple? exp)
      (cases expression exp
        (if-exp (test-exp true-exp false-exp)
          (cps-of-if-exp test-exp true-exp false-exp k))
        (primapp-exp (prim rands)
          (cps-of-primapp-exp prim rands k))
        (app-exp (rator rands)
          (cps-of-app-exp rator rands k))
        (letrec-exp (proc-names idss bodies letrec-body)
          (cps-of-letrec-exp
            proc-names idss bodies letrec-body k))
        (let-exp (ids rands body)
          (cps-of-let-exp ids rands body k))
        (else
          (eopl:error 'cps-of-expression
            "Can't call on ~s" exp)))
      (csimple exp k))))

(define csimple
  (lambda (exp k)
    (cases expression k
      (proc-exp (ids body)
        (let-exp ids (list (cps-of-simple-exp exp)) body))
      (else (app-exp k (list (cps-of-simple-exp exp)))))))
```

Figure 8.6 cps-of-program and cps-of-expression

```
(define gensymbol
  (let ((n 0))
    (lambda (s)
      (set! n (+ n 1))
      (let ((s (if (string? s) s (symbol->string s))))
        (string->symbol
          (string-append s (number->string n)))))))

(define var-exp?
  (lambda (x)
    (cases expression x
      (var-exp (id) #t)
      (else #f))))
```

Figure 8.7   Auxiliaries for generating identifiers and variables

This transformation can be implemented by the following code:

```
(define cps-of-primapp-exp
  (lambda (prim rands k)
    (let ((pos (list-index non-simple? rands))
          (v-id (gensymbol "v")))
      (cps-of-expression (list-ref rands pos)
        (proc-exp (list v-id)
          (cps-of-expression
            (primapp-exp prim
              (list-set rands pos (var-exp v-id)))
            k))))))
```

Here we use two procedures that were defined in section 2.3.2. The procedure `(list-index pred lst)` returns the zero-based index of the first element of `lst` that satisfies the predicate `pred`. Since the primitive application is known to be non-simple, this is guaranteed to succeed. The new call to p is built with `list-set`. The procedure `(list-set lst n x)` returns a list like `lst`, except that the nth element, using zero-based indexing, is `x`.

We next consider procedure applications. For a procedure application, we need to decide whether the rule C_{app} or the rule C_{head} applies. If both the rator and all of the rands are simple, then C_{app} applies:

$$[\![(S_0 \ \ldots \ S_n)]\!] \bullet [\![K]\!] = (\langle\!\langle S_0 \rangle\!\rangle \ \ldots \ \langle\!\langle S_n \rangle\!\rangle \ K) \qquad\qquad (C_{app})$$

If there is a non-simple subexpression, then we need to use C_{head}:

$$[\![\,(S_1, \ldots, S_{i-1}, E_i, E_{i+1}, \ldots, E_n)\,]\!] \bullet [\![K]\!]$$
$$= [\![E_i]\!] \bullet [\![\text{proc}\,(v)\,[\![\,(S_1, \ldots, S_{i-1}, v, E_{i+1}, \ldots, E_n)\,]\!] \bullet [\![K]\!]\,]\!] \qquad (C_{head})$$

Although this notation treats operators and operands uniformly, our abstract syntax trees treat them separately. We therefore begin the implementation of these rules by testing to see if the operator is non-simple. If it is, then it will be the expression selected for evaluation by C_{head}:

```
(define cps-of-app-exp
  (lambda (rator rands k)
    (if (non-simple? rator)
        (let ((v-id (gensymbol "v")))
          (cps-of-expression rator
            (proc-exp (list v-id)
              (cps-of-expression
                (app-exp (var-exp v-id) rands)
                k))))
        (cps-of-app-exp-simple-rator rator rands k))))

(define cps-of-app-exp-simple-rator
  (lambda (rator rands k)
    (let ((pos (list-index non-simple? rands)))
      (if (number? pos)
          (let ((v-id (gensymbol "v")))
            (cps-of-expression
              (list-ref rands pos)
              (proc-exp (list v-id)
                (cps-of-expression
                  (app-exp rator
                    (list-set rands pos (var-exp v-id)))
                  k))))
          (app-exp (cps-of-simple-exp rator)
            (append
              (map cps-of-simple-exp rands)
              (list k)))))))
```

For a simple operator, we use list-index to find the position of a non-simple operand. If there is one, we apply C_{head} much as we did for primitive applications. Otherwise, we apply the C_{app} rule.

The next case is `letrec`. The only rule that applies to a non-simple `letrec` expression is C_{letrec}:

$$
\begin{aligned}
&[\![\texttt{letrec} \\
&\quad p_1\,(x_1\,,\,\ldots\,,x_{n_1})\ = E_1 \\
&\quad \ldots \\
&\quad p_m\,(z_1\,,\,\ldots\,,z_{n_m})\ = E_m \\
&\quad \texttt{in } E]\!] \bullet [\![K]\!] \\
&= \qquad\qquad\qquad\qquad\qquad\qquad\qquad (C_{letrec}) \\
&\texttt{letrec} \\
&\quad p_1\,(x_1\,,\,\ldots\,,x_{n_1},\texttt{k})\ = [\![E_1]\!] \bullet [\![\texttt{k}]\!] \\
&\quad \ldots \\
&\quad p_m\,(z_1\,,\,\ldots\,,z_{n_m},\texttt{k})\ = [\![E_m]\!] \bullet [\![\texttt{k}]\!] \\
&\quad \texttt{in } [\![E]\!] \bullet [\![K]\!]
\end{aligned}
$$

As mentioned on page 315, however, this can cause variables in K to be captured if they are declared in the `letrec`. For example, consider

```
[[(fact letrec
          fact(n) = ...
        in (fact 6))]] • [[k]]
= create a continuation for the letrec                (C_head)
[[letrec
    fact(n) = ...
  in (fact 6)]] • [[proc(v)[[(fact v)]] • [[k]]]]
= transform the call to fact                          (C_app)
[[letrec
    fact(n) = ...
  in (fact 6)]] • [[proc(v)(fact v k)]]
= transform the letrec                                (C_letrec)
letrec
    fact(n, k) = [[...]] • [[k]]
in [[(fact 6)]] • [[proc(v)(fact v k)]]
```

Now the reference to `fact` in the continuation will be captured by the definition of `fact` in the `letrec`, when it originally referred to some other binding. We can avoid this difficulty by using the rule

$$
[\![E]\!] \bullet [\![K]\!] = \texttt{let } \texttt{k} = K \texttt{ in } [\![E]\!] \bullet [\![\texttt{k}]\!] \qquad\qquad (C_{bindk})
$$

when K is not a variable. (Here `k` is the initial continuation variable bound to `k-id`). This reduces the problem of transforming the `letrec` to the case in which the continuation is a variable, when no capture is possible.

```
(define cps-of-letrec-exp
  (lambda (proc-names idss bodies letrec-body k)
    (if (var-exp? k)
      (letrec-exp
        proc-names
        (map
          (lambda (ids)
            (append ids (list k-id)))
          idss)
        (map
          (lambda (body)
            (cps-of-expression body k-var-exp))
          bodies)
        (cps-of-expression letrec-body k))
      (cbindk
        (letrec-exp proc-names idss bodies letrec-body)
        k)))))

(define cbindk
  (lambda (exp k)
    (let-exp (list k-id) (list k)
      (cps-of-expression exp k-var-exp)))))
```

For our example above, we then get

$$
\begin{aligned}
&= \quad \textit{transform the call to } \texttt{fact} & (C_{app}) \\
&\llbracket \texttt{letrec} \\
&\quad\quad \texttt{fact(n) = ...} \\
&\quad \texttt{in (fact 6)} \rrbracket \bullet \llbracket \texttt{proc(v)(fact v k)} \rrbracket \\
&= \quad \textit{bind the continuation to a variable} & (C_{bindk}) \\
&\texttt{let k = proc(v)(fact v k)} \\
&\texttt{in } \llbracket \texttt{letrec} \\
&\quad\quad \texttt{fact(n) = ...} \\
&\quad\quad \texttt{in (fact 6)} \rrbracket \bullet \llbracket \texttt{k} \rrbracket \\
&= \quad \textit{transform the } \texttt{letrec} & (C_{letrec}) \\
&\texttt{let k = proc(v)(fact v k)} \\
&\texttt{in letrec} \\
&\quad\quad \texttt{fact(n, k) = } \llbracket \texttt{...} \rrbracket \bullet \llbracket \texttt{k} \rrbracket \\
&\quad\quad \texttt{in } \llbracket \texttt{(fact 6)} \rrbracket \bullet \llbracket \texttt{k} \rrbracket
\end{aligned}
$$

and the call to `fact` in the continuation is safely out of the scope of the `letrec` declarations.

This leaves `let` expressions. For a non-simple `let` expression, there are two possibilities: if all of the right-hand sides are simple, then C_{let} applies:

$$\begin{aligned}&[\![\texttt{let } v_1 = S_1 \ldots v_n = S_n \texttt{ in } E]\!] \bullet [\![K]\!] \\ &= \texttt{ let } v_1 = \langle\!\langle S_1 \rangle\!\rangle \ldots v_n = \langle\!\langle S_n \rangle\!\rangle \texttt{ in } [\![E]\!] \bullet [\![K]\!]\end{aligned} \qquad (C_{let})$$

In this case, we need to worry about variables in K being captured by the `let` variables, so we once again use C_{bindk} to avoid capturing whenever K is not a variable. The other possibility is that there is a non-simple right-hand side in the declarations; in that case we use C_{head}, which becomes

$$\begin{aligned}&[\![\texttt{let } v_1 = S_1 \ \ldots \ v_{i-1} = S_{i-1} \\ &\qquad v_i = E_i \\ &\qquad v_{i+1} = E_{i+1} \ \ldots \ v_n = E_n \\ &\quad \texttt{in } E]\!] \bullet [\![K]\!] \\ &= \\ &[\![E_i]\!] \bullet [\![\texttt{proc (z)}[\![\texttt{let } v_1 = S_1 \ \ldots \ v_{i-1} = S_{i-1} \\ &\qquad\qquad\qquad\qquad v_i = z \\ &\qquad\qquad\qquad\qquad v_{i+1} = E_{i+1} \ldots v_n = E_n \\ &\qquad\qquad\qquad \texttt{in } E]\!] \bullet [\![K]\!]\end{aligned} \qquad (C_{head})$$

The procedure `cps-of-let-exp` applies this C_{head} rule repeatedly until it is no longer applicable. Then it applies the C_{let} rule.

```
(define cps-of-let-exp
  (lambda (ids rands body k)
    (if (var-exp? k)
      (let ((pos (list-index non-simple? rands)))
        (if (number? pos)
          (let ((z-id (gensymbol "z")))
            (cps-of-expression
              (list-ref rands pos)
              (proc-exp (list z-id)
                (cps-of-expression
                  (let-exp ids
                    (list-set rands pos (var-exp z-id))
                    body)
                  k))))
          (let-exp ids (map cps-of-simple-exp rands)
            (cps-of-expression body k))))
      (cbindk (let-exp ids rands body) k))))
```

This completes the implementation of the CPS transformation. Go have a nice dinner.

Exercise 8.20 [⋆⋆] Implement and test this transformation. Make sure that the tests consider every case. Then have an even nicer dinner.

Exercise 8.21 [⋆] Modify the transformer so that arguments to primitive applications and procedure applications are evaluated from right to left.

Exercise 8.22 [⋆] The transformation of `cps-of-if-exp` copies the continuation `k`. This can cause an exponential increase in the size of the transformed program (see exercise 8.15). Modify the `if` clause of `cps-of-expression` to avoid this by first invoking the rule C_{bindk} when K is not a variable.

Exercise 8.23 [⋆] Each occurrence of C_{bindk} dispatches through `cps-of-expression` to the same procedure from which it was called. Utilize this fact to avoid the calls to `cps-of-expression` in C_{bindk}.

Exercise 8.24 [⋆] The code contains several occurrences of the call `(cps-of-expression exp k-var-exp)`. Abstract these into `(cps-of-tail-pos exp)`, and rewrite the code to use this abstraction instead.

Exercise 8.25 [⋆⋆⋆] Another way of avoiding variable capture in `let` and `letrec` is to rename any variables in the `let` or `letrec` declaration that would capture a free variable in the continuation expression. Modify the transformer to avoid capture in this way, rather than using C_{bindk}.

Exercise 8.26 [⋆⋆] The C_{head} rule on page 335 can often be rewritten by replacing z by v_i, thereby removing the $v_i = z$ `let` declaration. This only works when v_i is not free in $S_1, \ldots, S_{i-1}, E_{i+1}, \ldots, E_n$. When it is free, the `let` declaration can still be removed, but instead v_i must be renamed to z and substituted for all free occurrences of v_i in E. Redefine `cps-of-let-exp` to incorporate this approach.

Exercise 8.27 [⋆⋆] Modify the transformer to use $C_{simple-proc'}$ as in exercise 8.16 instead of $C_{simple-proc}$.

Exercise 8.28 [⋆] Our CPS algorithm is correct only if the program does not contain variables `k0, k1, ..., v0, v1, ...,` and `z0, z1, ....` If these variables appear in our program, then those created by `gensymbol` will not be fresh. To specify the algorithm correctly, we must use `fresh-id` from exercise 2.10. The arguments to `fresh-id` include an expression, and `fresh-id` is guaranteed to return a symbol that does not occur in that expression.

Modify the transformer to replace every occurrence of `gensymbol`, `k-id`, or `k-var-exp` by an appropriate call to `fresh-id`.

Some Scheme systems include a procedure `gensym`, which generates a unique, never-used-before symbol. How could `gensym` be used instead of `fresh-id` to correct our algorithm? Would that be more efficient than using `fresh-id`? Explain.

Exercise 8.29 [⋆⋆⋆] As written, this algorithm requires $O(n^2)$ time, because it potentially calls `non-simple?` $O(n)$ times, and each call to `non-simple?` requires $O(n)$ time. Rewrite the algorithm to avoid this by using two passes: one to annotate each node of the abstract-syntax tree to indicate whether or not it contains a simple expression, and then a second pass to perform the transformation.

Exercise 8.30 [★★★] Modify the algorithm of this section to handle the typed language of section 4.2. It should take a typed expression and produce another type expressions. Consider the following questions: if an expression is of type int, what type of continuation should it take? What should the type of the transformed expression be? Next, consider a proc expression. If it is of type (int -> int), what should the type of the transformed expression be? What if it were of type ((int -> int) -> int)?

Exercise 8.31 [★★★] Here is an implementation of a different CPS algorithm that builds from exercise 8.23 and exercise 8.24. First, use this definition of cps-of-tail-pos:

```
(define cps-of-tail-pos
  (lambda (exp)
    (cps-of-expression exp
      (lambda (res)
        (app-exp k-var-exp (list res))))))
```

Instead of passing k-var-exp to cps-of-expression, we pass in a procedure that will create the application of k-var-exp.

We change csimple to acknowledge that k is indeed a procedure and not a proc-exp. Moreover, since k is a procedure, we can no longer create a let-exp as we did for $C_{simple\text{-}proc}$.

```
(define csimple
  (lambda (exp k)
    (k (cps-of-simple-exp exp)))))
```

What remains is to implement each of the auxiliary procedures. Two of them, cps-of-app-exp and cps-of-let-exp are presented in figure 8.8.

The procedure cps-of-rands is like eval-rands on page 263, but it does not take an environment and the call to eval-expression is replaced by a call to cps-of-expression.

First, implement and test this algorithm. Next, add cps-of-primapp-exp, cps-of-if-exp, and cps-of-letrec-exp. Finally, apply the ideas for making more readable outputs as described in exercises 8.25–8.28.

The algorithm as described often generates continuations of the form proc (v) (k v). Modify the algorithm to generate k instead.

By restricting the definition of simple to include only literal, variable, and procedure expressions, this CPS transformer becomes a one-pass algorithm. Revise our implementation so that it, too, becomes a one-pass algorithm. In what fundamental ways do these two one-pass algorithms differ?

```
(define cps-of-app-exp
  (lambda (rator rands k)
    (let ((cont-exp
            (let ((v-id (gensymbol "v")))
              (proc-exp (list v-id)
                (k (var-exp v-id)))))))
      (cps-of-expression rator
        (lambda (rator-res)
          (cps-of-rands rands
            (lambda (rands-res)
              (app-exp rator-res
                (append rands-res
                  (list cont-exp)))))))))))

(define cps-of-let-exp
  (lambda (ids rands body k)
    (let ((cont-exp
            (let ((v-id (gensymbol "v")))
              (proc-exp (list v-id)
                (k (var-exp v-id)))))))
      (let ((exp (cps-of-rands rands
                   (lambda (rands-res)
                     (let-exp ids rands-res
                       (cps-of-tail-pos body)))))))
        (if (var-exp? cont-exp)
          exp
          (cbindk exp cont-exp)))))))
```

Figure 8.8   Two auxiliaries for exercise 8.31

8.5   Modeling computational effects

Another important use of CPS is to provide a model in which computational effects can be made explicit. A computational effect is an effect like printing or assigning to a variable, which is difficult to model using equational reasoning. By transforming to CPS, we can make these effects explicit in a way that allows us to use equational reasoning even on programs that have such effects. In this section, we will study three effects: printing, variable assignment, and non-local control flow.

Let us first consider printing. In our defined language, printing would ordinarily be considered a primitive that printed the value of its operand and returned 1. (See exercise 3.5.) It has a computational effect, however, so (`f print(3) print(4)`) and (`f 1 1`) have different effects, even though they return the same answer. The effect also depends on the order of evaluation of arguments; up to now our languages have always evaluated their arguments from left to right, but other languages might not do so. We can model these considerations by modifying our CPS transformation in the following ways:

- We modify the definition of a simple expression so that `print(e)` is never simple. Here *e* is in head position.

- If the operand of `print` is simple, the rule is

$$[\![\texttt{print}\,(S)\,]\!] \bullet [\![K]\!] = \texttt{printc}\,(\langle\!\langle S \rangle\!\rangle, K)$$

where `printc` is a new expression like `print`, except that it takes two arguments, which are expected to be a value and a continuation. The `printc` expression prints the value and then sends 1 to the continuation.

- If the operand of `print` is not simple, we use C_{head} to transform it:

$$[\![\texttt{print}\,(H)\,]\!] \bullet [\![K]\!] = [\![H]\!] \bullet [\![\texttt{proc}\,(v)\,\texttt{printc}\,(v, K)\,]\!]$$

Thus $[\![$ (`f print((g x)) print(4)`) $]\!] \bullet [\![\texttt{k}]\!]$ is

```
(g x
  proc(v4)
    printc(v4,
      proc(v2)
        printc(4,
          proc(v3)
            (f v2 v3 k)))))
```

Here, having received the continuation `k`, we call `g` in a continuation that calls the result `v4`. The continuation prints the value of `v4` and sends 1 to the next continuation, which binds `v2` to its argument 1, prints 4 and then calls the next continuation, which binds `v3` to its argument 1 and then calls `f` with 1, 1, and `k`. In this way the sequencing of the different printing actions becomes explicit.

Now the CPS transformation is from a source language (the one with `print`) to a slightly different target language (the one with `printc`). Figure 8.9 shows the code to implement this transformation.

```
(define cps-of-expression
  (lambda (exp k)
    (if (non-simple? exp)
        (cases expression exp
          (print-exp (exp) (cps-of-print-exp exp k))
          ...)
        (csimple exp k))))

(define cps-of-print-exp
  (lambda (exp k)
    (if (non-simple? exp)
        (let ((v-id (gensymbol "v")))
          (cps-of-expression
            exp
            (proc-exp (list v-id)
              (printc-exp (var-exp v-id) k))))
        (printc-exp (cps-of-simple-exp exp) k))))
```

Figure 8.9   CPS transformation for `print`

We next consider variable assignment. To do variable assignment, we need to make two effects explicit: assignment to variables and dereferencing of variables. Therefore we will add a target-language expression for each of these. We can describe the transformation of set (figure 8.10) much as we did the transformation of print.

- A set expression is never simple, and its right-hand-side expression is in head position.

- If the right-hand-side expression of set is simple, the rule is

$$[\![\texttt{set } x = S]\!] \bullet [\![K]\!] = \texttt{setc } x \; \langle\!\langle S \rangle\!\rangle \; K$$

where the expression setc x e K evaluates the expression e, stores the result in the reference to which variable x is bound, and then sends 1 (the value of the analogous set) to the continuation K.

- If the right-hand-side expression of set is not simple, we use C_{head} to transform it and then assign the result using setc:

$$[\![\texttt{set } x = H]\!] \bullet [\![K]\!] = [\![H]\!] \bullet [\![\texttt{proc}\,(v)\,\texttt{setc } x \; v \; K]\!]$$

- Since evaluation of a variable involves a dereference, *a variable from the source language is no longer simple*. Since a generated variable (one created by gensymbol) is never mutated, we can treat it as an unsettable variable, not a source language (reference) variable. Therefore *a generated variable is simple*. Since we must distinguish these two cases, we add genvar-exp as a new variant of expression and define genvar-exp?. At every place in the transformation where we had previously applied var-exp to a generated variable, we use genvar-exp instead. Furthermore, since k-id is a generated variable, everywhere we used var-exp? to test to see whether a continuation was a variable, we now use genvar-exp? instead. See figure 8.10.

- We transform source, but not generated, variables as

$$[\![x]\!] \bullet [\![K]\!] = \texttt{derefc}\ x\ K$$

where the expression derefc x K retrieves the binding of the identifier x and sends its contents to the continuation K.

Hence $[\![\texttt{set x = add1(x)}]\!] \bullet [\![\texttt{k}]\!]$ is

```
derefc x
  proc(v9)
    let v8 = add1(v9)
    in setc x v8 k
```

First, x is dereferenced and v9 is bound to the result. Then add1 is applied to v9, and v8 is bound to the result. Last, the value of v8 is assigned to the reference to which x is bound, and the continuation k is invoked.

Here is a subtler example: $[\![\texttt{(f set x = add1(x) +(2,x))}]\!] \bullet [\![\texttt{k}]\!]$ is

```
derefc f
  proc(v2)
    derefc x
      proc(v7)
        let v6 = add1(v7)
        in setc x = v6
              proc(v3)
                derefc x
                  proc(v5)
                    let v4 = +(2,v5)
                    in (v2 v3 v4 k)
```

```
(define-datatype expression expression?
  (var-exp
    (id symbol?))
  (genvar-exp
    (id symbol?))
  ...)

(define genvar-exp?
  (lambda (x)
    (cases expression x
      (genvar-exp (id) #t)
      (else #f))))

(define k-var-exp (genvar-exp k-id))

(define cps-of-expression
  (lambda (exp k)
    (if (non-simple? exp)
      (cases expression exp
        (var-exp (id) (derefc-exp id k))
        (varassign-exp (id exp)
          (cps-of-varassign-exp id exp k))
        ...)
      (csimple exp k))))

(define cps-of-varassign-exp
  (lambda (id exp k)
    (if (non-simple? exp)
      (let ((v-id (gensymbol "v")))
        (cps-of-expression
          exp
          (proc-exp (list v-id)
            (varassignc-exp id (genvar-exp v-id) k))))
      (varassignc-exp id (cps-of-simple-exp exp) k))))
```

Figure 8.10 CPS transformation for variable assignment

The code shows the sequence of dereference and assignment operations: first f is dereferenced, yielding v2, and x is dereferenced twice: once before the setc (yielding v7) and once afterwards (yielding v5).

As a last example, we consider letcc from exercise 7.31. A letcc expression letcc ⟨identifier⟩ in ⟨expression⟩ binds the current continuation to the variable ⟨identifier⟩. The only operation on continuations is throw. We use throw ⟨expression⟩ to ⟨expression⟩, which evaluates the two subexpressions. The second expression should return a continuation, which is applied to the value of the first expression. The current continuation of the throw expression is ignored.

We first analyze these expressions according to the paradigm of this chapter. These expressions are never simple. The expression part of a letcc is a tail position, since its value is the value of the entire expression. Since both positions in a throw are evaluated, and neither is the value of the throw (indeed, the throw has no value, since it never returns to its immediate continuation), they are both head positions.

We can now write down the rules for converting these two expressions. For letcc, the rule is

$$[\![\texttt{letcc } x \texttt{ in } E]\!] \bullet [\![K]\!] = \texttt{let } x = K \texttt{ in } [\![E]\!] \bullet [\![x]\!] \qquad C_{letcc}$$

For throw, the rule is

$$[\![\texttt{throw } S_1 \texttt{ to } S_2]\!] \bullet [\![K]\!] = (\langle\!\langle S_2 \rangle\!\rangle \ \langle\!\langle S_1 \rangle\!\rangle) \qquad C_{throw}$$

and K is ignored, as desired. If either of the operands of throw are non-simple, than C_{head} should be applied.

Exercise 8.32 [⋆] Implement these transformations.

Exercise 8.33 [⋆ ⋆] If a variable never appears on the left-hand side of a set expression, then it is immutable, and could be treated as simple. Revise the implementation so that all such variables are treated as simple.

Exercise 8.34 [⋆ ⋆] Add an expression begin E_1 E_2 to the language of this chapter.

Exercise 8.35 [⋆ ⋆] Extend the previous exercise to include begin expressions with more than one subexpression.

Exercise 8.36 [⋆ ⋆] Extend exercise 8.31 to include letcc expressions.

Further Reading

Steele's RABBIT compiler (1978) uses CPS conversion as the basis for a compiler. In this compiler, the source program is converted into CPS and then into iterative form, which can be compiled easily. This line of development led to the ORBIT compiler in (Kranz, Kelsey, Rees, Hudak, Philbin, & Adams, 1986) and to the Standard ML of New Jersey compiler (Appel & Jim, 1989).

(Plotkin, 1975) gives a very clean version of the CPS transformation and presents its theoretical properties. A very similar version of the transformation is given in (Fischer, 1972; 1999); a more complex version with some interesting theoretical properties is given in (Danvy & Filinski, 1992). The CPS algorithm in chapter 8 is taken from (Sabry & Wadler, 1997), which improved on (Sabry & Felleisen, 1993), which in turn was motivated by the CPS algorithm of chapter 8 of the first edition of this book.

A *The SLLGEN Parsing System*

Programs are just strings of characters. In order to process a program, we need to group these characters into meaningful units. This grouping is usually divided into two stages: *scanning* and *parsing*.

Scanning is the process of dividing the sequence of characters into words, punctuation, *etc*. These units are called *lexical items*, *lexemes*, or most often *tokens*. Parsing is the process of organizing the sequence of tokens into hierarchical syntactic structures such as expressions, statements, and blocks. This is much like organizing a sentence into clauses.

SLLGEN is a package for generating scanners and parsers in Scheme. In this appendix, we first review the basics of scanning and parsing, and then consider how these capabilities are expressed in SLLGEN.

Scanning

The problem of scanning is illustrated in figure A.1. The figure shows a small segment of a program, and the way in which it is intended to be broken up into atomic units.

The way in which a given stream of characters is to be broken up into lexical items is part of the language specification. This part of the language specification is sometimes called the *lexical specification*. Typical pieces of lexical specification might be:

- Any sequence of spaces and newlines is equivalent to a single space.

- A comment begins with % and continues until the end of the line.

- An identifier is a sequence of letters and digits starting with a letter.

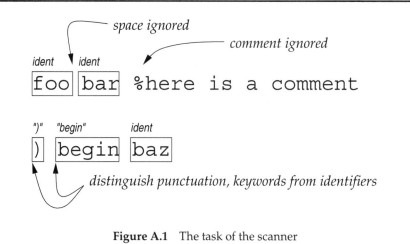

Figure A.1   The task of the scanner

The job of the scanner is to go through the input and analyze it to produce data structures with these items. In a conventional language, the scanner might be a procedure that, when called, produces the "next" token of the input.

One could write a scanner from scratch, but that would be tedious and error-prone. A better approach is to write down the lexical specification in a specialized language. The most common language for this task is the language of *regular expressions*. We define the language of regular expressions as follows:

$$\langle R \rangle ::= \langle \text{character} \rangle \mid \langle R \rangle \langle R \rangle \mid \langle R \rangle \cup \langle R \rangle \mid \langle R \rangle^* \mid \neg \langle \text{character} \rangle$$

Each regular expression matches some strings. We can use induction to define the set of strings matched by each regular expression:

- A character c matches the string consisting of the character c.

- $\neg c$ matches any 1-character string other than c.

- RS matches any string that consists of a string matching R followed by a string matching S. This is called *concatenation*.

- $R \cup S$ matches any string that either matches R or matches S. This is sometimes written $R \mid S$, and is sometimes called *alternation*.

- R^* matches any string that is formed by concatenating some number n ($n \geq 0$) of strings that match R. This is called the *Kleene closure* of R.

Some examples may be helpful:

- *ab* matches only the string ab.

- $ab \cup cd$ matches the strings ab and cd.

- $(ab \cup cd)(ab \cup cd \cup ef)$ matches the strings abab, abcd, abef, cdab, cdcd, and cdef.

- $(ab)^*$ matches the empty string, ab, abab, ababab, abababab, ...

- $(ab \cup cd)^*$ matches the empty string, ab, cd, abab, abcd, cdab, cdcd, ababab, ... cdcdcd, ...

The specifications for our example may be written using regular expressions as

$\langle\text{whitespace}\rangle = (\langle\text{space}\rangle \cup \langle\text{newline}\rangle) \, (\langle\text{space}\rangle \cup \langle\text{newline}\rangle)^*$
$\langle\text{comment}\rangle = \text{\%} \, (\neg\langle\text{newline}\rangle)^*$
$\langle\text{identifier}\rangle = \langle\text{letter}\rangle \, (\langle\text{letter}\rangle \cup \langle\text{digit}\rangle)^*$

When scanners use regular expressions to specify a token, the rule is always to take the *longest* match. This way xyz will be scanned as one identifier, not three.

When the scanner finds a token, it returns a data structure consisting of at least the following pieces of data:

- A *class*, which describes what kind of token it has found. The set of classes is part of the lexical specification. SLLGEN uses Scheme symbols to distinguish these classes; other syntactic analyzers might use other data structures.

- A piece of data describing the particular token. The nature of this data is also part of the lexical specification. For our system, the data is be as follows: for identifiers, the data is a Scheme symbol built from the string in the token; for a number, the datum is the number described by the number literal; and for a literal string, the datum is the string. String data are used for keywords and punctuation.

In an implementation language that did not have symbols, one might use a string (the name of the identifier), or an entry into a hash table indexed by identifiers (a *symbol table*) instead. Using Scheme spares us these annoyances.

• Some data describing the location of this token in the input. This information may be used by the parser to help the programmer identify the location of syntactic errors.

In general, the internal structure of tokens is relevant only to the scanner and the parser, so we shall not describe it in any further detail.

Parsing

Parsing is the process of organizing the sequence of tokens into hierarchical syntactic structures such as expressions, statements, and blocks. This is like organizing or diagramming a sentence into clauses. The syntactic structure of a language is typically specified using a BNF definition, also called a *context-free grammar* (section 1.1.2).

The parser takes as input a sequence of tokens, and its output is an abstract syntax tree (section 2.2.2). The abstract syntax trees produced by an SLLGEN parser can be described by `define-datatype`. For a given grammar, there will be one data type for each nonterminal. For each nonterminal, there will be one variant for each production that has the nonterminal as its left-hand side. Each variant will have one field for each nonterminal, identifier, or number that appears in its right-hand side. A simple example appears in section 2.2.2. To see what happens when there is more than one nonterminal in the grammar, consider a grammar like the one in section 3.9:

$$\begin{aligned}
\langle\text{statement}\rangle & ::= \{ \ \langle\text{statement}\rangle \ ; \ \langle\text{statement}\rangle \ \} \\
& ::= \texttt{while} \ \langle\text{expression}\rangle \ \texttt{do} \ \langle\text{statement}\rangle \\
& ::= \langle\text{identifier}\rangle \ \texttt{:=} \ \langle\text{expression}\rangle \\
\langle\text{expression}\rangle & ::= \langle\text{identifier}\rangle \\
& ::= (\langle\text{expression}\rangle \ \texttt{+} \ \langle\text{expression}\rangle)
\end{aligned}$$

The trees produced by this grammar could be described by this data type

```
(define-datatype statement statement?
  (compound-statement
    (stmt1 statement?)
    (stmt2 statement?))
  (while-statement
    (test expression?)
    (body statement?))
  (assign-statement
    (lhs symbol?)
    (rhs expression?)))
```

```
(define-datatype expression expression?
  (var-exp
    (id symbol?))
  (sum-exp
    (exp1 expression?)
    (exp2 expression?)))
```

For each nonterminal in a right-hand side, the corresponding tree appears as a field; for each identifier, the corresponding symbol appears as a field. The names of the variants will be specified in the grammar when it is written in SLLGEN. The names of the fields will be automatically generated; here we have introduced some mnemonic names for the fields. For example, the input

```
x := foo; while x do x := (x + bar)
```

produces the output

```
(compound-statement
  (assign-statement x (var-exp foo))
  (while-statement (var-exp x)
    (assign-statement x
      (sum-expression (var-exp x) (var-exp bar)))))
```

Throughout this appendix, abstract syntax trees are displayed as lists.

Scanners and Parsers in SLLGEN

Specifying Scanners

In SLLGEN, scanners are specified by regular expressions. Our example would be written in SLLGEN as follows:

```
(define scanner-spec-a
  '((white-sp
      (whitespace)                        skip)
    (comment
      ("%" (arbno (not #\newline)))       skip)
    (identifier
      (letter (arbno (or letter digit))) symbol)
    (number
      (digit  (arbno digit))              number)))
```

If the scanner is used with a parser that has keywords or punctuation, like `while` or `=`, it is not necessary to put these in the scanner manually; the parser-generator will add those automatically.

A scanner specification in SLLGEN is a list that satisfies this grammar:

⟨scanner-spec⟩   ::= {{⟨regexp-and-action⟩}*}
⟨regexp-and-action⟩ ::= (⟨name⟩ ({⟨regexp⟩}*) ⟨outcome⟩)
⟨name⟩   ::= ⟨symbol⟩
⟨regexp⟩   ::= ⟨string⟩ | `letter` | `digit` | `whitespace` | `any`
                      ::= (`not` ⟨character⟩) | (`or` {⟨regexp⟩}*)
                      ::= (`arbno` ⟨regexp⟩) | (`concat` {⟨regexp⟩}*)
⟨outcome⟩   ::= `skip` | `symbol` | `number` | `string`

Each item in the list is a specification of a regular expression, consisting of a name, a sequence of regular expressions, and an action to be taken on success. The name is a Scheme symbol that will become the class of the token.

The second part of the specification is a sequence of regular expressions, because the top level of a ⟨regexp⟩ in a scanner is almost always a concatenation. A regular expression may be a Scheme string; one of four predefined testers: `letter` (matches any letter), `digit` (matches any digit), `whitespace` (matches any Scheme whitespace character), and `any` (matches any character); the negation of a character; or it may be a combination of regular expressions, using a Scheme-like syntax with `or` and `concat` for union and concatenation, and `arbno` for Kleene star.

As the scanner works, it collects characters into a buffer. When the scanner determines that it has found the longest possible match of all the regular expressions in the specification, it executes the *outcome* of the corresponding regular expression.

An outcome can be one of the following:

- The symbol `skip`. This means this is the end of a token, but no token is emitted. The scanner continues working on the string to find the next token. This action is used for whitespace and comments.

- The symbol `symbol`. The characters in the buffer are converted into a Scheme symbol and a token is emitted, with the class name as its class and with the symbol as its datum.

- The symbol `number`. The characters in the buffer are converted into a Scheme number, and a token is emitted, with the class name as its class and with the number as its datum.

- The symbol `string`. The characters in the buffer are converted into a Scheme string, and a token is emitted, with the class name as its class and with that string as its datum.

If there is a tie for longest match between two regular expressions, `string` takes precedence over `symbol`. This rule means that keywords that would otherwise be identifiers are treated as keywords.

Specifying Grammars

SLLGEN also includes a language for specifying grammars. The simple grammar above would be written in SLLGEN as

```
(define grammar-a1
  '((statement
       ("" statement ";" statement "")
     compound-statement)
    (statement
       ("while" expression "do" statement)
     while-statement)
    (statement
       (identifier ":=" expression)
     assign-statement)
    (expression
       (identifier)
     var-exp)
    (expression
       ("(" expression "+" expression ")")
     sum-exp)))
```

A grammar in SLLGEN is a list described by the following grammar:

⟨grammar⟩   ::= ({⟨production⟩}*)
⟨production⟩ ::= (⟨lhs⟩ ({⟨rhs-item⟩}*) ⟨prod-name⟩)
⟨lhs⟩   ::= ⟨symbol⟩
⟨rhs-item⟩   ::= ⟨symbol⟩ | ⟨string⟩
                ::= (arbno {⟨rhs-item⟩}*)
                ::= (separated-list {⟨rhs-item⟩}* ⟨string⟩)
⟨prod-name⟩ ::= ⟨symbol⟩

A grammar is a list of productions. The left-hand side of the first production is the start symbol for the grammar. Each production consists of a left-hand side (a nonterminal symbol), a right-hand side (a list of ⟨rhs-item⟩'s) and a production name. The right-hand side of a production is a list of symbols or strings. The symbols are nonterminals; strings are literal strings. A

```
(define scanner-spec-1 ...)

(define grammar-1 ...)

(sllgen:make-define-datatypes scanner-spec-1 grammar-1)

(define list-the-datatypes
  (lambda ()
    (sllgen:list-define-datatypes scanner-spec-1 grammar-1)))

(define just-scan
  (sllgen:make-string-scanner scanner-spec-1 grammar-1))

(define scan&parse
  (sllgen:make-string-parser scanner-spec-1 grammar-1))

(define read-eval-print
  (sllgen:make-rep-loop  "--> " eval-program
    (sllgen:make-stream-parser scanner-spec-1 grammar-1)))
```

Figure A.2   Using SLLGEN

right-hand side may also include arbno's or separated-list's; these are discussed below. The production name is a symbol, which becomes the name of the define-datatype variant corresponding to the production.

In SLLGEN, the grammar must allow the parser to determine which production to use knowing only (1) what nonterminal it's looking for and (2) the first symbol (token) of the string being parsed. Grammars in this form are called *LL*(1) grammars; SLLGEN stands for Scheme *LL*(1) parser GENerator. This is somewhat restrictive in practice, but it is good enough for the purposes of this book. SLLGEN produces a warning if the input grammar fails to meet this restriction.

SLLGEN operations

SLLGEN includes several procedures for incorporating these scanners and grammars into an executable parser. Figure A.2 shows a sample use of SLLGEN to define a scanner and parser for a language.

The procedure `sllgen:make-define-datatypes` generates each of the `define-datatype` expressions from the grammar for use by `cases`. The procedure `sllgen:list-define-datatypes` generates the `define-datatype` expressions again, but returns them as a list rather than executing them. The field names generated by these procedures are uninformative because the information is not in the grammar; to get better field names, write out the `define-datatype`.

The procedure `sllgen:make-string-scanner` takes a scanner and a grammar and generates a scanning procedure. The resulting procedure may be applied to a string and produces a list of tokens. The grammar is used to add keywords to the resulting scanning procedure. This procedure is useful primarily for debugging.

The procedure `sllgen:make-string-parser` generates a parser. The parser is a procedure that takes a string, scans it according to the scanner, parses it according to the grammar, and returns an abstract syntax tree. As with `sllgen:make-string-scanner`, the literal strings from the grammar are included in the scanner.

SLLGEN can also be used to build a read-eval-print-loop (section 3.2). The procedure `sllgen:make-stream-parser` is like the string version, except that its input is a stream of characters and its output is a stream of tokens. The procedure `sllgen:make-rep-loop` takes a string, a 1-argument procedure, and a stream parser, and produces a read-eval-print loop that produces the string as a prompt on the standard output, reads characters from the standard input, parses them, prints the result of applying the procedure to the resulting abstract syntax tree, and recurs. For example:

```
> (define read-eval-print
    (sllgen:make-rep-loop  "--> " eval-program
      (sllgen:make-stream-parser
        scanner-spec-3-1
        grammar-3-1)))
> (read-eval-print)
--> 5
5
--> add1(2)
3
--> +(add1(2),-(6,4))
5
```

The way in which control is returned from this loop to the Scheme read-eval-print loop is system-dependent.

arbno's and separated-list's

An `arbno` is a Kleene star in the grammar: it matches an abitrary number of repetitions of its entry. For example, the production

⟨statement⟩ ::= begin {⟨statement⟩ ;}* end

could be written in SLLGEN as

```
(define grammar-a2
  '((statement
      ("{" (arbno statement ";") "}")
      compound-statement)
    ...))
```

This makes a compound statement a sequence of an arbitrary number of semicolon-terminated statements.

This `arbno` generates a single field in the abstract syntax tree. This field will contain a *list* of the data for the nonterminal inside the `arbno`. Our example generates the following datatypes:

```
(define-datatype statement statement?
  (compound-statement
    (compound-statement32 (list-of statement?))))
  ...)
```

A simple interaction looks like:

```
> (define scan&parse2
    (sllgen:make-string-parser scanner-spec-a grammar-a2))

> (scan&parse2 "x := foo; y := bar; z := uu;")
(compound-statement
  ((assign-statement x (var-exp foo))
   (assign-statement y (var-exp bar))
   (assign-statement z (var-exp uu))))
```

We can put a sequence of nonterminals inside an `arbno`. In this case, we will get several fields in the node, one for each nonterminal; each field will contain a list of syntax trees. For example:

```
(define grammar-a3
  '((expression (identifier) var-exp)
    (expression
      ("let" (arbno identifier "=" expression) "in" expression)
      let-exp)))
```

```
(define scan&parse3
  (sllgen:make-string-parser scanner-spec-a grammar-a3))
```

This produces the datatype

```
(define-datatype expression expression?
  (var-exp (var-exp4 symbol?))
  (let-exp
    (let-exp9 (list-of symbol?))
    (let-exp7 (list-of expression?))
    (let-exp8 expression?)))
```

Here is an example of this grammar in action:

```
> (scan&parse3 "let x = y u = v in z)")
(let-exp
  (x u)
  ((var-exp y) (var-exp v))
  (var-exp z))
```

The specification `(arbno identifier "=" expression)` generates exactly two lists: a list of identifiers and a list of expressions. This is convenient because it will let our interpreters get at the pieces of the expression directly.

Sometimes it is helpful for the syntax of a language to use lists with separators, not terminators. This is common enough that it is a built-in operation in SLLGEN. We can write

```
(define grammar-a4
  '((statement
      ("{" (separated-list statement ";") "}")
      compound-statement)
    ...))
```

This produces the datatype

```
(define-datatype statement statement?
  (compound-statement
    (compound-statement103 (list-of statement?)))
    ...)
```

Here is a sample interaction:

```
> (define scan&parse4
    (sllgen:make-string-parser scanner-spec-a grammar-a4))
> (scan&parse4 "{ }")
(compound-statement ())
> (scan&parse4 "{x:= y; u := v ; z := t}")
(compound-statement
  ((assign-statement x (var-exp y))
   (assign-statement u (var-exp v))
   (assign-statement z (var-exp t))))
> (scan&parse4 "{x:= y; u := v ; z := t ;}")
Error in parsing: at line 1
Nonterminal <seplist3> can't begin with string "}"
```

In the last example, the input string had a terminating semicolon that did not match the grammar, so an error was reported.

As with arbno, we can place an arbitrary sequence of nonterminals within a separated-list. In this case, we will get several fields in the node, one for each nonterminal; each field will contain a list of syntax trees. This is exactly the same data as would be generated by arbno; only the concrete syntax differs.

We will occasionally use nested arbno's and separated-list's. A nonterminal inside an arbno generates a list, so a nonterminal inside an arbno inside an arbno generates a list of lists.

As an example, consider a compound-statement similar to the one in grammar-a4, except that we have parallel assignments:

```
(define grammar-a5
  '((statement
      ("{"
        (separated-list
          (separated-list identifier ",")
          ":="
          (separated-list expression ",")
          ";")
        "}")
      compound-statement)
    (expression (number) lit-exp)
    (expression (identifier) var-exp)
    ))

> (define scan&parse5
    (sllgen:make-string-parser scanner-spec-a grammar-a5))
```

This generates the following datatype for `statement`:

```
(define-datatype statement statement?
  (compound-statement
    (compound-statement4 (list-of (list-of symbol?)))
    (compound-statement3 (list-of (list-of expression?)))))
```

A typical interaction looks like:

```
> (scan&parse5 "{ x,y := u,v ; z := 4; t1, t2 := 5, 6 }")
(compound-statement
  ((x y) (z) (t1 t2))
  (((var-exp u) (var-exp v))
  ((lit-exp 4))
  ((lit-exp 5) (lit-exp 6))))
```

Here the `compound-statement` has two fields: a list of lists of identifiers, and the matching list of lists of expressions. In this example we have used `separated-list` instead of `arbno`, but an `arbno` would generate the same data.

Exercise A.1 [⋆] The following grammar for ordinary arithmetic expressions builds in the usual precedence rules for arithmetic operators:

⟨arith-expr⟩	::= ⟨arith-term⟩ {⟨additive-op⟩ ⟨arith-term⟩}*
⟨arith-term⟩	::= ⟨arith-factor⟩ {⟨multiplicative-op⟩ ⟨arith-factor⟩}*
⟨arith-factor⟩	::= ⟨number⟩
	::= (⟨arith-expr⟩)
⟨additive-op⟩	::= + | -
⟨multiplicative-op⟩	::= ⋆ | /

This grammar says that every arithmetic expression is the sum of a non-empty sequence of terms; every term is the product of a non-empty sequence of factors; and every factor is either a constant or a parenthesized expression.

Write a lexical specification and a grammar in SLLGEN that will scan and parse strings according to this grammar. Verify that this grammar handles precedence correctly, so that, for example 3+2*66-5 gets grouped correctly, as $3 + (2 \times 66) - 5$.

Exercise A.2 [⋆⋆] Why can't the grammar above be written with `separated-list`?

Exercise A.3 [⋆⋆] Write an interpreter that takes the syntax tree produced by the parser of exercise A.1 and evaluates it as an arithmetic expression. The parser takes care of the usual arithmetic precedence operations, but the interpreter will have to take care of associativity, that is, making sure that operations at the same precedence level (*e.g.* additions and subtractions) are performed from left to right. Since there are no variables in these expressions, this interpreter need not take an environment parameter.

Exercise A.4 [★★] Extend the language and interpreter of the preceding exercise to include variables. This new interpreter will require an environment parameter.

Exercise A.5 [★] Add unary minus to the language and interpreter, so that inputs like 3*-2 are handled correctly.

B For Further Reading

The most important books are those that change the way one looks at the world. So we will begin our reading list with two books in this category. The first is *Structure and Interpretation of Computer Programs*, by Hal Abelson and Gerry Sussman with Julie Sussman (1985; 1996). This is a challenging introduction to programming that emphasizes general problem-solving techniques and uses Scheme throughout. We often list this book as a required text in our courses, just because every computer scientist and programmer should read it. A second mind-expanding book is *Gödel, Escher, Bach: An Eternal Golden Braid* by Douglas R. Hofstadter (1979). If you have not read this book, take some time off and get acquainted with it. It is a joy to read and will open your mind to new and exciting ways to think about recursion, especially as it occurs in the real world, and the meaning of symbols. We hope our book has as deep an effect on you as these books did on us.

General Readings

Two conferences on the history of programming languages, HOPL I (Wexelblat, 1981) and HOPL II (Bergin & Gibson, 1996) provide useful histories of many languages. (Horowitz, 1983) anthologizes many classic papers on programming language design. (Knuth & Pardo, 1977) traces the earliest development of programming languages. Earlier important books include (Braffort & Hirschberg, 1963; Steel, 1966).

The major professional organizations in computing, the Association for Computing Machinery (ACM) and the IEEE Computer Society (IEEE-CS), are rich sources for learning more about programming languages. They sponsor several major conferences and publish several journals that cover this field. Some of the major conferences are the ACM Symposium on Principles of Programming Languages (POPL), the ACM Symposium on Programming Language Design and Implementation (PLDI), the ACM International Conference on Functional Programming (ICFP), the ACM Conference on Object-Oriented Programming Systems, Languages, and Applications (OOPSLA), and the IEEE International Conference on Computer Languages (ICCL). In addition, new conferences are created almost every year. For details, see the listings that are published regularly in the *Communications of the ACM* and *IEEE Computer*.

Some of the journals that publish important papers in programming languages are *ACM Transactions on Programming Languages and Systems*, *Journal of Functional Programming*, *Higher-Order and Symbolic Computation* (previously entitled *Lisp and Symbolic Computation*), *IEEE Software*, *Journal of Computer Languages*, and *Software: Practice and Experience*.

We hope we have given you some useful directions. Enjoy!

Bibliography

Abadi, Martín, & Cardelli, Luca. 1996. *A Theory of Objects.* Berlin, Heidelberg, and New York: Springer-Verlag.

Abelson, Harold, & Sussman, Gerald Jay. 1985. *The Structure and Interpretation of Computer Programs.* Cambridge, MA: MIT Press.

Abelson, Harold, & Sussman, Gerald Jay. 1996. *Structure and Interpretation of Computer Programs.* Second edition. Cambridge, MA.: McGraw Hill.

Appel, Andrew W., & Jim, Trevor. 1989. Continuation-Passing, Closure-Passing Style. *Pages 293–302 of: Conf. Rec. 16th ACM Symposium on Principles of Programming Languages.*

Arnold, Ken, & Gosling, James. 1998. *The Java Programming Language.* Second edition. The Java Series. Reading, MA: Addison-Wesley.

Backus, J. W., *et al.*. 1957. The Fortran Automatic Coding System. *Pages 188–198 of: Western Joint Computer Conference.*

Barendregt, Henk P. 1981. *The Lambda Calculus: Its Syntax and Semantics.* Amsterdam: North-Holland.

Barendregt, Henk P. 1991. *The Lambda Calculus.* Revised edition. Studies in Logic and the Foundations of Mathematics, no. 103. Amsterdam: North-Holland.

Bergin, T. J., & Gibson, R. G. (eds.). 1996. *History of Programming Languages.* New York, NY: Addison-Wesley.

Birtwistle, G. M., Dahl, O. J., Myhrhaug, B., & Nygaard, K. 1973. *Simula Begin.* Philadelphia: Auerbach.

Braffort, P., & Hirschberg, D. (eds.). 1963. *Computer Programming and Formal Systems.* Amsterdam: North-Holland.

Church, Alonzo. 1941. *The Calculi of Lambda Conversion.* Princeton, NJ: Princeton University Press. Reprinted 1963 by University Microfilms, Ann Arbor, MI.

Clinger, William, *et al.*. 1985. *The Revised Revised Report on Scheme or The Uncommon Lisp*. Technical Memo AIM-848. Massachusetts Institute of Technology, Artificial Intelligence Laboratory.

Clinger, William, Rees, Jonathan, *et al.*. 1991. The Revised[4] Report on the Algorithmic Language Scheme. *ACM Lisp Pointers*, **4**(3), 1–55.

Clinger, William D. 1998. Proper Tail Recursion and Space Efficiency. *Pages 174–185 of: Proceedings of the ACM SIGPLAN '98 Conference on Programming Language Design and Implementation*.

Clinger, William D., Hartheimer, Anne H., & Ost, Eric. 1999. Implementation Strategies for First-class Continuations. *Journal of Higher Order and Symbolic Computation*, **12**, 7–45.

Clocksin, William F., & Mellish, Christopher S. 1994. *Programming in Prolog*. Fourth edition. Berlin, Heidelberg, and New York: Springer-Verlag.

Danvy, Olivier, & Filinski, Andrzej. 1992. Representing Control: A study of the CPS transformation. *Mathematical Structures in Computer Science*, **2**(4), 361–391.

Dybvig, R. Kent. 1987. *The Scheme Programming Language*. Englewood Cliffs, NJ: Prentice-Hall.

Dybvig, R. Kent. 1996. *The Scheme programming language: ANSI Scheme*. Second edition. Upper Saddle River, NJ 07458, USA: Prentice-Hall PTR.

Ellis, Margaret A., & Stroustrup, Bjarne. 1992. *The Annotated C++ Reference Manual*. Reading: Addison-Wesley.

Federhen, Scott. 1980. *A Mathematical Semantics for PLANNER*. Master's Thesis, University of Maryland.

Felleisen, Matthias, & Friedman, Daniel P. 1996. *The Little MLer*. MIT Press.

Fischer, Michael J. 1972. Lambda-Calculus Schemata. *Pages 104–109 of: Proceedings ACM Conference on Proving Assertions about Programs*. SIGPLAN Notices, 7(1), January 1972.

Fischer, Michael J. 1993. Lambda-Calculus Schemata. *Lisp and Symbolic Computation*, **6**(3/4), 259–288.

Flatt, Matthew, Krishnamurthi, Shriram, & Felleisen, Matthias. 1998 (Jan.). Classes and Mixins. *Pages 171–183 of: Proceedings ACM Symposium on Principles of Programming Languages*.

Friedman, Daniel P. 1974. *The Little LISPer*. Palo Alto, CA: Science Research Associates.

Friedman, Daniel P., & Felleisen, Matthias. 1996. *The Little Schemer*. Fourth edition. MIT Press.

Gamma, Erich, Helm, Richard, Johnson, Ralph, & Vlissides, John. 1995. *Design Patterns: Elements of Reusable Object-Oriented Software*. Reading, MA, USA: Addison Wesley.

Goldberg, A., & Robson, D. 1983. *Smalltalk-80: The Language and its Implementation*. Reading, MA: Addison-Wesley.

Gosling, James, Joy, Bill, & Steele, Guy L. 1996. *The Java Language Specification*. The Java Series. Reading, MA, USA: Addison-Wesley.

Hankin, Chris. 1994. *Lambda Calculi: A Guide for Computer Scientists*. Graduate Texts in Computer Science, vol. 3. Oxford: Clarendon Press.

Haynes, Christopher T., Friedman, Daniel P., & Wand, Mitchell. 1986. Obtaining Coroutines with Continuations. *J. of Computer Languages*, **11**(3/4), 143–153.

Hewitt, Carl. 1977. Viewing Control Structures as Patterns of Passing Messages. *Artificial Intelligence*, **8**, 323–364.

Hieb, Robert, Dybvig, R. Kent, & Bruggeman, Carl. 1990. Representing Control in the Presence of First-class Continuations. *Pages 66–77 of: Proceedings of the ACM SIGPLAN '90 Conference on Programming Language Design and Implementation*.

Hindley, R. 1969. The Principal Type-Scheme of an Object in Combinatory Logic. *Transactions of the American Mathematical Society*, **146**, 29–60.

Hofstadter, Douglas R. 1979. *Gödel, Escher, Bach: An Eternal Golden Braid*. New York: Basic Books.

Horowitz, Ellis. 1987. *Programming Languages: A Grand Tour*. Third edition. Rockville, Maryland: Computer Science Press.

Hudak, Paul, *et al.*. 1990. *Report on the Programming Language HASKELL*. Technical Report YALEU/DCS/RR-777. Yale University, CS Dept.

Hughes, R. J. M. 1982. Super Combinators: A New Implementation Method for Applicative Languages. *Pages 1–10 of: Proc. 1982 ACM Symposium on Lisp and Functional Programming*.

IEEE. 1991. *IEEE Standard for the Scheme Programming Language, IEEE Standard 1178-1990*. IEEE Computer Society, New York.

Kelsey, Richard, Clinger, William, & Rees, Jonathan. 1998. Revised[5] Report on the Algorithmic Language Scheme. *Higher-Order and Symbolic Computation*, **11**(1), 7–104. Also appeared in *SIGPLAN Notices* 33:9, September 1998.

Kiczales, G., des Rivières, J., & Bobrow, D. G. 1991. *The Art of the Meta-Object Protocol*. Cambridge (MA), USA: MIT Press.

Knuth, Donald E., & Pardo, L. T. 1977. The Early Development of Programming Languages. *Pages 419–493 of:* Belzer, J., Holzman, A. G., & Kent, D. (eds.), *Encyclopedia of Computer Science and Technology*, vol. 6. New York: Marcel Dekker.

Kranz, David A., Kelsey, Richard, Rees, Jonathan A., Hudak, Paul, Philbin, James, & Adams, Norman I. 1986. Orbit: An Optimizing Compiler for Scheme. *Pages 219–223 of: Proceedings SIGPLAN '86 Symposium on Compiler Construction.*

Liskov, Barbara, Snyder, Alan, Atkinson, R., & Schaffert, Craig. 1977. Abstraction Mechanisms in CLU. *Communications of the ACM*, **20**, 564–576.

McCarthy, John. 1960. Recursive Functions of Symbolic Expressions and their Computation by Machine, Part I. *Communications of the ACM*, **3**, 184–195.

McCarthy, John. 1962. Towards a Mathematical Science of Computation. *Pages 21–28 of:* Popplewell (ed.), *Information Processing 62*. Amsterdam: North-Holland.

McCarthy, John, *et al.*. 1965. *LISP 1.5 Programmer's Manual*. Cambridge, MA: MIT Press.

Milner, R. 1978. A Theory of Type Polymorphism in Programming. *Journal of Computer and Systems Science*, **17**, 348–375.

Milner, Robin, Tofte, Mads, & Harper, Robert. 1989. *The Definition of Standard ML*. Cambridge, MA: MIT Press.

Milner, Robin, Tofte, Mads, Harper, Robert, & MacQueen, David B. 1997. *The Standard ML Programming Language (Revised)*. MIT Press.

Morris, Jr., James H. 1968. *Lambda Calculus Models of Programming Languages*. Ph.D. thesis, MIT, Cambridge, MA.

Naur, P., *et al.*. 1963. Revised Report on the Algorithmic Language ALGOL 60. *Communications of the ACM*, **5**(1), 1–17.

Nielson, Flemming, Nielson, Hanne Riis, & Hankin, Chris. 1999. *Principles of Program Analysis*. Berlin, Heidelberg, and New York: Springer-Verlag.

Okasaki, Chris. 1998. *Purely Functional Data Structures*. Cambridge, UK: Cambridge University Press.

Parnas, David L. 1972. A Technique for Module Specification with Examples. *Communications of the ACM*, **15**(5), 330–336.

Paulson, Laurence C. 1996. *ML for the Working Programmer*. Second edition. New York, NY: Cambridge University Press.

Peyton Jones, Simon L. 1987. *The Implementation of Functional Programming Languages*. Prentice-Hall International.

Plotkin, Gordon D. 1975. Call-by-Name, Call-by-Value and the λ-Calculus. *Theoretical Computer Science*, **1**, 125–159.

Pratt, Terrence W., & Zelkowitz, Marvin V. 1996. *Programming Languages: Design and Implementation*. Third edition. Englewood Cliffs, NJ: Prentice-Hall.

Rees, Jonathan A., Clinger, William D., *et al.*. 1986. Revised[3] Report on the Algorithmic Language Scheme. *SIGPLAN Notices*, **21**(12), 37–79.

Reynolds, John C. 1972. Definitional Interpreters for Higher-Order Programming Languages. *Pages 717–740 of: Proceedings ACM National Conference.* Reprinted as (Reynolds, 1998).

Reynolds, John C. 1975. User-Defined Types and Procedural Data Structures as Complementary Approaches to Data Abstraction. *In: Conference on New Directions on Algorithmic Languages.* IFIP WP 2.1, Munich.

Reynolds, John C. 1993. The Discoveries of Continuations. *Lisp and Symbolic Computation,* **6**(3/4), 233–248.

Reynolds, John C. 1998. Definitional Interpreters for Higher-Order Programming Languages. *Higher-Order and Symbolic Computation,* **11**(4), 363–397.

Robinson, J. Alan. 1965. A Machine-Oriented Logic Based on the Resolution Principle. *Journal of the ACM,* **12**, 23–41.

Sabry, Amr, & Felleisen, Matthias. 1993. Reasoning about Programs in Continuation-Passing Style. *Lisp and Symbolic Computation,* **6**(3/4), 289–360.

Sabry, Amr, & Wadler, Philip. 1997. A Reflection on Call-by-Value. *ACM Transactions on Programming Languages and Systems,* **19**(6), 916–941.

Scott, Michael L. 2000. *Programming Language Semantics.* San Francisco: Morgan Kaufmann.

Sethi, Ravi. 1996. *Programming Languages: Concepts and Constructs.* Second edition. Reading, MA.: Addison-Wesley.

Smith, Brian C. 1982 (Jan.). *Reflection and Semantics in a Procedural Language.* Technical Report MIT/LCS/TR-272. Massachusetts Institute of Technology, Cambridge, MA.

Smith, Brian C. 1984. Reflection and Semantics in Lisp. *Pages 23–35 of: Conf. Rec. 11th ACM Symposium on Principles of Programming Languages.*

Springer, George, & Friedman, Daniel P. 1989. *Scheme and the Art of Programming.* New York, NY: McGraw-Hill.

Steel, T. B. (ed.). 1966. *Formal Language Description Languages for Computer Programming.* Amsterdam, NL: North-Holland. Proceedings of the IFIP Working Conference, Vienna.

Steele, Guy L. 1978. *Rabbit: A Compiler for Scheme.* Artificial Intelligence Laboratory Technical Report 474. Massachusetts Institute of Technology, Cambridge, MA.

Steele, Guy L. 1990. *Common Lisp: the Language.* Second edition. Burlington MA: Digital Press.

Steele, Guy L., & Sussman, Gerald Jay. 1978. *The Revised Report on SCHEME.* Artificial Intelligence Memo 452. Massachusetts Institute of Technology, Cambridge, MA.

Stoy, Joseph E. 1977. *Denotational Semantics: The Scott-Strachey Approach to Programming Language Theory.* Cambridge, MA: MIT Press.

Strachey, Christopher, & Wadsworth, C. P. 1974. *Continuations: A Mathematical Semantics for Handling Full Jumps.* Technical Monograph PRG-11. Oxford University Computing Laboratory. Reprinted as (Strachey & Wadsworth, 2000).

Strachey, Christopher, & Wadsworth, C. P. 2000. Continuations: A Mathematical Semantics for Handling Full Jumps. *Higher-Order and Symbolic Computation,* **13**(1/2), 135–152.

Sussman, Gerald J., & Steele, Jr., Guy L. 1975. *SCHEME: An Interpreter for Extended Lambda Calculus.* Artificial Intelligence Memo 349. Massachusetts Institute of Technology, Cambridge, MA.

Ullman, J. D. 1998. *Elements of ML Programming.* ML97 edition. Prentice-Hall.

Wand, Mitchell. 1980a. Continuation-Based Multiprocessing. *Pages 19–28 of:* Allen, J. (ed.), *Conference Record of the 1980 LISP Conference.* Palo Alto, CA: The Lisp Company, republished by ACM. Reprinted as (Wand, 1999).

Wand, Mitchell. 1980b. Continuation-Based Program Transformation Strategies. *Journal of the ACM,* **27**, 164–180.

Wand, Mitchell. 1999. Continuation-Based Multiprocessing. *Higher-Order and Symbolic Computation,* **12**(3), 285–299. Originally appeared as (Wand, 1980a).

Wexelblat, R. L. 1981. *History of Programming Languages.* New York: Academic Press.

Index

Colophon

The authors prepared camera-ready electronic copy for this book using emacs and LaTeX2$_\epsilon$ on Sun and PC workstations, with the help of bibtex, makeindex, and dvips. Graphic figures were prepared using xfig.

Custom software, running under Chez Scheme, incorporated the contents of Scheme-code figures from independent source files. This allowed convenient testing of this code, again using Chez Scheme.

The overall book design was derived from the LaTeX fbook class and style files of Christopher Manning. These were in turn partly derived from the LaTeX3 Project.

The body text font is Palatino, set 10 on 12 and magnified to about 11 on 13. Program text is Courier, set 9 on 10 and magnified to about 10 on 12.